TRUTHS AND MYTHS OF CYBER-BULLYING

new
literacies

AND DIGITAL EPISTEMOLOGIES

Colin Lankshear, Michele Knobel,
and Michael Peters
General Editors

Vol. 38

PETER LANG
New York • Washington, D.C./Baltimore • Bern
Frankfurt am Main • Berlin • Brussels • Vienna • Oxford

TRUTHS AND MYTHS OF CYBER-BULLYING

International Perspectives on Stakeholder Responsibility and Children's Safety

Edited by Shaheen Shariff and Andrew H. Churchill

PETER LANG
New York • Washington, D.C./Baltimore • Bern
Frankfurt am Main • Berlin • Brussels • Vienna • Oxford

Library of Congress Cataloging-in-Publication Data

Truths and myths of cyber-bullying: international perspectives on stakeholder responsibility
and children's safety / edited by Shaheen Shariff, Andrew H. Churchill.
p. cm. — (New literacies and digital epistemologies vol. 38.)
Includes bibliographical references and index.
1. Cyberbullying. 2. Internet and children. 3. Internet in education.
4. Internet—Safety measures. I. Shariff, Shaheen. II. Churchill, Andrew H. III. Title.
LB3013.3S468   371.5'8—dc22   2009043508
ISBN 978-1-4331-0467-1 (hardcover)
ISBN 978-1-4331-0466-4 (paperback)
ISSN 1523-9543

Bibliographic information published by **Die Deutsche Nationalbibliothek**.
Die Deutsche Nationalbibliothek lists this publication in the "Deutsche
Nationalbibliografie"; detailed bibliographic data is available
on the Internet at http://dnb.d-nb.de/.

The paper in this book meets the guidelines for permanence and durability
of the Committee on Production Guidelines for Book Longevity
of the Council of Library Resources.

© 2010 Peter Lang Publishing, Inc., New York
29 Broadway, 18th floor, New York, NY 10006
www.peterlang.com

Printed in the United States of America

*This volume is dedicated to the many children
and young adults whose lives have been
negatively impacted by cyber-bullying.*

*We sincerely hope the following conversations
help all those interested in creating kinder,
safer communities.*

▪ Table of Contents

▪ Acknowlegments

I wish to acknowledge first and foremost, the dedicated efforts and commitment of my co-author and research assistant, Andrew H. Churchill, without whom this book would not have come to fruition. Andrew has done some excellent editing, formatting work and writing for this book. He has also overseen submission of chapters and edits from all our contributors. Thanks also to series editor Professor Colin Lankshear for his support of our work and for his incredible insight and scholarship on digital literacies. Much of what I have learned about the conceptual differences or "mindsets" between adult and youth understandings of on-line communication originated in long and interesting conversations with Colin when he spent time with us at McGill University. I am greatly indebted to the Social Sciences and Humanities Research Council of Canada (SSHRC) for funding the research that has resulted in my current knowledge of cyber-bullying. SSHRC funding also enabled the fruitful international collaborations with scholars, networking organizations, schools, legal academics and law enforcement personnel that have culminated in this publication. I wish to thank my research assistant Lisa Trimble for her prompt and efficient edits of chapters at the last minute. Finally, a big thank you to our chapter authors for your excellent and timely contributions and for agreeing to collaborate on this publication under such short timelines, and to Chris Myers of Peter Lang for his support throughout the publication process.

Shaheen Shariff, Ph.D., Associate Professor
McGill University

I also wish to acknowledge our chapter authors. When we started this project, we hoped that this book would address the pedagogical, moral, legal and ethical complexity of helping young people more safely and compassionately navigate their newly emerging on-line worlds. I believe the authors have exceeded our expectations, and I am deeply grateful for the privilege of helping collect and edit their work. Of course, I also wish to thank the series editors Colin Lankshear, Michele Knobel and Michael Peters as well as our publisher Chris Myers at Peter Lang. But most importantly, I want to thank Shaheen Shariff, who invited me to collaborate on this project. I deeply appreciate her guidance, support, and trust. She has been an important teacher, from whom I continue to learn.

Andrew H. Churchill, Ph.D. student
McGill University

▪ Foreword

(or, Beyond 'Reify, Measure and Treat')

Colin Lankshear and Michele Knobel

*T*ruths and Myths of Cyber-bullying is a most welcome contribution to the
'New Literacies' series. During this first decade of the new millennium,
cyber-bullying has emerged as a major preoccupation for diverse social actors
and agencies inhabiting and experiencing many different points of connection
among new computing and communication tools, social institutions, and everyday
cultural practices. Cyber-bullying quickly has joined the ranks of internet fraud,
identity theft, and breaches of copyright law and intellectual property rights (a.k.a.
'piracy') as a major 'trouble spot' along the digital electronic frontier (Lankshear
& Knobel, 2008). As with these other trouble spots, we find that once we move
beyond the media storms 'cyber-bullying' becomes a signpost to complexity that
is beggared by common responses to its tidy accommodation under a deceptively
simple and singular term.

From the outset *Truths and Myths of Cyber-bullying* invites its readers to look
beyond surface appearances and easy generalizations and to consider what is
often overlooked, glossed, or rendered invisible within everyday discourse about
cyber-bullying, along with what cyber-bullying properly calls attention to. The
book insists that we attend carefully to those broader social, legal, ethical, policy-

making and pedagogical concerns that are often bypassed or sidelined when cyber-bullying is discussed and addressed at institutional levels. The editors of this volume insist that the issues surrounding and constituting cyber-bullying are complex. They "cannot be simplified to focus solely on the behaviours of children and youth without adequate consideration of the systemic influences that intersect and interlock to result in such behaviour."

Notwithstanding the short time that has elapsed since 'the cyber-bullying phenomenon' was first named, considerable work has already been undertaken in many parts of the world to 'recognize and raise awareness of the systemic complexities involved in cyber-bullying.' *Truths and Myths of Cyber-bullying* mobilizes interesting and challenging work being developed internationally by educators, academic researchers, legal practitioners, and child safety networking organisations to address the complexity of issues pertaining to cyber-bullying. These individuals and groups are variously engaged—alone and in collaboration—in scholarly and research inquiry, developing online programs and resources of a practical nature, and establishing stakeholder networks.

Such work is crucial if attempts to address 'cyber-bullying' in theory and in practice are to play significant roles within sustained efforts to enhance human relationships and interpersonal dealings—especially within educational settings, where pursuit of quick fixes is all too common. Much of what passes for educational improvement tinkers with symptoms while leaving deeper underlying factors untouched and, in many cases, unrecognized. Too often we find a familiar logic of 'Reify, Measure and Treat' being played out in response to 'troubles at school.' It is important that efforts to address the kinds of practices and interpersonal relations associated with 'cyber-bullying' move beyond this reductionist simplifying logic and onto stronger ground.

Reification is the process of turning complex relationships, processes and practices into *things* (Berger & Pullberg, 1965; Taussig, 1980). It is often referred to as "thingifying" and involves a distinctive kind of reduction, or reductionism. (Ironically, of course, in order to discuss 'reification' it is difficult to avoid reifying it!) When complex relations among diverse elements are objectified as some singular *thing*, this thing inevitably acquires the status of an agent that acts causally—as a cause—to bring about all kinds of consequences and effects. Amelioration becomes focused on trying to 'knock this agent' out. In fact, the 'agent' may be an illusion or, more likely, a proxy for many different kinds of practices, processes, interactional relationships that have been abstracted from concrete contexts, purposes, goals, intentions, forethoughts and the like. If we 'fire' at such a generic target we are likely to miss most of what is important in making a qualitative difference to how people relate to and interact with one another.

The risks of reification in the area of cyber-bullying are high. This becomes apparent when we look at what typical attempts to *measure* cyber-bullying subsume. Even a cursory sampling of how cyber-bullying is defined in academic texts and popular media reveals an ontological minestrone comprising, among many others, the following list of items:

- Saying mean or hurtful things to another person
- Stealing passwords and impersonating or pretending to be some other person online
- Threatening another person
- Making fun of another person
- Subjecting another person to vulgar or sexual suggestions or to sexually explicit images
- Calling another person mean or hurtful names
- Completely ignoring or excluding someone else from one's group
- Attributing same sex preference to another person
- Impugning another person's sexual preference
- Deliberately leaving another person out of things
- Telling lies or spreading false rumours about another person
- Sending mean notes about another person
- Mocking another person's disability
- Sending malicious code
- 'Polling' other people
- Trying to make others dislike a particular person
(cf., for example, Lenhart, 2007; Li, 2007; Patchin & Hinduja, 2006; Smith et al., 2005)

This mix is, to say the least, eclectic, and that is without taking into account the endless possible variations in contexts, antecedents, discourse memberships, affinities, intentions, personal histories, identity constitutive practices, and so on that may pertain from case to case. Thus reified, 'cyber-bullying' has quickly generated a widely publicized, measurement 'industry' concerned with estimating the scale and extent of cyber-bullying.

Two of the best-known measurement exercises conducted to date in Britain are that undertaken on behalf of the National Children's Home charity (NCH, 2005) and the study conducted by the Unit for School and Family Studies at the University of London's Goldsmiths College (Smith et al., 2005) for the Anti-bullying Alliance. These survey-based studies received responses from 770 youth aged 11–19 and 92 students in the London area aged 11–16, respectively. The former reported that 20% of respondents claimed to have been bullied through electronic media, and the latter study reported 22% of respondents have experienced cyber-bullying at least once in the previous 2 months, and 6.6% reported having been cyber-bullied more frequently during that period.

In the U.S., three of the largest scale and best known studies are those conducted by i-SAFE America (Carlson, 2004), Harris Interactive, (Harris Interactive, 2007; Moessner, 2007) and Pew Internet (Lenhart, 2007).

i-SAFE America, an Internet safety education foundation, conducted a national study among 1,566 students (grades four to eight) who were described by the researchers as being "online" (Carlson 2004). In this study, 57% of respondents reported experiences of someone saying hurtful or angry things to them online, with 13% saying it happens to them 'quite often'; 35% reported experiences of having been threatened online, with 5% of these respondents saying it happens to them 'quite often'; and 42% said they had been bullied online, with 7% claiming it happens to them quite often.

In 2006, Harris Interactive polled a nationally representative sample of 824 middle and high school students aged 13–17 years. Forty-three percent of participants reported having experienced "some form of cyber-bullying in the previous year" (Harris Interactive, 2007: no page; Moessner, 2007: 1), with a peak of 54% among 15-year-olds experiencing cyber-bullying, and a higher rate of incidence among females.

Pew (Lenhart 2007) conducted a nationally-representative call-back phone survey of 935 teenagers of 12–17 years, with follow-up focus groups. Pew reports 32% of their participants acknowledging that they had been victims of 'harassing or "cyber-bullying" behaviors' (no page). Two key patterns emerged: girls are more likely to be targets than boys, as are teens who 'share their identities and thoughts online' as opposed to those 'who lead less active online lives' (Lenhart 2007: no page).

Such reports are widely reported by media and anti-bullying groups as authoritative cyber-bullying data, yet it is far from obvious that they establish anything that could reasonably be considered scientifically robust. Whatever they are talking about it is clearly *not* the same thing.

For example, the i-SAFE study distinguishes between 'being bullied' and having 'hurtful or angry things said to them' online. Yet 'having hurtful or angry things said about them online' is central to the cyber-bullying incidence survey questionnaire used in the Goldsmiths' College study. Similarly, whereas the Goldsmiths College study takes seriously the idea that bullying refers to *repeated* instances where the victim finds it difficult to defend her or himself because of the greater strength of the bully, the Pew Internet study asks participants whether they have *ever* experienced any of the following actions:

- Someone else makes one of your private communications public
- Someone spreads a rumour about you online
- Someone sends you a threatening or aggressive message
- Someone posts an embarrassing picture of you online without permission.

Any of these had to occur just once for it to register as an instance of cyber-bullying. Pew's figure of 32% of respondents reporting being the target of cyber-bullying comprises the total number of respondents who had replied "Yes" to at least one of the items, which had to have occurred at least once. In addition, whereas some studies specifically ask respondents to exclude cases that are enacted in fun or that can be seen as cases of being teased by friends, others make no such discrimination.

Seen in this light, measurement begs scrutiny. Yet, such figures are widely used by different interested parties to support cyber-bullying 'treatments.' In a typical example, during September 2007, the British Secretary of State for Children, Schools and Families launched an updated package of anti-bullying guidance and resources for schools in England. This package contained 'new separate *sections*' on cyber-bullying and homophobic bullying (DCSF, 2007: no page). The press release published on the Department's website, however, began by saying that the Secretary had launched '*an online cyber-bullying campaign,* new guidance and a short film to help schools tackle bullies *who use the internet or mobile phones* to bully other children or abuse their teachers' (emphases added; DCSF, 2007: no page). The Secretary was quoted as recognising that 'the vast majority of schools' provide safe learning environments, while recognizing that bullying is 'a key concern for parents,' and that 'bullying of any kind is unacceptable.' Notwithstanding this brief, the website release follows immediately with the statement that

> Estimates vary but a recent study by the DCSF showed that up to 34% of 12–15 year olds had experienced some form of cyberbullying. There is also growing concern from teaching unions that school staff are increasingly becoming the victims of cyberbully-ing (ibid.).

Two maneuvers are noteworthy here. First, what was basically an expanded, updated and improved anti-bullying package was presented in the first instance as a response to *cyber-bullying.* Second, the quite considerable statistic of 34% was wheeled out in the context of foregrounding the cyber-bullying aspect of the package.

Our point here has less to do with the *kind* of treatment proposed in this particular case than with the close 'alliance' between measurement and treatment. This is because statistics can be used to support *any* kind of response, from informed and educative to draconian and authoritarian. Of course, the higher the incidence statistics for cyber-bullying, the more readily they can be used to justify (further) stifling internet use within school-based learning and for intensifying surveillance in young people's internet use generally. The simple truth is that schools, communities, and governments do not need an endless stream of numbers to justify taking acts of bullying seriously, and seeking to address them in ways that genuinely encourage bullies to see their practices—along with those of other bullies—as distasteful. As soon as bullying, of any kind, occurs on a visible scale the situation is unacceptable.

Lest the kinds of concerns we are raising here seem unduly 'academic' or tangential to the importance of addressing harmful forms of social interaction and communication, it is perhaps worth considering what has happened over the past three cases with respect to literacy—since literacy is probably the classic instance of applying the logic of 'Reify, Measure, and Treat' within education. At the level of moment by moment interaction and communication among human beings, literacy consists in innumerable and endlessly variable relationships between people, tools, bits of knowledge, goals, values, purposes and so on. There is endless variety, and each instance plays out in its own way, adding something—however small—to the shape of human life. Within education, however, these intricacies and multiple dimensions have been reduced to a single, homogenous, objective 'thing': a 'tool' or 'skill' or 'technology' called literacy, which is credited with far-reaching powers and consequences. This (reified) literacy can, of course, be measured in various ways, including measuring the scale and extent of illiteracy.

Since the 1970s, measuring literacy has become a fetish on a major scale. By the mid-1970s a literacy 'crisis' had been proclaimed throughout almost every 'developed' Anglo-American country (Shor, 1986; Lankshear, 1987). Treatment was prescribed on a massive scale, in the form of various intervention packages (assessment, diagnosis, remediation), a move to phonics-based instructional approaches, basics-oriented education reform, and the elevation of literacy from the status of a learning medium to that of a major goal, if not *the* goal, of education. It is now an established fact of life throughout the Anglo-American world that schooling will be an endless procession of standardized tests undertaken in the context of hollowed-out substantive curricula, and that teaching will involve reporting and teaching to tests on a scale previously unknown.

Reification-Measurement-Treatment is a potent triumvirate, and the directions it can take us in are not necessarily directions in which we would want to travel. Unfortunately, by the time this logic has established its grip the directions may be exceedingly difficult to change. At the very least we should be alert to this logic and reflect upon the extent to which and the ways in which it operates within our daily institutional settings, inside and outside of education. The contributing authors to *Truths and Myths of Cyber-bullying* provide a range of resources with which to transcend this logic in the context of promoting responsible and ethically acceptable forms of communication and interpersonal interactions and relationships mediated by the technologies of our times. From our perspective as series editors, that constitutes a most valuable contribution to the 'New Literacies' series. From our perspective, as people interested in human beings working together to build better social worlds, it represents a most valuable contribution to informed reflection and action in relation to what is widely called 'cyber-bullying.'

References

Berger, P. & Pullberg, S. (1965). Reification and the sociological critique of consciousness. *History and Theory* 4(1): 196–211.

Carlson, E. (2004). National i-SAFE survey finds over half of students being harassed online. Press release. Retrieved April 21, 2009, from http://www.tinyurl.com/cv974e

Department for Children, Schools and Families (DCSF) (2007). No hiding place for bullies. Press release 21 September 2007. Retrieved April 21, 2009, from http://tinyurl.com/58zyge

Harris Interactive (2007). Teens and Cyberbullying: Executive Summary of a Report on Research Conducted for the National Crime Prevention Council. Retrieved April 21, 2009, from http://tinyurl.com/bafxa4

Lankshear, C. (1987). *Literacy, Schooling and Revolution.* London: Falmer Press. Chapter 4.

Lankshear, C. & Knobel, M. (remixers) (2008). Digital literacy and the law: Remixing elements of Lawrence Lessig's ideal of "free culture." In C. Lankshear & M. Knobel (eds.), *Digital Literacies: Concepts, Policies and Practices.* New York: Peter Lang, 279–306.

Lenhart, A. (2007). Pew Internet & American Life Project Memo: Cyberbullying and Online Teens. Retrieved April 21, 2009, from http://tinyurl.com/dc84cg

Li, Q. (2007) Bullying in the new playground: Research into cyberbullying and cyber victimization. *Australasian Journal of Educational Technology* 23(4): 435–54.

Moessner, C. (2007). Cyberbullying. *Trends and Tudes* 6(4). Retrieved April 21, 2009, from http://tinyurl.com/2k4xr6

National Children's Home (NCH) charity (2005) *Putting U in the Picture.* NCH and Tesco Mobile. Retrieved April 21, 2009, from http://tinyurl.com/djzvvd

Patchin, J. & Hinduja, S. (2006). Bullies move beyond the schoolyard: A preliminary look at cyberbullying. *Youth Violence and Juvenile Justice,* 4(2): 148–169.

Shor, I. (1986). *Culture Wars.* New York: Routledge.

Smith, P., Mahdavi, J., Carvalho, M. & Tippett, N. (2005). An investigation into cyberbullying, its forms, awareness and impact, and the relationship between age and gender in cyberbullying. A report to the Anti-bullying Alliance. London: University of London. Goldsmiths College, Unit for Studies of Families and Schools. Retrieved April 21, 2009, from http://tinyurl.com/aqphxe

Taussig, M. (1980/02).Reification and the consciousness of the patient. *Social Science & Medicine. Part B: Medical Anthropology* 14(1): 3–13.

SECTION I

Introduction and Background

1 · Appreciating Complexity

Detangling the Web of Stakeholder
Influence and Responsibility

Shaheen Shariff
Andrew H. Churchill

FOUR MYTHS ABOUT CYBER-BULLYING

Over the last three years, both editors have been highly fortunate to engage in critically informed, inspiring conversations with Professor Colin Lankshear during his short visits to McGill University. We conversed on a range of matters relating to the enormous learning potential that technologies provide contemporary society. Our discussions highlighted one common concern that we felt needed to be addressed in a way that reached academics, policy-makers and educational practitioners. We have all noticed a disturbing trend by educators, government officials, lawmakers, educational practitioners, teachers' unions and parents to control, curb and restrict electronic on-line communications. Ultimately such restrictions diminish the potential for relevant and shared learning opportunities for young people and their educators. We challenge four myths about traditional and cyber-bullying. These myths have become entrenched in the public's understanding of cyber-bullying as a "trouble spot" or "battle" that pits kids and parents against schools with harsh policies and legislative responses designed to control student expression, especially when it is on-line and affects the reputations of authority figures such as school administrators and teachers (Asthana & Smith, 2007; Bernstein & Hanna, 2005).

Reconsidering this approach and challenging these myths is slowly gaining wider acceptance among leading academics and politicians. Consider, for example, the September 2009 testimony to the US Congress Committee on the Judiciary from the chairman of the Attorney General commissioned Internet Safety Technical Task Force, Dr. John Palfrey of Harvard Law School. In this testimony, that took place as part of the "Hearing on Cyberbullying and other Online Safety Issues for Children", Dr. Palfrey states:

> The data that show a sharp increase in bullying online need to be considered in light of a series of additional bits of context. First, overwhelmingly, most of the ways in which young people use digital technologies is positive…. Digital technologies themselves do not have a "nature." The Internet, as one core part of the digital architecture, is famously a "stupid" network. A key design principle of the Internet, the end-to-end principle, calls for it to "pass all packets." The network, and the applications that are built upon it, is not inherently "good" or "bad"; it is merely a conduit for human and machine-to-machine interaction…. No single solution to cyberbullying – or, more properly, bullying in general – exists. There is no one thing that we can do that will protect America's young people from being harmed online. The behavior that we would like to curtail – most commonly, young people saying or doing harmful things to other young people online – is part of typical adolescent behavior to some extent. In many cases, what concerns us is behavior that we want to stop, but not to criminalize; the image of filling our prisons with teenagers and young adults who have been teasing one another online is plainly unattractive. And many of the more aggressive responses to online bullying would curtail First Amendment freedoms that minors ought to enjoy as their parents and teachers do. All the same, it's too great a worry to make throwing up our hands an adequate response. (Palfrey, 2009)

Building on the foreword and in light of these statements to Congress by Dr. Palfrey, we invite you to consider the following myths that are not mutually exclusive, but which collectively mask the complex realities of cyber-bullying. The chapters in this book peel away the layers to expose how cyber-bullying as a phenomenon has been reified to levels that diminish young people's learning by depriving them of potentially collaborative and empowering learning opportunities *and* endanger their emotional health and well-being by failing to address the root causes of bullying behaviours.

Myth No. 1: Cyber-bullying and Bullying as "Thing" That Can Be Controlled

Cyber-bullying is often conceptualized by schools as a "trouble spot" or "thing" to be controlled. As Colin Lankshear and Michel Knobel aptly point out, the notion of cyber-bullying, and indeed, traditional bullying, has been reified, or as they describe it, "thingified" so that "it" can be controlled, managed, and packaged, bucketed and blueprinted. This oversimplification to fit a manageable blueprint for policy makers has brought the topic of cyber-bullying to the forefront of national and international policy agendas. The United Nations has identified it as a priority for international discussion and dedicated a full day on June 16, 2009, to symposia and workshops as part of its "unlearning intolerance" seminar series (see http://www.un.org/en/unlearningintolerance/index.html). Our extensive research on traditional and cyber-bullying over the last six years (Shariff 2004–2009) evidences that both are grounded in intersecting and interlocking systemic and social forms of expression, abuse, and threats rooted in homophobic, sexist, racist and discriminatory attitudes. Regrettably, most academic research on this subject over the last two decades persistently ignores these systemic barriers and discriminatory attitudes that are rooted, reinforced and modeled in adult society (Razack, 1998; boyd & Jenkins, 2006; Shariff, 2008–09). Bullying is conceptualized and defined by prominent research authorities as an entity on its own—separate from these endemic societal attitudes. Hence, the general approach of hundreds of academic and government funded studies in the last decade has been a narrow focus on statistics relating to prevalence and increases in the "behavior" of children and youth who are labeled "bullies" and "victims," without attention to the fact they are actors within specific contexts and may react or respond to a variety and range of complex influences on their lives at particular times (Shariff, 2008–09). Studies that draw from either Skinnerian measure and treatment models or behavior modification and relational aggression theories proliferate in the field of research on cyber-bullying (Pepler & Craig, 1997). Even when they give lip services to the importance of systemic and contextual factors, such studies remain fixated on statistical reports that warn the public about the increasing prevalence of cyber-bullying and its psychological and social impact. While these are reasonable concerns (especially when young people commit suicide or drop out of school as a result of cyber-bullying), narrowly focused statistical findings are widely disseminated and over-reported through the media, perpetuating the myth and spreading fear among educators and parents that cyber-bullying is out of control (Edwards, 2005; Dolmage, 2000; Shariff, 2009).

Such an approach ignores the significant influence and role of teacher attitudes, the impact of out-dated and irrelevant curricula, issues of poverty, neglect, parenting influences, as well as health, and social circumstances within school contexts. In cyber-space, these factors can highly complicate supervision of student communication and learning as we have traditionally known it because, for many young people, the virtual world is where they can express themselves freely, take on new and several identities, and stay connected with friends at a physical distance. Edwards (2005) for example has found that girls in India and Japan can maintain their traditionally domestic roles at home while living in an entirely different world in cyber-space. Their forays into the cyber-world open up learning and career opportunities they could only have dreamed of in the past. Shariff has argued elsewhere (Shariff & Hoff, 2007) that leaving kids to their own devices in the vast open spaces of the cyber-world and expecting them to respect narrowly defined school rules is like marooning them on Golding's mythical deserted island in his novel, *Lord of the Flies*. Young people are still developing their identities and need guidance and support—without such guidance it is not surprising that social norms break down, as they did on Golding's island. And yet, even Golding alluded to the fact that the boys marooned away from adult supervision were indeed mimicking what they had learned from adults in their home society. In that regard, we cannot overemphasize the fact that the only models of behavior that most kids have are those demonstrated by the adults who raise and teach them. We need not go far to find that adults are not exemplary models of respectful and inclusive behavior, on or offline. We simply need to remind ourselves of the Holocaust, numerous wars and genocides globally, and the many other abuses of power in the name of democracy in contemporary adult society. On a smaller scale, we can examine how often parents bully referees and coaches of the children's teams or how often white collar middle class adults treat with disdain the work done by people they hire to clean and care for their homes. Needless to say, we need not search hard for examples of how adults model the negative treatment of marginalized groups in many societies to appreciate that children are not the ones who epitomize bad behavior. Lori Drew, a 49-year-old parent in the United States is only one infamous example of adult cyber-bullying. In a highly sensationalized case, this adult woman assumed the identity of "Josh" (a teenage boy) and cyber-bullied thirteen-year-old Megan, who suffered from depression, resulting in her tragic suicide.

Moreover, there is ample evidence to suggest that dysfunctional relationships among administration and staff, and staff and their students in some schools can result in a prevalence of traditional and cyber-bullying incidents (McNeil, 1998; DiGuilio, 2001; Butler-Kisber & Portelli, 2003; Shariff, 2004–09). Consider, for example, a cyber-bullying controversy at one Montreal high school in 2007. Twenty-six students were suspended for apparently defaming their teachers on Facebook. The students joked and discussed one teacher who had problems with hygiene, which was something widely agreed upon, They talked about a teacher who was a lesbian, who was openly gay. They criticized an older teacher for her didactic teaching approach. This, too, was an accurate observation on the part of the students. Conversations with the school's new administrators clarified that not only were the students' observations correct but that the school had a history of dysfunctional and negative relations between the school administration and faculty as well as within the faculty. Butler-Kisber and Portelli found in their 1998 study of 10 schools across Canada (published in 2003), that violence among students was reduced greatly when staff and administration got along. Similar results were reported by McNeil (1998) in her study of various school administrator leadership styles. Autocratic leaders created a hostile environment in schools that resulted in student disengagement, boredom and violence; whereas administrators who adopted a more democratic and distributive leadership approach fostered successful environments where students thrived in their learning and social relationships. Fullan (2006) and Evans (1996) have also highlighted these considerations as indicators for schools with reduced violence. Nonetheless, students are most often blamed when such dysfunctional models of social interaction are identified on public websites. These students then find themselves suspended or even expelled for their online expressions. While we do not suggest that all students who engage in cyber-bullying are blameless or not responsible for their actions, we do argue for more in depth consideration of the systemic influences that motivate young people's on-line expressions and behavior instead of disrupting and holding in abeyance their educational process as punishment for immature actions. A more practical and ethical alternative might be to engage them in dialogue to determine their underlying motivations and gain a more accurate assessment of what concerns they have about their administrators, teachers and school in general.

Myth No. 2: Reification of Technologies as a "Thing" or "Technology"

A second myth or mistaken perception is that the Internet and range of related electronic forms of communication, social networking sites, cellular and video technologies are all part of a single technology that ensnares our children and youth, giving them too much power over adults in authority. This myth is magnified and fueled by sensationalist media through headlines that describe cyber-bullying as a "battle" or "war" between kids and schools: "Cyber-Bullying: The Internet Is the Latest Weapon in a Bully's Arsenal" (Leishman, 2002); "Teachers Declare War on Cyber-bullying" (Brown, 2007); "Cyber-bullying Can Spin Out of Control: Study" (Maughan, 2008; Shariff, 2008; Edwards, 2005). These provocative headlines and framing of news reports that pit students against teachers create the illusion that the Internet and related forms of electronic communication give young people too much power. This myth results in a sense of panic experienced by teachers, parents and the general public alike, fueling calls for increased controls through criminal legislation, increased police involvement and zero-tolerance policies and disciplinary practices in schools. Those who support such measures, however, also buy into Myth No. 1 and rarely give significant thought to the systemic context. Moreover, they believe that oversimplified responses will resolve "the problem" as sustained by two related myths.

Myth No. 3: Filters and Bans Will Reduce Cyber-bullying

Teacher education and communications curricula in many North American schools remain outdated, irrelevant, and disconnected from Internet learning or communication. They are largely Eurocentric despite youth on-line proficiency and increasingly diverse school populations (see http://www.youtube.com/watch?v=dGCJ46vyR9o). These critical factors are rarely addressed in studies that advocate increased police involvement, behavior modification and zero-tolerance approaches. Further ignored is the prevalent adult mindset of many adults towards on-line learning and communication as explained earlier, where most adults conceptualize and reify technologies as a singular, almost physical entity that can be boxed and controlled. Fear of too much power in the hands of young people has resulted in wide application of firewalls on school websites that prevent students from accessing a broad range of educational resources and social communications sites (see details in Shariff, 2008–09). Cellular phones and laptops are also increasingly banned from school classrooms except for officially designated computer classes, where students learn computer techniques but not social etiquette (boyd & Jenkins, 2006) Firewalls are assumed to function like brick walls. Online filters are thought to reduce the potential for cyber-bullying and other forms of on-line abuse (Lankshear & Knobel, 2006), and yet students repeatedly demonstrate their proficiency in hacking through these barriers to access prohibited information. Consider the example of sixteen-year-old Melbourne student Tom Wood who broke through the Australian Government's new $84 million Internet porn filter in less than thirty minutes (Higginbottom & Packham, 2007). In the story about the incident Tom was interviewed at length and talked about how the filters missed the mark by a long way, regardless of how easy they were to break:

> Filters aren't addressing the bigger issue anyway…. Cyber-bullying, educating children and how to protect themselves and their privacy are the first problems I'd fix…. They really need to develop a youth involved forum to discuss some of the these problems and ideas for fixing them. (Higginbottom & Packham, 2007)

Myth No. 4: Zero-tolerance Will Control Kids and Reduce Cyber-bullying

The combined effect of sensational media and the "measure and treat" approach of researchers who reify both traditional and cyber-bullying has also mobilized teachers who in turn pressurize their unions to call for legislation to criminalize cyber-bullying. Schools increase zero-tolerance approaches to "control" offending students through suspensions, expulsions and criminal charges. Zero-tolerance responses, as Skiba & Petersen (1999) observe, are largely rooted in authoritarian models of control whose origin is the United States military. In keeping with this punitive model, the Canadian Teachers' Federation, despite its efforts to better understand the issues towards improved professional development of its member teachers, succumbed to pressure from its members in 2008 and called upon the Canadian government to amend certain sections of the Canadian Criminal Code to include criminal sanctions for cyber misconduct and cyber-bullying in section 264 (harassment); section 298 (defamatory libel); section 372 (1–3 false messages), and section 320.1/164.1 (hate propaganda). The irony of this punitive reaction by educators is that rarely is there any realization or recognition that an educational, rather than a reactive and restrictive approach ought to be considered first. Given that the primary role of the teacher is to *educate* young people and help them learn from their mistakes, not abandon them by suspending or expelling them from school, education should be one of the core responses. As DiGuilio (2001) points out, there are many more opportunities for trouble on the streets and now on-line for young people who believe that adults do not support or value them. Our research in Quebec schools (Shariff, 2007) disclosed that many young people do not report either engaging in or being at the receiving end of cyber-bullying because "their teachers will not do anything about it" (Shariff, 2006) or because they fear losing their computer and cell phone privileges. Moreover, we found that in schools where students reported higher incidents of cyber-bullying, they also indicated that there would probably be less cyber-bullying if their school were a happier place. In those very same schools, teachers and school administrators appeared oblivious to cyber-bullying among their students, often relying on the assumption that the existence of school policies against cyber-bullying was sufficient to prevent their students from engaging in such forms of expression. There was a lack of dialogue and discussion about such expression and its impact when the situation could have been discussed in many areas of the curriculum.

The Misdirected Reactive Response: Control the Technology and Control the Kids and You Will Control Cyber-bullying

As Lankshear and Knobel observe in the foreword, once we reify a complex issue to become a "thing," especially one that appears to be out of control (like cancer), it becomes a *cause* that relies on drawing significant public attention. Politicians become involved to reassure the public by throwing funding to researchers and organizations who call loudest for bans and filters. For example, proposing such amendments as the Deleting Online Predators Act (2006—H.R. 5319—'DOPA'), to the Online Decency Act that would provide state governments with power to fine teachers and librarians who allowed students to access any social networking sites. This legislation would have had the effect of blocking numerous valuable and innocuous resources. Furthermore, the legislation would have potentially criminalized numerous everyday on-line searching activities. For example, educational sites such as Media Awareness Network, NetSafe and Childnet, which provide resources for teachers, students and parents, would be out of bounds. Teachers and librarians would simply have avoided using computers at all to avoid fines, ultimately reducing students' learning opportunities. Fortunately civil rights activists supported by the national library associations were successful in arguing against implementation of DOPA.

School officials also perpetuate this myth by convincing parents that they are in control by enlisting the help of police officers. As Larson (1997) discovered, when incidents at schools become public, school administrators are often galvanized into action to preserve school reputation and demonstrate that their house is in order and to reassure parents that they are in charge. They, like the media, resort to using language that describes the cyber-bullying as a "battle" to show that they will win. As Lankshear and Knobel explain, we attempt to manage the "thing"—that problem that makes us look inefficient. We try to keep it down, and shoot blindly into the air, hoping we will hit it and make it go away. However, the more we ignore the nuances and deep complexities, the intersecting and interlocking barriers, and the rapidly evolving legal and ethical boundaries, the more we support the myth that zero-tolerance will frighten young people into treating each other nicely. The more we believe that simply because we have developed codes of conduct and mission statements with the stated intent of having "safe and caring schools" or "bully-free schools," that we are obliged to do no more, the more we fail (DiGiulio, 2001). The "shoot em down" approach fails to recognize and take advantage of educational opportunities staring us in the face. The more we fail to control, the more obsessed we become. Our research (Shariff, 2004-09) finds evidence that this obsession with control persists, regardless of the fact that even the media are now moving towards highlighting proactive learning options based on feedback to their news reports from public bloggers (see Zinga, Chapter 5). As the foreword notes, the risks of reification are high, and we have lost too much time. Ultimately, we sacrifice the educational and emotional well-being of too many children and youth as a result of this approach (Anand, 1999; boyd & Jenkins, 2006; Campbell, 2005; DiGiulio, 2001; Lankshear & Knobel, 2006).

A second glaring irony that confounds us is the fact that it is adult society that models and largely sustains the forms of hostile, abusive and discriminatory behavior that we expect our children to avoid. Zero-tolerance punishes young people for mimicking the precedents that society has set for them. The act of engaging in zero-tolerance punishment without engaging in thoughtful dialogue and reasoning with perpetrators of cyber-bullying is itself an act of intolerance. It is time to end this cycle, and we hope that this book will begin that process.

To that end, this is the first publication on cyber-bullying in which researchers, community and corporate partners have come together globally to study a range of concerns relating to the use of social communications/networking devices;

illuminate joint strategies that reduce the potential for cyber-bullying from early childhood to young adulthood; learn its psychological and legal impact; and keep kids and schools out of court. We are indeed fortunate to have this opportunity to present comprehensive and well-researched perspectives on cyber-bullying, and to address the many myths that currently abound in the public sphere. Our book is unique because its contents place less emphasis on acts of cyber-bullying or the specific behaviors of perpetrators and those they select to victimize. Rather, the chapters that follow engage in conversations that address the broader social, legal, ethical, policy-making and pedagogical concerns that are often overlooked when cyber-bullying is discussed. We attempt to detangle the "web" or "networks" (metaphoric and technological) of stakeholders and institutional influences on the ways in which children, youth and adults conceptualize, approach, express themselves, and respond to those expressions in the world of cyber-space without minimizing the complexities of navigating free expression, privacy, supervision and safety in virtual environments.

We have included chapter contributions by experts involved in international and interdisciplinary research on cyber-bullying and on-line social networking, from early childhood to young adulthood, drawing on legal, educational, behavioural, social and technological perspectives. Some of our contributors have been involved in collaboration with researchers in education, sociology, psychology, criminology, the humanities, policy and law from Canada, the United States, India, Australia, Britain, New Zealand and Japan.

CONTEXT, BEHAVIOURS, AND MYTH SHAPERS

It is no secret that the rapid evolvement of new technologies has increased cellular phone and computer use by children internationally. As global communications networks connect youth and children day and night, social interactions and activities on websites such as Facebook, MySpace and YouTube for youth, Webkinz and Club Penguin for children have become extremely popular. Social computing and networking ("SC tools") are relatively new phenomena, especially for children (grades 1 to 7), who can now interact with peers instantly, regardless of location, and connect with parents through text-messaging and email. Corporations increasingly market their information technology products to younger audiences, but these captive children are not necessarily aware of the social impact of these products. As noted in the introduction to this chapter, cyber-bullying currently tops many public policy and research agendas (Fitzpatrick, 2008; Morris, 2008; Shariff, 2008). To develop relevant resources for children who seek support in dealing with cyber-bullying, it is critical that we understand their social networking behavior on the web and their approaches to searching for on-line information and resources. It is also important to examine how corporations ("IT corporations"), parents, teachers and librarians ("IS specialists") (collectively "stakeholders") can be better prepared for their responsibilities regarding cyber-bullying and children's related social interactions. Some of these important considerations include:

Educational and behavioral context: Monitoring this covert form of electronic bullying is difficult because it occurs on personal devices and raises important issues about supervision, free expression, privacy, and safety in cyber-space. Students can post modified photographs of peers or defame teachers on-line. Two forms of cyber-bullying have emerged: 1) peer against peer, where school-mates are singled out for ridicule and harassment through blogs, chat rooms and related sites; and 2) anti-authority forms of cyber-expression (Shariff, 2008). Through social networking sites such as Facebook and YouTube, educators have found themselves in the public eye as the brunt of on-line sexual jokes, films, modified photographs, insults and dangerous rumours (e.g., falsely labelled as pedophiles). Students often deny that they are directly bullying authority figures. Instead, they assert their free expression rights to have "private" conversations with friends despite the fact that those conversations can be viewed on-line by anyone.

Impact of technology providers: Youth are a captive audience for corporations who market their SC tools to increasingly younger audiences. Consider the impact of the following television commercial by Rogers, a telephone company, which appeared approximately two years ago and received significant airtime before academics and organizations such as the Canadian Teachers' Federation contacted the company's marketing department to make their concerns heard: The advertisement begins with five teenagers riding in an SUV. All of them except the driver are holding cellular phones. The passenger in the front seat uses her phone to take a photograph of the driver and emails it to her friends. She informs the driver that they are going to post his photograph on-line, and send it to all their friends for comments. The other passengers laugh and begin to text rapidly. The driver asks: "You're laughing at me, right?" His female passenger coyly replies: "Of course not, we're laughing *with* you!" Her grimace, unseen by the driver, suggests to the viewing audience that his peers really are laughing *at* him, not *with* him. The message in the commercial comes through: "Buy our cellular phones with photographic and internet capabilities and you'll have more fun." The advertisement clearly targets a teenage buying audience. At first glance this commercial is about selling cellular phones; however, it taps into the teenage tendency to put others down for fun. Similarly, a T-Mobile ad shows a high school student photographing younger students in the cafeteria. He compares their photos with those of animals on his phone—a turtle, a chicken, a horse. The camera focuses on his face as he laughs and snorts like a pig. The other children laugh to themselves. When this commercial is presented to high school students for analysis, they are divided in their opinions as to whether it encourages or discourages cyber-bullying. They question whether the marketing strategy intended to suggest that it is okay to take pictures of others and match them up with animal pictures or whether the marketing objective included a subtle public policy message to inform young people that bullying is not "cool." A third advertisement by koodomobile.com entices young girls to "Parlez et textez sans culpabilité" ("speak and text without culpability or blame"). These commercials illustrate that technology corporations have an important stake in cyber-bullying and suggest that marketing strategists need to become critically aware of the impact of their messages on young people. We are convinced that corporate technology firms and ISP providers could become powerful advocates for responsible use of their products, without sacrificing financial gain, if they can better appreciate their impact on young people's tendency to push the boundaries and engage first in innocent teasing and horseplay, that sometimes crosses over to result in serious cases of cyber-bullying using SC tools.

Impact of news media: The news media wield substantial power as a policy shaper. Public outreach on cyber-bullying is widely carried out by the news media, and in most cases, the daily news is the primary source of information for parents and policy makers. The competitive demands of news production and dissemination in a knowledge society where breaking headlines reach the on-line public only seconds after incidents occur, has increased the tendency of reporters and journalists to sensationalize cyber-bullying as a conflict between kids and schools. This framing of the issues in the media was highly problematic, because it raised considerable public fear that the Internet provides young people with too much power. This fear resulted in calls by teachers' unions, universities, and parent groups for banning of communications technologies (CTs) such as YouTube, Facebook, MySpace (boyd & Jenkins, 2006) and increased spending on filters and lobbies to amend criminal laws to account for negative on-line uses (Fitzpatrick, 2008). It often invited public policy responses grounded in military models of zero-tolerance such as suspension of suspected perpetrators from school (Rusk, 2007; Campbell, 2005). More recently however, and as one of our contributors, Dawn Zinga observes in Chapter 5, this trend is slowly changing, as media outlets reach out to audiences through the Internet. Many newspapers, television and radio stations provide websites that invite feedback and comments on their news reports. Ironically, bloggers on these websites have felt the impact of policing or monitoring biased or sensational framing of news stories, forcing journalists to consider writing more balanced reports that address the legal and ethical considerations as well as policy and programmatic challenges. Zinga's chapter discusses media reports that draw attention to approaches and programs that have a positive impact by reducing cyber-bullying and related on-line abuses. This is good news. It is imperative that the media, our primary information sources for the public at large, learn to appreciate that ignoring the systemic contexts of cyber-bullying (racism, sexism and homophobia), glossing over political and social tensions, demographics, economics, and modeling of adult behaviors, ultimately keeps the public misinformed and ignorant about the real issues. We believe that the news media could, in collaboration with technology firms, be a powerful contributor to the dialogue towards socially responsible use of SC tools and that both these powerful stakeholders ought to engage with front-line users such as children, youth, educators and parents, to promote improved educational policies and practices on cyber-safety.

We reinforce our point made elsewhere (Shariff, 2008; 2009) that it is essential to remember that it was our generation, not the children or youth, who developed and continue to introduce the SC tools that create children's digital realities. They are growing up in a world that is simultaneously physical and virtual. Cyber-space is very much an integral aspect of their world. Discriminatory attitudes and hegemonies that permeate our societies are embedded within the structures of our institutions. We often fail to recognize or acknowledge their existence and model behaviours and expressions that are internalized by our children and youth. And yet, when they reflect those behaviours and hurtful forms of expression, we suspend and expel them from schools and punish them with little explanation as to why we hold them to a double standard. While the stated intent of our school mission statements is to foster inclusive and respectful school environments, there seems to be a disconnect between mission and practice in many schools. The Internet has simply provided the wide open spaces that allow society's prejudices and disrespect to surface, opening up a Pandora's box of challenges. Lankshear and Knobel (2006) make an important observation, namely, that adult mindsets against technologies are as culpable as any negative behaviours or forms of expression that take place on-line. Efforts to control and manage on-line expression through filters, firewalls and criminal legislation comprise band-aid measures that exacerbate, rather than reduce, the problems.

Hence our objective in this book is to demonstrate that not only are the issues complex and varied but that important and interesting work is being undertaken globally by academics, educators, legal practitioners, and child safety networking organizations. These stakeholders work individually and collaboratively to address the issues through rigorous scholarly research, development of practical on-line programs, and establishment of stakeholder networks that recognize and raise awareness of the systemic complexities involved in cyber-bullying.

We present chapters by authors who embrace the complexities to identify focused, supportive and inclusive educational responses instead of reactive and punitive measures. As mentioned earlier in this introduction, at one level, the task is not easy. It involves the delicate balancing of constitutional rights such as free expression, with valid considerations of privacy, supervision and safety. The task becomes even more difficult as the legal boundaries shift and blur in cyber-space. The courts balk at opening the floodgates to litigation and hesitate when it comes to clarifying stakeholders' legal expectations and responsibilities, because laws have generally not caught up to the realities of a globalized world that now relies on communication technologies. There are moral considerations at play here too, as well as the age and maturity level of young people when they choose to tell lies. It is important to examine children's understanding of the motives, rights and responsibilities of on-line activity and determine what constitutes a violation of those rights. Children's lie-telling is related to perceived consequences to self, balanced with consideration of consequences to others (Talwar et al., 2004; Talwar, Gordon, & Lee, 2007). While younger children often lie indiscriminately, they rate lies more negatively and also show greater guilt or shame at being caught than do older children (Bussey, 1992; 1999; Talwar & Lee, 2002). Older children are more nuanced in their evaluations, taking the intentions of the transgressor as well as the degree of harm into consideration (Lee & Ross, 1997). It remains unclear how children view such transgressions and degrees of harm on-line and the frequency, nature and motives of their lying behaviour. From the social domain perspective, children may view on-line activity as part of the personal domain or subject to conventional rules of their peer group rather than moral standards of conduct. Social cognitive theory suggests that children and adolescents may be influenced differently by fear of repercussions or punishment, external factors (e.g., peer group evaluation, schools, parents, media) and internal factors (e.g., internalized moral standards of behaviour (Bandura, 1991)). Poststructuralist approaches (Davies, 2006; Kofoed, 2008), and a Foucauldian-inspired a focus on power as productive also shed light on power relations that develop when children cyber-bully or gossip on-line about peers and authority figures. This also suggests the need to understand the systemic power relationships within schools as institutions and the power of parents and the policy shapers we have mentioned earlier. It involves detangling the harm caused and considering when the line between teasing among friends and bullying has been crossed or when the critique of an authority figure, while unpleasant, may well be justified. This book attempts to cover much of this ground by looking at the points at which free expression crosses over to become cyber-libel and at what point children can be expected to leave their rights to free expression at the school house gates.

On another level, the task is simple. Our use of technology can be understood simplistically as an expression of our humanity. In this way, the choices we make, and those of our children, schools, and corporate citizens, can be understood as either a compassionate expression of our humanity or as an accurate reflection of the social relationships our society tacitly condones. Moral directives such as "Be kind, do unto others…, walk in another's footsteps, consider the results of your actions," can and do make a difference when they are considered carefully, and applied consistently, in the way each of us approaches technology to either benefit or destroy our social conditions.

As you read the following contributions by scholars and program directors from around the globe, we urge you to consider your own potential roles and responsibilities towards making the Internet a safer, more human place for our youth. Whether you are a teacher, administrator, researcher, politician, lawyer, youth advocate, corporate CEO, software developer, ISP provider—whatever your role(s)—we invite you to read this book with an eye towards how you can make a difference.

AN OVERVIEW OF THE BOOK

We have organized the volume into three distinct sections, each with a theme. Section 1 provides background and research about young people's use of technology as well as the media and legal discourses about them both. Section 2 explores legal issues around freedom of expression, privacy rights and supervisory responsibilities. In Section 3, our contributors discuss specific programs and educational pedagogy that they have developed and implemented with stakeholders and communities of young people.

Section 1: Background and Influences

Section 1 provides the background necessary to help readers understand the range of research on young people's online activities, and helps them to critically examine the role and potential culpability of technologies, media, legal and educational institutions in shaping young people's behavior. Taken together these chapters should help readers develop a sophisticated appreciation for not only what is happening on-line, but also become able to consider *why* it is happening. It will also provide insight into how policy shapers such as the media and technology corporations influence resulting policy approaches in schools.

Chapter 2, *Towards understanding the potential triggering features of technology* by Michel Walrave and Wannes Heirman provides an analysis of young people's online behaviours. While the research is primarily based in the home country of the chapter's authors, Belgium, they also cite comprehensive research from other countries that corroborates their findings. Their approach is consistent with our own work in Canada. Although the chapter provides some statistical information about the specific nature and the frequency of on-line bullying behaviours, the authors conclude that it is not the technologies that "trigger" these behaviours but rather, online cyber-bullying behaviour can be more accurately understood as the morphing of traditional bullying *attitudes* into a new medium. With this in mind, they alert readers to positive and pedagogically important on-line interactions that balance negative interactions. In that regard, Chapter 2 provides a balanced, thoughtful and informative perspective.

Professors Dianne Hoff and Sidney Mitchell adopt a unique approach to exploring the relationship between gender, on-line behaviours, and the reporting of those behaviours in Chapter 3: *Gender and cyber-bullying: How do we know what we know?* Their chapter challenges the growing body of research that purports to find significant differences in bullying behaviour of girls and boys without considering reporting norms. Their review of data discloses some interesting and important reporting patterns among both genders that warrant attention by researchers and educators alike. They detail how socially accepted gender differences influence the reporting patterns between boys and girls and that such reports may not accurately report the behaviors and social interactions that take place both on and off-line. The authors remind us that we must carefully analyze our own assumption relating to gender roles, experiences and expected reporting patterns. Accordingly, this chapter provides important insight into how gender may influence the messages we hear from young people.

In Chapter 4, Ellen Kraft examines *Juicycampus.com: How was this business model culpable of encouraging harassment on college campuses?* Her review involves a particularly troubling type of online space that seems designed to purposefully engender misogynist and hurtful behaviors that all adults who work responsibly with young people ought to minimize. The chapter provides a stark reality check of the types of hateful behaviors that unfortunately emerge on-line. This chapter also provides a preview of the serious legal challenges that can emerge and are discussed in Section 2. Importantly, the chapter also analyzes resistance to on-line communications sites like *juicycampus.com* and highlights issues relating to individual agency, thoughtful decision-making and responsibility on the part of young adults who use the site. Specifically, we see how many young people and their post-secondary institutions attempt to resist the imposition of this space on their social communities.

Chapter 5, *Boundaries in cyber-space: Media and stakeholders as policy shapers,* is the final chapter of our introductory section. Dawn Zinga undertakes a systematic review of ways in which a variety of news media stories have been framed to discuss cyber-bullying. As noted earlier, Dr. Zinga draws attention to the fact that while journalists and their producers and editors tend to sensationalize the stories with particular emphasis on children either gaining too much power or being too vulnerable on the Internet, there is also a new trend towards balanced reporting. This shift draws attention to the complex tensions between school authority, on and off-campus considerations, the extent of school responsibilities to intervene, emerging legal considerations, issues of legal and ethical accountability, and proactive and well-informed programming. That shift is mirrored in media framing of the issues as influenced by the new on-line police, namely, the bloggers who represent public perspectives through frank on-line discussion of the issues relating to specific cases of cyber-bullying, school, police, legislative and judicial responses.

Section 2: Legal Considerations

The legal context is crucial to any discussion involving social networking and cyber-bullying in contemporary society. Public educators, legislators, and the judiciary are generally considered to be the primary policy-makers because of their fiduciary positions as state agents. The legal boundaries that address these forms of expression have blurred as young people increasingly engage in more sophisticated online socializing. While most legal cases in Canada have been settled out of court, a number of claims against schools and cyber-perpetrators have been decided in the United States, many of which are discussed in this book.

Cyber-bullying is difficult to monitor because it occurs on personal computers and cell-phones outside of school hours and off school campuses, raising constitutional dilemmas about supervision, free expression, privacy, and safety in cyber-space. Although it currently tops many public policy and research agendas, the law has not kept pace with rapidly evolving technologies. There is a lack of knowledge about the role of stakeholders, such as technology corporations, news media and teachers' unions, as policy "shapers" and their legal responsibilities to proactively address cyber-bullying. Research at international levels reveals a behavioural focus without adequate attention to legal, policy and systemic barriers created within schools. Sensationalist media reports about cyber-bullying as noted above, have in some cases, increased fear that the Internet gives youth too much power, resulting in reactive and legalistic school policies grounded in zero-tolerance that suspend rather than educate children, and fuel calls for legislation to control cyber-bullying.

Our international policy guidelines on cyber-bullying drew from five legal frameworks under existing and emerging law, as they apply to cyber-bullying (Shariff, 2008–09), namely: i) tort law (cyber-libel); ii) constitutional law (balancing freedom of expression with safety and privacy considerations); iii) criminal law and youth justice provisions (criminal harassment and expressions of hate); iv) human rights provisions and jurisprudence (standards for institutional responsibilities to provide safe learning/working environments in physical and virtual settings); and v) school law (regulatory statutes and internal codes of conduct).

Canadian limits on free expression: Most students who are suspended under school zero-tolerance policies reject school definitions of anti-authority on-line expression as cyber-bullying. They claim infringement of their rights to free expression under Section 2 (b) of the Canadian Charter of Rights and Freedoms. They also assert their privacy rights to have personal conversations with friends on-line. No known cases of cyber-bullying have been heard by Canadian courts; however, the Supreme Court of Canada has provided direction in adult cases of cyber-libel. *In Hill v. Church of Scientology of Toronto* (1995) it held that a good reputation is closely related to the innate worthiness and dignity of the individual. Therefore, reputation must be protected in the same way as freedom of expression under Section 2(b). The court noted that a reputation tarnished by libel can seldom regain its formal luster. Accordingly, society has an interest in ensuring its members enjoy and protect their good reputation so long as it is merited. Along similar lines, in the case of *Newman et al v. Halstead* (2006), an adult was held liable for $626,000 for posting derogatory comments about teachers on-line.

American limits on free expression: American courts have developed a stronger body of jurisprudence on cyber-bullying in the school context. Chapter 6, *Legal issues related to cyber-bullying* by Jacqueline Stefkovich, Emily Crawford and Mark Murphy begin the legal conversation by providing details about the seminal cases informing current law. They provide a cogent and helpful summary of established and emerging cases in the United States and aptly point out that cases brought before the courts are not restricted to peer against peer conflicts. Perpetrators have been sued for anti-authority attacks that impact the entire school climate and students' feelings of safety. Significantly, a larger number of court challenges are launched against schools in response to student suspensions, fueling the debate about the limits of school intervention in off-campus student expression that occurs in cyber-space. The burden in these cases rests with school officials to justify that their decisions to discipline students do not infringe or unreasonably override rights to free expression.

The on and off-campus debate has dominated litigation on cyber-bullying. Although the boundaries of responsibility remain blurred in some cases, American courts have begun to establish guidelines. Relying on the exceptions to the right to free expression in the landmark decision in *Tinker v. Des Moines* (1969), U.S. courts have ruled that schools can intervene in off-campus expression only if it *materially or substantively disrupts learning* in the physical school setting. Moreover, in keeping with the precedent set in *Hazelwood v. Kuhlmeier* (1988), if the cyber-bullying occurs on school computers or websites, students can be held responsible for on-campus infractions of school policies and be subject to discipline. This chapter draws our attention to some of the following cases in which free speech trumped school authority and where the students mostly used home computers during off-school hours.

Free expression protected: In *A.B. v. State of Indiana* (Ind. App. 2007), a student posted a lewd comment protesting her school principal's decision to ban body piercings. The appeals court ruled that student opinions are constitutionally protected no matter how lewd the language used. The state Supreme Court, however, later vacated the appeals court decision and issued its own ruling (Ind. 2008). While the high court also sided with A.B., the justices disagreed with the appeals court's reasoning, finding instead that the state had failed to prove A.B.'s posting constituted harassment under state law. As Stefkovich et al. detail, courts have, in many cases, supported students whose rights have been overridden by school reactions to their forms of on-line expression.

School authority allowed: Both Chapter 6 (Stefkovich et al.) and Chapter 7 by Patrick Pauken, entitled Morse v. Frederick *and cyber-bullying in schools: The impact on freedom of expression, disciplinary authority, and school leadership* inform us that a few school boards have also successfully defended their right to discipline students for cyber-bullying by establishing either a nexus between speech and material disruption or between speech and school property (*Wisniewski v. Weedsport,* 2nd Cir., 2007; *Morse v. Frederick,* 127 S. Ct. 2618, 2007; *Ponce v. Socorro Indep. Sch. Dist.,* No. 06–50709, 2007 U.S. App.) In *J.S. v. Bethlehem Area School District,* 807 A.2d 847 (Pa. 2002), for example, a student created a website entitled "Teacher Sux" including vulgar images and threats. The court found that his expressions did not comprise *true* threats but held that the school had not violated his First Amendment rights because the site caused fear in the school environment. As this brief review of Canadian and American case law suggests, the legal standards to be met generally require a nexus between student speech and its effects on the entire school environment. As Professor Pauken explains in Chapter 7, a recent U.S. Supreme Court decision involving off-campus speech advocating drug use (*Morse v. Frederick,* 2007) could replace *Tinker* as the modern standard to inform policy on cyber-bullying. Pauken argues that although *Morse* did not directly relate to on-line expression, it did address location, content and the effect of off-campus speech. As newer law, that precedent is more readily applicable to the transformational challenges of technology than *Tinker, Bethel* and *Hazelwood.* Although it adhered to the *Tinker* standard of *material and substantial disruption,* the ruling also emphasized *reasonable interpretation* of student speech, which is supported by recent decisions outlined in Chapter 7. Pauken highlights recent cases in which the courts have directed that school administrators must be permitted to react quickly and decisively to the threat of physical or emotional violence against students and stressed that schools should not have to second guess their own judgment or worry about litigation, because indecision leaves school environments unprotected from "special danger" (*Ponce v. Socorro Indep. Sch. Dist.,* No. 06–50709, 2007 U.S. App. LEXIS 26862 (5th Cir. Nov. 20, 2007).

We caution schools not to interpret these recent decisions as free license to continue applying zero-tolerance policies rooted in military models that punish and suspend students. Such approaches are antithetical to their duty of care and purpose as educators and can perpetuate hostile, dangerous and poisoned environments. Schools would be better advised to interpret these legal guidelines as supporting proactive, ethical and informed policies and pedagogical practices that model respect, promote dialogue about empathy, and develop leadership, social and civil responsibility. Engaging this way with students shows greater promise of reducing cyber-bullying towards productive and healthy school environments, both physical and virtual. In that regard, human rights jurisprudence is instructive.

Importance of school environment: Canadian human rights and American Title IX jurisprudence has clarified an obligation on schools as public institutions to ensure their learning environments are inclusive, non-discriminatory and not *poisoned* or *deliberately dangerous*. To meet these obligations, school administrators need to be cognizant of the extent to which they can intervene to control student speech, whether it is on or off campus in cyber-space. Responsibility to ensure safe school environments was also made clear in *Davis v. Monroe County Board of Education* (1999) to ensure schools do not support *deliberately dangerous* environments. As with *Title IX* claims for sexual harassment in United States, Canada has developed a large body of jurisprudence in the area of sexual harassment within institutional settings. Sexual harassment is a prevalent aspect of cyber-bullying. Cases such as *Robichaud v. Canada* (1987) and *North Vancouver School District No. 44 v. Jubran* (2005) are instructive because they affirm: (1) an institutional responsibility to protect those victimized by co-workers or co-students outside the institution if they must face their perpetrators within the institution; and (2) an obligation that public institutions provide an environment free of discrimination, conducive to learning that is not *poisoned*. (See *Ross v. New Brunswick*, (1996)).

Chapter 8, *Mediated speech and communication rights: Situating cyber-bullying within the emerging global internet governance regime,* sifts our legal perspective to consider issues of global governance. For example, Marc Raboy and his co-author Jeremy Shtern draw our attention to the fact that although cyber-bullying is a relatively new phenomenon, the question of how acceptable speech is defined has been asked in regard to a series of successive "new" mass media for decades. They observe that although all public discourse and communication take place in a particular moral and ethical environment, media forms exhibit characteristics that demand particular forms of framing by public authorities. In this context the need to protect children has been a long-standing concern of media and communication policy. In this regard, Chapter 8 provides a comprehensive review of a range of emerging global governance treaties, conventions, summits and policies aimed at managing uses of the Internet and protecting society from cyber-crime and their particular application to cyber-bullying. The authors provide sound arguments as to why the global Internet governance regime, and within that regime, multi-stakeholder co-operation, offers opportunities through the "informal co-operation or the organization of dynamic coalitions" to pressure social networking sites such as Facebook and MySpace which are often media through which cyber-bullying occurs but are rarely interested or responsive to policy solutions. Lankshear and Knobel (2006) would likely agree with Raboy and Shtern's articulation that a more nuanced understanding of the Internet as fluid as opposed to static is needed:

> The view that the borderless nature of internet mediated communication creates jurisdictional conflicts that render it impossible to regulate is being discredited by the emergence of the global internet governance regime and a more nuanced understanding that the Internet should not be seen as a static technological tool, that its architecture and the values that are embedded into it are increasingly being subject to debate and institutional governance. (p. 30 of ch. 8).

Importantly, they note that while Internet governance may help to manage or in some cases curtail on-line expression, equal attention will need to be paid to the losses that children would suffer to their rights to free speech, and as such it would be important to ensure a balance between rights and responsibilities.

Given the important legal and governance policy considerations raised in this section, it is of significant importance that the conceptual research approach begins in early childhood to address the nuances and complexities, and that any forms of intervention, policy and programming are sensitive to these considerations. To that end, we provide in the third and more practice-based section, examples of some of the initiatives that are being undertaken. While we do not advocate that these responses will resolve the complexities, reduce or curtail cyber-bullying, we observe that our contributing authors are approaching their research and programming in thoughtful ways that are cognizant of the dynamic nature of expressions in cyber-space, and of the need to work with very young children to develop models and standards to guide them in use of the Internet in socially responsible, inclusive and educational ways.

Section 3: Towards Improved Interventions and Pedagogical Practice

The third section of the book is devoted to introducing readers to intervention programs and gives important insights about effective pedagogical practice. While by no means exhaustive, these chapters provide examples of different strategies being used to impact the behaviors of youth on-line. These examples include: developing a "safe" and "educative" on-line space for Australian youth, involving entire school communities to work towards being "bully-free" in New Zealand, and a nationwide education effort in the U.K. sponsored by the government designed to reach all youth and parents. In the final chapter, we share some of our own experiences working with groups.

Chapter 9, *Changing learning ecologies: Social media for cyber-citizens* by Jennifer Masters and Nicola Yelland provides insight into thoughtful structuring and monitoring of on-line social interactions beginning in early childhood. They describe an Australian initiative to build a safe educative on-line space for youth. We believe that this program, *SuperclubsPLUS Australia,* as introduced in early childhood is particularly important because it does not attempt to teach children about on-line safety independently of their on-line activity. Rather it creates an on-line community, similar to many of the social networking sites that exist, where adults are present and can help children reflect on socially hurtful or potentially dangerous behaviors in real time as they engage in these behaviors. Moreover it helps to develop empathy and an understanding of the impact of their comments from a very young age so that by the time they reach adolescence, considerate, inclusive and ethical use of social networking sites becomes second nature to these children. Moreover, this chapter emphasizes the use of technology as a safe teaching and learning space.

Chapter 10, *Kia Kaha: Police and schools working together to eliminate bullying, a New Zealand intervention,* shares a well-developed school intervention program developed by the New Zealand police that they conduct in partnership with school communities. In writing this chapter, Officer Gillian Palmer and Professor Juliana Raskauskus make the importance of community wide intervention programs, stakeholder buy-in, and working with partnerships abundantly clear. This well developed program can offer any school community important insights into the many steps of changing school cultures. This is a refreshing change from an approach focused wholly on policing as providing criminal sanctions to policing as educative and supportive.

Chapter 11, *Cyber-bullying: A whole-school community approach* is a nationwide initiative, sponsored by the U.K. government, to educate youth, teachers and parents about issues of on-line safety. In this chapter Will Gardner, CEO of Childnet International, shares some of the most sophisticated materials developed to date. This program is an excellent model for exemplifying how large scale interventions have the capacity to reach millions of people through the Internet. The Childnet story is important for politicians and governments to witness how well funded initiatives can have large-scale and long-term impact. These educational programs show far greater promise of reducing cyber-bullying, thereby saving the costs of putting cyber-offenders through publicly funded alternative schools or through the criminal justice system.

FINAL THOUGHTS

Although we had initially developed a concluding chapter to the book, on reviewing the strength of the chapters that follow our introduction, we have decided to let readers come to their own conclusions and ultimate responses to cyber-bullying. It is our goal upon completing this book that readers have a well developed appreciation for the complexity of issues and a good sense of the legal tensions and adult responsibilities to address cyber-bullying in educational, non-arbitrary and proactive, as opposed to reactive, ways. More importantly, we anticipate that they will come to recognize the four myths identified in this chapter (and throughout the book from our authors' perspectives) in their own schools and communities, as reification and oversimplification of the real complexities, and appropriate responses to cyber-bullying. Such realization and re-conceptualization will, we hope, mobilize collaborative stakeholder partnerships and informed dialogue (both on and off-line) in every aspect of teacher education, professional development and school curricula through a new lens.

It is essential that we ask ourselves whether we can be proud of the precedents we set for our children or of the environmental, financial, political or technological challenges we leave them as our legacy. Few would be proud of our current legacy. To the contrary, we owe it to our children to help them develop improved communications and relationships—both on and off-line towards a society that is significantly more mature, caring and intelligent than the one we cannot seem to escape. Young people are our future leaders. Given the state of our contemporary world, they are our only hope for a better future. It is time that we stop blaming them for emulating our behaviors and expressions and learn from them to develop a stronger and stable global society. We hope you will join us in this crucial endeavor and that this book will provide new insights into the complexities of cyber-bullying and other forms of on-line communication, and encourage thoughtful, informed and non-arbitrary responses towards inclusive, supportive and educational on-line teaching, learning and communication. To do this work we will need to re-conceptualize cyber-bullying as an indicator of deeper systemic challenges and learning opportunities within particular schools, communities and society as a whole, rather than sensationalizing cyber-bullying as a battle in which students are pitted against teachers, and parents against schools, and where unwieldy and out of control youth wield an "arsenal" of technological weapons against their authority figures. Instead of looking for scapegoats, we must seek collaborative partnerships that provide young people with opportunities to share their technological proficiency with adults who are having difficulty adjusting to rapidly changing technologies.

As the "guru" of research on bullying, Dan Olweus (1991; 1993) observed over a decade ago, bullying is significantly reduced when students are invited to contribute to development of school rules and school codes of conduct. Certainly, giving students "control" of developing disciplinary consequences for their own on-line expressions and behavior would empower and provide them with a sense of responsibility and accountability. Olweus' findings are supported by other studies (DiGiulio, 2001; Butler-Kisber & Portelli, 2003; boyd & Jenkins, 2006). This approach can easily be enhanced by increased opportunities for on-line discussions, feedback, dialogue and interaction between students at various ages with stakeholders such as parents, marketing strategists from technology corporations, media representatives, librarians and information systems experts, legal practitioners, law-makers and law enforcement officials, so that each of these stakeholder groups or policy shapers, including students, gains a broader appreciation of the complexities and collaborative learning opportunities that exist. Young people have enormous potential that can be enhanced and supported by information and communications systems technologies. If our educational stakeholders do not catch up now, it may be too late.

References

Anand, S. S. (1999) Preventing youth crime: What works, what doesn't and what it all means for Canadian juvenile justice. *Queen's Law Journal*, 25(1): 177–249.

Asthana, A. and Smith, D. (2007). Teachers call for YouTube ban over 'cyber-bullying' {electronic version}. *Guardian Unlimited*, 29 July. Retrieved 22 August 2007 from http://observer.guardian.co/uk_news/story/0,2137177,00.html.

Bandura, A. (1991). Social cognitive theory of moral thought and action. In W. M. Kurtines & J. L. Gewirtz (Eds.), *Handbook of moral behavior and development* (Vol. 1, pp. 45–103). Hillsdale, NJ: Lawrence Erlbaum Associates, Inc.

Bernstein, A. and Hanna, B. W. (2005). Cyberlibel: Defamation proofing your online world. Paper presented at the Ninth Annual Canadian IT Law Association Conference, Montreal, Quebec, Canada.

boyd, d. and Jenkins, H. (2006). MySpace and Deleting Online Predators Act (DOPA) [electronic version]. *MIT Tech Talk*, 26 May. Retrieved 13 August, 2007 from www.danah.org/papers/MySpaceDOPA.html.

Brown, L. (2007). Teachers declare war on cyber-bullying [electronic version]. TheStar.com. 13 July. Retrieved 13 August, 2007 from www.thestar.com/article/235675.

Bussey, K. (1992). Lying and truthfulness: Children's definitions, standards, and evaluative reactions. *Child Development, 63,* 129–137.

Bussey, K. (1999). Children's categorization and evaluation of different types of lies and truths. *Child Development, 70,* 1338–1347.

Butler-Kisber, L. and Portelli, J. P. (2003). The challenge of student engagement: Beyond mainstream conceptions and practices. *McGill Journal of Education, 38*(2): 207.

Campbell, M. (2005). Cyberbullying: An old problem in a new guise? *Australian Journal of Guidance and Counseling*, 15(1): 68–76.

Davies, B. (2006). Subjectification: The relevance of Butler's analysis for education. *British Journal of Sociology of Education*, 27 (4), 425–438.

DiGiulio, R. C. (2001). *Educate, mediate, or litigate: What teachers, parents, and administrators must do about student behavior.* Thousand Oaks, CA: Corwin Press.

Dolmage, W. R. (2000). Lies, dammed lies and statistics: The media's treatment of youth violence. *Education and Law Journal*, 10: 1–46.

Edwards, L. Y. (2005). Victims, villains, and vixens. In S.R. Mazzarella (ed), *Girl wide web*. New York: Peter Lang, pp. 13–30.

Evans, R. (1996) *The human side of school change: Reform, resistance, and real life.* San Francisco: Jossey-Bass.

Fitzpatrick, M. (12 July, 2008). Teachers urged to be careful on cyber-bullying: New policy likely to be ratified today. www.canada.com. CanWest News—received from McGill Media relations, July 12, 2008.

Fullan, M. (2006). *Turnaround leadership.* San Francisco: Jossey-Bass.

Higginbottom, N. and Packham, B. (2007). Student cracks government's 85M porn filter {electronic version}. *The Herald Sun*, 26 August. Retrieved 26 August 2007 from www.news.com.au/story/0,23599,22304224–421,00.html.

Kofoed, J. (2008) Social categories intersecting in school. In *Childhood*, Aug 2008; vol. 15: pp. 415—430

Lankshear, C. and Knobel, M. (2006). *New Literacies: Everyday practices and classroom learning.* 2nd edn. Maidenhead: Open University Press.

Larson, C. L. (1997). Is the land of Oz an alien nation? A sociopolitical study of school community conflict. *Educational Administration Quarterly*, 33(3): 312–50.

Lee, K., & Ross, H. (1997). The concept of lying in adolescents and young adults: Testing Sweetser's folkloristic model. *Merrill-Palmer Quarterly, 43*, 255–270.

Leishman, J. (10, October, 2002). Cyber-bullying: The Internet is the latest weapon in a bully's arsenal. *CBC News The National.* http://cbc.ca/news/national/cyberbullying/index.html. Accessed January 27.03.

Maughan, C. (3 June, 2008). Cyber-bullying can spin out of control: study. Report to English School Boards. Children gang up online, says study, which suggests students need codes of conduct. *The Gazette*, Montreal, A6.

McNeil, L. M. (1998). *Contradictions of control: School structure and school knowledge.* New York: Routledge.

Morris, H. (12, July, 2008). Online bullying should be a criminal offence: teachers. http://www.nationalpost.com/story-printer.html?id=651414. Accessed July 13, 2008.

Myers, D.A. (2006). Defamation and the quiescent anarchy of the Internet: A case study of cyber-targeting. *Penn State Law Review.* 110 (3): 667–86.

Olweus, D. (1991). Bully/victim problems among school children. Basic facts and effects of a school based intervention program. In D. J. Pepler and K. H. Rubins (eds), *The development and treatment of childhood aggression.* Hillsdale, NJ: Erlbaum.

Olweus, D. (1993). *Bullying at school: What we know and what we can do.* Oxford, Cambridge, MA: Blackwell.

Palfrey, Paul. (2009) Written testimony to the Committee on the Judiciary Subcommittee on Crime, Terrorism, and Homeland Security for the "Hearing on Cyberbullying and other Online Safety Issues for Children; H.R. 1966, the 'Megan Meier Cyberbullying Prevention Act'; and H.R. 3630, the 'Adolescent Web Awareness Requires Education Act (AWARE Act)." [electronic version] accessed October 1, 2009 from http://www.judiciary.house.gov/hearings/pdf/Palfrey090930.pdf.

Pepler, D. and Craig, W. (1997). *Bullying: Research and interventions. Youth update.* A publication of the Institute for the Study of Antisocial Youth.

Razack, S. (1998). *Looking white people in the eye: Gender race, and culture in the courtrooms and classrooms.* Toronto, Ontario: University of Toronto Press.

Rusk, J. (2007). High school suspends 19 for bullying principal on website [electronic version]. *The Globe and Mail,* 13 February. Retrieved 13 February 2007 from www.theglobeandmail.com/servlet/story/RTGAM.20070213.wxfacebook13/BNstory/.

Shariff, S. (2004). Keeping schools out of court: Legally defensible models of leadership to reduce cyber-bullying. Educational Forum. *Delta Kappa Pi,* 68(3): 222–23.

Shariff, S. (2006). Balancing competing rights: A stakeholder model for democratic schools. *Canadian Journal of Education,* 403(3): 476–96.

Shariff, S. (2007). 'What's the school's role? What about rights? And Would you report it?.' Data compiled by research assistant, Andrew H. Churchill, Julie D'Eon and Tomoya Tsutsumi. Tables and figures prepared by Andrew H. Churchill. Unpublished research conducted as part of a three year research project on cyber-bullying, funded by SSHRC. Shaheen Shariff, McGill University, Principal Investigator.

Shariff, S. (2008). *Cyber-bullying: Issues and solutions for the school, the classroom, and the home.* Abington, Oxfordshire, UK: Routledge (Taylor & Francis Group).

Shariff, S. (2009). *Confronting Cyber-bullying: What schools need to know to control misconduct and avoid legal consequences.* New York: Cambridge University Press (Spring, 2009)

Shariff, S. and Hoff, D. L. (2007). Cyber-bullying: Clarifying legal boundaries for school supervision in cyberspace {electronic version}. *International Journal of Cyber Criminology.* Retrieved 9 August 2007 from www40.brinkster.com/ccjournal/Shaheen&Hoffijcc.htm.

Skiba, R. and Petersen, R. (1999). The dark side of zero tolerance: Can punishment lead to safe schools? *Phi Delta Kappan,* 80(5): 372–6, 381–3.

Talwar, V., Gordon, H., & Lee, K.. (2007) "Lie-telling behavior in school-age children." *Developmental Psychology, 43,* 804–810.

Talwar, V., & Lee, K. (2002). The development of lying to conceal a transgression: Children's control of expressive behaviour during verbal deception. *International Journal of Behavioral Development, 26,* 436–444.

Talwar, V., Lee, K., Lindsay, R. C. L., & Bala, N. (2004). Children's lie-telling to conceal parents' transgressions: Legal implications. *Law and Human Behavior, 28,* 411–435.

2 · Towards Understanding the Potential Triggering Features of Technology

Michel Walrave
Wannes Heirman

INTRODUCTION

The double-edged nature of communication technology, continuously balancing between risks and opportunities, reveals itself clearly in an emerging societal problem called cyber-bullying. The same technologies that are employed constructively by youngsters to gain knowledge and to consolidate friendships with peers are also used in a destructive way with the purpose to inflict harm and pain. Cyber-bullying is a universal problem, spreading itself across cultures and countries worldwide. All of today's information societies have been confronted with the phenomenon, since information and communication technologies, initially only used in professional spheres, have permeated the households of our communities. In recent years, much academic research has devoted attention to this emerging online form of peer aggression. In Belgium, for instance, the authors of this chapter recently engaged in two large-scale surveys on cyber-bullying. These two studies have confirmed previous quantitative research, finding that a significant proportion of today's youngsters face the burden of being bullied by electronic means. We will start this chapter by exploring the Belgian victimization and perpetration rates of cyber-bullying and their relationship with important background variables: community of origin, gender, age, educational level and daily ICT uses. Next, we will explore a more conceptual level by critically evaluating some often raised issues and concerns about the mediation of technology in cyber-bullying. These issues are the new media's potential to safeguard anonymity, to intrude 24/7 in peers' lives, to circumvent adequate supervision by adults, to reach expanding audiences and to strip away non-verbal cues in online communication processes. We finish the chapter by providing some interesting insights into the question of why some pupils appear to be especially vulnerable to cyber-bullying and some are not.

PREVALENCE

Most international quantitative research shows a significant magnitude of cyber-bullying among pupils, although specific results deviate considerably. For example, one study reports in a special issue of the *Journal of Adolescent Health* victimization estimates range from 9% to 34%, and perpetration estimates fluctuate between 4% and 21% (David-Ferdon & Feldman, 2007). When exploring other studies, similar variations can be found. In the UK NCH study (2005) 770 children (between 11–19 years old) were surveyed: 20% have been cyber-bullied, and 11% claim to have sent a bullying or threatening message to someone else. Higher estimates were found in Li's Canadian study, for which 264 students (grade 7 to 9) were questioned: 25% were victims of cyber-bullying and 17% have cyber-bullied others (Li, 2006).

In Belgium, our research group found in the TIRO study (Teens and ICT: Risks and Opportunities) that one in three pupils in the total sample of 1,318 minors (between 12–18 years old) reports being victimized online (34.2%); whereas, approximately one out of five (21.2%) admits to have been a perpetrator of cyber-bullying. When including frequency, however, only a very small proportion of young people reports systematic perpetration (2.0%) or victimization (2.4%) (Walrave, Lenaerts, & De Moor, 2008). Since we were curious if parents were aware of these prevalence rates, we asked them whether they were suspicious of their teen engaging in bullying or being a victim in online environments. The stated results clearly show that cyber-bullying is an underestimated problem in parents' eyes: only one in four (24.3%) suspects that their son or daughter is being victimized, and less than one in ten (9.1%) believes that their teen is actively involved as a perpetrator.

In addition, we explored whether alternative questioning strategies would lead to different prevalence rates. Therefore the pupils were not only sounded out *explicitly* if they had ever engaged in cyber-bullying or been victimized, but they were also questioned in a more subtle, *implicit* way about their possible involvement in different deviant ICT-uses (see Table 1). This alternate questioning led to dramatically higher victimization and perpetration rates. More than six out of ten teens (64.3%) declared having experienced one or several of the described situations, while four out of ten (39.9%) reported having perpetrated at least one action. As can be observed in Table 1, the number of victims and perpetrators decreases or increases depending on the way involvement in cyber-bullying is questioned (explicit versus implicit). This difference might be an indication that the pupils' perception of cyber-bullying does not correspond with what academic researchers assume to be cyber-bullying.

In Table 1 the frequency with which students engage in the different deviant ICT uses is also summarized. These frequency rates are interesting, since only a very small minority of students engage systematically in cyber-bullying. Not minimizing the impact of an isolated cyber-bullying incident, it is encouraging to see that most victims do not have to face cyber-bullying as a daily recurring burden.

In follow up to this initial analysis, we have compared the prevalence rates between different groups of students (non-victimized, victimized and perpetrating minors) by taking into account some background variables: the community of origin, gender, age, educational level and daily ICT use.

Concerning the community of origin we compared the prevalence of cyber-bullying between the northern (Flemish) and the southern (French) region of Belgium. Table 2 shows that while 31.5% of surveyed pupils in the French Community (FR) had cyber-bullied other pupils, only 12.9% in the Flemish community (FL) admitted doing so. We found an even larger discrepancy in victimization rates between the two communities: 54.9% in the French-speaking part of Belgium versus only 17.6% in the Dutch-speaking part of Belgium. Since two different languages are spoken in these regions, the survey had to be formulated in both French and Dutch. Although the questionnaires were created by native speakers and tested among pupils, the impact of a different terminology on the results cannot be excluded. Despite this methodological explanation, we believe that the found discrepancies suggest that cyber-bullying to a certain degree is a culturally determined societal problem. In this regard we also refer to earlier findings by Qing Li, who found that notwithstanding the use of the same questionnaires in both countries, victimization and perpetration rates significantly differed among respondents in China and Canada (Li, 2007). Our study shows that also cultural differences within one country may well impact the extent of a societal problem. Therefore, we would be interested in further international comparative research, specifically research using insights concerning cultural differences, for instance, Hofstede's dimensions of national culture (Hofstede, 2003).

With regard to gender, no significant differences could be derived from our data with regard to perpetration rates; however, significantly more female students (42.5%) report being victimized than males (26.2%). In this regard, our findings

Table 1: Frequency of cyber-bullying (N=1282; explicit questioning and implicit questioning)

Frequency	Perpetrator				Victim			
	Never	seldom	once in a while	often	never	seldom	once in a while	often
Explicit questioning:								
Bullying via internet or mobile phone	78.8%	14.8%	4.4%	2.0%	65.8%	21.5%	10.4%	2.4%
Implicit questioning:								
Sending e-mails or mobile text messages although the receiver has clearly stated not wanting to receive them	88.6%	8.0%	2.3%	1.1%	54.6%	25.3%	14.8%	5.4%
Excluding another person from an online discussion	80.9%	11.6%	5.4%	2.1%	88.1%	9.2%	1.7%	1.0%
Making a picture or video without notice nor consent and making it publicly available on the internet	91.2%	5.7%	2.2%	0.9%	86.8%	9.2%	3.5%	0.6%
Breaking into the e-mail or MSN account and sending messages to the contacts	88.7%	7.4%	2.8%	1.0%	82.4%	13.2%	3.3%	1.2%
Breaking into the e-mail or MSN account and changing the password	84.6%	10.6%	3.2%	1.7%	79.5%	16.0%	3.4%	1.1%

coincide with a limited group of studies that state that boys are more involved as perpetrators in cyber-bullying (Kowalski, Limber, & Agatston, 2008; Ybarra & Mitchell, 2004). These studies conflict with other research that finds females are significantly more likely to become a cyber-victim (Li, 2006, 2007; Smith et al., 2008; Vandebosch, Van Cleemput, Mortelmans, & Walrave, 2006; Walrave et al., 2008). The topic of gender and its relationship to research on cyber-bullying frequency and behaviours are discussed in further detail by Diane Hoff and Sidney Mitchell in chapter 3 of this volume.

With regard to age, we found that perpetrators are significantly older than non-bullying youngsters. These results correspond partly with Ybarra and Mitchell's (2004) findings that online aggressors are older than their targets and bully-free pupils. Comparing the educational level of the respondents reveals interesting differences in both victimization and perpetration rates. Cyber-bullying appears to be especially an issue at the lowest and middle educational levels (vocational training and technical/artistic formation respectively). Despite lower victimization and perpetration rates, the highest educational level (General-theoretic forma-tion) is still affected by cyber-bullying. When reviewing the scientific literature on cyber-bullying, we were surprised that few studies have examined the relation between educational level and cyber-bullying. Our results are confirmed by a previous study by Vandebosch et al. (2006), who found in a survey among 2,052 Flemish pupils (between 9–18 years old) that cyber-bullying is especially an issue in vocational training and technical/artistic disciplines.

Concerning the daily use of ICT, our data suggest that both victims and perpetrators have an above average daily internet use and self-reported internet expertise. These findings confirm the image of especially ICT-savvy students getting involved in cyber-bullying (Vandebosch et al., 2006; Ybarra & Mitchell, 2004). Further we observed that perpetrators report remarkably high scores on internet dependency. Although Ybarra and Mitchell's study (2004) states that a more or less equal proportion of victims considered the internet to be extremely important to them, the victims in our study did not report significantly higher scores on the internet dependency scale. It is possible that this deviation can be partly ascribed to different measurement tools. Ybarra and Mitchell used a unique Likert scale in order to rate internet *importance,* and we used seven questions to measure internet *dependency.*

In addition to prevalence rates, we surveyed attitudes towards a variety of specific cyber-bullying acts. Of all the situations described, the respondents found that being a victim of someone who breaks into his or her e-mail or instant mes-saging and sends messages to his/her contacts or changes the password to be the most terrible experiences (a total of respectively 96.5% and 96.3% condemn these acts). These acts are closely followed by: a sneakily taken picture or video of them

Table 2: Perpetrator and victim of cyber-bullying, descriptive results (N = 1318)

Respondents' characteristics	All respondents (N=1318)	Perpetrator of cyber-bullying			Victim of cyber-bullying		
		No	Yes	p-value	No	Yes	p-value
Cyber-bullying		78.8%	21.2%		65.8%	34.2%	
Demographics:							
French community	45.2%	68.5%	31.5%	.000	45.1%	54.9%	.000
Flemish community	54.8%	87.1%	12.9%		82.4%	17.6%	
Male	50.5%	78.4%	21.6%	NS	73.8%	26.2%	.000
Female	49.5%	79.2%	20.8%		57.5%	42.5%	
Age (M:SD)	15.1 (1.9)	14.99 (1.85)	15.34 (2.02)	.006	15.01 (1.82)	15.13 (2.02)	NS
Education level*:							
Vocational training (FR)	7.0%	62.5%	37.5%	.000	42.7%	57.3%	.000
Artistic/technical (FR)	9.4%	48.7%	51.3%		35.8%	64.2%	
General-theoretic (FR)	28.4%	76.3%	23.7%		48.3%	51.7%	
Vocational training (FL)	13.4%	83.5%	16.5%		83.6%	16.4%	
Artistic/technical (FL)	20.1%	91.4%	8.6%		83.6%	16.4%	
General-theoretic (FL)	21.8%	84.9%	15.1%		80.6%	19.4%	
ICT use:							
Online frequency (hours/day) [M(SD)]	2.35 (1.39)	2.27 (1.41)	2.66 (1.44)	.000	2.37 (1.41)	2.29 (1.33)	NS
Online expertise [M(SD)]	5.70 (2.10)	5.59 (2.11)	6.31 (1.74)	.000	5.60 (2.11)	6.01 (1.95)	.001
Internet dependency [M(SD)]	1.68 (0.62)	1.64 (0.61)	1.83 (0.62)	.000	1.67 (0.62)	1.73 (0.62)	NS

M: mean; SD: standard deviation; NS: not significant; * Education level is differentiated into three levels in both communities, FR: French and FL: Flemish community education emerging on the web (89.1%), receiving unsolicited messages (83.6%), and being excluded from an online discussion (76.7%).

In this analysis of attitudes, we also conducted Pearson correlations between respondents' judgements of cyber-bullying and their experience both as a victim and an actor. To describe the strength of correlations, we follow Fink (2003) who names a value between (-) .11 and (-) .25 as indicating a weak (negative) correlation, between (-).25 and (-).50 a strong correlation and higher than (-).50 a very strong correlation. We found a strong negative correlation between electronic bullying and attitude towards perpetration (-0.428, p=0.000) or victimization of these acts (-0.313, p=0.000). In other words, teens who do not admit to cyber-bullying and teens who report that cyber-bullying has terrible consequences for the victim are less inclined to engage in cyber-bullying. Additionally, we found a very strong correlation between the pupils' attitude towards being a target of electronic bullying and the perpetration of these acts (0.741, p = 0.000). This correlation means that the more respondents are convinced of the negative impact of cyber-bullying on a victim, the more they condemn these acts. Finally, we found a weak negative correlation between victimization and judgment of the consequences of these offences (-0.242, p = 0.000) and a weak correlation between the gravity of perpetration of these acts (-0.216, p = 0.000). These findings seem to indicate the possibility of a certain habituation or development of strategies to cope with electronic bullying. However, they also could be explained by the strong positive correlation between both roles, namely victim and offender (0.458, p = 0.000). As stressed in previous research both roles are intertwined (Li, 2007; Vandebosch et al., 2006; Ybarra and Mitchell, 2004).

ACCUSING OR DEFENDING TECHNOLOGY?

Now that we have reviewed our survey data about the frequency of cyber-bullying, we want to examine the question of the role that specific characteristics of new technologies play (or do not play) in triggering these emergent behaviours. In reviewing the existing literature on cyber-bullying, we found recurring arguments that demonize the role of technology in cyber-bullying. These issues and concerns are not only addressed in the public debate but also by authors in diverse scientific publications. All of these issues can be classified into five groups, including the emerging technologies potential to: 1) safeguard anonymity (Kowalski & Limber, 2007; Patchin & Hinduja, 2006; Strom & Strom, 2005); 2) intrude 24/7 in peers' lives (David-Ferdon & Feldman, 2007; Kowalski & Limber, 2007; Patchin & Hinduja, 2006; Reid, 2005); 3) remain unnoticed by teachers, parents and educators (Williams & Guerra, 2007; Wing, 2005); 4) strip away non-verbal communication cues by the victim (Kowalski & Limber, 2007; Kowalski et al., 2008; Patchin & Hinduja,

2006; Reid, 2005); 5) quickly distribute online content to theoretically limitless audiences (David-Ferdon & Feldman, 2007; Kowalski & Limber, 2007; Kowalski et al., 2008; Sullivan, 2006).

In the following discussion, we will try to answer the question of whether we should act as a prosecutor, accusing communication technologies of being 'culpable' in triggering cyber-bullying, or whether it would be more justified to reject the hypothesis that communication technologies are to blame, and rather focus on the users' decision to utilize ICT in a socially harmful way. We will return to this question after having critically evaluated and interrogated the mediation of technology within the scope of the current knowledge on cyber-bullying. We do so by submitting the aforementioned concerns to two crucial questions:

(a)   Can these characteristics of emerging technology also have a beneficial outcome, when communication technologies are used in a pro-social way?

(b)   Do these characteristics of emerging technology solely manifest themselves in the context of cyber-bullying, or do they also have parallel characteristics in traditional forms of bullying?

We believe that, if emergent characteristics of technology have beneficial outcomes and if most appear to have parallel characteristics in traditional incidents of bullying, then information communication technologies themselves should not be accused of inherently triggering cyber-bullying, but rather, the way people choose to use new technologies should be seen as the problem. This distinction would suggest education and prevention programs should shift from being focused on monitoring and controlling new technologies to educating and inspiring teens to make better choices in how they use technologies.

ONLINE ANONYMITY

Many people worry about minors using the Internet and mobile phone to bully online anonymously. This concerns becomes clear in an illustrative quote provided by a pupil in a Belgian focus group interview: "I mean, I think it is safer to bully online, because who will find out that you were the bad guy sending the offending mail?" (Vandebosch, 2003). Such perception may lead pupils to think that they can get away with cyber-bullying without being sanctioned, thus suggesting that youngsters prefer to cyber-bully because of its perceived anonymity. Further, some authors suggest that anonymity online is commonplace, facilitated by the large availability of free communication services (e.g., IM, e-mail accounts) which allow teens to create multiple identities and pseudonyms (Kowalski & Limber, 2007; Li, 2007; Patchin & Hinduja, 2006; Strom & Strom, 2005). Similar possibilities are offered by anonymous re-mailers, a name that refers to the practice of forwarding e-mail messages without revealing their origin.

However, it is crucial to realize that anonymous online communication can in many conceivable situations turn out to have positive consequences for minors. For example, shy and introverted students can be more motivated to come out of their shells, since anonymity provides them with a certain degree of trust in online communication. Another reason why online conversation partners may benefit from anonymity is the possibility to separate thoughts and ideas from their real life worlds and identities. In psychology this is referred to as dissociative anonymity (Suler, 2004). This anonymity may bring people to tell each other the most intimate secrets of their lives to a complete stranger. This phenomenon, typically occurring during online conversations, is also called 'The-stranger-on-the-train'-effect (Bargh, McKenna, & Fitzsimons, 2002; Kowalski et al., 2008; Livingstone & Bober, 2004). In this way, people are able to express bottled-up emotions to a stranger (for example grief or anger) without the fear of being sanctioned socially.

Although many minors consider anonymity as being the main differing feature with traditional schoolyard bullying (Smith et al., 2008), we think that such a perception is debatable. One can easily conceive some examples of anonymous conventional bullying. Indirect types of traditional bullying, such as relational bullying (e.g., spreading gossip) and behavioural bullying (e.g., stealing things behind one's back), do not necessarily imply that the identity of the perpetrator is revealed. Thus anonymity is certainly not uniquely a characteristic related to cyber-bullying. For example in the 2007 study by Kowalski and Limber, the authors found that 48% of the victimized pupils in a sample of 3,767 middle schoolers did not know the name of the perpetrator. These findings were confirmed in many other studies, including Belgian survey data (Vandebosch et al., 2006; Ybarra, Mitchell, Wolak, & Finkelhor, 2006). Remarkably, Juvonen and Gross (2008) found in their cyber-bullying research that 73% of the victimized pupils in the survey sample were "pretty sure" to "totally sure" about the identity of the person who was harassing them online.

24/7 ATTAINABILITY

Communication technology enables minors to extend bullying episodes beyond the confines of the school environment. Unlike traditional bullying, the access to the victim of cyber-bullying is no longer limited by a circumscribed period of time. A student in our focus group interview said: "You can be caught virtually anytime, anyplace" (Vandebosch, 2003). In a television interview a victimized student said: *"The one thing about being beaten up at school is that you at least know you're at school from 9 o' clock in the morning until 3 o'clock in the afternoon and then you can go home where it is safe...*" (CBC, 2005). Whereas the home environment was considered as a safe retreat, a kind of sanctuary in traditional bullying cases, the walls of the home do no longer provide the youngster with an impenetrable bunker in cyber-bullying situations (Kowalski et al., 2008). In this way a victimized student can become a perpetual target for bullying-minded pupils, especially by their mobile phones since teenagers address great importance to their cellular being almost ceaselessly in the immediate proximity (Patchin & Hinduja, 2006). To summarize, the 24/7 attainability by mobile phone or internet may facilitate bullying behaviour since the boundaries of time and place, typically for traditional bullying, no longer apply in cyber-bullying (David-Ferdon & Feldman, 2007; Kowalski & Limber, 2007; Patchin & Hinduja, 2006; Reid, 2005).

Although we don't want to minimize the importance of bully-free environments and moments for victimized students, we wish to underline that 24/7 online communication may also have very beneficial outcomes for internet users. For example, at the psychological level, the world-wide introduction of cellular phones and notebooks has bridged private and public spheres and has founded 'privatised mobility': the opportunity to feel at home without even being home (Moores, 2000). Simultaneously, people get the 'global village' feeling: the distance between worlds, which are separated by time and space in reality, is shrinking. Today's generation of youngsters can maintain pen-friendships far more easily by using IM and e-mail instead of written postal letters. Further, youngsters today are liberated to a certain extent from adult imposed regulations and structures in communicating with their peers. In this way, personal experiences are connected and shared by electronic means beyond the confines of the school environment, which allows youngsters to consolidate their friendships with peers in the online environment (Kitzmann, 2004; Valentine & Holloway, 2001).

In a bullying context this 24/7 accessibility to the victim is a new issue. Traditional types of bullying occur mostly at school, on the school bus, or walking to and from school. Of course, conventional bullying can take place elsewhere in the community, for example, in youth movements or in sport clubs, but in all these situations the access to the victim is limited in time and space. These boundaries no longer apply in cyber-bullying. Several studies have found that cyber-bullying for the most part takes place off school grounds (Kowalski et al., 2008; Slonje & Smith, 2007; Smith et al., 2008). Also mobile phone bullying happens more outside the school. This can be explained by the fact that many schools regulate mobile phone use by their pupils very strictly (Smith et al., 2008).

ESCAPE DETECTION BY PARENTS AND TEACHERS

Much of what is said and done by youngsters online happens without adults noticing it. A 13-year-old teen in our focus groups said: "Cyber-bullying always happens in a sneaky way" (Vandebosch, 2003). Indeed many forms of cyber-bullying are hard to detect. It can be especially hard when the electronic bullying takes place beyond the boundaries of school supervision. Another reason why adult intervention is problematic in cyber-bullying is that a considerable proportion of victimized students choose not to tell anything about the harassment. In an English study 43.7% of cyber-victims did not report the online victimization to parents or teachers; in a Canadian study by Li (2007) this proportion was 65%. How can these findings be explained? Several authors suggest (Juvonen & Gross, 2008; Li, 2007) that some victimized pupils have given up their belief that adult intervention can ameliorate their painful situation, especially when the identity of the perpetrator is unknown. Juvonen et al.(2008) found that about one third (31%) preferred not to tell an adult because they feared that their internet and mobile phone access would be suspended in case parents and teachers found things out.

However, it is crucial to consider that without the private nature of online communication new media would probably never have boomed as a means used by teens to establish, maintain and reinforce friendships (David-Ferdon & Feldman, 2007; Patchin & Hinduja, 2006; Walrave et al., 2008). Online privacy is enabled in different ways: first, the visual framework of a computer screen or a cellular does not immediately lend itself to efficient control. Secondly, many tech-savvy teens are able to circumvent adult supervision by employing specific techniques, ranging from simply choosing a strategic hardly supervisible position in the classroom to using a smart-button on a keyboard which makes all messenger-windows disappear (BELSPO, in press). Thirdly, portable ICT devices such as notebooks, PDA and cellular allow teens to retire to rooms where they are alone and cannot be observed (for example, their bedroom), contributing to the so-called "Bedroom Culture," a concept that refers to the increasing amount of spare time spent by teenagers in their bedrooms (Bovill & Livingstone, 2001). However, we must remember that private communication may also be used in a pro-social manner. This feeling of exploring the online world without adult supervision can have beneficial outcomes such as sincere and intimate friendships made online and does not have to worry adults.

Furthermore we must acknowledge that many forms of traditional bullying share an increased likelihood of remaining unnoticed for teachers and school administrators. Especially, indirect types of bullying ('behind-the-back'-bullying) like relational bullying and verbal bullying are most likely to pass unnoticed (Griffin & Gross, 2004). It is not hard to imagine that social exclusion, for example not inviting one pupil of a group to a birthday party, and nasty oral remarks are difficult to detect by adult supervisors. Furthermore, Williams and Guerra found that young people may be facilitated to engage in covert types of bullying, because they believe that adults and bystanders are unlikely to intervene (Williams & Guerra, 2007). This may offer an explanation for a specific result found in the TIRO study, showing that students in possession of a personal computer share an increased likelihood of getting involved in cyber-bullying, certainly compared to those pupils not having such privileged access to a computer (Walrave & Heirman). In this regard, public (school and library) computers are subject to better supervision. One might conclude that this control is effective; nevertheless, conducted focus interviews in the US reveal that minors effectively use different techniques to circumvent supervision in the school context (Agatston, Kowalski, & Limber, 2007).

INFINITE AUDIENCES

An often mentioned concern is that by the easy online distribution of data a theoretically limitless audience can get involved in cyber-bullying. David Knight, a Canadian student being repeatedly cyber-bullied, said during a television interview: "Rather than just some people, say 30 in a cafeteria, hearing them all yell insults at you, it's up there for 6 billion people to see." (CBC, 2005). Whereas the extent of most traditional bullying episodes is limited to the local school community, the hurtful texts and images in cyber-bullying can be communicated to a theoretically unlimited audience in a very short period of time (Kowalski et al., 2008; Patchin & Hinduja, 2006; Shariff, 2005; Strom & Strom, 2005).

However humiliating this might be for some cyber-victimized minors, the quick distribution of online data also has many advantages. Whereas pupils in the pre-digital era had to pass very complex formal procedures to get in touch with experts from various organizations in order to complete for example their school tasks, most people can now easily be reached by means of e-mail. Further, it is relatively easy to quickly distribute online messages among large audiences by using, for example, mailing lists. Besides providing pupils with an endless library, the Internet also has the potential to increase students' social interaction and to enhance collaborative learning experiences by exchanging data files online through e-mail and instant messaging (Beran & Li, 2007; Li, 2006). Also other applications are available to reach a broad audience (e.g., posting a video on YouTube, Google Video). Nowadays, especially social networking sites (e.g., Facebook and MySpace) are very popular among young people. This technology allows them to express their feelings, needs and desires to a broad public of both offline and online contacts (Dwyer, 2007), which can be a very beneficial experience during adolescence, since in this period the development of one's own identity is very important (Calvert, 2002).

Despite the fact that the audiences in traditional bullying are smaller and more limited than in cyber-bullying, it must be underlined that the involvement of a more or less large audience is not exceptional in schoolyard bullying. What is more, spectators can have an important influence in the bullying process, since schoolyard bullying is a social process, often transcending the relationship between a bully and a victim. Different roles can be distinguished in the process of bullying: bullies, victims and bystanders (Salmivalli, 1999; Salmivalli, Lagerspetz, Bjorkqvist, & Kaukianinen, 2006). These bystanders, performing as assistants or "reinforcers," are believed to play an important part in school bullying episodes, since they provide bullying students with an audience. Extensive research has shown that bullies partially draw motivation for their behaviour out of this audience. This especially applies for proactive aggression, because then bullies will have the intention to display dominance with the goal to bolster power and to win admiration and support amongst peers (Unnever, 2005). The potential to reach theoretically *infinite* audiences is a feature that only occurs in cyber-bullying. However, it is important to realize that only in extreme cases will people beyond the confines of the local school community get involved as an audience in cyber-bullying. In many cases the extent of cyber-bullying remains limited to the local level (Kowalski et al., 2008).

LACK OF NON-VERBAL CUES

The lack of emotional feedback on behalf of the victim is often mentioned as a worrisome consequence of negative online communication forms. Cyber-bullying rarely occurs face-to-face, since perpetrator and victim mostly are in their home environments at a relatively great distance from one another. So when communicating online reactions such as crying, which might lead people to realize that their comments have been too harsh or have been misinterpreted, are no longer visible (Ybarra & Mitchell, 2004). Since emotional feedback is missing, cyber-bullies may assess quite wrongly the damage they are causing. We illustrate this with a quote from a 13-year-old pupil in the Belgian focus groups: *"It was a kind of joke to me, but when I saw him at school I realized that I had driven things too far"* (Vandebosch, 2003).

However, if communication technologies are used in a pro-social way, it may be that the absence of non-verbal communication motivates people to talk and share their most intimate stories and emotions, like fears and desires, with each other in the most sympathetic and honest way one can imagine (Kowalski & Limber, 2007; Patchin & Hinduja, 2006). The lack of face-to-face cues takes away restraintson the telling of stories, which in case of a physical meeting probably never would be told. For example, even a negligible change in the facial expression of an offline conversation partner, can prevent the other from telling what's on his mind. Conversely, the interpretation of online communication, by lack of non-verbal cues, is sometimes challenging and can easily derail into misunderstandings (Ybarra, Diener-West, & Leaf, 2007). When this dis-inhibition generates positive effects like relief and elevated levels of trust in the conversation partners, psychologists refer to this phenomenon as a 'benign dis-inhibition effect.' Yet, the dis-inhibition can also result in a 'toxic effect,' when it brings people to make rude remarks, to spread hatred and threats in the online conversation environment (Suler, 2004). In this latter case, a computer or mobile phone display acts as a mirror, so that by consequence people feel less restraint about really saying what's on their mind and how they feel. Much of what is written in e-mail and text messages far surpasses what people would daer to say to another person's face. When ICTs are used in an antisocial way, this allows people to be extremely vicious against one another without any fear of retaliation and seeing the other person suffer (Kowalski et al., 2008; Suler, 2004).

Furthermore, it makes sense to argue that this lack of direct contact is not atypical of some traditional bullying contexts. Especially, in behavioural bullying several situations are easily conceivable in which the perpetrator does not have to see any emotion and suffering of the victimized student—for example, when the personal belongings of a pupil are deliberately damaged by a schoolyard bully during playtime.

A crucial consideration, however, is that in real life people usually modulate or adjust their behaviours or comments, when they notice they have (un)willingly hurt someone based on emotional feedback. So, observing tears, a frown, a bored expression and other more or less subtle face-to-face cues can slam the brakes on what people are saying or doing. By actually being able to 'read' the emotional reactions of the other person, one is able to scan the faces of potential bullies for signs that a tease is really just a tease and not bullying (Suler, 2004).

Due to a striking analogy between pupils perpetrating cyber-bullying and fighter pilots, we refer to the disinhibiting and separating mechanism in cyber-bullying as the 'cockpit-effect.' Various psychologists, like Lorenz (1974) and Kulka (1990) have studied the mental condition of soldiers after being part of World War II and the Vietnam War. Their studies show that infantrymen with high war-zone exposure, constantly facing death in direct confrontation with individual enemies, report a higher level of post-traumatic stress syndromes (PTSD) than fighter pilots, who dropped bombs which devastated entire villages and killed hundreds of people each time they flew. *"Good husbands and fathers have laid carpets of bombs on civilized people and societies"* (Lorenz, 1974). Sitting in a cockpit, at a great distance from their (human) targets, pilots did not directly have to observe the suffering and the killing they caused, making it easier to kill more with less psychological damage for the perpetrator (De Laender, 1996). Foot soldiers however caused comparatively less pain and death but suffered more of post-traumatic stress syndromes during their postwar lives (Lorenz, 1974). In a similar way, due to absent face-to-face-cues, the perpetrator sitting in front of his/her computer display, like a pilot in a cockpit, feels disinhibited and is facilitated in his/her bullying behaviour since he/she cannot directly observe the emotional reaction of his/her 'target'. Like modern weapon technology modern information communication technology, if used in an antisocial way, has created distance between perpetrator and target and thereby has eliminated pity and empathy as powerful inhibitors of human aggression (De Laender, 1996).

Does the lack of face-to-face contact lead to merciless online bullies and does this 'cockpit-effect' differentiate the impact of cyber-bullying? There are two sides to this question. The three primary motivations for conventional bullying are the need to demonstrate dominance, to receive a reward (e.g. admiration by peers) and finally, the satisfaction of causing suffering and injury a victim (Olweus, 1993; Olweus et al., 2007; Salmivalli et al., 2006). In cyber-bullying, the 'cockpit-effect' may undermine these core motivations, since no suffering is visible, and perpetrators do not have a peer audience to whom their power can be demonstrated. So in cyber-bullying, the perpetrator is less likely to see any suffering from the victim, which might reduce the gratification for cyber-bullies who enjoy watching pain and suffering. The other side of the coin is that the inhibition of inflicting pain might be reduced due to a lack of empathy (Smith et al., 2008). Further, not seeing the victim may cause some perpetrators to remain unconvinced that they are actually harming or hurting someone badly. In psychology this phenomenon is referred to as 'dissociative imagination' (Suler, 2004). People may be convinced that their virtual characters only exist in cyberspace, which they consider to be a dream world or a fictional computer game, because they dissociate online fiction from offline reality. Cyber-perpetrators who argue this way may be genuinely convinced that they are not doing anything wrong, since they consider cyber-bullying to be an imaginary act of bullying (Kowalski & Limber, 2007).

RECONSIDERING THE CULPABILITY OF TECHNOLOGY

So, after having discussed the mediation of technology we now come back to the question of whether we should accuse or defend communication technologies in the context of a societal problem like cyber-bullying. Is it justified to talk about technology's culpability? Should we condemn the Internet and mobile phone as instigators of bullying episodes? We think that the previous discussion provides us with two good reasons to argue against demonizing technology.

First, all distinguished ICT-related issues can have beneficial outcomes, such as, for example, establishing new and consolidating existing youngsters' friendships and guaranteeing online privacy. So, rather than merely being destructive, on the contrary ICT also lays the necessary foundations of many peer friendships and other pro-social behaviours.

Secondly, most of the public concerns related to ICT in cyber-bullying are anything but new in a bullying context. We've indicated that much of traditional bullying occurs anonymously and in a sneaky way without direct face-to-face contact with the victim. Further we have mentioned that traditional bullies get motivated by a large audience witnessing the harassment. Only the 24/7 attainability was a completely new issue in a bullying context.

We therefore believe that rather than accusing technology, it would be a better idea to address the way in which some young people decide to use technology. In this regard, we believe that the importance of media education, literally educating young people how to handle new media, becomes highly relevant. That is why, within a more global prevention program, augmenting media literacy should be one key pillar of approaching cyber-bullying. This might mitigate the negative effects of some of the above raised ICT-related concerns and may bring young people to be well aware that their online behaviour may have serious offline consequences.

WHY DO SOME GET INVOLVED AND OTHERS DO NOT?

In the preceding section we have argued strongly in favour of communication technologies by posing that what really matters in approaching cyber-bullying as a societal problem is recognizing the fact that these media can be used in either a pro-social or an antisocial way. This plea may lead to the conviction that young people are free to decide whether they engage in cyber-bullying or not. Of course, to a certain extent they are free to choose, especially with regard to perpetration in cyber-bullying. However, being cyber-bullied does not really seem to be a choice, but rather an awkward consequence of another peer's choice. How can we reconcile the belief of free individual decision making, if we, based on the statistical analyses of the TIRO data, find that some children are particularly vulnerable to get involved as a perpetrator or a victim? Although we cannot exactly answer this question, we can provide the reader with a further insight into the risk factors (or so-called 'predictors') of be(com)ing an online victimized or perpetrating youngster. As we will see, not all of these factors are so easily escapable and some of them even are determined. To investigate which variables contribute most to the likelihood of perpetration and victimization in cyber-bullying, we applied logistic regression analysis to our data. In the next paragraphs we will discuss the most striking results found with regard to risk factors for both victimization and perpetration in cyber-bullying.

RISK FACTORS

Victimization

Although this might seem contradictory at first sight, Table 3 shows that the number one predictor (see (1)) of victimization in cyber-bullying is one's involvement as a perpetrator. The interpretation of the odds ratio (see last column) shows that cyber-bullies share an approximately six-fold increased likelihood of becoming a cyber-victim ($chi^2(1) = 48.79$, p = 0.000). This finding induces us to conclude that there is a strong interrelation between victimization and perpetration and that those students who bully online are at the same time the ones that run the greatest risk of being an online victim themselves. Our data also show that two other risk factors of victimization are the involvement in other online risk behaviour: chatting with older merely virtually known contacts (see (2): $chi^2(1) = 15.33$, p=0.000) and entrusting passwords of e-mail and Instant Messaging to online chat-partners (see (3): $chi^2(1) = 17.39$, p = 0.000). Translating the odds ratios these statistics mean that those pupils chatting with older virtually known chat partners and those entrusting passwords run, respectively, 2.339 and 1.839 higher chances of being victimized. An additional significant risk factor we have found is that teens who publish personal information about themselves on a blog also share an increased likelihood of becoming an online victim ($chi^2(1) = 13.26$, p = 0.000). Concerning gender, and in addition to the descriptive results mentioned above, female internet users appear to be more likely to become a victim of cyber-bullying than male users ($chi^2(1) = 9.79$, p = 0.002). And a final predictor of online victimization is the use of chatboxes, either open (where virtually anyone can contact one another;

Table 3: Determinants of cyber-bullying victimization (N=1185)

	Beta	S.E.	Wald Chi^2	Df	Sig.	Exp(Beta) (odds ratio)
Gender (male/female)	.437	.140	9.790	1	.002	1.548
Cyber-bullying perpetrator	1.897 (1)	.272	48.798	1	.000	6.668
Using closed chat	.518	.263	3.877	1	.049	1.678
Using open chat	.400	.148	7.307	1	.007	1.492
Chatting with older online partners	.850 (2)	.217	15.331	1	.000	2.339
Own blog	.548	.150	13.269	1	.000	1.730
Entrust password	.609 (3)	.146	17.399	1	.000	1.839
Constant	-.825	.259	10.103	1	.001	.438

chi^2(1) = 7.30, p = 0.007) or closed (where one has to accept someone else before adding him/her to a contact list; chi^2(1) = 3.87, p = 0.049).

Perpetration

Table 4 shows that especially previous involvement in cyber-bullying as a victim (see (1)) serves as the most influential risk factor for future perpetration (chi^2(1) = 67.67, p = 0.000). In other words, derived from the odds ratios, we see that victims of cyber-bullying have a nine times greater chance of engaging in electronic bullying. The next most important predictor of involvement is attitude (see (2)), meaning that teens who reject electronic bullying are less inclined to commit it (chi^2(1) = 15.42, p = 0.000). Conversely, those pupils who do not reject cyber-bullying by nature, run approximately four times more likely to actually perpetrate cyber-bullying. A third risk factor is identity fluidity (see (3)), namely teens who have been experimenting with different identities while chatting are approximately three times more likely to commit electronic bullying (chi^2(1) = 16.46, p = 0.000). Other less influential but significant predictors of perpetration are gender and age: boys are more inclined to engage in electronic bullying than girls are (chi^2(1) = 4.21, p = 0.040) and cyber-bullying frequency increases slightly with age (chi^2(1) = 6.74, p = 0.009). Young people who spend more time on the internet are marginally more likely to become online bullies (chi^2(1) = 5,121, p = 0.024). Teens who have their own computer (chi^2(1) = 4.32, p = 0.038) and go online more frequently in their own bedroom or study and not in a family room (chi^2(1) = 2.31, p = 0.129) also have an increased likelihood of being an online

Table 4: Determinants of cyber-bullying perpetration (N = 1185)

	Beta	S.E.	Wald's Chi^2	Df	Sig.	Exp(Beta) (odds ratio)
Gender (female/male)	.447	.218	4.215	1	.040	1.563
Age	.178	.069	6.745	1	.009	1.195
Online frequency	.172	.076	5.121	1	.024	1.187
Online expertise	.065	.039	2.715	1	.099	1.067
Cyber-bullying victim	2.235 **(1)**	.272	67.670	1	.000	9.348
Gravity of cyber-bullying	-1.376 **(2)**	.350	15.421	1	.000	.253
Place PC	.387	.255	2.305	1	.129	1.473
Own PC	.481	.231	4.323	1	.038	1.617
Identity fluidity	1.116 **(3)**	.275	16.464	1	.000	3.053
Constant	-3.749	.716	27.410	1	.000	.024

bully. Finally, teens who report higher scores on the ICT expertise scale have higher odds of being a bully ($chi^2(1) = 2.72$, p = 0.099).

Although the risk factors for victimization and perpetration in cyber-bullying slightly differ, the similarities are compelling. Key factors in both victimization and perpetration in electronic bullying are one's previous experiences with cyber-bullying. This corresponds with other studies which have accentuated the crucial influence of variables related to previous engagement in bullying behaviour (Kowalski & Limber, 2007; Li, 2007; Patchin & Hinduja, 2006; Slonje & Smith, 2007; Vandebosch et al., 2006). For victimization this key predictor is followed by other influential predictors related to engagement in online risk behaviour, namely, chatting with older online contacts and entrusting passwords of Instant Messaging and e-mail to others. For perpetration, second order predictors differ slightly (in comparison with those for victimization): especially important are the perceived gravity of cyber-bullying and experimenting with different online identities.

These insights induce us to put the liberty of choice into perspective. If the previous involvement as a victim in cyber-bullying is at the same time the most influential risk factor for perpetration, we can rightly wonder if youngsters are in fact able to freely choose whether they engage in cyber-bullying or not. No minor will deliberately choose awkward situation of being cyber-bullied, but this is precisely what often precedes the actual perpetration according to our data. This realization obviously raises interesting questions about the appropriateness of harsh disciplinary responses for perpetrators. Additionally the realization that those who by nature strongly reject cyber-bullying towards peers have a much declined likelihood of be(com)ing a cyber-bully suggests that strong community-wide pedagogical interventions, focused on ensuring students realize the gravity of cyber-bullying, may prove successful.

CONCLUSION

The current study shows that cyber-bullying is a manifest problem in Belgium, with about a third of the pupil population being victims. For some of them, the so-called 'global victims,' this means that they are now confronted with both offline and online victimization. We have discussed some common perceptions with regard to technology's role in cyber-bullying and concluded that all of these issues can also have beneficial outcomes, and most of them are not new issues solely pertaining to cyber-bullying but present in traditional bullying as well. We thus reject blaming technologies and instead consider the user's decision to use ICT for antisocial purposes. Here we find that perpetrators are often first victims and that attitudes towards cyber-bullying and its consequences can impact the decision to be a perpetrator.

These findings have important consequences for school intervention programs. Special attention is needed to impact the normative climate concerning (cyber-)bullying. Teachers need to be familiar with popular communication tools to be able to dialogue with their ICT-savvy pupils. Moreover, technology itself, ICT competences, as well as the creativity of children and teens can be used to create prevention tools tailored to their information and communication habits. Many authors support the call for the inclusion of electronic bullying prevention in conventional anti-bullying programs (Campbell, 2005; Kowalski et al., 2008; Williams & Guerra, 2007). The *whole school approach* proposed by Olweus, including pupils, teachers, and parents seems to have proven its efficiency in traditional bullying (Olweus, 1994; Peterson & Rigby, 1999; Stassen Berger, 2007). Schools implementing this holistic approach need to share their experiences in order to offer other schools possibilities of updating their knowledge and adapt their policy. In addition, collaboration with internet service providers (ISP) and online services are of the utmost importance. Codes of conduct could be adopted by ISPs, schools, families, website administrators (especially chatrooms and social networking sites) to clearly indicate unacceptable online behaviour and possible sanctions (Wolak, Mitchell & Finkelhor, 2007). Besides, policy, research and prevention programs will have to be flexible, as the convergence of internet applications and mobile telephony brings forth growing possibilities for bullies to hit their targets independent of time and space.

ACKNOWLEDGMENTS

The results referred to concerning Belgian minors were obtained via two research projects. The first project dedicated to the study of cyber-bullying was ordered by IST—het Instituut Samenleving & Technologie is an independent and autonomous institute, associated with the Flemish Parliament—at the request of the Commission for Culture, Youth, Sports and Media of the Parliament. This survey was conducted in October 2005 among 636 primary school children and 1,416 secondary education pupils in Flanders by Prof. Dr. Heidi Vandebosch, Katrien Van Cleemput, Prof. Dr. Dimitri Mortelmans and Prof. Dr. Michel Walrave from the University of Antwerp (http://www.samenlevingentechnologie.be/ists/nl/publicaties/rapporten/rapport_cyberpesten.html).

A second survey dealing with teens & ICT was conducted in March 2007 among 1,318 secondary education pupils in both the French and Flemish Community of Belgium. This research was conducted within the framework of and financed by the Federal Science Policy's programme Society & Future. The survey and focus groups were conducted by Prof. Dr. Michel Walrave, Sunna Lenaerts and Sabine De Moor. The research project entitled TIRO (Teens & ICT: Risks & Opportunities) did not only focus on the risks teens can be confronted with online, the use of ICT at home and at school has also been surveyed. Next to the survey and focus groups which were taken care of by the University of Antwerp, in-depth interviews and an online diary research were conducted by SMIT VUB (Brussels) and CITA FUNDP, whereas the legal aspects were analysed by CRID FUNDP (Namur) (http://www.ua.ac.be/tiro).

References

Agatston, P. W., Kowalski, R. M., & Limber, S. P. (2007). Student's perspectives on cyber bullying. *Jounal of Adolescent Health, 41*(6), 59–60.

Bargh, J. A., McKenna, K. Y. A., & Fitzsimons, G. M. (2002). Can you see the real me? Activation an expression of the "true self" on the internet. *Journal of Social Issues, 58,* 33–48.

BELSPO. (In press). *Eindrapport TIRO—Teens and ICT: Risk and Opportunities.*

Beran, T., & Li, Q. (2007). The relationship between cyber-bullying and school bullying. *Journal of Student Wellbeing, 1*(2), 15–33.

Bovill, M., & Livingstone, S. (2001). Bedroom culture and the privatization of media use (online): London: LSE Research Online.

Calvert, S. L. (2002). Identity construction on the Internet. In S. L. Calvert, A. B. Jordan & R. R. Cocking (Eds.), *Children in the Digital Age: Influences of electronic media on development.* Westport, CT: Praeger.

Campbell, M. A. (2005). Cyber-bullying: An old problem in a new guise? *Australian Journal of Guidance and Counselling, 15*(1), 68–76.

CBC. (2005). Item on cyber-bullying. On *CBC News.*

David-Ferdon, C., & Feldman, M. H. (2007). Electronic media, violence and adolescents: An emerging public health problem. *Journal of Adolescent Health, 41*(6), s1-s5.

De Laender, J. (1996). *Het hart van de duisternis: psychologie van de menselijke wreedheid.* Leuven: Davidsfonds.

Dwyer, C. (2007). *Digital Relationships in the 'MySpace'-Generation: : Results From a Qualitative Study.* Paper presented at the 40th International Conference on System Sciences Hawaii.

Fink A. (2003). *How to manage, analyse, and interpret survey data.* Thousand Oaks, CA: Sage Publications.

Griffin, R. S., & Gross, A. M. (2004). Childhood bullying: Current empirical findings and future directions for research. *Aggression and Violent Behaviour, 9,* 379–400.

Hofstede, G. (2003). *Culture's consequences: Comparing values, behaviors, institutions and organizations across nations.* Thousand Oaks: Sage Publications, Inc.

Juvonen, J., & Gross, E. G. (2008). Extending the School Ground? Bullying Experiences in cyberspace? *Journal of School Health, 78*(9), 496–505.

Kitzmann, A. (2004). *Saved from oblivion: Documenting the daily from diaries to web cams.* New York: Peter Lang Publishing.

Kowalski, R. M., & Limber, S. P. (2007). Electronic bullying among middle school students. *Journal of Adolescent Health, 41*(6), 22–30.

Kowalski, R. M., Limber, S. P., & Agatston, P. W. (2008). *Cyber bullying: Bullying in the Digital Age:* Blackwell Publishing Ltd.

Kulka, R., Schlenger, W., Fairbank, J., Hough, R., Jordan, B., Marmar, C., et al. (1990). *Trauma and the Vietnam war generation.* New York: Brunner-Mazel.

Li, Q. (2006). Cyber-bullying in schools: a research of gender differences. *School Psychology International, 27*(2), 157–170.

Li, Q. (2007). Bullying in the new playground. *Australasian Journal of Educational Technology, 23*(4), 435–455.

Livingstone, S., & Bober, M. (2004). *UK children go online: surveying the experiences of young people and their parents.* London: London School of Economics and Political Science.

Lorenz, K. (1974). *Das sogenannte Böse. Zur Naturgeschichte der Aggression.* Amsterdam: Ploegsma.

Moores, S. (2000). *Media and everyday life in modern society.* Edinburgh: Edinburgh University Press.

Olweus, D., Limber, S. P., Flerx, V. C., Mullin, N., Riese, J., & Snyder, M. (2007). *Olweus Bullying Prevention Program: Schoolwide Guide.* Center City, MN: Hazelden

Olweus, D. (1994). Bullying at school: Long-term outcomes for the victims and an effective school-based intervention program. In R. Huesmann (Ed.), *Aggressive behavior: Current perspectives* (pp. 97–130). New York: John Wiley.

Olweus, D. (1993). Victimization by peers: Antecedents and long-term outcomes. In K. H. Rubin & J. H. B. Asendort (Eds.), *Social withdrawal, inhibition, and shyness.* Hillsdaly, NJ: Erlbaum.

Patchin, J., & Hinduja, S. (2006). Bullies move beyond the schoolyard: A preliminary look at cyber-bullying. *Youth, Violence and Juvenile Justice, 4*(2), 148–169.

Peterson, L., & Rigby, K. (1999). Countering bullying at an Australian secondary school with student as helpers. *Journal of Adolescence, 22,* 481–492.

Reid, A. S. (2005). The rise of third generation phones: The implications for child protection. *Information & Communication Technology Law, 14*(2), 89–113.

Salmivalli, C. (1999). Participant role approach to school bullying: Implications for interventions. *Journal of Adolescence, 22,* 453–459.

Salmivalli, C., Lagerspetz, K., Bjorkqvist, K., & Kaukianinen, A. (2006). Bullying as a group process: Participant roles and their relations to social status within the group. *Aggressive Behaviour, 28*(1), 30–44.

Shariff, S. (2005). Keeping schools out of the court: Legally defensible models of leadership. *The Educational Forum, 68*(3), 222–233.

Slonje, R., & Smith, P. K. (2007). Cyber-bullying: Another main type of bullying? *Scandinavian Journal of Psychology, 49*(2), 147–154.

Smith, P. K., Mahdavi, J., Carvalho, M., Fisher, S., Russell, S., & Tippett, N. (2008). Cyber-bullying: its nature and impact in secondary school pupils. *Journal of Child Psychology and Psychiatry, 49*(4), 376–385.

Stassen Berger, K. (2007). Update on bullying at school: A science forgotten? *Developmental Review, 27*, 90–126.

Strom, P. S., & Strom, R. D. (2005). When teens turn cyber-bullies. *The Educational Digest, 71*(4), 35–41.

Suler, J. (2004). The online disinhibition effect. *Cyberpsychology and Behaviour, 7*(3), 321–326.

Sullivan, B. (2006). *Cyber bullying newest threat to kids.* Retrieved 8/10/2008, 2008, from http://www.msnbc.msn.com/id/14272228/

Unnever, J. D. (2005). Bullies, aggressive victims, and victims: Are they distinct groups? *Aggressive Behaviour, 31*, 153–171.

Valentine, G., & Holloway, S. (2001). Online dangers: Geographies of parents' fears for children's safety in cyberspace. *The Professional Geographer, 53*(1), 71–83.

Vandebosch, H. (2003). *Questioning cyber-bullying in Flanders.* Unpublished. Leeronderzoek, University of Antwerp, Antwerp.

Vandebosch, H., Van Cleemput, K., Mortelmans, D., & Walrave, M. (2006). *Cyberpesten bij jongeren in Vlaanderen: een studie in opdracht van het IST.* Brussel: IST.

Walrave, M., & Heirman, W. (under review). Predicting Victimization and Perpetration in Cyber-bullying.

Walrave, M., Lenaerts, S., & De Moor, S. (2008). *Cyberteens @ risk ? Tieners verknocht aan internet, maar ook waakzaam voor risico's?* Brussel: Samenvatting survey van het project TIRO in opdracht van BELSPO.

Williams, R. W., & Guerra, N. G. (2007). Prevalence and predictors of Internet bullying. *Journal of Adolescent Health, 41*(6), s14-s21.

Wing, C. (2005). *Young Canadians in a wired world.* Retrieved 31/5/2008, 2008, from http://www.media-awareness.ca

Wolak, J., Mitchell, J.M., Finkelhor, D. (2007) Does online farassment constitute bullying? An exploration of online harassment by Known Peers and Online-Only contacts. *Journal of Adolescent Health,* 41(6), 51–58.

Ybarra, M. L., Diener-West, M., & Leaf, P. J. (2007). Examining the overlap in Internet-Harassment and school bullying: Implications for School Intervention. *Jounal of Adolescent Health, 41*(6), 42–50.

Ybarra, M. L., Espelage, D. L., & Kimberly, J. M. (2007). The Co-occurence of internet harassment and unwanted sexual solicitation, victimization and perpetration: associations with psychosocial indicators. *Jounal of Adolescent Health, 41*(6), 31–41.

Ybarra, M. L., & Mitchell, K. J. (2004). Online aggressor/targets, aggressor and targets: A comparison of youth characteristics. *Journal of Child Psychology and Psychiatry, 45*(7), 1308–1316.

Ybarra, M. L., Mitchell, K. J., Wolak, J., & Finkelhor, D. (2006). Examining Characteristics and associated distress related to internet harassment: Findings from the second youth internet safety survey. *Pediatrics, 118*(4), 1169–1177.

3 · Gender and Cyber-bullying

How Do We Know What We Know?

Dianne L. Hoff
Sidney N. Mitchell

INTRODUCTION

An advertisement for Tonka toys featured trucks "built for the 3 stages of boyhood: smashing, crashing, and bashing." The corresponding Tonka™ (2007) website clearly identifies these as toys for boys, with descriptors like "mighty," "tough," and "bad boy." The home page for Hasbro, Inc. (2007), the parent company of Tonka, lets visitors "browse by boys" or "browse by girls." For boys there are action figures and toys for outdoor play. For girls, there are easy bake ovens, art supplies, and care-giving toys. Most of the toys are color coded—blue and brown for boys, pink and purple for girls.

These and other advertisements are part of social messages that children receive that clearly define socially acceptable roles for masculinity and femininity. From a very early age, boys and girls receive cues about gender-appropriate behavior and emotional responses from the actions and reactions of parents, teachers, coaches, peers, and the media (Pleck, 1995). These messages affect how children dress, what games they play, how they interact with others, and ultimately, their sense of self worth (Lorber, 1992; Lytton & Romney, 1991; Messner, 2001; Valian, 1999). Boys, for example, learn that certain behaviors and emotions fall within an acceptable range of what is considered masculine, including assertiveness, competition, not backing down from a fight or confrontation, and not showing emotions considered to be feminine. For girls, on the other hand, desirable traits associated with femininity include being passive, supportive, yielding, and fragile (Allan, 2004; Kivel, 1999; Valian, 1999; Thompson & Goodvin, 2005).

Gender socialization not only influences desirable behavior but also negative behaviors, such as violence and young people's reactions to it. In their 2003 study of middle school students, Tolman, Spencer, Rosen-Reynoso, and Porche found that male sexual aggression was considered "just the way things were" (p. 174) and that dating violence had been normalized by both the female and male students. They also found that adult intervention was most often designed to "fix and fiddle with the girls" (p. 176), including a focus on girls' tendency to enter or stay in such relationships as opposed to prevention for boys.

That aggressive behavior in boys is more prevalent (and normalized) is clearly rooted in the social construction of masculinity and femininity. Although boys and girls enter the world as biologically unique, the development of temperament, emotion, and expression are, at least in part, socially constructed and become a part of their self-identities. (Johnson, 2005; Thompson & Goodvin, 2005). A study on aggressive behavior in males and females playing video games illustrates this point. Researchers found that when the participants wore nametags and were watched by evaluators, their behavior complied more closely with socially accepted norms for masculinity and femininity. Females were far less aggressive when they thought they could be identified; males were somewhat more aggressive. When the participants believed they were anonymous and could not be seen, their behavior was much more similar. In fact, females acted more aggressively than their male counterparts. When asked later about their actions during the game, male participants more accurately reported their aggressive behavior. Female participants consistently under-reported aggression in line with their socialized norms of appropriate behavior (Lightdale & Prentice, 1994).

This study illustrates that behavior is normalized along gender lines, creating what Sandra Bem (2001) calls "mutually exclusive scripts for males and females," which "defines any person or behavior that deviates from these scripts as problematic" (p. 63). Consequently, the pervasiveness of gender socialization, and the desire of most people not to be marginalized into an "abnormal" group, makes studying behaviors that are closely linked to norms of femininity and masculinity a challenging task indeed. Studies in which participants are asked to talk about being victimized or asked about emotional responses, for example, may have fewer (or more veiled) responses from males than from females. In contrast, studies that ask participants about behaviors associated with aggression or taking charge may have fewer (or more veiled) responses from females than from males. This tendency for responses to shift toward socially accepted norms suggests that understanding the voices of respondents may not be as straightforward as some might suggest (Currie, Kelly, & Pomerantz, 2007).

As researchers, we began to wonder whether the emerging data on cyber-bullying might be somewhat skewed because of the influence of gender socialization. Briefly, cyber-bullying is a modern variation on traditional youth bullying, aggravated by new technology and is defined as, "willful and repeated harm inflicted through the medium of electronic text" (Patchin & Hinduja, 2006, p. 152). Instead of face-to-face threatening, perpetrators send messages and images that are sexually explicit, degrading, and/or threatening via instant messaging (IM), cell phones, blogs, chat rooms, websites, email, and on personal online profiles (Shariff & Hoff, 2007). It clearly puts young people into roles of victim, perpetrator, and/or retaliator—and all of these behaviors closely identify with norms for femininity and masculinity.

In order to examine the influence of gender socialization on cyber-bullying data, we returned to a study we conducted in 2007 on the prevalence and nature of cyber-bullying, as well as the psychological impact on their lives (Hoff & Mitchell, 2009). We surveyed over 300 students, asking whether respondents had been the victims of cyber-bullying, the nature of their reactive behavior, and their emotional responses. The survey contained 28 limited choice and scaled response questions, which we had analyzed using descriptive and inferential statistics. In our initial analysis we transposed and sorted the qualitative data from six open-ended questions, first by research question (related to their experience with cyber-bullying, their reactive behavior, and the effect it had on their lives), and then by emergent themes. These findings pointed to significant differences in the experiences of males and females. For example, females more often than males reported being victims of cyber-bullying, whereas males reported that they were not victims of cyber-bullying but had engaged in retaliatory behavior. These findings, along with other inconsistencies that we detected, left us wondering about the authenticity of the data. Were the differences a true representation of students' cyber-bullying experiences? Or, were students' responses influenced by their socialization into gender-appropriate roles—that is, were males really victims of cyber-bullying more often than they were willing to admit, and did females actually retaliate against the cyber-bully, although they did not report doing so? And how would we know?

REEXAMINING WHAT WE KNOW ABOUT CYBER-BULLYING

We decided to reexamine our initial study on cyber-bullying using secondary data analysis, which Schutt (2006) describes as analyzing data or information gathered by someone else, or gathered in a pervious study, for some other purpose. In this case, our purpose was to reexamine the data from our previous study to explore possible effects of gender socialization on student reporting of cyber-bullying. Originally, the quantitative data had been examined in aggregate, and the qualitative data had been sorted according to four broad categories: the prevalence of cyber-bullying, the specific content of the messages, students' reactive behavior, and the emotional effects they experienced. It represented a vertical analysis, which combined the responses from all participants and then compared the results of male and female respondents. When re-examining the data, we instead looked across each survey horizontally, looking for internal consistency and noting the language the respondent used in describing experiences with cyber-bullying.

From there we considered what types of evidence we would look for in determining whether gender socialization affected the data. We came up with four types of evidence—skewed patterns, distancing, inconsistencies, and gendered language—to create what we term a four-pronged Analysis of Coherence Test (ACT), which gave us multiple interpretive frames to analyze and triangulate the data across all sources, as follows:

Analysis of Coherence Test

a. *Skewed Patterns*—Did males or females respond noticeably differently depending on the topic? And did these differences align with gender-socialized norms of femininity and masculinity?

b. *Distancing*—Was there a difference by sex in students owning the response (this happened to me) or using strategies to deny or distance themselves from the experience (e.g., "othering" the experience—*this happened to a friend*)? Did these differences align with gender-socialized norms of femininity and masculinity?

c. *Inconsistency*—Were there inconsistencies within individual responses or within the patterns we found between males and females? Did inconsistencies show influences of gender norms for femininity and masculinity?

d. *Gendered Language*—Did males and females use language aligned with socialized norms for masculinity and femininity to describe their experiences? For this aspect of the analysis, we identified Allan's (2004) list of gender-polarized attributes as an interpretive frame.

Taken together, we believed the four prongs of the Analysis of Coherence Test would illuminate whether gender socialization influenced students' reporting of cyber-bullying.

The reexamination of the data focused on the major categories of the original study, including: the prevalence of cyber-bullying, the nature of the messages, the students' responses to being cyber-bullied, and the psychological effects on them. For each category, we explored the influence of gender socialization, applying the

Analysis of Coherence Test (ACT) described above. The findings presented here represent re-interpretations of the original data.

Prevalence of cyber-bullying

The quantitative data pointed to a large gender discrepancy in the prevalence of cyber-bullying, with females more than males admitting to being cyber-bullied (72% to 28%, respectively). It is in the qualitative data, however, that we found interesting nuances which made us question the accuracy of this discrepancy. First, we noticed a difference in how respondents described the incidents. In the qualitative examples students provided, 81% of the females reported experiences that had happened to them personally. In contrast, 65% of the male participants reported the incidents as happening to *friends*. However, the specificity of the examples provided by males led us to question if they were misreporting incidents in order to avoid being labeled as victims. We also noted that male respondents, who had previously indicated in the quantitative data they had not been bullied, were able to provide specific examples of cyber-bullying incidents. A few examples from male respondents illustrate that although male respondents disassociated with the experiences, they were still able to provide detailed examples:

- *I have a friend who everyone said was gay. Kids made a website made about him, and he gets hate messages. In high school he was threatened all the time.*
- *In an IM, my friend received the comment, "I'm going to f**king kill you."*
- *The message said, "I want to rape your big ass then come on your back and laugh at you crying."*

In one case the student claimed the message was for a friend but then later mentions himself inside the text:

- *My friend received an email message that said, 'I'll burn your house down.' This had escalated from friendly messaging, to requests for dates, which I declined, and then threats.*

Overall, in applying the Analysis of Coherence Test to the data on the prevalence of cyber-bullying, we found three gender-socialized patterns. First, we noticed a skewed pattern of response, with females reporting being cyber-bullied far more than males. This subtopic asked participants to admit being victimized, a role that identifies only with femininity, and the disparity between female and male reporting was dramatic. Only 28% of the males reported having this experience, compared to 72% of the females, who readily supplied specific examples. So the first prong of our test was met.

The second pattern was that while males did provide examples of cyber-bullying, they overwhelmingly distanced themselves from revealing that they had been victimized. The most common pattern was for them to "other" the problem—reporting incidents that had happened to "friends" in 65% of the incidents they recounted. The pattern was so pervasive that some degree of distancing (prong 2 of our test) appeared to have influenced their responses, especially when compared to the responses from females who typically recounted experiences they had personally experienced, only relating the experiences of friends 20% of the time.

There were also inconsistencies (prong 3 of our test) within their responses. Males provided very specific information, sometimes starting with describing a friend's experience but then switching to "I" part way through the response. Also, male respondents who indicated they had not been cyber-bullied frequently admitted retaliating later in the survey. Moreover, 81 percent of males indicated in the survey that they would not tell adults or friends about cyber-bullying; whereas only 16 percent of females reported that they would not tell friends or adults. If this were true, however, we question how male survey participants knew of all of the incidents that they claimed happened to friends.

In summary, the *skewed pattern* of responses (more females reporting victimization than males), the *distancing* (as seen in males "othering" the problem), and the *inconsistencies* led us to suspect that gender socialization could be affecting participant response to our inquiries about the prevalence of cyber-bullying. It led us wonder whether the data accurately reflected their experience or whether our original analysis had not revealed the complexity of this phenomenon. We explored further by examining the content of the messages they received.

The Content of the Messages

The content of the cyber-bullying messages that students reported was closely linked to gender norms. Females gave examples illustrating that they were taunted mostly about their appearance and sensuality (91% of the messages fell into these categories), and to a lesser extent about their ability, disability, race, religion, or sexual orientation. For males, sexual orientation was cited most often as the reason they had been cyber-bullied and being put down for lack of ability (especially athletic) followed closely behind. Within the messages that males indicated had been sent to them (as opposed to friends), sexual orientation and ability accounted for 77% of the messages. Factors such as appearance, race, and religion were all mentioned, but to a much lesser extent in the case of boys.

We noticed that the messages fell into two major categories: *out-group* abuse and *object abuse,* both of which have roots in gender socialization and social psychology (Hewstone & Brewer, 2004; Tajfel & Turner, 1979). *Out-group abuse* we defined as cruelty to anyone not in the "in group." This kind of bullying is directed at someone based on his/her popularity, ability, sexual orientation, and so on. Although out-group abuse affected both males and females, females were more often targeted for appearance, sexual promiscuity, and popularity; whereas males were more often targeted for their sexual orientation or lack of athleticism. *Object-abuse,* on the other hand, is directed at a specific individual independent of group membership. We use the term "object" deliberately instead of "target" because the victim is most often objectified in the abusive messages. This type of bullying occurs when the person becomes the object of another's abusive treatment. It can stem from sexual desire, the need for power over the person, or from specific incidents, such as relationship break-ups.

In our original study, females reported being cyber-bullied with messages that fell into both out-group abuse (for weight, popularity, etc.) and object-abuse (sexually explicit messages), while males reported messages that most frequently represented out-group abuse for sexual orientation and lack of manly ability. Here are some examples:

Out-group abuse (females)

▪ *People would make rude remarks about my weight and appearance (online). Others who didn't even know me chimed in.*
▪ *They would send me hundreds of messages saying that everyone hated me.*

Not one male reported cyber-bullying taking the form of chiding them for weight, popularity, etc.

Object abuse (females)

▪ *The person would write words like cunt, stupid bitch, and more. I told him to leave me alone, but he would make a new screen name and find me again.*
▪ *A boy kept making sexual remarks like 'meet me on the corner by the Seven 11...you like the corner. You belong there. Fuck me, you want it.'*

Out-group abuse (males)

▪ *These kids know I'm not gay, but they posted it anyway. Now my life is hell, and it won't stop.*
▪ *Messages telling my friend he's a wimp.*

We applied the Analysis of Coherence Test to the messages students reported receiving, and noted the following. In terms of the first prong—skewed patterns of responses along gender lines—females (almost exclusively) reported being objectified sexually. Almost no males reported this experience, with the exception of a few who are (or are perceived to be) gay and had received sexually objectifying messages. Further, although both males and females reported being victims of out-group abuse, the topic within these experiences varied according to gender-socialized norms. Females were most often bullied for traits associated with femininity (e.g. popularity, appearance), whereas males were most often bullied for "manly" topics—such as sports ability.

We also noted gendered language (prong 4) within the text of the messages students recounted. The messages that females reported had literally hundreds of words such as "threatening," "hunting down," "waiting for [me]," "watching"—all aligned with stalking and submission. Males rarely used such language to recount their messages, and the few times they did, indicated they were reporting messages girl friends had received. The messages the males reported overwhelmingly included language such as, "kill," "stomp out," "beat up," and "get the shit kicked out of me"—all aligned with aggression and dominance. There was a clear pattern of females reporting messages that placed them as victims in a helpless role, whereas males reported messages that placed them at the opposing side of a fight.

Both the *skewed patterns* on what males and females reported, coupled with the *gendered language* embedded in the messages, provided further evidence that gender socialization seemed to affect participants' accounts of their experiences. While, of course, the data could reflect actual gender differences in bullying, our point is that these patterns point to gender socialized reporting. If so, we may be missing important incidents of cyber-bullying that do occur but go unreported. We continued our analysis by examining how students reported their reactive behavior to cyber-bullying, which is reported next.

Students' Reactive Behavior

Students' reactive behavior to cyber-bullying experiences also showed alignment with gender norms. When females were confronted with cyber-bullying, they reported most often changing their own behavior, which included changing their phone numbers/screen names, avoiding certain websites (or not going onto the Internet at all), trying to find new friends, or hoping the behavior would stop if they ignored it. Females also were more likely to report incidents to adults. Of the responses that indicated either changing one's own behavior or reporting to adults, 80% came from females. While these actions are commendable, they still represent a gendered pattern of girls being expected (far more than boys) to change their own behavior (Tolman, et al., 2003). Here are some examples from females:

- *I deleted accounts—that's the only way I could get it to stop.*
- *I decided just not to go online, but that wasn't fair to me. So it's a problem.*
- *I just waited and hoped they would graduate.*
- *My parents called the police.*

The number one reactive behavior reported by males, on the other hand, was retaliatory behavior. Here are examples from males:

- *I physically assaulted the bully.*
- *I threatened the bully back—that ended it.*
- *I took care of it.*

It is noteworthy that not once did male respondents claim that they were reporting retaliatory behavior that a friend had done (as had been the case when reporting about being a victim).

In contrast, when females reported retaliatory behavior, it was less physical:

- *I spread nasty rumors about them.*
- *I went to the bullier (sic) and told her she'd better stop—she was so surprised, it shocked her out of it.*

When females did report physical retaliatory behavior, they frequently attributed the action to others acting on their behalf:

- *My brother took over—bullied back.*
- *The older sister of the victim went to talk to the bully and took care of it. Let's just say it never happened again.*
- *Someone 'took care of it' or it would have continued.*

The contrast in the responses can be further examined by applying our Analysis of Coherence Test. First, we clearly saw skewed patterns of reporting (prong 1). Males, far more than females, reported retaliatory behavior that was active and aggressive, whereas females typically reported more passive reactive behavior. Their reported responses closely aligned with gender-socialized norms: for males, it is considered appropriate for behavior to be assertive and confrontational; for females, the appropriate behavior is passive and yielding (Allan, 2004; Kivel, 1999; Valian, 1999; Thompson & Goodvin, 2005).

We also saw evidence of distancing behavior (prong 2), where respondents distanced themselves from actions that are not socially accepted with gender norms. It is interesting to note that when males were earlier asked about being *victims,* they were the ones engaging in distancing behavior, attributing their experiences to that of "friends." Females had no trouble reporting being victimized. In terms of *reactive behavior,* however, it was now the girls' turn to "other" the problem—attributing the retaliation to the actions of friends or relatives. Males had no problem owning retaliatory behavior.

We also saw evidence of internal inconsistencies (prong 3). Males, who had earlier reported not being victims, reported later that they had retaliated. Females, who earlier had reported feelings of anger to the same degree as male participants, did not report acting aggressively in reaction to cyber-bullying incidents.

Finally, we also can point to gendered language (prong 4) in students' responses about their reactive behavior. Females, for example, used language that describes passive, gentle, and/or dependent behavior:

- "I *changed*" [my phone number, email address]
- "I *stopped visiting*" [the blog, website]
- "I *waited* and *hoped*" [it would go away]
- "I *told*" [parents, authorities].

This language suggests that female respondents believed they needed to change their own behavior (a common pattern for female victims) or that as females they should turn to others for assistance to end the bullying. Both are gender-socialized responses.

Males on the other hand used language like "assaulted," "threatened," "watched," and "took care of" which align with the masculine traits of aggression, taking charge, and being in control. This language reflects a common pattern among male respondents and suggests they wanted to be seen as capable of ending the cyber-bullying and handling things on their own.

The *skewed patterns, distancing, inconsistencies,* and *gendered language,* taken together, made us question the veracity of the reports given by both males and females about their own reactive behavior, and led us to suspect that a pattern of gender socialization was affecting participants' responses. We see this further in the last category of the study, psychological effects of cyber-bullying.

Psychological Effects

Data also reveal differences in how students say they were affected by victimization. Female and male respondents equally reported psychological effects as a result of cyber-bullying including anger, fear, helplessness, and loss of concentration. In the quantitative data, gender differences were not significant. However, within the qualitative data, where students wrote about their experiences, the language of boys tended to express anger, whereas girls expressed fear and helplessness. The examples below illuminate the psychological effects.

The responses from females indicated a pattern of shutting down and losing self-confidence:

- "*I became less confident in myself.*"
- "*I'm more timid at school.*"
- "*I fought depression and had to see a therapist.*"

The responses from males, on the other hand, indicated a pattern of becoming emboldened and taking action:

- "*I physically assaulted the bully.*"
- "*I watched the person and when I got him alone, I ended it.*"

▪ *"I got fed up—found the bully and threatened him."*

When we applied the Analysis of Coherence Test to these data, we found very skewed response patterns (prong 1) in line with socialized gender norms (Thompson & Goodvin, 2005). Males tended to use feelings of anger and fear to propel them to take action and take control. Females overwhelmingly reported letting feelings of anger and fear paralyze them.

We also noted inconsistencies (prong 2). Whereas the quantitative data had shown no significant differences in the emotional effects of cyber-bullying on males and females, it was clear from this data that this experience was affecting them differently, as evidenced by their descriptions of reactive behavior. Not only did males report taking action, as noted above, their aggressiveness in dealing with the cyber-bully had the effect of allowing them to feel they had "dealt with the problem." Taking action, even if it is somewhat questionable, provides a form of closure and perpetuates feelings of competence and control. It is important to remember, however, that retaliatory action often triggers another round of bullying, creating an escalating cycle that is difficult to interrupt. In contrast, females' more passive responses, while helpful in not escalating the conflict, do not lend themselves to feelings of competence or control but rather perpetuate victimization. Thus, the reactive behaviors reported by males and females each had problematic elements, and understanding them is further complicated when their reporting is influenced by gender norms.

Overall, the responses from both males and females about their experiences with cyber-bullying, the nature of the messages, their reactive behavior, and the psychological effects were all quite skewed toward patterns of behavior aligned with conventions of gender-appropriate roles. This led us to conclude that gender socialization was a factor that had dramatically influenced the students' responses.

A COMPLEX PICTURE OF CYBER-BULLYING

The re-examination of the data from our study on cyber-bullying led us to several new understandings. First, the re-examination of the data led us to ask ourselves what kind of evidence would help us uncover the effects of gender socialization on qualitative responses. We came up with four factors—skewed responses, distancing, inconsistencies, and gendered language—which, taken together, we term the Analysis of Coherence Test. To uncover evidence for the four prongs of the test, we were forced to look within surveys for patterns and inconsistencies, as opposed to conducting analysis on the aggregated data. This was a very time-intensive process, but it revealed nuances we had not noted in our initial investigation. The Analysis of Coherence Test thus proved useful for illuminating differential response patterns of males and females (particularly related to behaviors closely associated with societal norms for femininity and masculinity), which were not readily evident in either a strictly quantitative or qualitative analysis. We believe it is a test that could be applied usefully to other data sets.

Second, the re-examination of the data has led us to new interpretations of our cyber-bullying data. Originally we reported with confidence that females had been much more victimized by cyber-bullying than males and that males more often retaliated. In digging deeper, however, we saw patterns suggesting that students' responses were affected by gender norms and their insecurities around how they might be viewed by others.

Among male respondents, for example, we saw inconsistencies (e.g., they claimed not to have been cyber-bullied but then switched to "I" in the examples or later reported retaliating), and we saw distancing of the problem (e.g., they attributed the incidents to friends). There was a pattern among males not to admit victimization. While males did report feeling fear and helplessness on the quantitative data to the same degree as female respondents, when asked about their reactive behaviors, they instead frequently used gendered ("macho") language to report physical retaliatory behaviors. Further, there was a repeated pattern indicating males felt they had to "take care of" cyber-bullying on their own—a position that can potentially be non-productive and even dangerous. Our current analysis of the data suggests that male students were victims of cyber-bullying more often than they cared to admit, had a much wider range of reactions than they were willing to report, and lacked social/emotional skills to understand or deal with incidents appropriately.

For females, who had readily admitted being victims of cyber-bullying, we found patterns that suggest unwillingness on their part to admit retaliation (e.g., they were able talk about retaliatory behavior but attributed it to "friends"). It was much more common for them to report helplessness or that they ignored the situation, both more socially acceptable positions for girls. Our current analysis of the data suggests that female students were most likely retaliators more often than they admitted, had a much wider range of reactive behavior than they were willing to report, and that they also lacked social/emotional skills to understand or deal with incidents appropriately.

Finally, a word about our interpretation. The analysis from this study is not meant to suggest that all males and females experience or report cyber-bullying in ways described here. It was also impossible to sort out the degree to which *behavior* had been affected by gender norms (e.g., females are cyber-bullied more frequently because of gender norms that cast them as victims; males retaliate more because it is in line with socialized behaviors) or whether it was the students' *reporting* that was colored by their own gender socialization. We suspect that it is some of both. Even without clarity on his point, however, it is evident that gender socialization can be a confounding factor in efforts to understand social phenomena, especially when the research has embedded implications for respondents' sense of femininity and masculinity. By acknowledging this potential confounding variable and then applying our Analysis of Coherence Test to the data, we were able to reveal a more complete (and complex) story about cyber-bullying and its impact on students.

If school leaders were to consider this new interpretation of the data, it might help them take new and inventive steps to curb and respond to incidents of cyber-bullying. This could include creating "safe contacts," who have training in what to look for when boys and girls report incidents of victimization or retaliation, and who go beneath the surface to understand the significance of what is being said and, more importantly, what is not being said. It could also help school leaders recognize the need for more educational emphasis on how students might handle social tensions more appropriately—including cyber-bullying—in a manner less driven by their fears of acting outside of gender-socialized norms. Finally, these findings might help educators break down gender stereotypes that work to perpetuate victimization and the desire to appear passive among girls, and the tendency toward aggression and denial in boys. Cyber-bullying is a serious issue for students, and schools are relying on emerging data to help create policies to respond appropriately. Yet studies that just report means and percentages may not reveal the complicated ways in which this social phenomenon is grounded in students' sense of self and their insecurities about how they are seen by others. In order to "know what we know" about cyber-bullying, it is therefore important to understand how it affects boys and girls differently, looking beyond what is being openly reported. Only then can schools hope to create the safe, accepting environment all students deserve.

References

Allan, E. J. (2004). Hazing and gender: analyzing the obvious. In H. Nuwer (Ed.) *The hazing reader* (pp. 275–294). Bloomington, IN: Indiana University Press.

Bem, S. L. (2001). In a male-centered world, female differences are transformed into female disadvantages. In P. S. Rothenberg (Ed.) *Race class and gender in the United States* (pp. 47–57). New York: Worth Publishers.

Currie, D., Kelly, D., & Pomerantz, S. (2007). Listening to girls: Discursive positioning and the construction of self. *International Journal of Qualitative Studies in Education, 20*(4), 377–400.

Hasbro, Inc. (2007). Website retrieved October 27, 2007 at *http://www.hasbro.com*.

Hewstone, M. & Brewer, M. (2004), *Self and social identity*. New York: Blackwell Publishing Professional.

Hoff, D. L. & Mitchell, S. N. (2009, in press). Cyberbullying: Causes, effects, and remedies. *Journal of Educational Administration*.

Johnson, A. G. (2005). *The gender knot: Unraveling our patriarchal legacy.* Philadelphia, PA: Temple University Press.

Kivel, P. (1999). *Boys will be men.* Gabriola Island, B.C., Canada: New Society Publishers.

Lightdale, J. R., & Prentice, D. A. (1994). Rethinking sex differences in aggression: Aggressive behavior in the absence of social roles. *Personality and Social Psychology Bulletin,* 20, (1), 34–44.

Lorber, J. (2001). The social construction of gender. In P. S. Rothenberg (Ed.) *Race, class and gender in the United States* (pp. 47–57). New York: Worth Publishers.

Lorber, J. (1992). Gender, in E. F. Borgatta, & M. L. Borgatta (Eds.), *Encyclopedia of Sociology,* 2, 748-765. NY: Macmillan.

Lytton, H., & Romney, D. M. (1991). Parents' differential socialization of boys and girls: A meta-analysis. *Psychological Bulletin,* 109, 267–96.

Messner, M. 2001. Ah, ya throw like a girl. In P. S. Rothenberg (Ed.) *Race, class and gender in the United States* (pp. 57–59). New York: Worth Publishers.

Patchin, J. & Hinduja, S. (2006). Bullies move beyond the schoolyard: A preliminary look at cyberbullying. *Youth Violence and Juvenile Justice,* 4 (2), 148–169.

Pleck, J. H. (1995). The gender role strain paradigm: An update. In R. F. Levant & W. S. Pollack (Eds.) *A new psychology of men* (pp. 11–32). New York: Basic Books.

Schutt, R. K. (2006). *Investigating the social world: The process and practice of research.* Thousand Oaks, CA: Pine Forge Press.

Shariff, S., & Hoff, D. L. (2007). Cyber-bullying: Clarifying Legal Boundaries for School Supervision in Cyber-Space. *International Journal of Cyber Criminology,* 1 (1), 76–118.

Tajfel, H. & Turner, J. (1979), "An integrative theory of intergroup conflict," in Austin, W. & Worchel, S., *The Social Psychology of Intergroup Relations.* Monterey, CA: Brooks Cole.

Thompson, R., & Goodvin, R. (2005). The individual child: Temperament, emotion, self, and personality (pp. 391–428). In M. Bornstein and M. Lamb (Eds.), *Developmental ccience* (5th Ed.). Mahwah, NJ: Lawrence Erlbaum.

Tolman, D. L., Spencer, R., Rosen-Reynoso, M., & Porche, M. V. (2003). Sowing the seeds of violence in heterosexual relationships: Early adolescents narrate compulsory heterosexuality. *Journal of Social Issues,* 59 (1), 159–178.

Tonka™ (2007). Website retrieved October 27, 2007 at *http://www.hasbro.com/tonka/.*

Valian, V. (1999). *Why so slow?* Cambridge, MA: The MIT Press.

4 · Juicycampus.com

How Was This Business Model Culpable of Encouraging Harassment on College Campuses?

Ellen M. Kraft

INTRODUCTION: WHAT WAS JUICYCAMPUS.COM?

Juicycampus.com was an online gossip site about campus life at over 500 colleges and universities that was started in October 2007. College students flocked to the site and revealed sexual escapades, commented on who was the biggest slut, who was the hottest sorority or fraternity member on campus, discussed who had what STDs, who used drugs, what happened at parties, spread nasty rumors, and came out of the closet. Derogatory comments were made about physical appearance, ethnicity, race, and implied sexual experiences of students. Many students were humiliated, maligned, had their reputation tarnished, left school, and sought professional help as a result of posts made to the site. The website caused controversy on college campuses across the United States. Some students liked the site for entertainment, while others found it offensive. There was also disagreement among administrators, parents, and government officials regarding how to address the content of the postings. Students expressed their opposition to the site by creating groups on Facebook.com, creating websites to address issues about Internet speech, writing editorials in their college newspaper, posting comments directly on

Juicycampus.com, filing complaints with their state Attorney General's office, and complaining to college administrators. Juicycampus.com was under investigation by New Jersey and Connecticut state Attorney General's offices for violating its terms of agreement. This chapter reviews the issues surrounding the website and discusses the reaction students and administrators had to the launch, expansion, and shutdown of Juicycampus.com. It analyzes how JuicyCampus's business model and website were culpable of encouraging college students to spread online gossip that was racist, sexist, homophobic, and antireligious. Litigation against the site by the New Jersey and Connecticut state Attorney General's offices is also discussed. Finally, the potential for the problem to continue on CollegeACB.com, a website that bought the traffic from Juicycampus.com, is explored.

Matthew Ivester, a 2005 Duke University graduate started the site with the intention of creating a site about "all the ridiculous things we did and the hilarious stories" (McNiff & Varney, 2008) about college life. According to the site all postings were "always anonymous, always juicy" (JuicyCampus, 2009a). Attorney General Anne Milgram of New Jersey argued that instead of being a lighthearted look at campus life, derogatory comments were made on the site about "physical appearance, ethnicity, race, and implied sexual experiences of students" (State of New Jersey Department of Law and Public Safety Press Release, 2008). Posts from the site exhibited racism, homophobia, and anti-Semitism (eschoolnews.com, 2008). Furthermore, the site was a forum that encouraged behavior that was an escalation of high school cyber-bullying into online sexual harassment. Many students were humiliated, maligned, left school, or had their reputation tarnished. Some even had to seek professional help as a result of posts made to the site. The reactions of college students to the online harassment on this site were similar to the reaction of students who experience serious incidents of cyber-bullying in high school.

Consider the examples in Figure 1, which provides a screen shot of the most viewed posts on Juicycampus.com on May 25, 2008 (JuicyCampus, 2008a).

All of the 9 most viewed posts contained sexually explicit content. The most viewed post was "Who is the sluttiest girl?" (Anonymous, 2008a) with 98,223 views. Names, e-mail addresses, and phone numbers of students were included in the posts. Under the same theme of exploiting the implied sexual experiences of students was the "Sluttiest Girls at Cornell" (Anonymous, 2008b) and "Biggest Slut at Baylor?" (Anonymous, 2008c) placing not only their reputations at risk but also their physical safety. The posts on this site described sexual characteristics about women named in detail. The next theme expressed in the most viewed posts was about who is the "hottest" on campus. The three posts discuss the "Hottest People on Campus" (Anonymous, 2008d), "Hottest Freshman Girl on Campus" (Anonymous, 2008e), and "Hottest Sorority" (Anonymous, 2008f). The originator of the "Hottest People on Campus Posts" requested that respondents

Figure 1: Most Viewed Post on Juicycampus.com as of May 25, 2008

| Latest Posts | Latest Replies | Most Discussed | Most Viewed | Juiciest |

New Post

● Who is the sluttiest girl?????? 01-29-2008	70% JUICY 749 votes 98221 views	#Replies 155
● Sluttiest Girls at Cornell 01-26-2008	64% JUICY 222 votes 34096 views	#Replies 45
● Hottest People on Campus 02-05-2008	64% JUICY 346 votes 33336 views	#Replies 90
● Biggest Slut at Baylor? 01-24-2008	59% JUICY 236 votes 32822 views	#Replies 86
● Hottest Freshman Girl On Campus 01-23-2008	66% JUICY 128 votes 23064 views	#Replies 60
● Jenna Hirsch 01-31-2008	47% JUICY 141 votes 21141 views	#Replies 88
● Samson Mesele = cheater? 12-03-2007	51% JUICY 229 votes 18629 views	#Replies 87
● Hottest Sorority? 01-20-2008	52% JUICY 164 votes 17326 views	#Replies 57
● ALL URBANA BOYS RANKED 02-07-2008	59% JUICY 59 votes 16688 views	#Replies 83

include the name, house, and year of the hottest people on campus (Anonymous, 2008d). Specific girls were named in the "Hottest Freshman Girl on Campus" with one girl being accused of having herpes and another of being on drugs (Anonymous, 2008e). The girls in a particular sorority on the "Hottest Sorority" post were called "whores" (Anonymous, 2008f). The "All Urbana Boys Ranked" post classified the students as top tier, Indie boys, party boys, Allen Hall boys, art boys, child molesters, and totally useless (Anonymous, 2008g). The names of the students from the University of Illinois were listed under each category.

The child molesters category was the most reputation-damaging category for the Urbana boys. One person was accused of faking a car accident as an excuse for missing an economics exam as well as attempting to hire another student to take an exam for him. He was called a "resume padder," accused of lying and cheating, and called a "f***ing nigger" (Anonymous, 2008h). The discussion in the replies was essentially a flame war attacking the person's character as well as attacking participants in the discussion.

ANONYMITY ON JUICYCAMPUS.COM

In reality the Internet is not truly anonymous, as posts can be traced. There have been at least two incidents of threatening posts on Juicycampus.com that have led to students being arrested. The first incident occurred in December 2007 when a student posted a message to the site threatening that he would start a campus shooting and commit suicide afterwards (Morgan, 2008; Young, 2008a). The student was arrested but not charged with any crimes.

The second incident occurred when a student posted the following message to Juicycampus.com:

> I wonder if i could shut down the school…by saying I'm going to shoot as many people as i can in my second class tomorrow. I hope I get more than 50……….. For liability reasons and ip tracking I won't leave it at that. But seriously, this site is ridiculous (sic), if it got big, and someone put the effort into writing a big long serious suicide note informing all readers that he would kill over 100 kids, they could shut down the school. Nice. (Young, 2008a)

A Colgate University student reported the posting to campus police who reported the incident to the local police. The student who posted the original message was arrested and charged with second degree aggravated assault. He was released on $1,000 bail (Morgan, 2008).

To discuss anonymity (and show users how to bypass traditional IP tracking software) Juicycampusrevealed.com website was created by someone who wanted to show users how Juicycampus.com uses cookies to track their visits to the site and how they have information about a user's IP addresses. Juicycampus.com kept track of the users and what they posted by linking postings to the IP address that the post came from. The site explained how IP cloaking software modifies an IP address so that a fake IP address will be recorded in a router log. Libel is also explained on the site.

JUICYCAMPUS.COM CONSULTED ITS CLIENTS

Juicycampus.com created a space within the site allowing users to comment about the site during March 2008. According to its instigator, Matt Ivestor, the thoughts and opinions of its users would be taken into consideration as policies evolved (JuicyCampus, 2008b). Mr. Ivestor requested feedback about moderation asking users to identify for him, "which posts are juicy and which are trash" and "where they should draw the line." In response to his request for feedback, there were many posts requesting that a particular college or university be added or removed from the list of university campuses that the web site supports. Other common suggestions were that posts to Juicycampus.com should expire after a period of time (Anonymous, 2008i; Anonymous, 2008j; Anonymous, 2008k) there should be a way to report posts to have them removed (Anonymous, 2008j; Anonymous, 2008l), and that users should be able to modify what they have posted (Anonymous, 2008j). There were requests from Baylor University (Anonymous, 2008m), Colgate University (Anonymous, 2008n), Cornell University (Anonymous, 2008o), Emory University (Anonymous, 2008p), and Michigan State University (Anonymous, 2008g), to have their campuses removed from Juicycampus.com. Moreover, there was a suggestion that racist language be blocked (Anonymous, 2008j) or deleted (Anonymous, 2008r).

Users indicated that the layout and speed of the site needed to be improved. A post was made that having the site hosted by Blogspot and the lack of quality advertisers made the site look like a "pathetic get-rich-quick scheme" (Anonymous, 2008s). On the subject of trash, the post "2005 Grad Working as a Pro," suggested that Matt Ivestor is a "Recent grad, with advanced degree, is now working the world's oldest profession, because it's more 'lucrative'" (Anonymous, 2008t). Another post, "This Does Not Help Anybody!" simply stated, "GET RID OF IT" (Anonymous, 2008u).

A major concern expressed by users was the moderation of the site. Many viewers suggested that defamatory posts needed to be deleted. A comment posted as "Constructive Criticism" asked, "Why can't you spend just as much effort censoring malicious posts as you do censoring good ones?" (Anonymous, 2008w). Another comment that supported this view was made in a post requesting "More Moderation" remarking that "You censor good posts and don't delete the malicious ones" (Anonymous, 2008y). The respondent also stated "We understand that you think this is all a big joke, but many of the personal attacks have had a detrimental effect on the victims" (Anonymous, 2008w). Site viewers voiced concerns about the effects of the posts damaging reputations.

There was a thread "From a Parent to Mr. Ivestor" posted by a parent whose family had been torn apart because of postings on the site, begging that posts with vicious personal attacks be deleted. In the same post it is also stated "you provide a good platform for discussion and fun, but what good is it if you ruin lives, even one life?" (Anonymous, 2008x).

Other users believed that JuicyCampus should not censor posts as the site should be a place where people can freely express themselves. The excerpt from the post "Advice" explains that:

> People like juicy campus for the reason that it shows the truth about a lot of things. Most posts are true, and if they arent, there are enough replies that really do let everyone know the truth about something or someone. Yes there are a lot of offensive posts but i feel like it is up to the students to learn about and decidewhat is and is not appropriate to write online—it is NOT the job of juicy campus to screen posts and/or delete what they deem is inappropriate. (Anonymous, 2008y)

Other participants did not believe that for the most part posts are true. College students should be able to discern what is true and what is not true. A post was made stating "anyone who takes this site seriously needs to get a life!! It's just the next internet fad" (Anonymous, 2008z).

Participants posting to the site can defend themselves or other people if they do not think a post is true. Concerns were voiced on the site that people post comments on Juicycampus.com because they do not have the gumption to make the comments directly to the person (Anonymous, 2008aa; Anonymous, 2008ab; Anonymous, 2008ac). One participant who posted "High School All Over Again" wondered:

> What is the deal with bashing other students on here? This isn't highschool. If you have a problem with someone, tell it to their face instead of hiding behind your computer and writing crap about them. Last I checked you have to be an adult to be in college. Act like one. (Anonymous, 2008aa)

Viewers of Juicycampus.com appear to like the site because it is fun and entertaining. However, some of these same people did have concerns about the site having harmful effects (Anonymous, 2008ad). A respondent who was in favor of free speech asked Juicycampus.com to "Stop the Censorship!" (Anonymous, 2008ae). The participant gave specific guidelines about when to remove posts:

> There are only a couple times when the delete button needs to be used—ever: 1. posting contact info2. posting long, disruptive spam of the constitution, the same word 802432564 times, or the like with no substance added to the conversationAny other thing needs to be left alone. (Anonymous, 2008ae)

Several students have commented that people like the site until they are the victim. There was considerable discussion about the issue in replies to the post "Everything on This Site is Hilarious Until it Says Your Name" (Anonymous, 2008af). Comments such as "It is all fun and games until the target is YOU!" (Anonymous, 2008y) express this point of view.

A post from Facebook.com sums up the problem that Juicycampus.com "is so popular because it is funny as hell to laugh about the stupid stuff that happens to your friends or things that happen to people you don't know. Nobody gets mad until its themselves that are talked about" (Shelton, 2008). Another Facebook.com post to the Students Against Juicy Campus discussion board viewed the group as "you're all just a bunch of people that probably got made fun of and now you're mad about it. Maybe you shouldn't take things written on a website that everyone knows is ridiculous so seriously" (Francisco, 2008).

THE SUCCESS OF JUICYCAMPUS.COM: UPGRADES AND REDESIGN

Despite controversy surrounding the site, Juicycampus.com underwent an extensive upgrade and expanded. On September 1, 2008 the site was temporarily closed to upgrade the technology with servers that are ten times faster to prepare to accommodate traffic of over one million viewers at a time (JuicyCampus, 2008c). The site was re-launched the next day with 185 new schools. The interface was redesigned to allow users to link posts to other sites and vote on whether they agree with a post.

During September Juicycampus.com added schools daily based on a theme. The "most requested schools" were added first along with campuses by geographic area. During October they added the "the Biggest Stoners," "Top Party Schools," and top "Top Greek Schools." On October 6, 2008, Juicycampus.com reached its goal of 500 campuses by adding Gettysburg College. JuicyCampus CEO Matt Ivestor selected Gettysburg College as the 500th campus making an analogy that:

> as Gettysburg was the turning point during the Civil War, we hope Gettysburg will be the turning point where JuicyCampus moves past the resistance put up by campus Administrations and students are free to discuss the topics that interest them most. JuicyCampus is, in Lincoln's famous words, the website 'of the people, by the people, and for the people.' (JuicyCampus, 2008d)

With this statement Mr. Ivestor was expressing his hope that the site would be a place where there is a free exchange of ideas. He was fully aware of the negative publicity that the site had received for the racist, sexist, homophobic, and anti-religious comments. In his statement he said that students will use the site to discuss topics that interest them most. The site home page asked users to "spill the juice about all the crazy stuff going on at your campus" (JuicyCampus, 2009a).

LEGAL ISSUES AND JUICYCAMPUS.COM

In its terms and conditions Juicycampus.com made a disclaimer to absolve itself of any liability from posts by stating that:

> JuicyCampus is not responsible for, does not control, does not endorse and does not verify the Content posted to the Site or available through the Site, and that it makes no guarantee regarding the reliability, accuracy, legitimacy or quality of any such Content (JuicyCampus, 2009b).

The Communications and Decency Act of 1996 section 230, was federal legislation passed by Congress to protect website hosts from third party liability for defamation and other torts. Under section 230, protection for private blocking and screening of offensive material, website hosts cannot be held liable for third party communications. As Shariff (2008) has explained, this is because in the United States, website hosts and ISP providers are defined as "distributors" of expression and not "publishers" based on the landmark *Zeran* case (*Zeran v. America Online, Inc.*, 1997). However, as stated in the terms and conditions of the site, JuicyCampus has "the right (but not the obligation) to access, re-arrange, modify and remove or restrict access to any Content on the Site in its sole discretion" (JuicyCampus, 2008f; JuicyCampus, 2009b). Users of the site agreed not to post anything "unlawful, threatening, abusive, tortuous, defamatory, obscene, libelous, or invasive of another's privacy" (JuicyCampus, 2008e). In addition users were not required to register for the site.

The Attorney General's Office in New Jersey received complaints from parents and students about Juicycampus.com. Specifically, a student filed a complaint with the Attorney General's Office in New Jersey about having her address posted to the site and being severely harassed online (e-School News.com, 2008). Attorney General Anne Milgram launched a formal investigation in March 2008 of JuicyCampus to determine whether the organization is "violating the New Jersey Consumer Fraud Act through unconscionable business practices and misrepresentations to users" (State of New Jersey Department of Law and Public Safety Press Release, 2008). The state of New Jersey issued a subpoena to Lime Blue, LLC of Reno Nevada requesting information regarding how the company selects 'supporting campuses'; how it verifies the campus affiliation of posts, and how it enforces the parental consent form for participants under age 18 (State of New Jersey Department of Law and Public Safety Press Release, 2008). The state also issued subpoenas to Abdrite.com and Google.com to determine information about the business relationships of these organizations with JuicyCampus. Google confirmed that it has severed its business relationship with JuicyCampus and no longer has advertising provided through the Adsense Online Program.

Three days after New Jersey commenced its investigation against JuicyCampus, Connecticut Attorney General Richard Blumenthal began an investigation of

JuicyCampus to determine whether it was following rules that prohibit libelous, defamatory and abusive postings. Similar to the investigation commenced by the State of New Jersey, the Connecticut Attorney General's office was investigating the manner in which JuicyCampus selects campuses; verifies that postings come from a particular campus; tracks repeat violators of its policies and unlawful content. Both states were also investigating how the site enforces the parental consent form for participants under age 18. Mr. Blumenthal stated:

> I am personally appalled by this site's contents—and business model. Juicycampus seeks profit from the pain inflicted by gossip. Making money by providing anonymity to those wishing to spread malicious, malignant gossip is repugnant and repulsive. (State of Connecticut Attorney General Press Release, 2008)

If registration were required to use Juicycampus.com or if users had to identify themselves on the site it would be less likely that they would have made the defamatory comments. Consequently, JuicyCampus was profiting from the lack of accountability it gives users through anonymity. The states of Connecticut and New Jersey commenced legal investigation into JuicyCampus's business practices as both Attorneys General believed that JuicyCampus was responsible for the suffering of the victims who have been defamed on its site. These investigations did not result in any charges being filed against JuicyCampus.

During the investigation, JuicyCampus changed its privacy policy and terms of use in June 2008 to avoid liability. These changes were made following the start of the legal investigation and are worth reviewing. The website's new policy had the TRUSTe Web Privacy Seal. The TRUSTe privacy seal is a "seal of quality" that identify sites that have agreed to comply with privacy guidelines set forth by TRUSTe (Turban et al., 2008). On their website the TRUSTe organization says that their program helps businesses develop privacy policies that are "100% accurate to their business policies" (TRUSTe, 2009). By having this privacy seal, JuicyCampus had agreed to comply with the TRUSTe's guidelines for gathering data responsibly. A safe harbor is a self-regulating policy and enforcement mechanism that does not have government enforcement because it meets government objectives. However, the TRUSTe seal that JuicyCampus had was not considered a "safe harbor." There has been criticism that privacy seal programs are not effective in protecting the privacy of users (Laudon & Traver, 2008). Hence, having the TRUSTe seal gave users the impression that JuicyCampus was highly committed to developing responsible privacy policies even though the TRUSTe seal is not necessarily effective for ensuring compliance to a company's privacy program.

While the previous privacy policy protected users by providing the statement: "It is not possible for anyone to use this website to find out who you are or where you are located. We do not track any information that can be used by us to identify you" (Haynes, 2008; Magid, 2008; Stringer, 2008; JuicyCampus, 2008e), the modified policy explicitly stated that the site would gather certain information automatically and store it in log files. This information includes internet protocol (IP) addresses, browser type, the internet service provider (ISP) information, referring/exit pages, operating system, date/time stamp, and clickstream data, facilitating the identification of users and in that regard, making it significantly easier to identify abusive users (JuicyCampus, 2009c).

Juicycampus.com in its updated privacy policy stated that it used cookies to identify users and that their third party advertisers may also use cookies on the site (JuicyCampus, 2009c). The site provided a link to a reference on Wikipedia.com about cookies, and moreover, it warned users that its administrators would collect and share aggregate demographic information with their third party advertisers (JuicyCampus, 2009c). The section "Tips for Extra Cautious" (JuicyCampus, 2008e) that previously guided users on how to cloak their IP addresses using cloaking software was replaced by a statement referring participants to learn about free IP cloaking by searching Google.com.

To increase visibility of the terms of agreement, a pop-up menu appeared before entering the site warning that "this is a juicy site." There was a link to the terms and conditions. Although there was no way of proving that users are over 18 years of age, the site also warned that users must be over 18. Accordingly, with these changes, the IP address of users' computers could be tracked; however, identifying an IP does not necessarily identify a specific user. The new pop-up menu did at least call attention to the fact that the site did have terms and conditions.

Moreover, the revised terms of agreement had been expanded from the original not to post anything "unlawful, threatening, abusive, tortuous, defamatory, obscure, libelous, or invasive of another's privacy" (JuicyCampus, 2008f). The revised version also stated: "You agree not to post content that is obscene or that violates laws relating to sexually explicit material, that infringes the rights of any third party (including intellectual property and privacy or publicity rights), that is defamatory, or that constitutes hate speech under applicable law" (JuicyCampus, 2009b). The new terms also explicitly asked users to agree that they will not "post the private information of yourself or another such as addresses, phone numbers, Social Security numbers or credit card numbers" (JuicyCampus, 2009b).

In regards to its codes of conduct, Juicycampus.com had user conduct rules; however, it stated that the site "cannot and does not assure that other users are complying" (JuicyCampus, 2009b). The site provided an e-mail address for reporting content that violated user conduct. It also made disclaimers that "it will take any particular action, or any action whatsoever, in response to such reports" (JuicyCampus, 2009b) and "cannot and does not guarantee that it will read your report, or respond to it, in any particular time frame or at all" (JuicyCampus, 2009b).

Did these modifications to the terms and conditions of the website make a significant difference? Did they in effect protect privacy and avoid libel and a ruined reputation? Not quite. According to Connecticut Attorney General Richard Blumenthal the revision by JuicyCampus of its terms of agreement in June 2008, whereby they reserve the right not to enforce compliance, abdicated responsibility for defamatory or hateful racist or anti-religious posts (Kinzie, 2008). After JuicyCampus closed, the New Jersey State Attorney General's office issued a press release about the site. The press release noted the changes in the privacy policy including the TRUSTe seal, the pop-up menu asking users to verify that they are 18 years old, and making the terms and conditions of the site more prominent that occurred after the office began their investigation but did not change the site's operation. With regard to the changes the Attorney General's press release commented that:

> Despite these changes, JuicyCampus.com retained many of its most problematic features, including the encouragement of anonymous postings, and the failure to assure those who reported abuse that their complaints would be responded to and acted upon (State of New Jersey Department of Law and Public Safety Press Release, 2009).

Clearly, Juicycampus.com, as its name indicates, earned its profits from "juicy" gossip and controversial content. It did not want to be held accountable for any of the content posted on its site and merely put in place superficial provisions on its website that provided a perception of due diligence in reducing negative content. By allowing users to remain anonymous, gossip escalated to libelous, defamatory, and abusive posts which attracted attention to the site, increasing viewer traffic. Without question, JuicyCampus sought to profit financially from paid advertisements that needed traffic to the site to increase along with the "juicy" content— without such content it might as well have close down.

Matt Ivestor had stated in interviews with ABC News and *The Washington Times* that JuicyCampus would remove posts that contain spam, illegal hate speech, or contact information (Goff, 2008; Lisson, 2008). His interpretation of the term "illegal hate speech" was not well defined. An ABC News reporter asked him what hate speech would include. Mr. Ivestor's response was that if there was not "real discussion" and the people making the posts were "just being negative" (Lisson, 2008) about race, homosexuality or religion that he considered the post to be hate speech. He made a similar statement to *Saturday Night Magazine* claiming that he would remove posts that contained "rampant hate speech" and did "not say anything" (*Saturday Night Magazine*, 2008) In other words, it was up to the discretion of JuicyCampus's staff to determine whether the speech was in some way "fostering a healthy debate" (Lisson, 2008) about an issue such as race, homosexuality, or religion. In some cases, JuicyCampus actually did remove posts that should be considered hate speech. For example, a student from Santa

Clara University reported that JuicyCampus removed a post about her in which someone suggested she should kill herself (Tan, 2008).

Accordingly, it is argued that while the site claims to support the First Amendment of free speech, they were quick to censor and remove negative posts about their site. A Marquette University student posted the thread "Boycott this Site" as one of the first topics in Marquette University's new forum on Juicycampus. com (Hren, 2008). The post warned students not to post on the site. It was removed by a site moderator within minutes of being posted (Hren, 2008). Another student posted a message on Facebook that JuicyCampus promptly removed her post that said that the site was retarded (Meyer, A., 2008). A post "Clarification from JuicyCampus" asked the JuicyCampus administration "Can you please just enlighten us as to what type of posts you remove?" (Anonymous, 2008ag). No one from the JuicyCampus team responded to the post; however, someone complained that a post was removed that told students from a particular school that they should go to a better school if they wanted JuicyCampus to care about them (Anonymous, 2008ah). Although the post was hearsay, the content of this alleged post did not appear to be severe enough to be considered hate speech. Another user complained that a post had been removed because it asked if other people had been to another online gossip site (Anonymous, 2008ai). JuicyCampus may have removed this message because they believed it was a violation of the user condition not to "disseminate off-topic messages on boards, including but not limited to messages promoting any product, service, web site, board or venture" (JuicyCampus, 2009b).

Mr. Ivestor, CEO of JuicyCampus, allowed posts that bashed him personally because they were "juicy" and continued to encourage people who didn't like him to go to the site and read those posts. Some examples of those types of posts were calling him a "low-life scumbag" (English, 2008), "a money seeking ASS HOLE who is willing to put people's lives on the line to make a buck" (Anonymous, 2008af), and a "little pansy ass faggot" (Anonymous, 2008aj). Even posts that made potentially threatening statements towards Mr. Ivestor such as "im planning to rip off his testes if i ever see him" (Anonymous, 2008ak) or ask that "someone needs to punch that fagget right in his goatse" (Anonymous, 2008ak) were not removed.

In its terms of agreement JuicyCampus had users agree not to post material that "violates laws relating to sexually explicit material, that infringes the rights of any third party (including intellectual property and privacy or publicity rights, that is defamatory, or that constitutes hate speech under applicable law" (JuicyCampus, 2009b). Several students who had posted in the Defamation, Libel, and Slander Law discussion board of the Students Against Juicy Campus Group on Facebook.com learned that after asking JuicyCampus to remove posts they found defamatory JuicyCampus did not want to honor their requests to remove those posts. The reason given by JuicyCampus for not removing the posts was because they had no way to detemine whether the post was actually defamatory (Alford, 2008; Diggs, 2008). When the students asked JuicyCampus to delete a defamatory post, they received the same e-mail reply from the JuicyCampus team encouraging them to "reply to the post with additional information or a differing opinion, start a new thread entirely, and/or encourage your friends to do the same" (Alford, 2008; Diggs, 2008).

Mr. Ivestor was willing to remove posts that violated laws against hate speech, but not defamatory posts because he claimed that the JuicyCampus staff did not know whether the post was defamatory (Goff, 2008; Hahn, 2008). Mr. Investor was correct to the extent that a determination of what is "defamatory" speech and what is not ought to be left to the courts to determine. Nonetheless, libel was not the only consideration here. As Professors Stefkovich and Pauken explain in their discussions of the legal issues relating to cyber-bullying in Chapters 6 and 7, some expressions also breach criminal codes and anti-hate laws. It is against breach of these statutes that JuicyCampus needed to be vigilant with respect to its users' forms of expression.

On October 21, 2008 JuicyCampus modified its terms and conditions again. The modifications included a statement that, "JuicyCampus reserves the right, but disclaims any obligation or responsibility, to remove any content that does not adhere to these guidelines, in its sole discretion" (JuicyCampus, 2009b). The site also stated that, "by using the site, you agree that JuicyCampus shall have no obligation to monitor content on the site or to delete content from the site, even if JuicyCampus is notified that such content violates this agreement" (JuicyCampus, 2009b). Hence, the site staff decided what posts they were going to remove regardless of feedback from users. Their user conduct provisions listed rules, but the site disclaimers helped them avoid enforcement of those rules. These creatively worded terms and conditions undermined the actions of JuicyCampus staff members to remove posts they found unfavorable because as stressed earlier, the "juicy" expressions were essential to attracting profitable traffic to the site. In that regard, Juicycampus.com had side-stepped being held accountable for allowing the expressions, or being held legally responsible when it failed to address the legitimate concerns expressed by users about removing defamatory posts.

CONSIDERING USER RIGHTS AND FREEDOMS

The FIRE (FIRE, 2009), Foundation for Individual Rights in Higher Education, is an organization whose primary mission to is to defend the free speech rights of individuals on American college and university campuses. Through its Individual Rights Defense Program, the FIRE refers cases to pro bono lawyers to defend students or faculty who believe they have had their free speech rights violated on college campuses. The organization makes frequent press releases to the media and on its website about current First Amendment rights issues happening on college and university campuses. It is the opinion of FIRE that JuicyCampus was exactly what its users make of it (Shibley, 2008), simply because the content on JuicyCampus was user generated and not written by third parties. Celebrity gossip blogs such TMZ.com (TMZ Productions, Inc., 2009) or Perez Hilton (PerezHilton.com, 2009) , or even political gossip blogs like Wonkette (Wonkette, 2009), have contributions from third parties gossiping and reporting about people or events, that are not directly under the control of the user (Shibley, 2008). According to the FIRE, if the users of JuicyCampus stopped posting salacious gossip on the site, that gossip simply would not exist (Shibley, 2008). In other words, students who chose to use the website, chose it because it is known as a place for negative and hateful speech.

Accordingly, it could be argued that the content of the posts on Juicycampus.com was the decision of those who used the site. The site title and design provided cues as to what was said and promoted the perception that users would remain anonymous, although technology lawyers confirm that all on-line content can be traced (Claessens, 2003; Meyer, R, & Mollad, 2008). "This site became popular because of its anonymity and the capabilities it gave us—to truly and freely express ourselves without repercussions" (Anonymous, 2008y) as stated by a Juicycampus.com user. Students liked being able to express their free speech rights in this anonymous forum. Many students believe that even though students did not like Juicycampus.com the site should still be allowed to operate because of First Amendment free speech rights and that those who disapproved of the site should simply not visit the site (Anonymous, 2008al; Anonymous, 2008am). Other students advocated not visiting the site in the form of a boycott in posts on Facebook.com. (Diemand-Yauman, 2008; Fortuna, 2008; Murphey, C., 2008). As suggested by the FIRE, if students banned the site altogether, that would destroy the business model. The suggestion by FIRE was in effect true as JuicyCampus eventually closed due to not having enough advertising revenue.

Did JuicyCampus really respect First Amendment free speech rights? Many users made posts said they did not believe so (Anonymous, 2008ag; Anonymous, 2008ai; Anonymous, 2008an; Meyer, A., 2008). Students were warned in the post "Beware" that Mr. Ivestor did not honor free speech rights. He was accused of disclosing information to schools that had caused students to be expelled (Anonymous, 2008ao). In the replies to the "Beware" post there were two posts claiming that students were expelled because of what they had posted on Juicycampus.com. Despite the comments that were made on the site disagreeing with the censorship, JuicyCampus still continued to monitor and remove posts within minutes that might hurt their profits—seemingly incompatible with a defense of the site based on free speech.

DID JUICYCAMPUS.COM INFLICT REAL HARM?

Matt Ivestor stated that what was said on Juicycampus.com should be taken with a grain of salt. He believed that any reasonable person reading Juicycampus.com knew what they were reading (Crisp, 2008). Users of Juicycampus.com that posted feedback had also expressed views that what was posted on the site was ridiculous; the information should not be taken seriously, and that the posts are not true. Many college students lack the ability to discern the reliability of information on the Internet (Graham & Metexas, 2003; Metzger et al., 2003). Nonetheless, there is research evidence that college students find information on the Internet to be more credible than the adult population does (Graham & Metexas, 2003; Metzger et al., 2003). To compound this problem, some of the posts on Juicycampus.com were true (Bercovici, 2008; Jarosz, 2008; NPR, 2008).

Chelsea Gorman, a Vanderbilt University student spoke publicly about her experience with the site on the ABC news magazine *20/20* (McNiff & Varney, 2008). During her freshman year at Vanderbilt University she was raped. She had told only a few friends about the experience. One of her friends made a post to Juicycampus.com with the title "Chelsea Gorman Deserved It." The post described the rape. After the post, Ms. Gorman became the target of campus gossip. She was approached by students on campus who asked her about the rape. As a result of the abuse she left campus for the remainder of the semester. For Chelsea Gorman the gossip started on Juicycampus.com escalated to a level of her feeling as though she had been raped for a second time.

When posts were true, students could be ostracized within the college community. Leaving campus or dropping out of school was a common reaction for other victims of posts on Juicycampus.com. Students experienced strong emotions such as anger, crying, betrayal, and depression (McNiff & Varney, 2008). College communities are small enough that victims can be harassed in person about posts that are true or may be perceived to be true. Moreover, students live in close on-campus communities personal information such class schedules, residence hall addresses, and e-mail addresses is easy to access or observe (Finn, 2004). When a student's name was posted to Juicycampus.com that information may have been enough to locate the student, and it is difficult to get away from the stares, gossip and ridicule because of the close proximity of living quarters and classroom confines.

STUDENT REACTION TO JUICYCAMPUS.COM

Students reacted to Juicycampus.com in a variety of ways. Examples include:

1. Contacted the Attorney General's Office

2. Wrote comments expressing dissatisfaction on the site in response to requests by JuicyCampus for feedback
3. Replied to posts with additional information or differing opinion
4. Wrote editorials in school newspapers speaking out against the site
5. Suggested that users make the content interesting and substantial
6. Boycotted the site
7. Requested college administrators contact the site to have posts removed.
8. Requested that the site be blocked from the campus network
9. Spammed the site
10. Ignored the site
11. Wrote gossip about fictitious people
12. Took what's said on the site with a grain of salt

Not surprisingly, and despite the fact that from its inception students responded to the site's requests for feedback, their comments did not influence the moderation of the site. This avoidance strategy is worth brief analysis in this section.

Upon review of the site, it was noted that some students expressed their opposition to the posts on the site by posting their views in the discussion thread of the offensive post. For example, the opening response in the post for "Who's the Sluttiest Girl" was "This is retarded! Can we not bash on individuals…What's the point?" (Anonymous, 2008a). This initial comment did not stop any further discussion on the topic. A post in the "Hottest Freshman Girl on Campus" simply stated "This is slander! Stop now!"(Anonymous, 2008e), however, the discussion continued. A respondent lashed out to those replying to "Who's the Biggest Slut at Baylor" by stating:

> How pathetic is it that this is the most viewed? Why does everyone give a crap who the biggest slut at Baylor is? I mean seriously is it really worth you feeling better about yourself to know that other people are being openly judged? All I can say is pathetic and the people that are responding and placing names of this deal are way worse off and have more issues than any person's name on this list. Keep it up see where it gets you in life. (Anonymous, 2008c)

Bystanders play an important role in bullying in the physical world (see Shariff, 2008). Some may encourage the perpetrator to carry out their own cruel impulses (Imperio, 2001). Others feel empathy towards the victim, making them reluctant to stand up to the instigators because they want to avoid involvement in the encounter (Imperio, 2001). Bystanders are an important part of the bullying experience as they provide an audience for the bullying. In the case of online bullying, the audience is the online community viewing the website. The dynamics of the members of an online community deciding whether to encourage or prevent online bullying is different than in-person bullying. Confronting a perpetrator of bullying or abuse on Juicycampus.com may seem to be easier because the bystander can remain anonymous and not have to face the bully. However, when reviewing posts on Juicycampus.com bystanders would find it very difficult, if not impossible, to stop the cyber-bullying. The reason lies with the underlying dynamics that allow bullying to continue once it is started. When bullies receive the desired reactions from victims and bystanders they want to continue the bullying (Joy, 2007). In the online community cyber-bullying is in the form of continuing to post cruel comments.

According to Matt Ivestor, censorship was not the answer to bad speech (Lisson, 2008; U-Wire, 2008). Instead he encouraged more speech in the form of responding to posts. The problem with the strategy was that when students defended other students or themselves, hence engaging in more speech, they often became the target of cyber-bullying. What really happened when students provided additional information was that they were giving the reaction that the cyber-bully wanted. In the case of the online community, there were members that enjoyed reading these reactive messages and were encouraged to join the cyber-bullying. Others in the online community may be angered by the posts. Their negative emotions intensified because they did not know who the bully was (McKenna, 2007). The anonymity of Juicycampus.com increased the confrontation and cruel posts (McKenna, 2007). One astute user of Juicycampus.com noted that "when people are spurred on by anonymity there's a moral shift and the comments become more and more vicious" (Anonymous, 2008ap). Thus, perceptions about the anonymity of the site reduced inhibitions allowing people to act on vindictive impulses causing bullying to intensify.

A vicious cycle developed in which members of the online community that reacted to the cruel posts by the cyber-bullies encouraged the cyber-bullies to make more mean posts that were followed by a reaction and more cyber-bullying. Moreover, some speculate that there was content on Juicycampus.com that was written by JuicyCampus staff members posing as students to incite reactions from the online community. These accusations were made in posts directly on Juicycampus.com and in college newspapers (Weiner, 2008; Anonymous, 2008aq). Furthermore, the JuicyCampus staff could decide to remove content from the website that did not give a cyber-bully the desired reaction or reflected negatively on the site (Anonymous, 2008ar; Anonymous, 2008as). Hence, the reactions provided by the additional information to the threads on Juicycampus.com prolonged and intensified the bullying rather than stopped it, making it virtually impossible to effectively stand up to a bully online at this website. Meanwhile, the additional posts and views to Juicycampus.com added value to their advertising business model.

ADMINISTRATORS' REACTIONS TO JUICYCAMPUS.COM

College administrators across the United States had received complaints from students about posts on Juicycampus.com. The site was not affiliated with any of the campuses, giving college administrators no control about its content. Anonymous comments made it difficult, if not impossible, for administrators to determine who made the defamatory comments (Jarosz, 2008; indy.com, 2008).

Matt Ivestor, CEO of JuicyCampus, is a recent Duke University graduate. When a Duke University student affairs staff member who knew him contacted him to express concerns about the pain students were suffering from the posts on the site, Ivestor expressed no concern. Instead he refused to change the moderation of the site and appeared to be enjoying the notoriety (Young, 2008b). As with many official efforts to censor controversial expression (Shariff & Johnny, 2007), censored material or venues often attract even more attention, because people want to know what was so controversial in the content that warranted censorship. Hence, when certain books are censored by public schools for example, more people go out and buy them to read the offensive content. In this regard, by contacting Mr. Ivestor, Duke University indirectly gave him the publicity he desired. This was evident as Mr. Ivestor proudly displayed links to articles from the press and university newspapers on the Juicy Campus blog.

Officials at Pepperdine University took a different (and strategic) approach than that of Duke University. They took action against JuicyCampus by contacting its advertisers, impacting the offending website's revenues through paid advertisements. Officials from Pepperdine University complained to Google. Adsense is a program that analyzes a website's content in order to place advertisements for companies that have the website's users advertise to a target market. Advertisements geared towards the website's target market are placed inside an "Ads by Google Frame." Google decided to terminate its business relationship with JuicyCampus because the website violated its terms of use (Hall, 2008; McNiff & Varney, 2008; Young, 2008b). Adbrite, another company that does online ad placement, also severed its relationship with JuicyCampus. The termination of both Google and Adbrite cost Juicycampus.com $25,000 a month in advertising (McNiff & Varney, 2008). The web site had to close due to declining advertising revenues, making only $136 a day in advertising revenues (Cubestat.com, 2009a). For a 31-day month this left advertising revenues at a mere $4,216. The $25,000 loss in revenues from Google and Adbrite (Cubestat.com, 2009a) appears to have been a fatal blow.

The Pepperdine University Student Government Association had requested the administration to block the site. They felt that by having the site blocked from the campus network that they would be making a symbolic public statement that Pepperdine did not support harmful and libelous gossip (Young, 2008c). The administration decided not to ban Juicycampus.com.

As noted above, when deciding whether to block a site from the campus network administrators are faced with the issue of censorship. If they had decided to censor Juicycampus.com, then what criteria would they use to determine how will they handle future requests to block sites (Creeley, 2008)? Even if a site is blocked from the campus network students can still access it off campus. Blocking sites is not an effective way of handling the underlying issue of the harmful speech on the site. However, some private religious colleges and universities have chosen to block the site (Echegaray, 2008). On November 12, 2008 Tennessee State University (TSU) became the first public university to block the site from the campus network (Butler, 2008). According to Michael Freeman, TSU vice president for student affairs, Tennessee State University's network was a private forum for the purpose of academic work and research (Carter, 2009). It was not considered a public forum where the issue of free speech would apply (Carter, 2009). TSU's legal opinion was that the student technology fee "pays for student technology needs" that are for academic work, that JuicyCampus is not considered as meeting the requirement for the technology fee (Carter, 2009).

Gabriel Reif, Assistant Director of Greek Life at Binghamton University, had received many complaints from students about Juicycampus.com. He tried having students make "copious non-nonsensical posts" (Reif, 2008) to the site. Within 15 minutes of making the posts these posts had "dissappeared" (Reif, 2008). This same strategy, mentioned earlier, was discussed in the student newspapers the *GW Patriot* (Flanigen, 2008) and *The Colonialist* (Travis, 2008). According to the *Chronicle of Higher Education* many college administrators believed that the best way to respond to JuicyCampus was to ignore it (Young, 2008c). Their reasoning was that if the site does not have any visitors it will lose its advertisers and eventually be shut down. Visitors to the site started to decline in December 2008. Eventually JuicyCampus did not have enough advertising revenue to survive. The site has since closed, but the issues of hatred that surfaced on the site still need to be addressed. The posts reflected attitudes of racism, sexism, homophobia, and intolerance of religious beliefs. These attitudes will remain in the minds of students even though the site has shut down. Administrators, who deliberately ignore the issues, hoping the problem will go away, are culpable to students for tacitly promoting and indirectly condoning continuation of this type of behavior.

Colleges and universities are intended to be places where free expression is encouraged. However, they are also places where there is equal opportunity for education. The racist, sexist, anti-religious, and homophobic speech on JuicyCampus is against the educational philosophies of equal opportunity and creates a hostile campus environment. Some colleges and universities responded to JuicyCampus by educating the college community about speech and privacy on the Internet. According to the *Chronicle of Higher Education*, some campus administrators say that JuicyCampus should be used to teach students to rise above the kind of hateful speech posted there (Young, 2008c). Emory University created a conference panel with representation among student organizations to address hate speech in response to JuicyCampus (Tamul, 2008).

ATTEMPTS AT INTERVENTION

At Carnegie Mellon University an editorial was published in the student newspaper suggesting that students make the site "interesting and substantial" (Tartan Board, 2008). The author suggested that students should "take advantage of the anonymity and get the campus's dirty laundry—and ideas for change—out in the open" (Tartan Board, 2008). Readers were encouraged to share advice about classes and professors; buy and sell textbooks; publicize an event their organization was having on campus; ask questions about how certain university procedures work; or how to get around campus; and thank another student for helping them out. (Tartan Board, 2008).

The posts from Carnegie Mellon University did not change as a result of the editorial. Students were reluctant to use the site to discuss controversial issues on campus. A user on the site commented:

> This site could be so great for finding info about greensboro, other colleges in the area, good parties/events, or getting some honest details about organizations on campus. but instead, posts have to pop up about certain girls being hoes, certain guys being gay ormanwhores, or whatever. i'd rather see a debate on the upcoming election or something. (Anonymous, 2008at)

A different intervention strategy suggested that posters destroy by inundating it with posts that were "utterly ridiculous and benign" (Flanigen, 2008). The author asked users to post poetry or material copied from Wikipedia. Students decided to do this with the posts being disguised under juicy titles. Other campuses, such as Williams College and Cornell, were automating computers to post full text of novels and Bible verses (Guess, 2008). This strategy did not work to shut down JuicyCampus. The problem with this strategy was that it was considered spamming the site and violated the site's terms of agreement, resulting in removal of the posts.

A more creative Juicycampus.com user suggested e-mailing the advertisers on the site to let them know about the content as many are unaware of the content on the site (Anonymous, 2008au). This strategy seems to have been on the right track. Not long after their major advertisers closed their accounts, the site shut down.

Interestingly, some students opted to use websites to voice their opposition to online attacks. Facebook.com, a social networking site, is often used as a place where students can express their opposition to malicious gossip. More than 50 discussion groups were formed about JuicyCampus with varying participation

(Facebook.com, 2009a; Facebook.com, 2009b). The most prominent groups were Students Against JuicyCampus (Murphey, C., 2008), BAN JuicyCampus!! (Palisoc, 2008), and Boycott Juicycampus.com (Diemand-Yauman, 2008).

STUDENTS SHAPING THE INTERNET

A "Boycott Juicycampus.com" group was started on Facebook.com with 1,046 members as of October 26, 2008. Members of Facebook.com did not like the fact that Juicycampus.com was "profiting at their expense" meaning that Juicycampus.com was diverting Facebook.com members to their site. They believed that "Juicycampus.com gives students an enormous amount of power to hurt others and to actively shape the way in which people on this campus are perceived" (Diemand-Yauman, 2008). The group expressed disdain for the anonymous nature of the site that allows for no accountability for what is posted and little or no concern for the veracity of such statement. They believed that the site encouraged them to expose classmates with the most personal, inappropriate, and shocking information. As a result the postings were exaggerations and even complete fabrications of information about others just to get a reaction. The group also expressed concern that people who are publicly attacked are left feeling hurt and insecure, and they have no opportunity to defend themselves or attest to the truthfulness of the claims (Diemand-Yauman, 2008).

Connor Diemand-Yauman, president of Princeton University's class of 2010 is leading students to take a stand "against character assassination, a culture of gossip, and all other acts of ethical and intellectual cowardice" (Ownwhatyouthink.com, 2009a). In response to the offensive postings on Juicycampus.com and other sites, OwnWhatYouThink.com was launched April 1, 2008, followed by a campaign at Princeton University during the first three weeks of April (Ownwhatyouthink.com, 2009b). The campaign started with having students sign the following petition:

> We, the undersigned, commit ourselves to taking a stand against anonymous character assassination, a culture of gossip, and all other acts of ethical and intellectual cowardice (Ownwhatyouthink.com, 2009a).

The first 320 students to sign the petition received t-shirts with the slogan "Anonymity = Cowardice" (Ownwhatyouthink.com, 2009b) that they wore on April 8 and 10, 2008. From April 10 to April 17, 2008 posters were hung on the Princeton campus with the phrase "You Can't Take Me Down" to symbolize the group's mission against individuals defacing and removing posters that are against their viewpoints. Two nights from April 12 to April 18, 2008 a 14 by 10-foot screen in front of the campus center displayed a "Love Wall" with comments by Princeton students affirming other Princeton students (Ownwhatyouthink.com, 2009b).

OwnWhatYouThink.com currently has 2,520 people as of March 15, 2009 that have signed their petition (Ownwhatyouthink.com, 2009a). Student-initiated anti-bullying campaigns have been successful in raising awareness and preventing bullying in schools. Perhaps this site will raise awareness of cyber-bullying and online harassment that is occurring at the college level. The creation of the site itself adds content to the Internet created by students.

Despite the defamatory comments on Juicycampus.com, students created their own discussion areas on sites like Facebook.com, where they continue to talk about free speech and privacy. High school students have been included in the discussions. In effect, JuicyCampus has caused students to think about issues such as free speech and privacy and fostered open discussion. These discussions did not take place on Juicycampus.com itself, but Facebook.com allows users to create groups. This site is not anonymous. Users must register and posts can be reported by clicking on the report abuse button. Users who do not abide by Facebook's terms of agreement can lose their privileges.

A Facebook.com member specifically voiced an opinion that he did not think that best way to boycott a site was to make a Facebook group about it because it calls attention to the site (Fortuna, 2008). The groups formed on Facebook.com have started discussions about regulating speech on the Internet, privacy, and hate speech. The JuicyCampus team even responded to the BAN JuicyCampus!! blog (Palisoc, 2008). More importantly, the groups have engaged students in discussions that address the underlying causes of the problems with Juicycampus. com such as hate speech. A greater understanding of the underlying causes of the problems that have evolved from Juicycampus.com can lead to addressing the root causes of the problem. Additionally these discussions are helping students to be our future leaders that will understand the social, legal, and ethical implications of the Internet in society.

JUICYCAMPUS SHUTS DOWN

JuicyCampus closed on February 5, 2009. The decision was made on February 2, 2009 and announced to the public on February 4, 2009. According to the final entry in the Juicy Campus blog the site was shut down because:

> JuicyCampus' growth outpaced our ability to muster the resources needed to survive the economic downturn and the current level of revenue generated is simply not sufficient to keep the site alive (JuicyCampus, 2009d).

JuicyCampus said that the "advertisers have spent less, but have remained loyal, and for that we are very much appreciative" (JuicyCampus, 2009d). Matt Ivestor claimed that the reason for the site shutting down was due to the site not having enough revenue to sustain itself after expanding to 500 campuses. He states in his blog that:

> We've expanded to more than 500 campuses across the US, and have more than a million unique visitors coming to the site every month. It's clear that we have provided a platform that students have found interesting, entertaining, and fun (Ivestor, 2009).

JuicyCampus states on its blog that its closing was not the result of legal investigations or lawsuits. "No charges were ever brought against JuicyCampus by any Attorney Generals. JuicyCampus' services and policies have always been well within the law" (JuicyCampus, 2009d). JuicyCampus does not intend to return after the economy recovers.

While the extent of JuicyCampus's legal issues and their potential role in the site's closing is unclear, Ivestor's claims about website traffic and advertiser loyalty appear to be false. As we have already noted, JuicyCampus' two major advertising sources, Google and Adbrite, had both terminated their contracts in the fall, resulting in a precipitous drop in ad revenues. Revenue estimations from Cubestat. com, an online service appraising websites, confirms this analysis. On February 4, 2009 Juicycampus.com advertising revenues were estimated to be $136 per day and the number of daily page views was 54,493 (Cubestat.com, 2009a). In a 31-day month Juicycampus.com had 1,689,283 views and earned $4,216 based on this data (Cubestat.com, 2009a).

Figure 2 is a graph of data from Compete.com. for an estimate of the number of unique visitors from the United States to Juicycampus.com for each month from January 2008 to January 2009. The unique visitors metric counts a person as one visitor to the site one time, regardless of the number of times they visit during the month (Compete.com, 2009). This metric is an indication of the number of unique

Figure 2: Estimated Number of Unique Visitors to Juicycampus.com

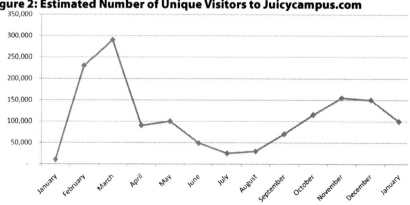

Source: www.compete.com

visitors visiting the site in a given month. After the expansion to 500 campuses it would be expected that there would be more unique visitors as additional campuses were added, and new users would come to the site to spread gossip on their newly added campus. Based on Figure 2 there was an increase in unique visitors from September to November, and the November peak was not as high as the traffic in the previous February and March. Since the site had upgraded their technology so that it could accommodate over one million viewers at a time (JuicyCampus, 2008c), we can conclude they had wildly overestimated traffic projections.

CURRENT STATUS OF LEGAL INVESTIGATION AGAINST JUICYCAMPUS

No charges from the Attorney Generals Offices in Connecticut or New Jersey were filed as of February 5, 2009. In an interview with WTNH News Channel 8, Connecticut Attorney General Richard Blumenthal expressed satisfaction that his efforts may have led to the site's demise. He stated:

> I'm delighted if our criticism contributed to this insidious site's collapse. JuicyCampus is deservedly dead—out of juice and financially ruined after our investigation revealed it was failing to fulfill its own promises to prohibit abusive and obscene posts (WTNH/Associated Press, 2009).

The New Jersey Attorney General's Office made a press release regarding the shutdown of JuicyCampus. Attorney General Anne Milgram said that:

> New Jersey's college students won't have to worry about their names and character being damaged anymore by the malicious anonymous gossip that was the backbone of JuicyCampus.com (State of New Jersey Department of Law and Public Safety Press Release, 2009).

In a proactive approach to cyber-safety as JuicyCampus expanded to ten New Jersey campuses the Division of Consumer Affairs Director worked with college administrators to offer programs on Internet safety and help college administrators develop their own best practices (State of New Jersey Department of Law and Public Safety Press Release, 2009).

Under the 1996 Communications Decency Act JuicyCampus cannot be held liable for damage from third party posts. However, they can be subpoenaed for records to find who made defamatory posts. Students are taking legal action against third parties for sexual harassment and discrimination. A University of Delaware student has filed a federal lawsuit against five people to determine who posted "vulgar, scurrilous and false" claims about her sexual history (Associated Press, 2008). Another student is taking legal action against an unnamed university (Lisson, 2009) under Title IX of the Education Amendments of 1972 that prohibits discrimination based on sex (20 U.S.C. §§ 1681–1688; Associated Press, 2009). If these cases are tried in the courts landmark precedents can establish cyber-libel resulting in pain and suffering by victims whose reputations and safety are jeopardized. New standards of accountability for content that is posted online could be set based on these precedents. It is yet to be determined whether the constitutional argument of freedom of expression trumps that of cyber-libel. In Canada, for example, the Supreme Court has established that free expression at the expense of individual reputations is not an unfettered right (see *Robichaud v. Canada* (Treasury Board [1987] 2 S.C.R. 84 and Shariff (2008).

REACTION TO JUICYCAMPUS SHUTDOWN

JuicyCampus users mourned the loss of the gossip forum with last minute gossip posts with the typical racist, sexist, and homophobic themes (Carter, 2009). One user made a goodbye post saying "You'll be missed….how will I ever know what tier my frat is or if the girl I was with last night is slutty…RIP" (Gink, 2009). Other students expressed their satisfaction that the site was shutting down with posts to the site such as "So Happy JC is SHUTTING DOWN" (Carter, 2009), "Juicy Campus Shutting Down—Goodbye and Good Riddance" (Young, 2009), and "Glad to See You Go"(Carter, 2009). Other users made comments about Mr. Ivestor saying, "He ruined many lives and relationships in the past year and a half" (Young, 2009) and "What goes around comes around." (Young, 2009).

Based on editorials in student newspapers, students do not believe that finances were the only reason Juicycampus.com shut down. "The issues of responsibility or morality due to the offensive nature of the posts on the site" were cited as reasons in Carnegie Mellon's The Tartan Online (Thurston, 2009). A similar statement was made in Baylor University's The Lariat Online also citing "apathy for bygone trends" (Lariat Online, 2009), noting that successful businesses can withstand hard economic times. Sites such as Facebook.com and YouTube.com that contain user generated content will be in business during the recession because they are "products of true innovation" not "passing fads like JuicyCampus" (Lariat Online, 2009).

According to the *Chronicle of Higher Education* college administrators are relieved that the site has shut down. As mentioned earlier in the chapter, Larry Moneta, Vice President for Student Affairs at Duke University, had contacted Mr. Ivestor to express concerns about the painful impact that Juicycampus.com was having on Duke University students. Mr. Moneta's efforts were unsuccessful in moderating of the site. He told the *Chronicle of Higher Education* that "JuicyCampus ran its course in some respects longer than I expected. Rest in peace." (Young, 2009).

Has the closing of Juicycampus.com due to insufficient advertising funds solved the problem of online gossip? Although students, faculty, and administrators are celebrating the closing of Juicycampus.com, others maintain that the site's demise will not solve the problem of online college gossip. In an article in the *Chronicle of Higher Education*, Professor Patrick Hornbeck states that "We cannot write off online gossip as site closed, case closed" (Hornbeck, 2009). Gossip has been around since the Middle Ages. Professor Hornbeck thinks that the root causes of the online gossip problem need to be examined in order to solve the problem (Hornbeck, 2009). He identifies anonymity as the underlying problem of gossip sites like Juicycampus.com allowing "user access at any time without site identification proof, or responsibility" (Hornbeck, 2009). He believes that educators need to teach students to "communicate and challenge one another empathetically and respectfully online and in person" as part of a liberal education (Hornbeck, 2009).

Danielle Citron, Associate Professor of Law at the University of Maryland, also agrees that closing Juicycampus.com is not the end to online gossip. She states that:

> Juicy Campus is but a small (but notorious) player in a crowded (and odious) outfield. Anyone who thinks that its closing heralds the demise of anonymous gossip sites and cyber harassment more generally is sadly mistaken. Online harassment (especially of women) is pervasive in our networked environment. Approximately 40% of female Internet users have experienced cyber harassment. Although the tough economy cost Juicy Campus its online ad revenue and financial support, it did not dampen the appetite for such destructive behavior. Indeed, one might imagine that job lay offs and light wallets would fuel dissatisfaction and the desire to abuse others online. Unfortunately, eradicating cyber harassment will take much more than shuttering Juicy Campus and their ilk (Citron, 2009).

Even though Juicycampus.com closed, college students still have many online gossip sites to choose from including CollegeACB.com, CollegeTrashTalk.com, Collegeconvo.com, and Usagonedirty.com. They have expanded the number of colleges that are listed on their sites. There still exists the opportunity for the same problems that arise from the defamatory speech that existed with Juicycampus.com to happen again on these sites. Users go to these sites with the expectation of gossiping. Traffic from Juicycampus.com is being redirected to CollegeACB.com, another anonymous online college gossip site. The speech could even become worse as Professor Citron points out that because of increased pressure and frustration of the economy. With the downturn in the economy fewer college students will have jobs allowing them more time to participate in online gossip. The next section reviews the site CollegeACB.com., which bought content and traffic redirection rights from juicycampus.com.

COLLEGEACB.COM REPLACES JUICYCAMPUS

According to Peter Frank, CollegeACB.com is different from Juicycampus.com because it "is devoted to promoting actual discussion, not promoting salacious attacks" (Wojnar, 2009). Its mission states:

> The College Anonymous Confession Board seeks to give students a place to vent, rant, and talk to college peers in an environment free from social constraints, and about subjects that might otherwise be taboo (Frank, 2009).

The site claims to target towards topics such as "college life, sexuality, keg parties, politics, and course selections" (Frank, 2009). Despite its mission of promoting actual discussion, students argue that by purchasing the traffic from Juicycampus. com, CollegeACB.com will become the new Juicycampus.com (Atkinson, 2009; Cline, 2009; Weiss, 2009). The same community that visited Juicycampus.com is now becoming the online community for CollegeACB.com as a result of the website traffic from Juicycampus.com (Atkinson, 2009; Cline, 2009; Weiss, 2009). CollegeACB.com may have hindered its own image as it will be thought of as a replacement for Juicycampus.com (Atkinson, 2009; Cline, 2009; Weiss, 2009). A student from Hofstra University stated "I think it would be a decent idea, but they can't be associated with Juicycampus.com" (Atkinson, 2009).

In retrospect Mr. Frank, the site's new owner, realized that purchasing Juicycampus.com may have injured CollegeACB.com's image. He stated in a March 7, 2009 interview with the *Los Angeles Times* that, "There's more hateful speech than we would like to see. I might have hurt our image in the short term." (Milian, 2009). The content of the posts on CollegeACB.com has been similar to the content of the posts made on Juicycampus.com. For example, students from Northwestern University initially made posts complimenting the site about its advertising free layout. The discussion quickly changed to posts about Greek life and how one student "gets around" (Bobrowsky, 2009). The posts on the Carnegie Mellon board are similar to those made on Juicycampus.com with many of them having "crude sexual comments" (Thurston, 2009). Mr. Frank admits that the users are not having discussions of the intellectual caliber that he would like to see but believes he can "mold them for the better." (Milian, 2009).

Mr. Frank thinks that the moderation of the site will make the difference between CollegeACB.com and Juicycampus.com (Murphey, M., 2009; Wojnar, 2009). He spends about 5–6 hours a day maintaining the site (Murphey, M., 2009; Wojnar, 2009). His friends help him with technical support and moderating the site. Users will be helping moderate the site by flagging posts they find objectionable. Criteria have been set to automatically delete posts that contain a certain number of flags (Murphey, M., 2009; Wojnar, 2009).

A Tufts University student thought the moderation on College ACB.com was a "step in the right direction" (Dreyer, 2009). The student said that, "These sites should police themselves through mechanisms to report offensive posts (Dreyer, 2009).

Other students do not think that moderation is the solution to the hate speech problems that occurred on Juicycampus.com. An editorial in the Berkeley Beacon places the responsibility on the students as members of the campus community for deciding how to treat each other online:

> The site's new philosophy does not heal anything until we as a campus community have matured. Gossip does not go away because someone decides to hit the report button. (Pashley, 2009)

Whether a site has a substantial discussion is up to the users. Having measures in place for accountability suggests that salacious attacks might not escalate to levels seen on Juicycampus.com. A CollegeACB.com user predicts that the site will "fizzle and die faster than a kitten thrown in ice water" (Pashley, 2009). The reason for this prediction is that users are coming to CollegeACB.com with expectation of gossiping in an anonymous environment. Users who register with CollegeACB.com will be giving the site their e-mail address, making them held accountable for their posts to the forum. Currently no registration is required to post to the discussion area, but it is anticipated that it will be required in the near future (Pashley, 2009). The posts will not show the user's e-mail address, but the posts can be traced to the e-mail address, holding the user accountable. The allure of Juicycampus.com was the juicy posts and not knowing who posted them. By having accountability measures this user predicted that people will no longer want to come to the site because they will be held accountable for their posts (Pashley, 2009). In other words people like to gossip and do not want to be held accountable for it. Hence the site will lose popularity by having accountability.

CONCLUSIONS

Juicycampus.com was an online rumor mill that allowed students to exploit each other with no repercussions. Juicycampus.com is considered to be a model for online gossip websites, which are becoming a new form of e-commerce relying on user generated content. Modifications of the Juicycampus.com website model are now being tested in terms of features, user accountability, and moderation.

College students are beginning to recognize the damage that online posts can cause to a person's reputation as well as the devastation in their lives. Time will tell what the long term consequences of this online harassment will be on its victims. As more employers are conducting online searches for information about applicants, college students will need to be more vigilant about information they reveal online and in posts made by others. Student initiated campaigns to boycott sites like Juicycampus.com may prove to be the most effective measure in stopping online harassment, as peers often have the most influence on college students' behavior. In that regard, Juicycampus.com has tested students about how they view their free speech rights and privacy on the Internet. While some college administrators are seeing the website as an educational opportunity, most of the controversy has been raised by students. Perhaps the answer lies in litigation where courts and statutes establish new standards for accountability of such websites. As the chapters that follow in this book on the emerging legal jurisprudence suggest, this process has already begun. However, it is evident that clear standards are not yet established. In the meantime, it will take awareness, education and strategic measures to sensitize college students to the fact that no one should make a profit through abusive and defamatory forms of expression, and that while free expression is a constitutional guarantee, in a democratic society, no speech is unfettered.

References

Alexa.com. (2009). JuicyCampus.com: Traffic Details from Alexa.com. Retrieved February 23, 2009, from http://www.alexa.com/data/details/traffic_details/juicycampus.com.

Alford, Emily Rachel. (2008, October 30). Message posted to the Defamation, Slander and Libel Law Discussion Board of Students Against Juicy Campus. Retrieved January 20, 2009, from Facebook web site: http://www.facebook.com/topic.php?uid=10089684487&topic=4757.

Anonymous. (2008a, January 29). *Who Is the Sluttiest Girl?* Retrieved January 14, 2009, from JuicyCampus web site: http://www.juicycampus.com/posts/permalink/UC%20 Irvine/32019.

Anonymous. (2008b, January 26). *Sluttiest Girls at Cornell.* Retrieved January 14, 2009, from JuicyCampus web site: http://www.juicycampus.com/posts/permalink/Cornell/31728.

Anonymous. (2008c, February 21). *Biggest Slut at Baylor.* Reply Retrieved January 13, 2009, from JuicyCampus web site: http://www.juicycampus.com/posts/permalink/Baylor%20 University/31523.

Anonymous. (2008d, February 5). *Hottest People on Campus.* Retrieved January 14, 2009, from JuicyCampus web site: http://www.juicycampus.com/posts/permalink/University%20of%20 Illinois/633.

Anonymous. (2008e, January 23). *Hottest Freshman Girl on Campus.* . Retrieved January 14, 2009, from JuicyCampus web site: http://www.juicycampus.com/posts/permalink/Vanderbilt%20 University/31342.

Anonymous. (2008f, January 20). *Hottest Sorority.* Retrieved January 14, 2009, from JuicyCampus web site: http://www.juicycampus.com/posts/permalink/University%20of%20Illinois/30952.

Anonymous. (2008g, February 2). *All Urbana Boys Ranked.* Retrieved January 14, 2009, from JuicyCampus web site: http://www.juicycampus.com/posts/permalink/University%20of%20 Illinois/1434.

Anonymous. (2008h, December, 12). *Samson Meale = Cheater.* Retrieved January 14, 2009, from JuicyCampus web site: http://www.juicycampus.com/posts/permalink/Duke/28801.

Anonymous. (2008i, November, 17). *Expire Posts After One Year.* Retrieved January 14, 2009, from JuicyCampus web site: http://www.juicycampus.com/posts/permalink/JuicyCampus/192250.

Anonymous. (2008j, September 10). *How to Make This Just a Little Less Offensive.* Retrieved January 14, 2009, http://www.juicycampus.com/posts/permalink/JuicyCampus/62986.

Anonymous. (2008k, November 19). *Proposal-Thread Delection After a Set Time.* Retrieved January 14, 2009, from JuicyCampus web site: http://www.juicycampus.com/posts/permalink/JuicyCampus/197195.

Anonymous. (2008l, July 31). *Can You Delete Posts.* Retrieved January 14, 2009, from JuicyCampus web site: http://www.juicycampus.com/posts/permalink/JuicyCampus/53714.

Anonymous. (2008m, March 16). *Remove Baylor University.* Retrieved January 16, 2009, from JuicyCampus web site: http://www.juicycampus.com/posts/permalink/JuicyCampus/19333.

Anonymous. (2008n, March 10). *Remove Colgate from This Site.* Retrieved January 16, 2009, from JuicyCampus web site: http://www.juicycampus.com/posts/permalink/JuicyCampus/17375.

Anonymous. (2008o, March 11). *Remove Cornell.* Retrieved January 16, 2009, from JuicyCampus web site: http://www.juicycampus.com/posts/permalink/JuicyCampus/17445.

Anonymous. (2008p, March 11). *Remove Emory.* Retrieved January 16, 2009, from JuicyCampus web site: http://www.juicycampus.com/posts/permalink/JuicyCampus/17635.

Anonymous. (2008q, March 13). *Remove MSU.* Retrieved January 16, 2009, from JuicyCampus web site: http://www.juicycampus.com/posts/permalink/JuicyCampus/18267.

Anonymous. (2008r, December 18). *Racial Slurs.* Retrieved January 13, 2009, from JuicyCampus web site: http://www.juicycampus.com/posts/permalink/JuicyCampus/245703.

Anonymous, (2008s, March 2). *The Layout Is Fucking Ugly.* Retrieved January 13, 2009, from JuicyCampus web site: http://www.juicycampus.com/posts/permalink/JuicyCampus/11742.

Anonymous. (2008t, March 21). *2005 Grad Working as a Pro.* Retrieved January 13, 2009, from JuicyCampus web site: http://www.juicycampus.com/posts/permalink/JuicyCampus/20514.

Anonymous. (2008u, March 13). *This Does Not Help Anybody!* Retrieved January 13, 2009, from JuicyCampus web site: http://www.juicycampus.com/posts/permalink/JuicyCampus/18488.

Anonymous. (2008v, March 1). *Constructive Criticism.* Retrieved January 13, 2009, from JuicyCampus web site: http://www.juicycampus.com/posts/permalink/JuicyCampus/14503.

Anonymous. (2008w, March 1). *More Moderation.* Retrieved January 13, 2009, from JuicyCampus web site: http://www.juicycampus.com/posts/permalink/JuicyCampus/14347.

Anonymous. (2008x, March 2). *From a Parent to Mr. Ivestor.* Retrieved January 13, 2009, from JuicyCampus web site: http://www.juicycampus.com/posts/permalink/JuicyCampus/9903.

Anonymous. (2008y, June 3). *Advice*. Retrieved January 13, 2009, from JuicyCampus web site: http://www.juicycampus.com/posts/permalink/JuicyCampus/41379.

Anonymous. (2008z, May 19). *This Type of Website Will Ruin the Internet*. Retrieved January 13, 2009, from JuicyCampus web site: http://www.juicycampus.com/posts/permalink/JuicyCampus/19959.

Anonymous. (2008aa, March 24). *High School All Over Again*. Retrieved January 17, 2009, from JuicyCampus web site: http://www.juicycampus.com/posts/permalink/Michigan%20State/8215.

Anonymous. (2008ab, June 24). *Kappa Zeta Phi*. Retrieved January 17, 2009, from JuicyCampus web site: http://www.juicycampus.com/posts/permalink/UC%20San%20Diego/45197.

Anonymous. (2008ac, October 27). *An Apology*. Retrieved January 17, 2009, from JuicyCampus web site: http://www.juicycampus.com/posts/permalink/Murray%20State/128477.

Anonymous. (2008ad, October 20). *Juicy Campus Sucks*. Retrieved January 17, 2009, from JuicyCampus web site: http://www.juicycampus.com/posts/permalink/University%20ofRochester/113832.

Anonymous. (2008ae, March 2). *Stop the Censorship!*. Retrieved January 13, 2009, from JuicyCampus web site: http://www.juicycampus.com/posts/permalink/JuicyCampus/12445.

Anonymous. (2008af, March 3). *Everything on This Site Is Hilarious Until It Says Your Name*. Retrieved January 16, 2009, from JuicyCampus web site: http://www.juicycampus.com/posts/permalink/JuicyCampus/15906.

Anonymous. (2008ag, March 11). *Clarification from JuicyCampus*. Retrieved January 23, 2009, from JuicyCampus web site: http://www.juicycampus.com/posts/permalink/JuicyCampus/17554.

Anonymous. (2008ah, March 12). *Re: Clarification from JuicyCampus*. Retrieved January 23, 2009, from JuicyCampus web site: http://www.juicycampus.com/posts/permalink/JuicyCampus/17554.

Anonymous. (2008ai, March 7). *My Post Got Deleted*. Retrieved January 16, 2009, from JuicyCampus web site: http://www.juicycampus.com/posts/permalink/JuicyCampus/16014.

Anonymous. (2008aj, May 27). *Ivestor*. Retrieved January 16, 2009, from JuicyCampus web site: http://www.juicycampus.com/posts/permalink/JuicyCampus/38963.

Anonymous. (2008ak, March 3). *Matt Ivestor*. Retrieved January 16, 2009, from JuicyCampus web site: http://www.juicycampus.com/posts/permalink/JuicyCampus/16047.

Anonymous. (2008al, October 12). *Juicy Campus Sucks. Get Rid of it*. Retrieved January 17, 2009, from JuicyCampus web site: http://www.juicycampus.com/posts/permalink/Texas%20Tech/108489.

Anonymous. (2008am, December 3). *Dude, What the Fuck?*. Retrieved January 17, 2009, from JuicyCampus web site: http://www.juicycampus.com/posts/permalink/Emerson%20College/221098.

Anonymous. (2008an, March 3). *The Censors Here are Fucking Nazis!!* Retrieved January 16, 2009, from JuicyCampus web site: http://www.juicycampus.com/posts/permalink/JuicyCampus/11401.

Anonymous. (2008 ao, October 16). *Beware.* Retrieved January 17, 2009, from JuicyCampus web site: http://www.juicycampus.com/posts/permalink/Drexel/118681.

Anonymous. (2008ap, June, 14). *Matt Ivestor* Retrieved January 16, 2009, from JuicyCampus web site: http://www.juicycampus.com/posts/permalink/JuicyCampus/44637.

Anonymous. (2008aq, July 15). *Re: Clarification from JuicyCampus.* Retrieved January 23, 2009, from JuicyCampus web site: http://www.juicycampus.com/posts/permalink/JuicyCampus/17554.

Anonymous. (2008ar, January 22). *Juicy Campus Sucks.* Retrieved January 17, 2009, from JuicyCampus web site: http://www.juicycampus.com/posts/permalink/USC/31184.-taking down posts

Anonymous. (2008as, October 12). *Re: JuicyCampus Sucks. Get Rid of It.* Retrieved January 17, 2009, from JuicyCampus web site: http://www.juicycampus.com/posts/permalink/Texas%20Tech/108489. -take down negative posts about the site, leave up the rest.

Anonymous. (2008at, October 17 Reply). *Here's an Idea.* Retrieved January 16, 2009, from JuicyCampus web site: http://www.juicycampus.com/posts/permalink/UNC%20Greensboro/120683.

Anonymous. (2008au, February 19). *Email and Boycott.* Retrieved January 17, 2009, from JuicyCampus web site: http://www.juicycampus.com/posts/permalink/Virginia%20Tech/5205.

Associated Press (2008, November 21) First public college blocks gossip Web site. Retrieved March 6, 2009 from http://www.firstamendmentcenter.org/news.aspx?id=20910.

Associated Press. (2009, February 5). Gossip Site Folds. *ABC News.* Retrieved February 23, 2009, from http://abclocal.go.com/wpvi/story?section=news/local&id=6642370#bodyText.

Atkinson, Jamie. (2009, February 12). JuicyCampus.com Replaced Money Problems Lead to Formation of Free Blog on Blogspot. Retrieved March 14, 2009, from http://media.www.hofstrachronicle.com/media/storage/paper222/news/2009/02/12/Features/Juicycampus.com.Replaced-3632790-page2.shtml.

Bercovici, Jeff. (2008, July/August). Cruel Intentions. *Radar Magazine.* Retrieved August 19, 2008, from http://www.radaronline.com/from-the-magazine/2008/06/juicy_campus_online_gossip_college_std_list_01.php.

Bobrowsky, Olivia (2009, February 9). JuicyCampus Closed, Northwestern Students Looking Elsewhere. Retrieved March 7, 2009 from http://www.uwire.com/Article.aspx?id=3730614.

Boyd, D. and Jenkins, H. (2006). MySpace and Deleting Online Predators Act (DOPA) [electronic version]. MIT Tech Talk, 26 May. Retrieved 13 August 2007 from www.danah.org/papers/MySpaceDOPA.html.

Butler, Jennifer. (2008, November 17). Juicy' web site wreaks havoc on campus. Campus gossip scene gets 'Juicy,' site banned. *The Meter.* Retrieved November 27, 2008, from http://www.tsumeter.com/home/index.cfm?event=displayArticlePrinterFriendly&uStory_id=529d8984–75a9–46bb-bb98–6a84f41c82b6.

Carter, Dennis (2009, February 6). Controversial Student Gossip Site Folds Citing Lack of Funds, JuicyCampus Shuts Down—Much to the Delight of Several Student Groups and Many Campus

Administrators. *eCampus News*. Retrieved February 22, 2009, from http://www.ecampusnews. com/news/top-news/index.cfm?i=57167;_hbguid=65b1299f-87d5–4adb-a13b-0f9cdc3cfd45.

Citron, Danielle. (2009, February 5). Juicy Campus: One Down, Too Many More to Go. Retrieved February 22, 2009, from http://www.concurringopinions.com/archives/ privacy_gossip_shaming/.

Claessens, J.; Díaz C.; Goemans, C.; Dumortier, J.; Preneel, B.; Vandewalle, J. (2003) Revocable anonymous access to the Internet? *Internet Research: Electronic Networking Applications and Policy*, 13,(4) 242–258.

Cline, John. (2009, February 16). N.C. State: Juicy Campus Redirected to New Site. Retrieved March 14, 2009, from http://education.tmcnet.com/news/2009/02/17/3994171.htm.

Communications and Decency Act of 1996, 47 U.S.C. § 230. US Code-Title 47- Section 230: Protection for private blocking and screening of offensive material

Compete.com. (2009). Snapshot of Juicycampus.com. Retrieved February 23, 2009, from http:// siteanalytics.compete.com/juicycampus.com/?metric=uv.

Creeley, William (2008, March 21). Regarding JuicyCampus.com. *FIRE'S the Torch*. Retrieved November 27, 2008, from http://www.thefire.org/index.php/article/9065.html.

Crisp, Elizabeth. (2008, October 10). Anonymous Website Site Offers Juicy College Gossip. *Clarion Ledger*. Retrieved October 25, 2008, from http://www.clarionledger.com/article/20081010/ NEWS/810100362/1001/news.

Cubestat.com. (2009a). Juicycampus.com: Estimated Worth and Web Stat From Cubestat. Retrieved February 23, 2009 from http://www.cubestat.com/www.juicycampus.com.

Dechter, Gadi. (2008, May 8). Site Keeps Students Posted. Johns Hopkins Senior Launches a Network of Anonymous, and Often Vulgar Message Boards. Retrieved February 23, 2009, from http://www.jhu.edu/clips/2008_05/02/site.html.

Diemand-Yauman, Connor. (2008). Boycott Juicycampus.com!. Retrieved January 23, 2009, from facebook.com website: http://www.facebook.com/group.php?sid=0ec592829092aab442d4f 887ad9250b5&gid=8978275804.

Diggs, Alesia. (2008, November 2). Message posted to the Defamation, Slander and Libel Law discussion board of Students Against Juicy Campus. Retrieved January 20, 2009, from Facebook web site: http://www.facebook.com/topic.php?uid=10089684487&topic=4757.

Dreyer, Annie. (2009, February 24). The Internet Takes Bullying to New Levels, Cyber-related Harassment Poses Unforeseen Problems for Students. *Tufts Daily*. Retrieved March 14, 2009, from http://www.tuftsdaily.com/features/the_internet_takes_bullying_to_new_levels-1.1570241.

e-School News staff and wire service reports. (2008, May). Prosecutors Tackle College Gossip Site. *e-School News*. p.12.

Echegaray, Chris. (2008, November 20). TSU Bans Racy, College-Themed Web Site. *The Tennessean*, Retrieved November 27, 2009, from http://www.tennessean.com/article/20081120/ NEWS04/811200338/1001/RSS6001.

English, Bella. (2008, December 29). Juicy Campus helps college students spread secrets and lies—and ruin one another's reputations. *The Boston Globe*. Retrieved January 18, 2009, from http://www.boston.com/ae/media/articles/2008/12/29/dorm_rumors?mode=PF.

Facebook Search: JuicyCampus (2009a). Retrieved January 23, 2009, from Facebook website: http://www.facebook.com/home.php#/s.php?init=q&q=juicy%20campus&ref=ts&sid=9ee 6460b476fee992bb411638f619b04.

Facebook Search: JuicyCampus (2009b). Retrieved January 23, 2009, from Facebook website: http://www.facebook.com/s.php?q=juicycampus&n=-1&k=400000000010&sf=r&init=q& sid=9ee6460b476fee992bb411638f619b04

Finn, J. (2004). A Survey of Online Harassment at a University Campus. *Journal of Interpersonal Violence,* 19(4), 468–483.

FIRE. (2009). *About FIRE.* Retrieved January 19, 2009, from the FIRE web site: http://www.thefire. org/index.php/article/4851.html

Flanigen, Bill. (2008, October 6). Engaging Juicy Campus. *GW Patriot.* Retrieved October 25, 2008, from http://thegwpatriot.blogspot.com/2008/10/engaging-juicycampus.html.

Fortuna, Nate. (2008, March 25). message posted to Students Against Juicy Campus Wall on Facebook website: http://www.facebook.com/s.php?q=students%20against%20juicy%20cam pus&init=s%3Agroup&k=200000010&n=-1&sid=e1db68dd22fe93d9e0b98aa09441d4b8#/ wall.php?id=10089684487&page=8&hash=0d890b96efdad065a64fbba26417173b.

Francisco, Pat. (2008, October 13). Retrieved January 14, 2009, from Students Against Juicy Campus Wall on Facebook website: http://www.facebook.com/group.php?sid=e1db68dd22 fe93d9e0b98aa09441d4b8&gid=10089684487#/wall.php?id=10089684487&page=2&hash= 224faf1571793ce251541730fe10a0fb.

Frank, Peter. (2009, February 5). CollegeACB.com to Offer Free Anonymous College Discussion. Retrieved March 15, 2009 from http://collegeacb.blogspot.com/2009/02/collegeacb-press-release.html.

Gink, Kelsey. (2009, February 6). Gossip Site's Demise Pleases Local Greeks. *The Daily Collegian Online.* Retrieved March 7, 2009, from http://www.collegian.psu.edu/archive/2009/02/06/ gossip_sites_demise_pleases_lo.aspx.

Goff, Karen Goldberg. (2008, October 15). Gossip Site Gives Access to Rumors. *The Washington Times.* Retrieved January 17, 2009 from http://www.washingtontimes.com/news/2008/oct/15/ gossip-sites-give-access-to-rumors/.

Graham, Leah and Metaxas, Panagiotis Takis. (2008, May). Of Course It's True; I Saw it on the Internet! Critical Thinking in the Internet Era. *Communications of the ACM.* 46(5), 71–75.

Guess, Andy. (2008, October 21). Using Juicy Campus As a Weapon Against Itself. *Inside Higher Ed.* Retrieved November 27, 2008, from http://www.insidehighered.com/news/2008/10/21/ juicy.

Hahn, Alice. (2008, October 3). Hate Isn't Juicy. *The Flat Hat.* Retrieved October 4, 3008, from http://flathatnews.com/content/68965/hate-isnt-juicy.

Hall, David. (2008, February 26). Google Pulls Ads from College Web Site. *TCU Daily Skiff.* Retrieved October 18, 2008, from http://media.www.tcudailyskiff.com/media/storage/paper792/ news/2008/02/26/News/Google.Pulls.Ads.From.CollegeGossip.Web.Site-3233999.shtml.

Haynes, Brad. (2008, March 19). 'Juicy' College Gossip Site Investigated. *USA Today,* Retrieved January 17, 2009, from http://www.usatoday.com/tech/webguide/internetlife/2008-03-19-juicycampus-investigation_N.htm.

Hornbeck, J. Patrick. (2009, February 27). JuicyCampus:Gone and Best Forgotten. *The Chronicle of Higher Education*. Retrieved March 7, 2009, from http://chronicle.com/weekly/v55/i25/25a09901.htm.

Hren, Megan. (2008, September 30). Marquette Is Better Than Juicy Campus. *The Marquette Tribune*. Retrieved October 19, 2008, from http://media.www.marquettetribune.org/media/storage/paper1130/news/2008/09/30/Viewpoints/Hren-Marquette.Is.Better.Than.Juicy.Campus-3458341.shtml.

Imperio, Winne Anne. (2001). Bullying Task Force Targets Bullies, Victims, and Bystanders. *Clinical Psychiatry News*. Retrieved October 26, 2008, from http://findarticles.com/p/articles/mi_hb4345/is_/ai_n28851082.

Indy.com Staff. (2008, October 15). JuicyCampus.com Exposes College Students to Ridicule, False Rumors. *Indianapolis Star*. Retrieved October 18, 2008, from http://www.indy.com/posts/12447.

Ivestor, Matthew. (2009, February 4). Official Juicy Campus Blog. Retrieved February 22, 2009, from http://juicycampus.blogspot.com/2009/02/juicy-shutdown.html.

Jarosz, Francesca. (2008, September 6). Critics Say Gossip on Juicy Campus Web Site Goes Too Far. *IndyStar*. Retrieved November 27, 2008, from http://m.indystar.com/detail.jsp?key=313095&full=1.

Joy, Kevin. (2007, January 31). Cyber-bullying: Type of Cruel Communication. *The Columbus Dispatch*, p. 01H.

JuicyCampus. (2009a). *Gossip Home Page*. Retrieved January 20, 2009, from JuicyCampus web site: http://www.juicycampus.com/posts/gossips/all-campuses/.

JuicyCampus. (2009b). Shutdown FAQ's. *Official Juicy Campus Blog*. Retrieved March 2, 2009, from http://juicycampus.blogspot.com/.

JuicyCampus. (2009c). *Terms and Conditions*. Retrieved January 20, 2009, from JuicyCampus web site: http://www.juicycampus.com/posts/terms-condition.

JuicyCampus. (2009d). *Privacy and Tracking Policy*. Retrieved January 20, 2009, from JuicyCampus web site: http://www.juicycampus.com/posts/privacy-policy.

JuicyCampus. (2008a, May 25). *Most Viewed Posts*. Retrieved May 25, 2008, from JuicyCampus web site: http://www.juicycampus.com/posts/gossips/all-campuses/.

JuicyCampus. (2008b, May 29). Juicy Campus Wants Your Help! *Official JuicyCampus Blog*. Retrieved October 19, 2008, from JuicyCampus web site: http://juicycampus.blogspot.com/2008_05_01_archive.html.

JuicyCampus (2008c, September 2). Juicy Campus Gets Even "Juicier" with Expansion and Re-launch of Website. *Official JuicyCampus Blog*. Retrieved October 17, 2008, from http://juicycampus.blogspot.com/2008_09_01_archive.html.

JuicyCampus (2008d, October 6). 500 Campuses!!!. *Official JuicyCampus Blog*. Retrieved October 19, 2008, from http://juicycampus.blogspot.com/2008/10/500-campuses.html.

JuicyCampus. (2008e). *Privacy and Tracking Policy*. Retrieved July 7, 2008, from JuicyCampus web site http://www.juicycampus.com/ privacy_policy.php.

JuicyCampus. (2008f). *Terms and Conditions*. Retrieved July 7, 2008, from JuicyCampus web site: http://www.juicycampus.com/ terms_conditions.php.

Kinzie, Susan. (2008, October 30). Juice, the Whole Juice and Nothing but the Juice. *The Washington Post.* Retrieved November 27, 2008, from: http://www.washingtonpost.com/wp-dyn/content/article/2008/10/29/AR2008102904345_pf.html

The Lariat Online Editorial Board. (2009, February 11). Editorial: Juicy Campus shutdown long overdue. *The Lariat Online.* Retrieved March 7, 2009, from http://www.baylor.edu/lariat/news.php?action=story&story=56150.

Laudon, Kenneth and Traver, Carol Guercio. (2008) *E-commerce: Business, Technology and Society.* Upper Saddle River, New Jersey: Pearson Prentice Hall.

Lisson, Meghan. (2008, October 9) Juicy Campus Founder Defends His Controversial website. *ABC News.* Retrieved October 18, 2008, from: http:abcnews.go.com/print?id=5985372.

Lisson, Meghan. (2009, February 9). Juicy Campus Folds, but Why? Retrieved March 14, 2009 from http://a.abcnews.com/m/screen?id=6811604&pid=5613749.

Magid, Larry. (2008, March 24). Connect Safely—JuicyCampus Haven for Cyberbullies. Retrieved January 17, 2009, from: *http://www.connectsafely.org/articles—advice/commentaries—staff/juicycampus-haven-for-cyberbullies.html.*

McKenna, Phil. (2007, July 21). The Rise of Cyberbullying: The Anonymity and Public Nature of Online Communication Encourages Aggression and Amplifies the Potential for Humiliation. *New Scientist.* 26–27.

McNiff, Eamon and Varney, Ann. (2008, May 14). College Gossip Crackdown: Chelsea Gorman Speaks Out: Juicy Campus' Cruel Online Postings Prompt Government Investigation. *ABC News.* Retrieved May 26, 2008, from: http://abcnews.go.com/2020/Story?id=4849927&page=1.

Metzger, Miriam J., Flanigan, Andrew J., and Zwarum, Lara. (2003). College Student Web Use, Perceptions of Information Credibility, and Verification Behavior. *Computers and Education,* 41(3), 271–290.

Meyer, Anne Marie. (2008, October 6). Message posted to Students Against Juicy Campus Wall. Retrieved January 20, 2009, from Facebook web site: http://www.facebook.com/group.php?sid=e1db68dd22fe93d9e0b98aa09441d4b8&gid=10089684487#/wall.php?id=1008968448 7&page=3&hash=f64d4f89bcc3f2b7e70f524b55deb49a

Meyer, Rauer L. and Mollad, Jonathan P. (2008) Social Network Site Litigation. *The IP Litigator: Devoted to Intellectual Property Litigation and Enforcement.* 14(4), 22–31.

Milian, Mark. (2009, March 7). Student Gossip Site CollegeACB Pick Up where JuicyCampus Left off. *LA Times.* Retrieved March 14, 2009, from http://latimesblogs.latimes.com/technology/2009/03/collegeacb.html.

Morgan, Richard. (2008, March 16). A Crash Course in Gossip Online. *The New York Times.* Retrieved May 26, 2008, from http://www.nytimes.com/2008/03/16/fashion/16juicy.html?pagewanted=1&_r=1&ref=fashion.

Murphey, Caitlyn. (2009, February 5). Retrieved February 23, 2009, from Students Against Juicy Campus Wall on Facebook website: http://www.facebook.com/s.php?init=q&q=juicy%20campus&ref=ts&sid=d29138a951112ca0b56b2e61ac7aea54#/group.php?sid=d29138a95111 2ca0b56b2e61ac7aea54&gid=10089684487.

Murphey, Caitlyn. (2008, February 20). Retrieved January 14, 2009, from Students Against Juicy Campus Wall on Facebook website: http://www.facebook.com/group.php?sid=e1db68dd22 fe93d9e0b98aa09441d4b8&gid=10089684487.

Murphey, Michael. (2009, February 10). CollegeACB will replace Juicy Campus. Retrieved February 22, 2009, from http://media.www.marquettetribune.org/media/storage/paper1130/news/2009/02/10/News/Collegeacb.Will.Replace.Juicy.Campus-3620158.shtml.

National Public Radio. (2008, August 25). *Rumors Fly on Anonymous College Gossip Sites.* Retrieved September 12, 2008, from http://www.npr.org/templates/player/mediaPlayer.html?action=1&t=1&islist=false&id=93948235&m=93948220.

Ownwhatyouthink.com-petition. (2009a). Retrieved January 20, 2009, from Ownwhatyouthink website: http://www.ipetitions.com/petition/ownwhatyouthink/.

Ownwhatyouthink.com-campaign. (2009b). Retrieved January 20, 2009, from Ownwhatyouthink website: http://www.ownwhatyouthink.com/campaign.html.

Palisoc, Rachelle. (2008). BAN JuicyCampus!!. Retrieved January 20, 2009, from Facebook web site: http://www.facebook.com/group.php?sid=0ec592829092aab442d4f887ad9250b5&gid=9749700026.

Pashley, Elizabeth. (2009, February12). It's Still an Insult: Juicy Campus Folds, Spawns a Doomed Heir. *The Berkeley Beacon.* Retrieved March 14, 2009, from http://media.www.berkeleybeacon.com/media/storage/paper169/news/2009/02/12/Opinion/Its-still.An.Insult-3626724.shtml.

PerezHilton.com. (2009) Celebrity Gossip Juicy Celebrity Rumors Hollywood Blog from Perez Hilton. Retrieved January 17, 2008, from http://perezhilton.com/.

Reif, Gabriel. (2008). Juicy Campus Censorship. Message posted in response to Guess, Andy (2008, October 21). Using Juicy Campus As a Weapon Against Itself. *Inside Higher Ed.* Retrieved November 27, 2008, from http://www.insidehighered.com/news/2008/10/21/juicy.

Robichaud v. Canada (Treasury Board [1987] 2 S.C.R. 84.

Saturday Night Magazine (2008) JuicyCampus Creator, Matt Ivestor. Retrieved January 22, 2009, from http://www.snmag.com/MAGAZINE/Destination-Success/JuicyCampus-Creator-Matt-Ivester.html.

Shariff, S. and Johnny, L. (2007). Cyber-libel and cyber-bullying: Can schools protect student reputations and free expression in virtual environments? Paper presented at the American Educational Research Association (AERA) Conference. Chicago, Illinois.)

Shariff, Shaheen. (2008). *Cyber-Bullying: Issues and Solutions for the School, the Classroom and the Home.* Canada: Routledge.

Shelton, Tim. (2008, October 22). *Students Against JuicyCampus.* Retrieved January 14, 2009, from Students Against Juicy Campus Wall: on Facebook website http://www.facebook.com/group.php?sid=e1db68dd22fe93d9e0b98aa09441d4b8&gid=10089684487#/wall.php?id=10089684487&page=2&hash=224faf1571793ce251541730fe10a0fb.

Shibley, Robert. (2008, November 20). Tennessee State Bans JuicyCampus.com from Network. *The Torch.* Retrieved November 27, 2008, from http://www.thefire.org/index.php/article/9960.html.

State of Connecticut Attorney General Press Release. (2008). *Attorney General Investigating College Gossip Website Juicycampus.com.* Retrieved May 26, 2008, from http://www.ct.gov/ag/cwp/view.asp?A=2341&Q=412190.

State of New Jersey Department of Law and Public Safety Press Release. (2008). *State Subpoenas Records from JuicyCampus.com As It Investigates the College Gossip Website.* Retrieved May 26, 2008, from http://www.nj.gov/oag/newsreleases08/pr20080318b.html.

State of New Jersey Department of Law and Public Safety Press Release (2009). *College Gossip Website Says It Is Shutting Down JuicyCampus.com Was Target of Attorney General's Investigation into Potential Violation of Consumer Fraud Act.* Retrieved March 2, 2009, from http://www. nj.gov/oag/newsreleases09/pr20090204c.html.

Stringer, Elizabeth. (2008, Too Much Juice? Gossip Website Facing Complaints, Possible Lawsuit. *Union Wire, 3,* Retrieved January 17, 2009, from http://www.acui.org/publications/unionwire/ article.aspx?issue=1020&id=7152.

Tamul, Matt. (2008, February 25). Emory to Respond to Gossip. *The Emory Wheel.* Retrieved October 18, 2008, from http://www.emorywheel.com/detail.php?n=25165.

Tan, Genna. (2008, November 6). Students Stand up to Juicy Campus Web Site Anonymous Online Blogging Affects Students' Self Esteem. *The Santa Clara.* Retrieved January 18, 2009, from http://media.www.thesantaclara.com/media/storage/paper946/news/2008/11/06/News/ Students.Stand.Up.To.Juicy.Campus.Web.Site-3529113.shtml.

Tartan Board. (2008, September 22). Make Juicy Campus Substantial and Interesting. *The Tartan.* Retrieved October 25, 2008, from http://www.thetartan.org/2008/9/22/forum/ juicycampus.

Thurston, Jessica. (2009, February 9). JuicyCampus Goes Sour-Students Rejoice in Flavor. *The Tartan.* Retrieved March 7, 2009, from http://www.thetartan.org/2009/2/9/news/juicy.

Title IX of the Education Amendments of 1972, 20 U.S.C. §§ 1681–1688.

TMZ Productions, Inc. (2009). *TMZ.com Your Official Gossip Site for the Latest Entertainment News, Celebrity Gossip, Hollywood Rumors, Celebrity Video, and Photo Gossip.* Retrieved January 17, 2009, from http://www.tmz.com/.

Travis. (2008, October 6). How to Defeat Juicy Campus. *The Colonialist.* Retrieved October 18, 2008, from http://www.thecolonialist.com/2008/10/how-to-defeat-juicy-campus/.

TRUSTe. (2009) *TRUSTe-Make Your Privacy Choice.* Retrieved January 18, 2009, from http://www. truste.org/businesses/web_privacy_seal.php.

Turban, Efraim, King, Davis, McKay, Judy, Marshall, Peter. (2008). *Electronic Commerce: Managerial Perspective 2008.* Upper Saddle River, New Jersey: Pearson Prentice Hall.

U-Wire Via Acquire Media NewsEdge. (2008, December 4). Kent State U.: Juicy Campus censor-ship an 'appropriateness' call at Kent State U., *TMC News.* Retrieved January 21, 2009, from http://www.tmcnet.com/news/2008/12/04/3833261.htm.

Weiner, Jenna. (2008, December 1). Juicy Campus: Struggling to Keep Georgetown? *The Georgetown Independent.* Retrieved January 18, 2009, from, http://www.thegeorgetownindependent.com/ home/index.cfm?event=displayArticlePrinterFriendly&uStory_id=a8362885-ce10-4ada-93b5-b97240b06875.

Weiss, Suzannah. (2009, March 4). CollegeACB Picks Up Where Juicy Campus Left off. *Brown Daily Herald.* Retrieved March 14, 2009, from http://media.www.browndailyherald.com/ media/storage/paper472/news/2009/03/04/HigherEd/Collegeacb.Picks.Up.Where.Juicy. Campus.Left.Off-3657908.shtml.

Wojnar, Liz. (2009, February 17). Freshman Develops CollegeACB Empire. *The Wesleyan Argus*. Retrieved March 1, 2009, from http://wesleyanargus.com/2009/02/17/freshman-develops-collegeacb-empire/.

Wonkette. (2009) *Wonkette: The DC Gossip*. Retrieved January 17, 2009, from http://wonkette.com/.

WTNH/Associated Press (2009, February 5) Economy squeezes Juicy Campus site dry. Gossip site had Yale section. Retrieved March 1, 2009 from http://www.wtnh.com/dpp/news/news_ap_economy_squeezes_juicy_campus_site_dry_200902051351.

Young, Jeffery. (2008a, February 12). Web Site Promising 'Juicy' Campus Gossip Faces Backlash. *Chronicle of Higher Education*. Retrieved on May 26, 2008, from http://chronicle.com/wiredcampus/article/?id=2736.

Young, Jeffery. (2008b, March 12). Colgate U. Student's Violent Message to a Gossip Web Site Leads to His Arrest. *Chronicle of Higher Education*. Retrieved May 26, 2008, from http://chronicle.com/wiredcampus/article/2813/colgate-u-students-violent-message-to-a-gossip-web-site-leads-to-his-arrest.

Young, Jeffery. (2008c, March 28). How to Combat a Campus-Gossip Web Site (and Why You Shouldn't). *Chronicle of Higher Education*. Retrieved October 19, 2008, from http://chronicle.com/weekly/v54/i29/29a01602.htm.

Young, Jeffrey. (2009, February 5). JuicyCampus Shuts Down, Blaming the Economy, Not Controversy. *Chronicle of Higher Education*. Retrieved February 9, 2009, from http://chronicle.com/free/2009/02/10973n.htm?rss.

Zeran v. America Online, Inc. 958 F. Supp. 1124, 1134 (E.D.) Va) aff'd, 129. F.3d 327 (4th Cir.1997).

5 · Boundaries in Cyber-space

Media and Stakeholders as Policy Shapers

Dawn Zinga

INTRODUCTION

Cyber-space is often perceived of as a boundary-free space where individuals are able to express their creativity and converse freely with others. This chapter will consider how cyber-bullying is challenging school personnel, parents, media, and students (collectively the stakeholders) to take responsibility for on-line actions while also establishing boundaries for on-line behaviour. Specifically, it will examine how stakeholders talk about boundaries and responsibility in cases of cyber-bullying. Examples from recent instances of cyber-bullying and the associated court cases as well as media responses will be used to examine these conversations. Consideration will also be given to various approaches of addressing cyber-bullying as well as emerging policy and practice within educational contexts.

Despite the many possibilities for creative exchange that the Internet offers young people, for many youth the cyber-world can be a very dangerous space. Being boundary free, it crosses regional jurisdictions and national borders, introducing complicated new issues around international definitions of crime. Furthermore, it presents challenges to the tensions between freedom of speech and protection from attacks or persecution. We are at an interesting crossroads. Adults have had to adapt to the internet and its rapidly changing technologies, while still being in positions of authority as parents and educators, over young people who are more technologically adept than themselves. As concerns about cyber-bullying and other internet safety issues become more prominent, we are increasingly forced to make sense of the tensions between free speech and protection, as well as jurisdiction and responsibility.

Other chapters within this volume have discussed cyber-bullying as an emerging phenomenon and identified the many issues associated with its occurrence and prevention. There have been discussions about responsibility on the part of various stakeholders as well as in depth considerations of the role that user decision-making, individual agency and personal choice play in the use of technology. This chapter focuses on cyber-bullying within the media, and the forum of public opinion. I do this by focusing on accounts of cyber-bullying as reported by media around the globe. Interestingly, there are many similarities and patterns in the ways media report on cyber-bullying cases, regardless of their country of origin. I focus on how media accounts locate cyber-bullying within society and what discussions are taking place around free speech and protection as well as boundaries and responsibilities. The majority of the references in this chapter are drawn from online sources as it is important to see what is being voiced in cyber-space about these issues that are at the heart of how cyber-space can be used and how it is abused.

These conversations around free speech, protection, boundaries, and responsibilities are vitally important for all stakeholders so that we can educate ourselves and our children to be active and respectful internet citizens. In examining media accounts related to cyber-bullying, I have found a shift in these discussions over time. Initially, there was talk of blaming and punishing those who engaged in cyber-bullying in combination with a lot of sentiment that called for young people who had been victimized to just shake it off, or log off, if they could not handle 'a little teasing.' With the widespread coverage of cyber-bullying cases, especially that of Megan Meier (Brady, 2008; Huffstutter, 2007; Michels, 2008a; Michels, 2008b; Price, 2008), there has been a shift to holding people accountable for their actions and enacting laws that better govern cyber-space abuses. There has also been more attention paid in the media to reporting on how to identify and address cyber-bullying as well as tips on how to protect children from experiencing such attacks. Where initially there had been a lot of reactive coverage, it seems as if the Meier case has opened space for a discussion around proactive responses to cyber-bullying issues and an increased focus on education that addresses those issues.

I will consider how these discussions around free speech, protection and responsibilities are taking place and what is missing from the conversation. Finally, I will predict different paths and outcomes for the discussions happening around cyber-bullying and what that could mean for the safety of young people in cyber-space.

CYBER-BULLYING AND THE LAW

There are serious concerns that on-line threats and plans can become physical acts in the real world, often with devastating consequences. A Finnish teenager who shot eight people at his school in 2007 had been engaged in on-line communications with a teen in the United States who also planned to target a local school (Goldman, 2007). The teen posted videos of himself and a gun on YouTube 30 minutes prior to his attack on the school. Goldman's article also discusses the concerns that law enforcement officials have over like-minded criminals meetings on the internet and sharing information in ways that were previously not possible. While law enforcement representatives are concerned about the vastness of the internet and state that it is not possible to monitor everything, it has not stopped them from catching whatever they can. Police were too late when they arrived at the address of the Florida teen who broadcast his suicide in real time on the internet (Florida boy's suicide live on web, 2008; Stelter, 2008a). However, ten days later police officers in Southwest Florida were able to successfully intervene when a twelve-year-old girl threatened to commit suicide while broadcasting live video of herself holding a knife at her throat (Mills, 2008). Many law enforcement agencies around the world are taking steps to address cyber-crimes and setting up specialized positions and units to address these issues. Recently, the FBI opened a cyber-crime lab in Omaha that will centralize internet related crime and has specialized units devoted to different aspects, including cyber-bullying (Molai, 2009). However, these actions on the part of law enforcement will only be helpful in addressing cyber-bullying if a given incident is considered to have broken the law.

Cases of cyber-bullying often cross the divide between the virtual and physical worlds and can lead to criminal charges. Young people who have been cyber-bullied often have been bullied at school and/or threatened with real world violence. A recent case that has invoked a new cyber harassment law involved a 16-year-old girl who had been nicknamed "pork and beans" by her tormentors (Currier, 2008). The girl received threatening and derogatory texts and voicemails in addition to having a can of beans dumped on the roof of her car. All of the texts and voicemails were traced to one cell phone, and police have charged the young woman who owns the phone. Two recent cases out of New Zealand resulted in assault convictions for two 18-year-old women after each physically assaulted other young women who they claimed were responsible for harassing them online (Chug, 2009). When cyber-perpetrators send threats to their victims the fear inspired by those threats may tragically result in young people choosing to take their own lives. Rachael Neblett was one of those young people who escaped threats through suicide. She took her life on October 9, 2006 after a cyber-perpetrator threatened that when they met in the real world she would not put her in the hospital but send her to the morgue (MacDonald, 2007). In Rachael's case no charges were laid as the 'bully' did not take any action, and despite police being able to track the on-line threats to a specific household, they have no evidence of intent. In many cases, victims of cyber-bullying are told that no crime has been committed and/or that since the incidents took place outside of school that the school cannot do anything (see Charles, 2009; Leishman, 2005; Meadows, 2008). However, there is evidence that ideas about boundaries and responsibility around cyber-bullying incidents may be shifting.

There are at least thirteen U.S. states that have enacted some form of legislation to address cyber-bullying (Rubinstein, 2009; Surdin, 2009). The media accounts report that legislation has already been enacted by Arkansas, California, Delaware, Idaho, Iowa, Michigan, Minnesota, Nebraska, New Jersey, Oklahoma, Oregon, South Carolina and Washington with several other states considering legislation at the time of this publication However, the new laws primarily focus on requiring schools to adopt policies to address all forms of bullying, including cyber-bullying. The schools are required to have plans for training school staff, educating students and parents, and having procedures for how to deal with incidents. In addition, school districts are often being empowered to suspend or expel students who have committed cyber-bullying. Chaker (2009) discussed the complexity of these new laws and the level of consultation that has often been involved in establishing the most appropriate language around cyber-bullying. Like many other journalists, she is well aware of the boundary issues around what is done on school campus and what is done off school campus, as well as the issues around free speech and First Amendment rights. As states enact these new laws, they are sending a clear message that schools have a responsibility to address these issues.

However, the issues around boundaries and free speech are not very clear, and states have not done much to address this aspect of the complexity surrounding cyber-bullying. The 1969 ruling in the *Tinker v. Des Moines School District* (1969) case provides some guidance for schools as it found that schools could suppress student speech on campus if it could be proven that in doing so the school was preventing a serious disruption to the school environment that is above and beyond the discomfort or disruption associated when unpopular views are expressed. While this provides some guidance in the case of on campus speech that can be extended to electronic media, it does not provide guidance around off campus speech. Guidance addressing issues of off campus speech is needed by schools in the case of cyber-bullying, for off campus posting can still directly affect the school environment. A case out of Juneau Alaska, in which a student was suspended for holding up a sign "BONG HITS 4 JESUS" at an off campus school event, seemed to hold promise that it would provide some guidance to schools (Mears, 2007). However, the decision of the Supreme Court was that the principal could suppress the speech in that specific case, but the language of the decision indicated that the incident was considered to be equivalent to on-campus speech because it was a school sanctioned event (*Morse et al. v. Frederick*, 2007). This does not shed much light on the issue of off-campus speech that does not involve a school sanctioned event. In addition, there were several dissenting opinions among the Justices around the interpretation of the *Tinker* case and associated principles around students' First Amendment rights. Some of the Justices disagreed with the decision that schools can suppress speech that includes a pro-drug opinion, viewing that decision as a direct violation of the principles. The statements of one dissenting Justice are most applicable to cyber-bullying. Justice Stevens stated that "In my judgment, the First Amendment protects student speech if the message itself neither violates a permissible rule nor expressly advocates conduct that is illegal and harmful to students" (*Morse et al. v. Frederick*, 2007). This case is detailed further in chapter 7.

Other countries are also interested in taking a stronger stance on cyber-bullying. The government of South Korea is reported to be promoting a new law that would punish those who abused others online, but the opposition party claims that such incidents can be addressed under existing laws that address slander and public insults (Sang-Hun, 2008). The Czech education ministry is taking a similar stance to the U.S. in enabling its teachers to take more action and providing them with a set of guidelines (Czech Move to Stop Cyber Bullying, 2008). Within Canada, the Ontario government has changed the Safe Schools Act to specifically include cyber-bullying and is enabling its schools and teachers to take stronger action in these cases, including suspension and expulsion (see Bill to Cover Internet Abuses, 2007; Cyber-bullying, 2007; Cyber-bullying Law Introduced at Queen's Park, 2007; Cyber-bullying Law Introduced in Ontario, 2007). In an editorial about the new legislation, the *Welland Tribune* called upon Canadians to recognize that free speech has limitations in so far as it can and should be overridden when it comes to "an individual's right to security of person" (Cyber-bullying, 2007).

There seems to be increasing social concern around cyber-bullying as high profile cases grab the attention of the media, and the public becomes aware that cyber-bullying is not rare or unusual but becoming an everyday occurrence. Even the recent media accounts on the presidential elections in the U.S. included small pieces about cyber-bullying. The Family Online Safety Institute has called for President Obama to create a national safety officer and dedicate $100 million to the internet safety education for youth as well as additional research (Group Calls on Obama to Appoint Internet Safety Specialist, 2008). The group is calling for a national campaign around internet safety like those that exist in the United

Kingdom and European Union (Gunn, 2008). Clearly, an increasing number of people are lobbying to ensure that something is done to address cyber-bullying and the general public appears to have this issue on their radar. Furthermore, the passing of new laws that position schools as needing to be empowered to address cyber-bullying sends clear messages about responsibility in terms of who needs to act. The push for legislation and ways of criminalizing cyber-bullying suggest a focus on punishment, and yet much of the research literature has identified the need for proactive approaches and education (see Belsey, 2005; Li, 2006; Patchin & Hinduja, 2006; Shariff, 2008; Stover, 2006; Willard, 2005). This leads me to wonder how news media depictions of cyber-bullying incidents influence public opinion and shape public policy.

MEDIA ACCOUNTS OF CYBER-BULLYING

The following section reviews media articles about cyber-bullying. In order to focus the review, I have divided media coverage into three distinct sections: i) reporting incidents of cyber-bullying, ii) resources to address cyber-bullying; and, iii) prevention and responses to cyber-bullying. While the divisions are somewhat imperfect (at times articles cover more than one area or review a topic not captured in my title descriptions), the divisions, nonetheless, provide a useful framework for discussion. Each section reviews multiple media articles from multiple countries.

Reporting Incidents of Cyber-Bullying

It is important to examine the ways that online media depict incidents of cyber-bullying and also the information that is provided in the media accounts. By examining media accounts of cyber-bullying cases, I have found that while there are some culturally related differences, cases of cyber-bullying from around the globe share many similarities. The cultural differences in cyber-bullying are usually connected to social norms within the society, for example isolating a student from a group in Japan is a particular tactic that is associated with the collective nature of the society. One of the most striking similarities is how often the victims choose to escape the situation by attempting suicide or succeeding in taking their own lives. Other similarities include the targeting of teachers and of young people who are seen to be 'different,' as well as subjecting the victim to public humiliation or humiliation within a certain group (i.e., school population).

British media have reported a suicide attempt associated with Bebo, an on-line social networking site (see BBC News, 2008; Stayton, 2008) whereby a sixteen-year-old boy from Brighton, UK, attempted suicide in response to being cyber-bullied by a former friend. The boy formed a romantic on-line friendship with another boy "Callum" through Bebo. The former friend had created Callum's fake profile and is reported to have lured his former friend into the relationship. When the boy accidently discovered that Callum was a fake profile, his former friend informed him that everyone including the teachers at his school knew about the relationship and had been laughing about it. The boy could not face returning to school and made a serious attempt on his life. The former friend demonstrated remorse and pled guilty to a charge of harassment. He was sentenced on February 8, 2008 and ordered to pay compensation to his victim. This is not the first instance of cyber-bullying that has troubled British authorities. A school in West Sussex struggled with cyber-bullying when a group of students used Bebo and Facebook to post threatening and abusive material about their teachers. At the University of Kent, a librarian discovered that he was the target of an on-line Facebook group (Gardham, 2008). A teacher at the Grey Coat Hospital School in England was also the subject of a Facebook group called "The Hate Society" that resulted in the suspension of 29 students who participated in the group (Nikkhah & Henry, 2009). In addition, a thirteen-year-old boy was successful in his suicide bid following on-line bullying. Sam Leeson hanged himself in his parents' home after being cyber-bullied for his taste in music and clothes. The bullying was apparently in response to his Bebo profile and took place over several months. (Gardham, 2008; Kiyani, 2008). A thirteen-year-old girl from England who has Marfan syndrome (a genetic syndrome resulting in excessive height) was physically bullied and bullied on-line by her classmates. Her parents removed her from the school (Tall Girl 'bullied' in Chatroom, 2006).

Cyber-bullying is also creating problems for students in Japan with cell phone texting and e-mails playing a major role. Kubota (2007) reported on a teen who attempted suicide twice following cyber-bullying from other peers at his school and the eighteen-year-old boy who committed suicide after classmates uploaded a nude photograph and demanded money via e-mail. The lack of monitoring and the prevalence of technology among youth are associated with the increase in cyber-bullying in Japan. A report from the Education Ministry in Japan states that there are over 38,000 school websites that are not monitored by the schools and are filled with material that is inappropriate and contributing to cyber-bullying (Cyber-bullying Common among Japan's Children, 2008). Another media report discussed the pattern for cyber-bullying combined with extortion attempts or physical attacks and reported that five Japanese school children had committed suicide from September 2006 to March 2007, including a twelve-year-old girl (Makino, 2007).

Japan is far from being the only country with websites schools that are unmonitored. A media report from the United States claims that there are almost 100 schools from Southern California that have sites based on the schools on schoolscandals.com. The attorney that represented the site stated that the comments posted there are not illegal as the website is for posting opinions and is operated by students (Parents, Schools Unite against 'Cyber Bullying,' 2003). However, the site was voluntarily suspended following a public campaign by some of the parents through media articles and radio talk shows (Guernsey, 2003). The United States has also faced other challenges around issues of cyber-bullying that have not ended as well as the schoolsscandal.com situation. One of the highest profile American cases of cyber-bullying is that of Megan Meier from Dardenne Prairie, Missouri. Megan hanged herself in her bedroom closet after becoming distraught over a series of comments directed at her through her Myspace.com account (Brady, 2008; Huffstutter, 2007; Michels, 2008a; Michels, 2008b; Price, 2008). The majority of the comments appeared to be from a boy named Josh Evans, who had become her friend through the social networking site. Megan was days away from celebrating her fourteenth birthday. In the aftermath of the suicide, it was discovered that "Josh Evans" did not exist but was a profile that had been allegedly created by three individuals: Lori Drew, her daughter, and one of Drew's business assistants. The Drews lived down the street from and were reported to have been friendly with the Meiers. Megan and the Drews' daughter had been friends for years although it was reported to be a rocky friendship that had ended. In addition, the Meier family claims that the Drew family was well aware that Megan had ADD and had battled with depression for years. The incident occurred on October 16, 2006 and has continued to be in the media as the resulting court case received coverage (see Ayres, 2008; Brady, 2008; Judge Delays Ruling on Mistrial in 'Cyber-bullying' Case, 2008; Michels, 2008a; Michels, 2008b; Mother Convicted in Internet Suicide Case, 2008; Patrick, Hunn & Currier, 2008; Price, 2008; Stelter, 2008b).

The notoriety of Megan's case has been attributed to the charges brought against Lori Drew in what has been dubbed in the media as the first 'cyber-bullying' case. While the jury in the Drew case found her guilty of three misdemeanor charges and no felony charges, Judge Wu overturned the verdict and acquitted Drew pending finalization by his written decision (see McCarthy & Michels, 2009; Zetter, 2009). The media storm triggered by Megan's suicide, convicted Drew in the court of public opinion and also spurred the introduction of new legislation. One such piece of proposed legislation is the "Megan Meier Cyberbullying Prevention Act" that was introduced to the House of Representatives on April 2, 2009 by Congresswoman Linda Sanchez, who claims the bill will preserve free speech while also providing protection from hostile and repeated communication made with the intent to harm (Sanchez, 2009). Megan Meier is not the first victim in the United States to have committed suicide; there have been many other cases including Ryan Halligan and Rachael Neblett. Ryan Halligan was in eighth grade when he committed suicide on October 7, 2003 after experiencing prolonged bullying at school and through the Internet (Flowers, 2006). Rachael Neblett was seventeen years old when she committed suicide after on-line bullying (MacDonald, 2007).

A case of "sexting" has also lead to the suicide of an eighteen-year-old girl, Jessica Logan. Sexting is the transmission of sexually charged materials or messages via cell phone texts and/or the posting of such materials on-line. Jessica committed suicide in July 2008 following bullying that was triggered by the distribution of nude pictures she had sent of herself to her boyfriend. After breaking up, the ex-boyfriend distributed the pictures to other girls in the school who harassed and bullied Logan (Celizic, 2009). While garnering less attention in the media than the Meier's case, the Logan case has also contributed to the introduction of new legislation. Senator Robert Menendez has introduced The School and Family Education about the Internet Act (SAFE Internet Act) (see LaVallee, 2009; Menendez, 2009). The act will establish an Internet safety education program that would initially fund research into best practices and then use the guidelines established by that research to fund partnerships between education agencies and other local partners to develop additional research as well as education and prevention programs and initiatives. The goal of the act is to protect children from Internet dangers. Jessica Logan's mother, who has been involved with the act, hopes it will prevent other suicides and help children living with the pain of cyber-bullying and sexting (see Menendez, 2009; Mom Fighting to End Cyber Abuse, 2009).

There are also many cases in the United States and elsewhere of young people who are living with the reality of cyber-bullying. A seventeen-year-old boy from California had his YouTube account taken over. The hacker posted pornographic material and derogatory comments on the site (Charles, 2009). Andrew from Tennessee discovered a MySpace account that had been set up as if it were his own and included content that stated he had raped girls and been involved in other inappropriate acts (Andrew's Story of an Imposter Profile on MySpace, 2008). In addition to the trauma suffered as a result of the cyber-bullying, Andrew worries that although the page has been taken down the information still exists on the Internet and could interfere with his future plans and job prospects. Harts Middle School in West Virginia is reported to have experienced a 'cyber-bullying outbreak' over students' use of a local news aggregate site called www.topix.net (O'Donoghue, 2009). Students are reported to be launching inappropriate polls and online conversations that target specific students and teachers.

Like the United States, Japan, and Britain, Canada has also experienced cases of problematic outbreaks of cyber-bullying in schools. Recently, a Facebook group launched a violent campaign against red-haired people called "National Kick a Ginger Day" that led RCMP to investigate the teenager who administers the group and take precautionary action in several British Columbia schools (Alphonso, 2008). The campaign was widespread, although the only media reported violence occurred in British Columbia. Ironically, the campaign took place in the middle of Bullying Awareness week. There have been other cases when internet bullying has spilled over into action in the real world. Two teenaged girls in Odessa,

Ontario, were charged with 15 counts of threatening as well as conspiracy to commit murder charges after online threats against their teachers and fellow students led to some undisclosed action by the teens (CTV.ca News Staff, 2006). An Ajax, Ontario teen committed suicide in response to being cyber-bullied and physically bullied after a former friend "outed" him as being gay (Rau, 2007). There was also the case of the Ontario high school principal who suspended 19 students for between three to eight days depending on their level of participation in a chat group on Facebook entitled "McMahon, The Grinch of School Spirit" (Rusk, 2007; Students Suspended for 'Cyber-bullying' Principal, 2007). The chat group included sexual content, derogatory comments, and inappropriate pictures that targeted the principal.

A similar case led to real world violence as a violent protest over the suspension of students who posted derogatory comments about their vice principal on Facebook resulted in arrests (Teens Charged in Protest over Facebook Freedom, 2007). The students involved in the protest contended that the administration had overreacted and had violated their freedom of speech by punishing students for "private" on-line comments. There were a number of other incidents that involved inappropriate online comments about teachers or school administration including the suspension of five grade eight students from a Thornhill elementary school over Facebook comments and five students from a Quebec high school following Facebook comments (Father: School Too Harsh on Son for Online Remarks, 2007). There have also been some high profile cases, including the David Knight case and a case that became known as "The Star Wars Kid" (Lampert, 2006a). In the David Knight case, the young teen was physically bullied and cyber-bullied. David discovered that there was a website that was devoted to making fun of him and also included accusations of inappropriate behaviour and derogatory comments (Leishman, 2005). The "Star Wars Kid" case involved the appropriation of a video made for a school project. The video depicted a student acting as a Jedi knight with an improvised light saber, and some classmates posted the video on the internet where it gained amazing notoriety (Ha, 2003). The video resulted in the parents of the victimized student launching a lawsuit against the parents of the boys who posted the video. It was revealed in court testimony that one site solely devoted to the video clip had recorded 76 million visits by late 2006 (Ha, 2006). The clip is still widely available on the internet including on YouTube in the original, and in 106 cloned variations. The lawsuit was recently settled out of court-eliminating the possibility of jurisprudence that could have been used in other cases (Ha, 2006; Lampert 2006b).

Resources to Address Cyber-Bullying

The media have also devoted some of their cyber-bullying coverage to the discussion of new and available resources to help address cyber-bullying. While many media accounts focused on local initiatives (Children Made Aware of the Dangers of 'Cyber bullying,' 2008; Labbe, 2008; Levy, 2008; Papprill, 2008; Preston, 2008) others (CYBERCOPS Software Helps Students Stay Safe On-line, 2005; Kurutz, 2008; Mead, 2008; Michael, 2008; Qwest Foundation, 2008; RCMP, 2008) have also focused on larger initiatives and resources that are more widely applicable. The media coverage on resources tends to be triggered by press releases, recent incidents of cyber-bullying, or associations with school initiatives that would also be considered good human interest stories. Media reports on resources have focused on two other associated areas that can be described as ways to combat or prevent cyber-bullying: 1) technological advances and services offered through social networking sites; and 2) information designed to keep kids safe on the internet and prevent or address cyber-bullying.

Media accounts of local initiatives tend to be narrow in scope and are situated in small geographic areas such as cities and towns, often with a focus on individual schools or people. This type of media report often reads like a human interest story and is less likely to have been triggered by press releases. As demonstrated by the following examples, the coverage from different countries tends to be very similar. A media story out of New Zealand stressed the importance of a team approach that brings schools, parents and students together to ensure that everyone is a good cybercitizen and knows how to conduct themselves appropriately as well as what steps to take if something inappropriate happens (Papprill, 2008). Coverage from Teeside, England, reported that a student's attempts to combat cyber-bullying through theatre and volunteer efforts has now moved into film, as the teen works with writers from a TV drama to develop a three-minute film on cyber-bullying (Levy, 2008). Another British newspaper reported on a unique approach to informing school children about how to deal with cyber-bullying that involved senior arts students performing a series of sketches that focused on cyber-bullying in chat rooms and other on-line formats (Children Made Aware of the Dangers of 'Cyber bullying,' 2008). Similarly, a story from the United States reported that Verizon Foundation, the philanthropic arm of Verizon, provided a $15,000 grant to Madison City schools to support their internet safety program (Labbe, 2008). Another article from the United States identified a local school that has been struggling to deal with "rampant" cyber-bullying and reported on how the police, teachers, and students have teamed up to deal with it (Preston, 2008). An article from Canada, focused on the improvements made to one school district's cyber-bullying prevention strategies over the four years since a student committed suicide after being bullied at school and on-line (Simms, 2008).

National coverage of initiatives is reserved for those that are broader in scope and tend to be triggered by formal press releases. For example, two media reports that discuss video components in cyber-bullying resources originated from press releases. One of these reports was out of Pennsylvania and focused on an award-winning 22 minute DVD that provides parents and other caregivers with a tutorial on internet safety, including a segment on cyber-bullying (Mead, 2008). The video resulted from collaboration between Pennsylvania's State Police, Department of Education, and Commission on Crime and Delinquency. Another report out of the United States also focused on a video component that was part of a unique cyber-bullying curriculum created by the Qwest Foundation (Qwest Foundation, 2008). The curriculum features an internet site with resources, a downloadable guide, and a series of videos that have been made available to education systems. The video can be found on YouTube where they have been getting hits or on www.intelligentinternet.com. A second curriculum package that has been released in the United States "CyberSmart!," was created in conjunction with the National School Boards Association's Technology Leadership Network, the Character Education Partnership, the National Association of School Psychologists, and the National Cyber Security Alliance. The news release that announced the curriculum program describes it as offering non-sequential lesson plans, technology supports and activities that focus on preventing cyber-bullying and extending learning out of the classroom into the home and the community (First Research-based Cyber Bullying Awareness Curriculum Launched in Partnership with Leading Education Organizations, 2007).

Similarly, a media account out of Canada also reports that under Premier Dalton McGinty, the government of Ontario has provided one million dollars to support the development of CYBERCOPS, an on-line safety program directed at junior high aged students and also provides resources for teachers (CYBERCOPS Software Helps Students Stay Safe On-line, 2005). A more recent report from Canada discussed how the RCMP and the Canadian Teachers' Federation are working together to deliver cyber-bullying presentations to students from grade four through to the end of high school (RCMP, 2008). The education program was designed with input from the Canadian Teachers' Federation and will be delivered as part of the RCMP's education program. The RCMP also have a youth website, www.deal.org, that has launched an interactive on-line game "Cyberbullying: The Dark Side of Technology." Irish media also reported on larger initiatives with a piece on Ireland's Office for Internet Safety's release of a booklet designed to address cyber-bullying by providing guidance on how to prevent it, identify it when it occurs and take steps to respond appropriately (Michael, 2008). Some stories discussed how multiple schools districts were addressing cyber-bullying. One, in a British newspaper, reported on how counties were adopting a multi-pronged approach to address cyber-bullying including peer mentoring, targeted curriculum, case studies, and other proactive approaches (Bid to Tackle the Problem of Cyber Bullying, 2008). The other media account is out of Pittsburgh and highlighted the anti-bullying programs implemented in various district schools (Kurutz, 2008). While the programs were diverse, with some taking a more hands-on approach, all of the programs were associated with the Pennsylvania requirement that school districts should have an anti-bullying policy incorporating all forms of bullying in place by January 1, 2009.

In addition to the coverage of local and larger initiatives, there has been some media coverage on technological advances and steps taken by social networking sites to protect kids from cyber-bullying. Two Irish companies, Anam and Sentry Wireless, have developed applications relevant to cyber-bullying via mobile phones. Anam offers a SIM-based application that blocks numbers upon the request of parents; Sentry Wireless offers an option called "Kidsafe" that requires parents to enter a white list of phone numbers and blocks all other incoming calls (O'Brien, 2008). The technology is already in use in Ireland and Singapore with interest expressed from other countries. Within two weeks of the media coverage on the mobile phone technology, the Irish Cellular Industry Association made news when it announced the release of its new guide, "Mobile Phones: A Parent's Guide to Safe and Sensible Use," that includes information on how to deal with issues around cyber-bullying (Minihan, 2008). Technology to combat cyber-bullying is also available from an American company, CyberPatrol, that offers "Chatguard" an application designed to prevent the sending or receiving of inappropriate language by children using IM, has enhanced that product to offer more blocked words including what the company identifies as "a comprehensive list of key cyber-bullying terms" (Rubenking, 2009). Cyberpatrol also offers "Threat Detector" an application that scans all URLs in the history and favorites and reports URLs that fall into what parents consider to be undesirable categories. It also suggests that parents use the scans as an opportunity to talk about internet safety and why access to certain URLs will be blocked by the parents.

Social networking websites have slowly been taking action to address cyber-bullying and other inappropriate behaviours largely since the highly publicized Drew trial in California. Many on-line media sources have included brief reports on the action taken by YouTube, MySpace, and Facebook (see Sarno, 2008; Shallenberger, 2008; Wright, 2008). YouTube has added an "Abuse and Safety Centre" that provides instructions on how to report online abuse as well as resources, while MySpace is in the process of developing technology to detect and delete inappropriate content before it is reported. Facebook is improving its content removal procedure and committing to a 24-hour complaint response time. One article offered praise for YouTube's introduction of its new centre from the National Centre for Missing and Exploited Children as well as support from Mark Neblett, whose daughter committed suicide in October 2006 (San Miguel, 2008). In addition to praising the action, Mark Neblett is also reported to be calling for more proactive actions by other social networking sites while at the same time wondering if such measures will ultimately protect children in situations like his daughter's. Surprisingly, despite the intensity of the coverage of the Megan Meier incident and the associated Lori Drew case, actions taken by the social networking sites in response have received little coverage.

It is less surprising to find a news story about the difficulties experienced by a California boy and his mother when they contacted YouTube to remove inappropriate content (Charles, 2009). According to the article, the boy requested that YouTube assist in resolving an incident that involved a hacker posting inappropriate material and derogatory comments on the boy's YouTube.com web page. The 17-year-old boy had no access to his account because the hacker had changed the password locking him out. Interestingly, the boy phoned and e-mailed Youtube on December 12—one day following media coverage (Sarno, 2008) of YouTube's introduction of its Abuse and Safety Centre. The Abuse and Safety Centre is designed for users of the site or what YouTube terms "YouTube community members." The boy or his mother would have to create a new account in order to access the service; however, they are both reluctant to do so since they have concerns about being on YouTube (Charles, 2009). This situation raises some interesting questions about how YouTube will address issues from individuals who are not members of the YouTube community or who have been locked out of their accounts. YouTube has posted a video on the site to introduce the new feature to its community members (Safety, Education and Empowerment on YouTube, 2008). While the video does a good job of orienting users to the new feature and walking the user through how to make a complaint, it does not address what to do if you have been locked out of your account or do not have an account. No offers of assistance are made if the complainant does not want to open a YouTube account.

Prevention and Responses to Cyber-bullying

The final area that falls within the resource theme for on-line media coverage focuses on providing tips on how to prevent and/or deal with cyber-bullying. These articles range in scope, including some that provide specific information or tips on how to recognize cyber-bullying or signs that a child is being cyberbullied and others that detail what adults should know about the Internet (Burns, 2008; Duffy, 2006; Hirsh, 2006; McIntosh, 2008; Murphy, 2007; Wasserman, 2008; Weinstein, 2008) as well as reports of educational initiatives available in the community such as presentations or classes on internet safety for parents (Choi, 2009; Fowler, 2008; Niswander, 2009). Many of the articles combine multiple aspects of these elements. For example, Weinstein (2008) talks about a presentation on internet safety and cyber-bullying, given to parents by the local police chief. In the article she provides definitions and several strategies that parents can use to remain in touch with what's happening when their children go on-line. Although the on-line media articles are somewhat limited in scope, numerous websites are devoted to cyber-bullying (i.e., www.cyberbullying.us, www.stopcyberbullying.org, www.netsafe.org.nz) or contain useful information on internet safety for parents and young people (i.e. Bullying online, n.d.; Cyber-bullying prevention, n.d.).

Clearly, the media are providing a great deal of coverage on cyber-bullying incidents and related issues. Google offers a new notification feature and after signing up for notification of any news that featured cyber-bullying, I received a daily notification that provided links for anywhere from one to fifteen new stories that had appeared on the Internet each day. On average over a three month period, there were five news reports related to cyber-bullying on a daily basis that were either reporting an incident, focused on one of the four resource areas, or discussed cyber-bullying and the law.

ENGAGING THE ISSUES

In this section, I again review media accounts of cyber-bullying but with a distinct focus on issue analysis. That is I have identified some key issues—free speech, protection, boundaries, and responsibilities—that were recurring themes in the previous analysis and now take a more analytical approach to probe what assumptions are being made about these issues and what does this suggest about future policy directions. Importantly, I have also incorporated the response forums to articles that allow the public to engage with the media in these discussions.

It is vitally important that all stakeholders engage in discussions around free speech, protection, boundaries, and responsibilities, as these issues are associated with cyber-bullying and conduct on the Internet that needs to be considered and debated. Engaging in these discussions is essential to furthering our collective understanding of social norms in cyber-space and in making informed decisions about how to deal with incidents that cross the boundaries between cyber-space and the real world. This section will consider how these discussions are taking place as evidenced in media framing of their reports and the patterns that have emerged within electronic postings in response to articles. These electronic debates are important because they provide an excellent window into which issues engender public discussion. I will also look at media reporting of criminal charges and lawsuits as well as the associated discussions on the implications of court decisions, with a special emphasis on free speech and the protection of individual security.

Journalists are expected to write articles that are informative and speak to the public. Thus, the way that articles are framed in terms of what is included and what left out provides information about the journalist's expectations and assumptions about public opinion. Two Canadian articles provide interesting insights into the emerging discussions around cyber-bullying issues. . The first focuses on the experiences of David Knight and his reaction to being a victim of cyber-bullying while the second article approached the issues from the perspective of the 'bully' who was disciplined by the school.

In the article about David Knight's experiences (Leishman, 2005), the journalist provides a very sympathetic account of David Knight's experiences of being bullied at school and highlights how those experiences culminated in, and were eclipsed by, the cyber-bullying he experienced. The article includes quotes from David and his mother, as well as an account of the frustration they experienced when informed that the police had limited ability to intervene unless death threats or other criminal offences were involved and that schools need clear evidence of the material being sent from a school computer. Of particular interest is the journalist's choice of 'experts' who are quoted in the article and the content of the quotes that were included. One of these individuals is Jay Thompson, reported to be the president of the Canadian Association of Internet Providers at the time of the article. He stated that Internet Service Providers are not involved in censorship, nor would their clients want them to take that role. The next 'expert' to be cited was Jeffrey Shallit, reportedly speaking for a group called "Electronic Frontier." Shallit suggests that any form of censorship undermines free speech and sends the wrong message to students by indicating that free speech is not an important value. He goes further to state that people should adhere to the old saying the "sticks and stones may break my bones, but names will never hurt me" because, after all, it's just name-calling. The journalist asked Shallit to look at the website that targeted David Knight, and he indicated that he had seen worse and that if it were his own child he would be upset but he would tell his child to hold his head high and ignore it. Shallit also indicated that the negatives associated with suppressing free speech outweighed any argument that derogatory comments on the Internet should be censored. The journalist then introduced questions about how serious cyber-bullying really is and why kids can't just log off and ignore the messages. Leishman included some quotes from David and other young people, but she failed to fully address the questions that she raised.

What I find most interesting about this article is how it was put together in terms of what the journalist chose to include and what that indicates about the state of discussions around cyber-bullying. Leishman framed her questions about the degree of harm caused by cyber-bullying to imply that victims should develop a thicker skin or avoid the situation. This suggests that, even in 2006, discussions were already focusing on the tensions between rights—particularly free speech, protection and participation. David's right to protection and to participation is in conflict with the bully's right to free speech and participation. While the tensions are laid out, there is little discussion of how to manage those tensions and balance the rights of individuals. It is also clear that freedom of speech is a highly charged topic and one that is easily triggered by cyber-bullying.

The second article also focused on issues around free speech and participation (*Father: School Too Harsh on Son for Online Remarks*, 2007). The incident that triggered this article involved five grade eight students who were suspended and not allowed to take part in a year-end trip to Montreal because of comments that they had posted on Facebook. In the article David Koch, the father of one of the suspended students, is quoted as saying that the school had gone too far in punishing the students and that he had concerns about free speech and boundary issues. While Mr. Koch agrees that his son's comments were inappropriate, he feels that his age should be taken into consideration as he describes his son as being only fourteen years old. He also indicated that he felt that the school had crossed a boundary and was addressing an issue that occurred in his home, as his son posted the comments from the home computer. He contends that as the incident was not on school grounds, not on school equipment, and not during a school event the incident should fall within parental bounds and not within the school's jurisdiction. Mr. Koch has even gone as far as to claim that when the school looked at his son's Facebook comments, they were invading his property since the comments originated from his home. Education Minister Kathleen Winn is quoted in the article as saying that students need help in understanding what is public and what is private when the Internet is involved. She also indicates that students need help in understanding these new technologies and how rules apply to the new technologies. The article provides brief summaries of other incidents in Ontario and Quebec in which students have been suspended for posting inappropriate comments on the Internet. It concludes with another quote, "You don't get a free pass on the Internet" that is attributed to a school board official.

While these two articles provide clear evidence that freedom of speech, personal security, and protection as well as boundaries are important issues that engage the public, they do not provide much insight into how these discussions are likely to evolve. While these articles were available on the Internet, they did not allow the option for the electronic posting of responses to the articles. An examination of online interactive media reports provides a better picture of how these issues are being engaged and the flow of discussions relating to these issues.

In cyber-space, media is less static and more interactive in many ways. Blogs and chat groups can take up information from the media and other sources and continue discussions that originated in the article or branch off in some new direction with the information. Zetter (2007b) discusses how the Internet can also act as a vehicle to express outrage through blogs. She reported on how an individual who was outraged by the Megan Meier case figured out that Lori Drew was the individual that the newspapers articles were identifying as the 'woman' involved. She posted Drew's identity and involvement in the MySpace hoax. Other individuals on the Internet took things farther by tracking down more information including her husband's name, the address and phone number of the family's home, cell phone number, the name of the family's advertising company, and contact information for their clients (Zetter, 2007a). The comments that were posted in response to the article were extensive and posted over a long period of time, from November 15, 2007 and continued until the writing of this article, January 2009. The comments reflect extreme opinions on both sides: some contributors trying to diffuse the situation and others being accused of creating an internet lynch mob. It is also interesting that many of the contributors use colourful or derogatory language and engage in accusations directed at both the Drews and the Meiers. There is a lot of talk about blame and responsibility, with Lori Drew being held responsible for her alleged actions on the Internet, and the Meiers being held responsible for Megan's state of mind as well as for leaving her alone when she was upset.

There are a number of other media articles about the Megan Meier incident that also allow posts in response. Two articles from a St. Louis media outlet report on an upcoming court response to a motion to dismiss charges against Lori Drew, and then about its delay (Ratcliffe, 2009a and b). The four comments following the second article were somewhat questionable when considered against the media outlet's commenting guidelines. The guidelines ask those who choose to comment to be "civil, smart, on-topic and free from profanity. Don't say anything you wouldn't want your mother to read!" (Ratcliffe, 2009b). While all but one comment could be considered to be 'on-topic' the comments either cast aspersions or made judgments about others. In response to the first article, there were 22 comments. While some were questionable with regard to the paper's purported guidelines, there was more engagement with the issues, including discussions around blame, the victim's mental health history, and whether or not the case should have gone to trial (Ratcliffe, 2009a). There were mixed opinions on the case going to trial: some individuals being of the opinion that there are no appropriate laws for the case and thus it should not go to trial and others agreeing with the lack of laws but arguing that loopholes should be found to litigate anyway.

One media article about a new law introduced in Dardenne Prairie that makes internet harassment a misdemeanor triggered 32 posts. These primarily discussed the notion of responsibility in connection with the Megan Meier's case (Michels, 2007). Most of the posts talked about holding people accountable for their internet actions (i.e., Lori Drew should be punished). They also reflected the belief that parents need to take responsibility for supervising their children's online activities. There were also comments that supported free speech and the dangers of overriding First Amendment provisions because someone's feeling are hurt by comments on the Internet. Another media article related to the Meier's case drew 100 posted comments, including reactions focusing on responsibility, freedom of speech, and children's safety on-line (Michels, 2008a). An article reporting on

Ashley Grills talking about her role in the MySpace hoax that targeted Megan Meier's (Brady, 2008) also attracted numerous posts. The 120 posts that responded to Brady's article primarily focused on responsibility with particular emphasis on the responsibility of the web service provider and parents.

An editorial in the *Los Angles Times* claims that the prosecutor in the Lori Drew case misused internet regulations to win her conviction (Government as cyber-bully, 2008). The internet regulations were developed and broadly written to address violations by hackers. However, they have been applied to this case through a claim that Lori Drew's use of MySpace to create a fake profile to purposefully target Megan Meier's constitutes 'unauthorized access,' since MySpace's terms of service do not allow users to use fake names or post abusive comments. The editorial cautions against the emotional need to punish and the possibility that this use of internet regulations could criminalize what millions of internet users do every day. The editorial attracted 51 comments, and there are a number of themes that can be identified in the resulting discussion through the posts.

One prominent component of the discussion was whether or not the government was justified in using whatever means it had to bring Lori Drew to trial. Many posters supported this position, accusing the editorial of taking an anti-government, pro-defendant position. Others took issue with it by arguing that there were state laws that should have addressed what happened or by agreeing with the editorial that the government had overstepped its authority in this case. In terms of discussions about responsibility, many postings argued that Lori Drew should be held accountable for her actions, while others suggested that MySpace needs to monitor its site more effectively. Some posts argued that it was the responsibility of parents to monitor their children's online activities. Finally a few comments were made about Megan's responsibility for her actions in logging onto the computer and reading the comments as well as in deciding to take her own life.

Another media article that argued against the prosecutor's use of the law (Magrid, 2008) elicited similar comments to its content. The postings included derogatory comments directed at Lori Drew as well as several emotional calls for justice and punishment. In terms of responsibility, there was some discussion around Lori Drew's responsibility, that of Megan Meier's parents and that of Megan herself. There was also support for the use of the law in this case as well as a minority who disagreed that it should be applied. What was different in this article was that the journalist called for an educational campaign, an aspect of the article that was not picked up on in any of the posts except one that stated, "Do you really think that spending money on an educational campaign will make a difference? NOOOOO. What does make a difference though is throwing these people in jail. What more education does anyone need?

While some journalists have argued that the use of the 'hacker' laws to prosecute Lori Drew was a misuse of the law that will have serious implications for all internet users, trial lawyer Nick Ackerman (2008) disagrees. He has argued that just because the Lori Drew case is the first time the statute has been applied to cyber-bullying that does not make it a misuse of the law. Drew was accused of violating MySpace's terms of service, a charge that has been pursued under the statute in the past. According to Ackerman, the main criticisms have been that the law was written with the intention of only prosecuting hackers and that the use of the law in the Lori Drew case puts everyone who lies on the Internet at risk of prosecution. He sees these criticisms as unfounded because he contends that the statute was not just designed with hackers in mind but was written more broadly to cover computer crimes. Furthermore, prosecutors have neither the time nor the inclination to go after individuals for smaller indiscretions such as lying about their age or name on the Internet. He argues that the case has more implications for web site providers as they need to be concerned about whether or not their terms of service provide enough protection for themselves in terms of liability and for their users.

US District Judge George Wu, the presiding judge in the Lori Drew case, disagrees with the position taken by Ackerman and that of the prosecutors in the case as he did have concerns about what he termed as the criminalization of breach of contract (Zetter, 2009). His concerns about the legalities of using the 'hacker' laws to prosecute Lori Drew were significant enough to result in his overturning of the guilty verdict returned by the jury. The jury found Drew guilty on three misdemeanor counts but failed to find her guilty on the four possible felony counts of unauthorized computer access. Drew is now officially acquitted of all charges. In his written ruling, Judge Wu applied the "void for vagueness doctrine" which specifies that if a person of ordinary intelligence cannot establish to whom the law applies, what type of conduct is prohibited, or the type of punishment that will be applied than the law is to be considered constitutionally vague. He concluded that the application of the My Space terms of service as a criminal breach would afford too much discretion to law enforcement and not enough notice to individuals who use the Internet. As a reasonably intelligent individual would not be able to ascertain when an action would be criminal under the terms of service, it is a constitutionally vague law that cannot be applied in this case. Legal experts commenting on the ruling have suggested that Wu was concerned about expanding the definition of what is considered criminal behaviour on the internet to include violating terms of agreement by service providers (McCarthy & Michels, 2009). Wu has also been quoted as stating that he was concerned that upholding the jury's decision would allow a website owner to determine criminal behaviour (Zetter, 2009) as the terms of service for individual providers would provide the definition of criminal behaviour on the internet. He also indicated that had Drew been convicted of the felonies, he would have upheld the jury's finding, but he was troubled by the misdemeanor charges given the vague wording of the Computer Fraud and Abuse Act (McCarthy & Michels, 2009; Zetter, 2009).

Other media articles have addressed the case against Lori Drew from the perspective of First Amendment rights. Holliday (2007) discussed Lori Drew's trial and the proposed Megan Meier Cyberbullying Prevention Act that is still sitting in a congressional subcommittee awaiting approval. According to Holliday, free-speech advocates have questioned the constitutionality of legislation to control cyber-bullying that has emerged in various states as well as the current bill in the congressional sub-committee. Some have identified such legislation as being the "censorship of free speech under the guise of protecting children." Similarly, in another article Christensen (2008) claims that cyber-bullying legislation could be a 'slippery slope' and that free speech is not subjective. She worries about how the wording of the proposed Megan Meier Cyberbullying Prevention Act will be interpreted. The proposed act defines punishable behaviour as being "severe, repeated and hostile behaviour." Christensen agrees with Holliday that the constitutionality of such legislation remains in question, arguing that the First Amendment protects all speech and does not discriminate between 'good' or 'bad' speech. She goes further by stating that the nature of the Internet and the illusion of anonymity in cyberspace, harassment or 'cyber-bullying' is to be expected. She advocates that a better approach would be to educate young people to not take cruel internet messages seriously.

Another media article addressed the problem of cruel internet messages from a different perspective. Guernsey (2003) compares teenage gossip as expressed verbally or through messages on the bathroom wall and teenage gossip in its electronic expression through blogs, e-mail, and social networking sites. She discusses sites like ratemyteacher.com, that allow students to post ratings about their teachers; the now defunct schoolscandals.com; and other similar sites that allow students to post anonymous messages. While students can post rebuttals and engage in heated discussions about the statements that are made, Guernsey argues that messages on the Internet have an exponentially greater impact than rumors on the bathroom wall. The administrators of such sites have no liability for on-line comments as long as they make no attempt to manage or edit the comments. A few, like ratemyteacher.com and ratemyprofessor.com, have added an option that allows the teacher to join in the conversation or post a rebuttal.

Recently, the BBC opened a forum on cyber-bullying and asked young people to post comments. The young people who participated ranged in age from ten to thirteen years old and were predominantly from England. While their posts were brief, the comments held interesting similarities to some of the themes that appeared in the electronic responses to articles about Lori Drew. The youth talked about how cyber-bullying was worse than physical or verbal bullying because there was no escape from it. Some also supported the need to inform parents or school officials about the cyber-bullying. These posts also recommended saving the texts or messages as proof of victimization, not to let the comments get to them, and not to give cell numbers or other information. There were also indirect references to responsibility, as many referred to cyber-perpetrators in negative terms. There were no posts in support of free speech or the bully's actions. However, there were posts suggesting that the victim was responsible for indiscriminately handing out their cell number or suggesting the victim was taking everything too seriously and letting the comments 'get to them.'

From these reviews of media articles and response forums, we begin to see how stakeholders are discussing boundaries and responsibility around cyber-bullying in various ways. Comments of young people quoted in media accounts and forums provide insights into their take on cyber-bullying as well as those of other stakeholders such as educators, parents, and concerned community members. There are concerns about freedom of speech and protecting the individual's security and safety from attacks, the boundaries or jurisdictions in terms of what falls under the purview of schools and what should be within the parental domain and responsibility. It is also clear that these discussions have not progressed very far nor have they introduced the idea of education in much detail at all. There has been a shifting over the past few years to more emphasis on punishment and expanding the reach of schools as evidenced by the increase in articles about schools addressing cyber-bullying as well as the push for and introduction of legislation targeting cyber-bullying.

CONCLUSION

In this chapter, I have argued that it is vitally important to engage in discussions about the core issues associated with cyber-bullying, namely: free speech in balance with personal security, boundaries (i.e., jurisdiction, public/private, cyberspace/physical space) and responsibilities. Such discussions are essential to educating ourselves and our children to be active and respectful internet citizens. In order to assess past and current state of these discussions, this chapter focused on media articles and associated electronic comments to provide a glimpse of how these discussions are evolving. It is apparent that there is heavy coverage of cyber-bullying with striking similarities in how cyber-bullying occurs within various countries. These include the use of social networking sites to target students and teachers either through direct attacks or the use of fake accounts as well as the tendency for cyber-bullying to blur the lines between virtual and physical space resulting in physical attacks and/or victims committing suicide or attempting to commit suicide to escape from the cyber-bullying. The examination of cyber-bullying resources as reported through the media underscored the importance of examining how the media chooses to report and discuss resources as well as identifying the limited coverage that social networking sites received when unveiling their new policies and procedures to address safety and abuse issues.

The chapter then shifted to an examination of how the media and other stakeholders talk about free speech, protection, boundaries, and responsibilities within media articles and on-line forums. While stakeholders discuss these core issues in various ways, it became clear that the discussions were somewhat limited and included little focus on educational approaches. The discussions have shifted over time, with increasing emphasis on extending the reach and power of the schools to address cyber-bullying as well as an increase in legislation targeting cyber-bullying. High profile cases have stimulated engagement with the issues, but the discussions tend to be reactive and have a punitive focus, with little consideration given to proactive or educational approaches. There are a number of issues such as young people's ability to understand the consequences of their virtual acts and educational advances that could be proactively applied to address cyber-bullying.

In conclusion, cyber-bullying will continue to be an issue until society chooses to engage fully in discussions about the issues of boundaries and responsibility. Currently the discussion on these issues is limited in scope, tending to focus on reacting to incidents and punishing perpetrators. There has been some movement towards more proactive approaches and clarifying boundaries through school policies and new legislation, but these actions have not fully engaged the issues. Social norms pertaining to the Internet are still evolving and could be shaped by strong educational programming that teaches students to consider others and the rights and responsibilities associated with it. Young people need to be guided in establishing an understanding of the long-term consequences of their virtual actions both for themselves and for others. Many youth still perceive some of their virtual acts as jokes with minimal consequences. They are stunned when they find themselves facing serious consequences. If we are unable to teach individuals how to navigate the boundaries between what is public and what is private and to develop an understanding of the impact that their internet actions have in the real world, we will continue to read about court cases that seek to define the boundaries between free speech and public attack or persecution of another individual as well as tragic news reports like that of Megan Meier.

References

Ackerman, N. (2008, December 22). Opinion: Criticism of woman's prosecution in cyberbullying case is off base. *Mercury News* (Silicon Valley, CA). Retrieved on December 23, 2008 from http://www.mercurynews.com/opinion/ci_11297835?nclick_check=1.

Alphonso, C. (2008, November 21). RCMP probe B.C. teen for Facebook's 'kick a ginger' forum. Retrieved on November 25 from Globe and Mail website.http://www.theglobeandmail.com/servlet/story/RTGAM.20081121.wredhead1122/BNStory/National/home.

Andrew's story of an imposter profile on MySpace (2008, October). Retrieved on November 15, 2008 from SafeWave website. http://www.safewave.org/index.php?option=com_content&task=view&id=337&Itemid=57.

Ayres, C. (2008, November 27). 'MySpace' bully Lori Drew escapes felony charge over suicide of Megan Meier. *TimesONLINE* (Los Angeles, CA). Retrieved on November 30, 2008 from http://technology.timesonline.co.uk/tol/news/ tech_and_web/the_web/article5246833.ece.

BBC News (2008, February 18). Bebo bully victim in suicide bid. *BBC News* (London, England). Retrieved on October 28, 2008 from http://news.bbc.co.uk/2/hi/uk_news/england/sussex/7251384.stm

Belsey, B. (2005). Cyberbullying: An emerging threat to the "always on" generation. Retrieved on March 14, 2007 from Bullying.org Canada website. http://www.bullying.org.

Bid to tackle the problem of cyber bullying. (2008, December 16). *Evening Star* (Ipswitch, England). Retrieved on December 23, 2008 from http://www.eveningstar.co.uk/content/eveningstar/news/story.aspx?brand=ESTOnline&category=News&tBrand=ESTOnline&tCategory=News&itemid=IPED15%20Dec%202008%2010%3A52%3A52%3A157.

Bill to cover internet abuses (2007, April 17). Retrieved on October 20 from *Globe and Mail* website. http://www.theglobeandmail.com/servlet/story/RTGAM.20070417.wbullying17/BNStory/Technology/Ontario/.

Brady, J. (2008, April 1). Exclusive: Teen talks about her role in web hoax that led to suicide. *ABC News* (New York, NY). Retrieved on October 12, 2008 from http://abcnews.go.com/GMA/story?id=4560582&page=1.

Burns, D. (2008, December 9). Mediacom: How parents can keep kids' net use safe and smart. *Daily Times Herald* (Carroll, IA). Retrieved on December 12 from http://www.carrollpaper.com/main.asp?SectionID=1&SubSectionID=1&ArticleID=7113&TM=52632.61

Celizic, M. (2009, March 6). Her teen committed suicide over 'sexting.' *Today Show* (New York, NY).

Chaker, A. (2007, January 24). Schools act to short-circuit spread of 'cyber-bullying.' *The Wall Street Journal* (New York, NY). Retrieved on October 20, 2008 from http://online.wsj.com/public/article/SB116960763498685883-g2Qbz2.

Charles, B. (2009, January 4). Cyber bullies target local boy. *The Signal* (San Clarita Valley, CA). Retrieved on January 5, 2009 from http://www.the-signal.com/news/article/7538/

Children made aware of the dangers of 'cyber bullying.' (2008, December 22). *Lytham Today* (Lancashire, England).Retrieved on December 23, from http://www.lythamstannesexpress.co.uk/lytham-news/Children-made-aware-of-dangers.4813700.jp

Choi, J. (2009, January 12). Parents, protect your kids. *Times Beacon Record* (Huntington, NY). Retrieved on January 14 from http://www.thetimesofhuntington.com/Articles-i-2009–01–08–77671.112114_Parents_protect_your_kids.html.

Christensen, M. (2008, December 1). Freedom of speech isn't subjective. Retrieved on December 10, 2008 from *The Rebel Yell* website. http://unlvrebelyell.com/2008/12/01/freedom-of-speech-isnt-subjective/.

Chug, K. (2009, January 15). Cyber bullying provokes street attack. *The Nelson Mail* (Wellington, New Zealand). Retrieved in January 15 from http://www.stuff.co.nz/4819453a11.html

CTV.ca News Staff (2006, April 27). Online threats result in charges for two teens. *CTV Toronto* (Toronto, ON). Retrieved on July 15, 2007 from file:///Users/dawnzinga/Documents/ Cyber%20 Media/Online%20threats%20result%20in%20charges%20for%20two%20teens. webarchive.

Currier, J. (2008, December 17). New cyber-bullying law is being used in St. Louis. *St. Louis Post-Dispatch* (St. Louis, MO). Retrieved on December 20, 2008 from http://www.stltoday. com/stltoday/news/stories.nsf/stcharles/story/A5F18B865AE42BB6862575220015CFA2? OpenDocument.

Cyber-bullying (2007, April 19). *Welland Tribune* (Welland, On). Retrieved on May 15, 2007 from http://www.wellandtribune.ca/webapp/sitepages/printable.asp?paper=...welland tribune.ca &contentID=492482&annewspapername=Welland+Tribune.

Cyber-bullying common among Japan's children (2008, April 18). *Mail & Guardian Online* (Johannesburg, South Africa). Retrieved on October 20, 2008 from http://www.mg.co.za/ article/2008–04–16-cyberbullying-common-among-japans-children.

Cyber-bullying law introduced at Queen's Park. (2007, April 17). Retrieved on May 15, 2007 from CTV Toronto website. http://toronto.ctv.ca/servlet/an/local/CTVNews/20070416/ cyberbullying_legislation_070417/20070416?hub=TorontoHome.

Cyber-bullying law introduced in Ontario. (2007, April 16). Retrieved on May 15, 2007 from *CityNews* website. http://www.citynews.ca/news/news_9878.aspx.

CYBERCOPS software helps students stay safe on-line. (2005, January 21). Retrieved November 15, 2008 from Ontario Newsroom—Hosted by CNW Group Ltd. Website. http://ogov.newswire. ca/ontario/GPOE/2005/01/21/c5375.html?lmatch=&lang=_e.html

Czech move to stop cyber-bullying (2008, December 30). *BBC News* (London, England). Retrieved on January 2, 2008 from http://news.bbc.co.uk/go/pr/fr/-/2/hi/europe/7804617.stm.

Duffy, M. (2006, March 19). A Dad's encounter with the vortex of Facebook. *Time* (New York, NY). Retrieved on October 20, 2008 from http://www.time.com/time/printout/0,8816,1174704,00. html.

Father: School too harsh on son for online remarks (2007, April 30). *CTV Toronto* (Toronto, ON). Retrieved on May 15, 2007 from http://www.ctv.ca/servlet/ArticleNews/story/CTVNews /20070430/facebook_punishment_070430/20070430?hub=CTVNewsAt11.

First research-based cyber bullying awareness curriculum launched in partnership with leading education organizations. (2007) Retrieved January 12, 2009 from *PR Newswire* Website. http://www.itnewsonline.com/showprnstory.php?storyid=29150.

Florida boy's suicide live on the web. (2008, November 21). *BBC News* (London, England) Retrieved on November 24, 2008 from http://news.bbc.co.uk/2/hi/americas/7743214.stm.

Flowers, J. (2006, October 19). Cyber-bullying hits community. *Addison Independent* (Middlebury, VT). Retrieved on October 20, 2008 from http://www.addisonindependent.com/print/280.

Fowler, J. (2008, January 15). Children plagued by cyber bullies. *BBC News* (London, England). Retrieved on November 15, 2008 from http://news.bbc.co.uk/2/hi/technology/ 7197023. stm.

Gardham, G. (2008). Facebook and Bebo used to bully teachers. The Telegraph (London, England). Retrieved on August 1, 2008 from http://www.telegraph.co.uk/scienceandtechnology/3357661/ Facebook-and-Bebo-used-to-bully-teachers.html

Goldman, R. (2007, November 17). How online plots lead to real world crimes. *ABC News* (New York, NY). Retrieved on October 20, 2008 from http://abcnews.go.com/Technology/ Story?id=3860920&page=1.

Government as cyber-bully (2008, December 3). *Los Angeles Times* (Los Angeles, CA). Retrieved on December 15, 2008 from http://www.latimes.com/news/opinion/ editorials/la-ed-myspace3-2008dec03,0,6238729.story.

Group calls on Obama to appoint internet safety specialist (2008, December 11). Retrieved on December 15 from SmartBrief website. http://www.smartbrief.com/news/cec/storyDetails. jsp ?issueid=49EA...9-81DD-142540E3CFCC&copyid=77DA4B2A-8995-4533-A97C-.

Guernsey, L. (2003, May 8). Telling tales out of school. *The New York Times* (New York, NY). Retrieved on October 20, 2008 from http://query.nytimes.com/gst/fullpage.html?res =9D0 4E2DC163FF93BA35756C0A9659C8B63&sec=&spon=&pagewanted=1.

Gunn, A. (2008, December 12). Group seeks kids' online safety in the White House. Retrieved on December 15 from BetaNews website. http://www.betanews.com/article/Group_seeks_ kids_online_safety_in_the_White_House/1229132038.

Ha, T. T. (2003, July 23). Parents file lawsuit over Star Wars kid video. *Globe and Mail* (Toronto, On). Retrieved on October 20, 2008 from http://www.theglobeandmail.com/servlet/ story/ RTGAM.20030723. gtuboyyn/BNStory/Technology/?query=star+wars+kid/.

Ha, T. T. (2006, April 7). 'Star Wars Kid' cuts a deal with his tormentors. *Globe and Mail* (Toronto, On). Retrieved on October 20, 2008 from http://www.theglobeandmail.com/ servlet/story/ RTGAM.20060407.wxstarwars07/BNStory/National/home.

Hirsch, J. (2006, May). Is student blogging the new social disease? *The School Administrator* (Arlington, VA). Retrieved on October 20, 2008 from http://www.aasa.org/publications/ saarticledetail.cfm?ItemNumber=6071

Holliday, C. (2007, November 20). MySpace-hoax trial shine light on federal cyber-bullying bill. Retrieved on December 10, 2008 from First Amendment Center website. http://www. firstamendmentcenter.org/news.aspx?id=20905.

Huffstutter, P. J. (2007, November 26). Girl's suicide after online chats leaves a town in shock. *Los Angeles Times* (Los Angeles, CA). Retrieved on November 29, 2008 from http://www. stumbleupon.com/toolbar/#topic=Cyberculture&url=http%253A%252F%252Fwww.boston. com%252Fbusiness%252Ftechnology%252Farticles%252F2007%252F11%252F26%252Fgi rls_suicide_after_online_chats_leaves_a_town_in_shock%252F.

Jacobson, S. (2009, January 13). Club gives students a chance to argue. *Payson Roundup* (Payson, AZ). Retrieved on January 15, 2009 from http://www.paysonroundup.com/news/2009/jan/13/ club_gives_students_chance_argue/

J.S. v. Blue Mountain School District, WL 954245 (M.D. Pa. 2008).

Judge delays ruling on mistrial in 'cyber-bullying' case. (2008, November 24). *KTLA News* (Los Angeles, CA). Retrieved on November 25, 2008 from http://www.ktla.com/ landing_ news/?Judge-Delays-Ruling-on-Mistrial-in cyber=1&blockID= 142035 &feed ID=171.

Kiyani (2008, June 12). Teenager commits suicide after being bullied on Bebo. *Intology-Intelligent Technology News* (Retrieved on October 20, 2008 from http://www.intology.com/computers-internet/teenager-commits-suicide-after-being-cyberbullied-on-bebo/

Kravets, D. (2008, December 9). Student who created Facebook group critical of teacher sues high school over suspension. Retrieved on October 20, 2008 from Wired Blog Network website. http://blog.wired.com/27bstroke6/2008/12/us-student-inte.html.

Kubota, Y. (2007, November 11). Cyber bullying bedevils Japan. *Reuters.* Retrieved on October 20, 2008 from http://www.reuters.com/article/internetNews/ idUST1761020071112?sp=true.

Kurutz, D. R. (2008, December 16). Anti-bullying programs aim to teach students empathy. *Pittsburgh Tribune-Review* (Pittsburgh, PA). Retrieved on December 23, 2008 from http://www.pittsburghtrib/news/today/s_603198.html.

Labbe, B. (2008, December 24). Schools get Verizon grant to aid internet safety. *The Huntsville Times* (Huntsville, AL). Retrieved on December 30, 2008 from http://www.al.com/news/huntsvilletimes/madison.ssf?/base/news/1230113797260760.xml&coll=1.

Lampert, A. (2006a, March 29). High school was time of torment. *The Gazette* (Don Mills, ON). Retrieved on October 20, 2008 from http://www.canada.com/montrealgazette/ news/montreal/story.html?id=6d98e618-702d-4f85-9a3e-dc1c06ada98c&k=68633.

Lampert, A. (2006b, April 8). Star Wars kid settles lawsuit. *Global TV Quebec* (Montreal, Quebec). Retrieved on October 15, 2008 from http://www.canada.com/globaltv/quebec/ news/story.html?id=e93a2a11-11c9-4d97-82ed-221d6cfa1ef2&k=14313.

LaVallee, A. (2009, July 2). Cyberbullying report opposes regulation. *The Wall Street Journal* (New York, NY). Retrieved on July 29, 2009 from http://blogs.wsj.com/digits/2009/07/02/ cyberbullying-report-opposes-regulation/.

Layshock v. Hermitage Sch. Dist., 496 F. Supp. 2d 587 (W.D. Pa. 2007).

Leishman, J. (2005, March). Cyber-bullying. *CBC News* (Toronto, ON). Retrieved on October 20, 2008 from http://www.cbc.ca/news/background/bullying/cyber_bullying.html.

Levy, M. (2008, November, 29). TV project will feature teenager's bid to beat cyber bullies. *Gazette Live* (Middlesborough, England) Http://www.gazettelive.co.uk/news/teesside-news/2008/11/29/ tv-project-will-feature-teenager-s-bid-to-beat-cyber-bullies-84229-223671138/

Li, Q. (2006). Cyberbullying in schools: A research of gender differences. *School Psychology International, 27*, 157–170.

MacDonald, J.(2007). Family of teen who took her own life pushing lawmakers for anti-bullying ordinance. Wave 3 (Louisville, KY). Retrieved on November 22, 2008 from http://www.wave3.com/Global/story.asp?S=6029598&nav=0RZF.

Magrid, L. MySpace prosecutors used wrong law. Retrieved on December 15, 2008 from *CBS News* Website. http://www.cbsnews.com/stories/2008/12/09/opinion/main4656719.shtml.

Makino, C. (2007, March 26) Bullying in Japan leads to student suicides. *News VOA.com* (Washington, DC). Retrieved on October 20, 2008 from http://www.voanews.com/english/ archive/2007-03/2007-03-26-voa14.cfm.

Mayo, M. (2008, December 14). Cyber-bullying or free speech? Now it's a federal case. *Sun Sentinel* (Orlando, FL). Retrieved on October 20, 2008 from http://www.sun-sentinel.com/news/ columnists/sfl-flbmayocol1214sbdec14,0,3657653.column.

McCarthy, T. & Michels, S. (2009, July 2). Lori Drew MySpace hoax conviction thrown out. *ABC News* (New York, NY). Retrieved on July 29, 2009 from http://abcnews.go.com/TheLaw/ story?id=7977226&page=1

McIntosh, E. (2008, December 11). Is the internet safe for children? *The News* (Salem, AR). Retrieved on January 8, 2009 from http://www.areawidenews.com/story/1484986.html.

Mead, T. (2008, December 23) 'Protecting Kids Online' video wins prestigious award. *PR Newswire*. Retrieved on December 23, 2008 from http://news.prnewswire.com/Display ReleaseContent. aspx?ACCT=104&story=/www/story/12–23–2008/004946548&edate

Meadows, R. (2008, December 30). Cracking down on bullying. Retrieved from Lancaster Online website. http://articles.lancasteronline.com/local/4/231971.

Mears, B. (2007, June 26). "Bong Hits 4 Jesus" case limits student rights. *CNN* (Washington, DC). Retrieved on October 20, 2008 from http://www.cnn.com/2007/LAW/06/25/free.speech/.

Menendez, R. (2009, May 13). Keeping children and teens safe online: Sen. Menendez, Rep. Wasserman Schultz propose national grant program from internet and wireless safety education. Press Release from the Office of Senator Menendez (Newark, NJ). Retrieved on July 29, 2009 from http://menendez.senate.gov/newsroom/record.cfm?id=312958.

Michael, J. (2008, December 9). Booklet aims to tackle cyberbullying. *The Irish Times* (Dublin, Ireland). Retrieved on December 12, 2008 from http://www.irishtimes.com/ newspaper/ breaking/2008/1209/breaking68.html.

Michels, S. (2007, November 22). Town rules internet harassment a crime. *ABC News* (New York, NY). Retrieved on November 20, 2008 from http://abcnews.go.com/TheLaw/story?id= 3888606&page=1.

Michels, S. (2008a, November 20). Teen's mom testifies in MySpace hoax trial. *ABC News* (New York, NY). Retrieved on November 20, 2008 from http://abcnews.go.com/ TheLaw/ story?id=6297275&page=1.

Michels, S. (2008b, December 24). Prosecutors bringing charges under law inspired by Megan Meier suicide. *ABC News* (New York, NY). Retrieved on December 27, 2008 from http:// abcnews.go.com/TheLaw/story?id=6520260&page=1.

Mills, B. (2008, December 7). Cyber suicide becoming more common. *Naples Daily News* (Naples, FL). Retrieved on December 15, 2008 from http://www.naplesnews.com/news/ 2008/dec/07/ cyber-suicide-becoming-more-common/.

Minihan, M. (2008, December 17). New guide warns parents of bullying by mobile phone. *The Irish Times* (Dublin, Ireland). Retrieved on December 18, 2008 from http://www.irishtimes. com/newspaper/ireland/2008/1217/1229035813621.html.

Molai, N. (2009, January 11). New FBI Centre in Omaha aims to combat cyber crimes. KPTM 42 (Omaha, NE) Retrieved on January 14, 2009 from http://www.kptm.com/Global/story. asp?S=9654633.

Mom fighting to end cyber abuse (2009, May 15). AOL News (New York, NY). Retrieved on July 29, 2009 from http://news.aol.com/article/cyber-abuse-sexting-jessica-logan/486080.

Morse et al. v. Frederick (2007, March 19). Retrieved on October 20, 2008 from http://caselaw. lp.findlaw.com/scripts/getcase.pl?court=US&vol=000&invol=06–278.

Mother convicted in internet suicide case. (2007, November 26). *KTLA News* (Los Angeles, CA). Retrieved on November 25, 2008 from http://www.ktla.com/ landing_news/?MySpace-Cyber-Bullying-Case-Goes-to-Jury=1&block ID=142 035&feedID=171.

Murphy, R. (2007, November 8). A MySpace lesson. WHAS 11 (Louisville, KY). Retrieved on October 20, 2008 from http://www.whas11.com/news/murphy/stories/110707whasmjd To pJourneyToTheCenterOfMySpace.1ea08a6ed.html.

Nikkhah, R. & Henry, J. (2009, January 11). Facebook bullying students 'should be expelled.' *The Telegraph* (London, England). Retrieved on January 12, 2009 from *http://www.telegraph. co.uk/scienceandtechnology/technology/facebook/4214234/Facebook-bullying-students-should-be-expelled.html*

Niswander, A. (2009, January 14). Programs help parents combat bullying in school. *Hudson Hub-Times* (Ravenna, OH). Retrieved on January 14, 2009 from http://www.hudsonhubtimes. com/news/article/4504321.

O'Brien, C. (2008, December 5). Technology firms determined to beat mobile bullying. . *The Irish Times* (Dublin, Ireland). Retrieved on December 9, 2008 from http://www.irishtimes.com/ newspaper/finance/2008/1205/1228337441045.html.

O'Donoghue, S. (2009, January 3). Concerns raised over cyberbullying in Harts. *The Lincoln Journal* (Hamlin, WV). Retrieved on January 4, 2009 from http://www.lincolnjournalinc. com/ default.asp?sourceid=&smenu=1&tw...ed=&rebath=&subname=&pform=&sc=218 6&hn=lincolnjournalinc&he=.com.

Niswander, A. (2009, January 14). Programs help parents combat bullying in school. *Hudson Hub-Times* (Ravenna, OH). Retrieved on January 14, 2009 from http://www.hudsonhubtimes. com/news/article/4504321.

Papprill, R. (2008, December 10). Team approach urged to stop cyber bullying. *Eastern Courier* (Auckland, NZ). Retrieved on December 15, 2008 from http://www.stuff.co.nz/stuff/sundaystartimes/ auckland/4787532a22395.html.

Parents, schools unite against 'cyber bullying.' (2003, April 23). *eSchool News Online* (Bethesda, MD). Retrieved on October 15, 2008 from http://www.eschoolnews.com/news/ showStory. cfm?ArticleID=4369

Patchin, J. W. & Hinduja, S. (2006). Bullies move beyond the school yard: A preliminary look at cyberbullying. *Youth Violence and Juvenile Justice, 4*, 148–169.

Patrick, R., Hunn, D. & Currier, J. (2008, November 20). Woman convicted of lesser charges in cyber-bullying case. *PHYSORG.COM*. Retrieved on November 22 from http://www.physorg. com/news147002322.html.

Preston, P. (2008, December 10). Cyberbullying. KULR-8 Television (Billings, Montana). Retrieved on December 15 from http://www.kulr8.com/news/wyoming/35941749.html.

Price, R. (2008, June 20). How cyber-bullies drove my daughter to commit suicide. *Daily Mail Online* (London, England) Retrieved on October 15, 2008 from http://www.daily-mail.co.uk/femail/article-1027554/How-cyber-bullies-drove-daughter-commit-suicide. html?printingPage=true.

Qwest Foundation. (2008, December 15). Foundation helps teachers fight cyberbullying. *Marketwatch* (New York, NY). Retrieved on December 20, 2008 from http://www.marketwatch.com/

news/story/First-Its-Kind-Curriculum-Sponsored/story.aspx?guid=%7BEA90BA47–1F8C-
4F13–87FD-79BF94782D08%7D.

Ratcliffe, H. (2009a, January 8). Lori Drew cyber-bullying decision expected today. *St. Louis Post-
Dispatch* (St. Louis, MO). Retrieved on January 9, 2009 from http://www.stltoday.com/stltoday/
news/stories.nsf/stcharles/story/F263399A28E8A3338625753800065825?OpenDocument.

Ratcliffe, H. (2009b, January 9). Judge defers decision on dismissing Lori Drew cyber-bullying
convictions. *St. Louis Post-Dispatch* (St. Louis, MO). Retrieved on January 9, 2009 from http://
www.stltoday.com/stltoday/news/stories.nsf/stlouiscitycounty/story/ 4EE818B8839615C18
6257539001498C6?OpenDocument.

Rau, K. (2007, December 6). Gay Ajax student kills himself. XTRA! (Toronto, ON). Retrieved on
October 20, 2008 from http://www.xtra.ca/public/Toronto/Gay_Ajax_student_kills_himself-
4020.aspx.

RCMP and Canadian Teachers' Federation join forces to fight cyberbullying (2008, December 17).
Retrieved December 29, 2008 from Royal Canadian Mounted Police website. http://www.
rcmp-grc.gc.ca/news-nouvelles/2008/2008–12–17-cyber-eng.htm.

Rubenking, N. J. (2009, January 1). CyberPatrol announces free scanner, ChatGuard enhancement.
PCMAG.com (Boulder, Colorado). Retrieved on January 2, 2009 from http://www.pcmag.
com/article2/0,2817,2338642,00.asp

Rubenstein, M. H. (2009, January 5). States enact cyber-bullying legislation. Retrieved on January
6, 2009 from *Huliq News* website. http://www.huliq.com/1/75462/states-enact-cyber-bullying-
legislation.

Rusk, J. (2007, February 13). High school suspends 19 for bullying principal on website. *Globe
and Mail* (Toronto, ON). Retrieved on March 10, 2007 from http://www.theglobeandmail.
com/ servlet/story/RTGAM.20070213.wxfacebook13/BNStory/National.

Safety, education and empowerment on YouTube [Online video]. (2008). Retrieved January 15,
2009 from http://www.youtube.com/watch?v=upzjXCZtm9g

Sanchez, L. (2009, April 6). Protecting victims, preserving freedoms. *The Huffington Post* (New
York, NY). Retrieved on July 29, 2009 from http://www.huffingtonpost.com/rep-linda-sanchez/
protecting-victims-preser_b_198079.html.

Sang-Hun, C. (2008, October 12). Korean star's suicide reignites debate on web regulation. *The
New York Times* (New York, NY). Retrieved on October 20, 2008 from http://www.nytimes.
com /2008/10/13/technology/internet/13suicide.html?fta=y.

San Miguel, R. (2008, December 12). YouTube aims to curb abuse with safety center. *TechNewsWorld*
(Encino, CA) Retrieved on December 14, 2008 from http://www.technewsworld.com/
story/65491.html

Sarno, D. (2008, December 11).Youtube creates Abuse and Safety Center. *Los Angeles Times*
(Los Angeles, CA). Retrieved on December 30, 2008 from http://latimesblogs.latimes.com/
technology/2008/12/you-tube-creates.html.

Shallenberger, S. (2008, December 22). Web sites offer tools to combat cyberbullying. *Baltimore
Sun* (Baltimore, Retrieved on December 30, 2008 from http://www.baltimoresun.com/
technology/bal-bully1222,0,6881159.story

Shariff, S (2008) *Cyber-Bullying: Issues and Solutions for the School, the Classroom and the Home.*
New York: Routledge (Taylor and Francis Group).

Simms, J. (2008, November). Cyber-bullying: The new schoolyard. *Niagara Falls Review* (Niagara Falls, ON). Retrieved on December 30, 2008 from http://www.niagarafalls review.ca/ ArticleDisplay.aspx?e=1274433&auth=JANE%20SIMS,%20SUN%20MEDIA

Slater, D. (2008a, September 16). On students, MySpace and the First Amendment. *The Wall Street Journal* (New York, NY). Retrieved on October 20, 2008 from http://blogs.wsj.com/ law/2008/09/16/on-students-myspace-and-the-first-amendment.

Slater, D. (2008b, December 11). Cyberbullying & the law: Free speech's next frontier. *The Wall Street Journal* (New York, NY). Retrieved on December 15, 2008 from http://blogs.wsj.com/ law/2008/12/11/cyberbullying-the-law-free-speechs-next-frontier.

Stayton, J. (2008, February 18). Cyber bully drove schoolboy to attempt suicide. *The Argus* (Brighton, England). Retrieved on October 20, 2008 from http://www.theargus.co.uk/ news/2053716. cyber_bully_drove_schoolboy_to_attempt_suicide/

Stelter, B. (2008a, November 24). Web suicide viewed live and reaction spur a debate. The *New York Times* (New York, NY). Retrieved on November 24, 2008 from http://www.nytimes. com/2008/11/25/us/25suicides.html?fta=y.

Stelter, B. (2008b, November 27). Guilty verdict in cyberbullying case provokes many questions over online identity. *New York Times* (New York, NY). Retrieved on December 1, 2008 from http://www.nytimes.com/2008/11/28/us/28internet. html?_r=1&ref=technology.

Stover, D. (2006). Treating cyberbullying as a school violence issue. *Education Digest, 72,* 40–42.

Students suspended for 'cyber-bullying' principal. (2007, February 13). *CTV Toronto* (Toronto, ON). Retrieved on March 10, 2007 from http://toronto.ctv.ca/servlet/an/local/CTVNews /20070212/cyberbullying_suspensions_070212?hub=TorontoHome.

Surdin, A. (2009, January 1). In several states, a push to stem cyber-bullying. *Washington Post* (Washington, DC). Retrieved on January 3, 2009 from http://www.washingtonpost.com/ wp-dyn/content/article/2008/12/31/AR2008123103067.html.

Tall girl 'bullied' in chatroom. (2006, February 3). *BBC News* (London, England). Retrieved on October 12, 2008 from http://news.bbc.co.uk/2/hi/uk_news/england/leicestershire/4679190. stm.

Teens charged in protest over Facebook freedom (2007, March 23). *CTV Toronto* (Toronto, ON). Retrieved on April 2, 2007 from http://toronto.ctv.ca/servlet/an/local/CTVNews /20070323/ student_protest_070223?hub=TorontoHome.

Tinker v. Des Moines School District (1969). Retrieved on October 20, 2008 from http://case-law.lp.findlaw.com/cgi-bin/getcase.pl?navby=case&court=US&vol=393 &invol=503& pageno=506.

Wasserman, E. (2008). Warning signs: Is your child having cyber issues? *KRISTV* (Corpus Christi, TX). Retrieved on November 20, 2008 from http://www.kristv.com/Global/ story. asp?S=9522479.

Weinstein, S P. (2008, December 18). Safe driving tips for information superhighway. *Raynham Call* (Raynham, MA). Retrieved on December 20, 2008 from http://www.wickedlocal.com/ raynham/archive/x1720701527/Safe-driving-tips-for-information-superhighway.

Willard, N. (2005). An educator's guide to cyberbullying and cyberthreats: Responding to the challenge of online social aggression, threats, and distress. Retrieved on March 14, 2007 from Centre for Safe and Responsible Internet Use website. http://www.csriu.org.

Wright, R. (2008, December 27). New Year brings change to social Web sites. *The Columbia Tribune* (Columbia, MO). Retrieved on December 30, 2008 from http://www.columbiatribune.com/2008/Dec/20081227Busi003.asp.

Zetter, K. (2007a, November 15). Blog readers out anonymous adults that newspaper refused to identify—Updated. *Wired* (New York, NY). Retrieved on October 20, 2008 from http://blog.wired.com/27bstroke6/2007/11/blog-readers-ou.html.

Zetter, K. (2007b, November 21). Cyberbullying suicide stokes internet fury machine. *Wired* (New York, NY). Retrieved on October 20, 2008 from http://www.wired.com/politics/ onlinerights/ news/2007/11/vigilante_justice.

Zetter, K.(2009, July 2). Judge acquits Lori Drew in cyberbullying case, overrules jury. *Wired* (New York, NY). Retrieved on July 29, 2009 from http://www.wired.com/threatlevel /2009/07/ drew_court/.

Legal Issues

6 · Legal Issues Related to Cyber-bullying

Jacqueline A. Stefkovich
Emily R. Crawford
Mark P. Murphy

INTRODUCTION

Although technology has had a profoundly positive impact on the way teachers teach and students learn, these technological innovations also present challenges. While the positive effect technology has on curriculum is well documented, it is less common to find sources that reference its negative influence on student life. Cyber-bullying—a modern day adaptation of traditional bullying that uses technology to harass, demean, or threaten an individual or group of students—undermines both school climate and the safe and supportive atmosphere that fosters student growth (Smith et al., 2008; Shariff & Johnny, 2007; National Crime Prevention Council, 2008). It manifests itself within schools in a variety of ways. Social networking sites such as MySpace.com and Facebook.com, for instance, have provided a forum for students to engage one another as friends or enemies. Text and picture messaging can be an expedient means of harmless dialogue, or they can circulate damaging words and images that have a lasting impact on the daily operation of schools. Email, instant messaging, and Internet blogs can serve the educational process in creative and stimulating ways, or they can uproot the process of education altogether. The misuse of technology in recent years has threatened school climate and given rise to a host of legal concerns for school authorities.

This chapter will examine legal issues relative to cyber-bullying in public schools; it will also argue that there are limitations to the law which administrators should be aware of when disciplining students engaged in cyber-bullying. The concluding argument will stress the need for educators' moral awareness as they maintain safe schools for all students and address practical implications of decision making related to cyber-bullying.

CYBER-BULLYING IN SCHOOLS

With the advent of cyber technology and the posting of threatening messages to personal web sites and blogs, educators have been forced to balance the rights of students against school safety issues. For example, it is not uncommon for a student to text message a damaging rumor, circulate humiliating photos via mobile phone, or post idle threats to personal web pages (Hinduja & Patchin, 2009; National Coalition for Parent Involvement in Education, 2008). These threats may go so far as to include "hit lists" (*Mahaffey*, 2002) or a detailed physical confrontation that the author may or may not intend to come to fruition.

Personal web pages, therefore, create an outlet for students to express themselves without fearing the immediate consequences that their self-expression might have on others. Whereas bullying has been traditionally viewed as a means to physically or emotionally dominate another person or group, it is now possible for students to engage in psychological dominance by waging a social war of words through technology (Smith et al., 2008). Citing Ybarra & Mitchell (2004), Raskauskas and Stoltz note the especially damaging effects of cyber bullying:

> Electronic bullying may have more impact on youth's emotional development and well-being than traditional bullying because of an even greater power imbalance created by the fact that many victims of electronic bullying may never know the identity of their bully. Another factor that can make electronic bullying more of a threat to psychological health than traditional bullying is its transcendence beyond school grounds and 24-hr availability such that children are not even safe from bullying in their own homes (2007, p. 565).

Cyber-bullying is therefore easier for a student to engage in because he is far removed from the fear of immediate danger or retaliation (Ybarra & Mitchell, 2004). In short, technology may temporarily cloak the identity or intent of an author's message and subsequently remove the individual from a feeling of being responsible for his actions.

The combination of photo imaging software, digital cameras, and cellular phones has given way to a host of damaging trends. The intent of these attacks is to distribute the information as quickly as possible to ridicule another or to redeem oneself in the eyes of others from a prior conflict (Hinduja & Patchin, 2009). By replacing headshots and physical attributes with files that are widely available on the World Wide Web and transposing them, students attack one another not with their words or fists but with embarrassing or threatening photos. With even minimal knowledge of common computer software and digital devices, students are able to generate virtual snapshots that oftentimes do not mirror reality.

Cyber-bullying, however, is not limited to student-to-student conflicts. Generic attacks on the school community are just as damaging to the school climate and students' feelings of safety. This form of cyber-bullying commonly takes aim at the entire school community because sometimes the bully thinks his words are humorous or clever and fails to realize the severity of his threat. Examples of this trend include threatening and harassing students or school personnel via commonly accessed web forums and personal web pages (Hinduja & Patchin, 2009; *Beussink*, 1998; *Latour*, 2005; *Layshock*, 2007; *Mahaffey*, 2007).

Strikingly, court cases are not brought on grounds that a cyber-bullying attack has been made. More frequently, cases related to cyber-bullying are generated by students when the administrator's decision to punish the student is perceived by the student as violating his or her rights. Therefore school officials have to justify in court not only their decision to discipline the student but also the nature of the punishment and the effect caused by the student's actions (*Beussink*, 1998; *Emmett*, 2000; *Latour*, 2005). Often the documentation required to show a nexus between student speech and a disruption in the educational process is too cumbersome or difficult for school authorities to gather.

While there are only a few court cases that address school disruptions caused by cyber-bullying, these disturbances are common and often require immediate administrative action. In extreme cases that affect student safety, for instance, educators may be forced to consider options like limiting access to school buildings, increasing security on campuses, or closing school for operations. How educational leaders choose to react often determines how quickly school operations can return to normal and how student performance is affected.

Understanding the legal context of cyber-bullying equips school officials with the tools necessary to properly examine and document the appropriate nexus between instances of cyber-bullying and its effect on the function of schools. The next section of this chapter addresses legal issues that govern student rights in relation to school leaders' responsibilities in carrying out their educational mission.

LEGAL BACKGROUND

Despite the rise of cyber-bullying behavior, there is a dearth of legal precedent upon which schools can draw to make decisions about how to handle cyber-bullying. The increasing prevalence of students who cyber-bully other students or school staff has required courts to clarify the boundaries between student rights and the authority of school leaders.

Thus far, no cyber-bullying cases in the United States have risen beyond the level of the lower courts. The implications are that school practitioners are largely left on their own to determine both how to discipline cyber-bullies and deter future incidents. However, several U.S. Supreme Court decisions have helped set the stage for schools to understand legal issues related to cyber-bullying. These decisions have set the standard by which claims of impingement on student rights are decided.

A 1969 Supreme Court opinion, *Tinker v. Des Moines Independent Community School District,* established that students have free speech rights but that these rights are limited within the public school setting. *Tinker* involved students and adults who met off campus and decided that they would wear black armbands for a designated period of time as a sign of protest against the Vietnam War. School officials learned of the plan and set a policy to discipline any student seen with a black armband on school grounds. Although they were aware of this policy, several students proceeded to wear the armbands to school and were subsequently suspended. These students sued the school district claiming violation of their free speech and due process rights.

The Court found that the students should have been afforded First Amendment rights to free speech through the symbolic representation of the armbands. This right is guaranteed for students even on school property. Further, the Court maintained that school officials did not have the right to take disciplinary action against the students due to a disagreement over political views. More importantly, the school had not successfully linked the wearing of armbands as a cause for material or substantial disruption of the school environment or school activities. Thus, this type of disruption is the standard courts use to determine if student speech is protected under the first amendment.

Cohen v. California (1971) also dealt with an individual's right to free speech, including the right to wear clothing bearing an expletive. The Court echoed the decision in *Tinker* (1969) to protect First Amendment rights by denying the state of California the power to curtail an individual's choice of self-expression with an accusation of "disturbing the peace." A more compelling, specific argument discriminating between the speech expressed itself and the subsequent behavior was required. Both *Tinker* and *Cohen* are noteworthy because courts evaluate cyber-bullying cases in part by determining if the speech caused a disruption in school operations. They weigh the student's rights of self-expression versus those of school officials to impose limits on student speech as a way to ensure a school environment conducive to learning for the entire student body.

The Supreme Court also addressed the extent to which students' rights to free speech could be controlled by school authorities. In *Bethel School District v. Fraser* (1986), Fraser, a student, used vulgar, sexually charged language in a speech during a school assembly in front of approximately 600 other students who visibly reacted to this language. The student was suspended for disruptive behavior which affected the educational process. The Supreme Court determined the school had the right to restrict speech that is lewd and disruptive in a school setting and that the school board should be allowed to judge whether the type of speech given in a classroom or assembly is appropriate.

Following along the same lines as *Tinker* (1969) and *Bethe* (1986), *Hazelwood School District v. Kuhlmeier* (1988) addressed students' rights to free speech in school newspapers. In *Hazelwood*, a high school principal removed several pages from a student newspaper due to a concern that an article would push the boundaries of protecting other students' privacy by revealing information that would lead to their identification. The school was sued on the basis that school officials had encroached upon the student journalists' First Amendment rights. The Court found that students do not shed their rights to free speech while on school property; however, a principal can restrict speech in a school paper because the school itself does not represent a public forum. Thus, thoughts expressed in the newspaper are subject to administrative oversight. In other words, school principals may use reasonable restraint in restricting the content of school newspapers.

In sum, newspapers are sponsored by the school, and therefore educators do not impinge upon student rights in their use of editorial control. The Court in *Hazelwood* opined that similar speech occurring off-campus would be permissible. The Court's ruling in *Bethel* (1986) also noted that off-campus speech has greater legal protection than that on school grounds.

More recently, the Supreme Court in *Morse v. Frederick* (2007) responded to questions regarding school regulation of off-campus conduct. Charges that a high school principal and school board violated a student's First Amendment rights were brought on the grounds that the principal wrongfully took a banner away from a student during an off-site activity. The student was later subject to discipline because the principal felt that the banner advocated illegal drug use by displaying the phrase "BONG HITS 4 JESUS." The Supreme Court held that the principal was justified to intercede even though the actions took place off school grounds because the event was approved by the school, and therefore student behavior was subject to the same district policies governing on-campus conduct. This court rejected the Ninth Circuit's assertion that the speech used on the banner had not caused a disruption in the educational process.

Protection for speech that takes place off-campus versus that which takes place on school grounds is an important distinction that has been a point of contention in cyber-bullying cases. Schools do not have an explicit right to interfere with speech in the privacy of a student's home. Nevertheless, this expression can negatively influence school climate and raise the stakes in school liability when off-campus student speech takes the form of written threats, derogatory language or images, and is aimed at fellow students or school teachers and administrators.

Although the speech may have occurred outside of the school building, it quickly enters a school context by virtue of ease of accessibility, widespread distribution, and psychological harm done to the individual—or entire school community—that either receives or is made aware of such messages. The ramifications of this speech is difficult to fully document because the forms of communication used to facilitate cyber-bullying limit school authorities' knowledge about who sees, reads, or is exposed to the material. Traditional methods of bullying like physical or verbal intimidation at school enabled administrators to take immediate disciplinary action. The sophistication of technology has hindered school officials' ability to immediately resolve incidents of bullying.

Cyber-bullying causes school staff and administrators to rethink how to discipline bullies, and it forces administrative action to take a new direction. A closer look at court cases that specifically address cyber-bullying and emerging trends in this area demonstrates how the distinctions between school authorities' responsibilities and students' rights have been blurred. Legal precedent has not adequately clarified where those distinctions lie, leaving school practitioners in the uncertain position of how to control for and discipline incidents of cyber-bullying.

COURT DECISIONS ON CYBER-BULLYING

Despite the rise in cyber-bullying incidents, surprisingly few turn into cases that are handled through the courts. Those that do have been decided by lower courts, which turn to decisions such as *Tinker* (1969), *Hazelwood* (1988), and *Bethel* (1986) for guidance. We will now turn to some of these decisions in an effort to demonstrate a contrast between those fact patterns and legal decisions which have not favored school districts and those which have. The choice of these cases is intended to be instructive and illustrative of key points rather than inclusive of all court decisions on cyber-bullying.

In the cases of *Buessink v. Woodland School District* (1998), *Emmett v. Kent School District* (2000), *Coy v. North Canton City Schools* (2002), *Layshock v. Hermitage School District* (2007), and *J.S. v. Bethlehem Area School District* (2003), students used home computers to create web sites that arguably cyber-bullied other students or school authorities. These cases pitted students' rights to privacy for content created outside of school against school authorities' right to discipline for derogatory or insulting material that caused either a perceived threat or negative effect on students or school staff. In their decisions, the courts looked at these cases and made judgments about the rights of student self-expression via the web based primarily on whether the educational process had been interrupted by the material created.

First, consider decisions where the school district lost. For example, in *Beussink v. Woodland School District* (1998), a student made a personal web page in the privacy of his home that used vulgar language to convey criticism of his high school and school officials. The principal disciplined Beussink immediately after learning of the site, not knowing if other students had viewed it. The student's subsequent suspension caused him to fail all of his classes. Beussink sued the Woodland School District on the grounds that school officials had impinged upon his First Amendment rights. The court granted a preliminary injunction in the student's favor because the school district had not proved through adequate documentation that the content contained on the web site had caused any substantial disruption in the educational process.

Insufficient documentation was also the same reasoning behind the court's decision in *Coy* (2002). Coy's web site had personal information about Coy and his two friends and pictures of the boys. The site stated it was meant to describe the adventures of a group of skateboarders going by the name "NBP." The pictures of the boys were under a section entitled "losers." Under the "losers" section were a couple of pictures showing the boys and also a few crude remarks. One picture showed boys giving the "finger." Under another picture was a sentence about how another boy's mother sexually aroused him. The court did not find the content on the web site obscene and maintained that it was questionable whether Coy was disciplined for violating school Internet policy or for the content he posted to the web site. Ruling for the student, the court noted that school authorities would have had grounds to discipline Coy for breaking the school policy on Internet use had it been combined with a "material and substantial interference" with the school's activities.

In *Flaherty v. Keystone Oaks School District* (2003), school authorities also argued for their right to discipline a student for violating school Internet policy. In this case, Flaherty used an online message board to discuss an upcoming volleyball game with its rival, Baldwin High School. Using computers at both his home and school. Flaherty compared each school's prospects of winning the game. In doing so, he made comments about a Baldwin volleyball player, Bemis. Among other things, he discussed Bemis' mother, who was an art teacher at Flaherty's school. Flaherty commented that Bemis would "…shed tears on the court," and that his "…dog could teach better than Bemis' mom" (*Flaherty*, p. 701).

The school claimed that Flaherty's messages and engagement in online conversation broke school handbook policy. However, the court agreed with Flaherty's assertion that the school's handbook policies were overly broad and vague, and no substantial disruption at the school had resulted from the student's postings made to the Internet from either his personal computer or the school's computer. Again, court decisions favor the protection of students' rights to off-campus speech unless the school sufficiently documents a nexus between the speech and disruption to the school environment caused by the speech.

This reasoning was also reflected in the Pennsylvania case, *Layshock v. Hermitage School District* (2007). This decision hinged on whether a nexus between student speech and disruption to the educational process could be found. Here, a popular social networking web site, MySpace.com, was used by a student to post disparaging remarks about his high school principal. The "profile" of his principal, Trosch, was created in Layshock's home but was later accessed by an indeterminable number of students while at school. Layshock created questions and answers that were purported to be by and about Mr. Trosch, and they used the word "big" as a kind of theme. For example, one question asked, "ever been beaten up?" and the corresponding answer was "big fag" (*Layshock,* p. 591).

Other questions and answers implied Mr. Trosch used steroids and drank heavily. Layshock added students to this MySpace web page so they could see the principal's "profile." Subsequently, a substantial proportion of the student body knew about the profile, and several students, including Layshock, viewed the profile while at school. The court found that Layshock should have been afforded his First Amendment rights to free speech because the profile had been created off campus. Several other profiles of the principal had been posted to the web site as well. The school district could not prove a nexus between the creation of Layshock's profile of the principal and any significant disruption to the school operations. Thus, the school did not have cause to discipline Layshock for his off-campus conduct.

Similarly, in *Killion v. Franklin Regional School District* (2001), school authorities were unable to show a nexus between off-campus actions and school disruption. Here, the court found that despite widespread electronic distribution of a "Top Ten" list mocking the high school athletic director, it was not the speech produced off campus that caused any disruption at school. Rather, the court cited the distribution of the list itself as disruptive and not the content; therefore, the student's First Amendment rights had been violated. The defendant, Zachariah Paul, also fought to prevent the school from investigating either the identities of students who had contributed to the Top Ten list or those who had actively distributed or received it. The court also agreed that this fact-finding would be irrelevant to the case.

In *Emmett v. Kent School District* (2000), the district court considered whether student speech on a web site constituted a threat. The court determined that the student's First Amendment rights had been violated when a school official disciplined a student after discovering a web site which had been created to post fake obituaries of fellow students. Visitors to the web site could give their opinion as to who should be next to "die." A local television station found out about the web site and stated that a "hit list" had been created, even though this was not the language used on the site. The content on the web site had been made in jest and during the student's private time, apparently modeled after a school creative writing exercise where students had written mock obituaries for themselves. As such, the district failed to prove that the student had used the web site to threaten anyone. Neither was there sufficient evidence to prove that anyone had felt threatened as a result of being exposed to the site.

While the majority of court decisions appear to favor students' claims, instances where school authorities have established a sufficient nexus between speech and a material disruption in school operations are instructive. For example, in *J.S. v. Bethlehem Area School District*, a student-created web site entitled "Teacher Sux" included vulgar language and images of the student's teacher and principal. J.S. posted a disclaimer on the site that anybody entering the site agreed not to tell school employees or district staff about it, nor would they identify him as the web site's creator. Regardless, there were no safeguards to prevent anyone from accessing the site if they chose to do so.

On the site, one image showed the teacher with her head severed from her body. The site listed reasons why the teacher should die and stated that money would be given to a hit man. Technology was also used to morph the teacher's face into that of Adolf Hitler. Another statement made on a different page on the web site claimed that their principal engaged in a sexual relationship with the principal from a neighboring school. J.S. proceeded to access the site at school and show it to friends. Other school faculty and students were also exposed to the web site.

Although the court did not find that the student was making a true threat via the Internet, neither did it find that the student's First Amendment rights were violated. Because it was targeted specifically at school staff and was accessed at school, the speech on the web site was considered lewd, offensive, and on-campus even though the student made the web site at home. The Bethlehem Area School District was able to prove that the speech caused fear and low morale within the school community which was detrimental to the educational process. As such, the nexus between student speech—in this case on-campus speech—and material disruption of school operations was strong enough to persuade the court to decide for the school. The chief justice of the court, concurring with the majority decision, cautioned, however, that student speech via the Internet cannot be considered as on-campus simply because a web site is accessed at school by the producer of the speech.

In *Wisniewski v. Weedsport Central School District* (2007), a middle-school student, Aaron Wisniewski, was suspended after school authorities learned he had used the instant messaging (IM) software to create a disturbing online icon that accompanied his messages. The icon shoved a pistol shooting at a person's head, and dots above the head which conveyed blood splattering. Underneath the image was the statement, "Kill Mr. VanderMolen" (p. 36).

At least fifteen other people viewed this icon in the process of chatting online with Aaron. Mr. VanderMolen was Aaron's English teacher. A classmate of Aaron's brought the icon to Mr. VanderMolen's attention. Mr. VanderMolen notified the police, school authorities, and Aaron's parents. As a result of his actions, Aaron was suspended. School officials argued that the icon represented a threat and disrupted school operations. Aaron's parents argued that school staff had not been adequately trained on how to assess threats and that their son's First Amendment rights were violated.

The United States Court of Appeals for the Second Circuit held that the icon represented a "true threat" and was not protected under the First Amendment. The court also held that the speech was not protected because of the high likelihood that school authorities would be made aware of the icon. As a result, it conceivably would have created a material disruption in the educational environment even though student communication had taken place off campus.

These examples of legal decisions demonstrate how the majority of courts have favored the protection of students' First Amendment rights over the responsibilities of school authorities to discipline for cyber content that makes its way into schools. The courts' decisions show how difficult it is for school authorities to gather evidence sufficient to prove that student speech emanating from technology in the privacy of a one's home materially and substantially disrupts the school environment.

In sum, the legal condition requiring a nexus between student speech and its effects on the school environment can be difficult to meet. The implication is that cyber-bullies are given wide latitude to say what they want without fear of repercussion from their school or the legal system unless school authorities are able to document that the students' actions disrupt the school. Nonetheless, a few schools have been able to do so successfully and school authorities are becoming more sophisticated in how to handle such incidents.

Another area that concerns educators is the issue of immunity, i.e., who is or can be liable for damages. Because so few court decisions on this topic apply directly to cyber-bullying, this discussion also includes other types of legal precedence that may provide some guidance.

SCHOOL LIABILITY

The issue of legal liability is a complicated, yet highly important, matter which must be discussed as it carries with it serious financial and policy implications for school districts. In its simplest terms, tort liability is defined as: "A private or civil wrong or injury...for which the court will provide a remedy in the form of an action for damages" (Garner, 2004, p. 1526). The remedy in this definition is money. In other words, if a school district loses a tort liability claim, that entity will need to pay financially for its transgressions. For this reason, tort liability carries with it severe consequences, and, in turn, courts are reluctant to impose such liability on government entities with limited resources, such as schools.

Torts do not include breach of contract claims. In addition, they involve civil and not criminal actions, although there can be some overlap if the behavior is willful (intended to hurt) and the standard of "beyond a reasonable doubt" is used to determine guilt. Having made this distinction, we will provide one brief example of a school-related case involving criminal charges after which the discussion will be confined to civil actions. The latter require a lesser standard than in criminal cases, i.e., a "preponderance of the evidence" to establish liability. Emphasis will be placed on those torts most likely to involve schools and those that could be related to cyber-bullying claims. These include intentional, non-intentional, and constitutional torts.

Criminal Actions

In the case, *I.M.L v. Utah* (2002), a student, I.M.L., was charged with criminal libel for creating a web site at home that fabricated sexual histories for fellow high school students and contained demeaning comments about his school principal and faculty. For example, I.M.L. stated the principal was the "town drunk," that a teacher possibly was a "...homosexual leading a double life," and another might be addicted to speed or some other illegal drug (p. 1040).

Because I.M.L. did not purport that his statements were true, and his comments were not made against people who were public figures, the court ruled that Utah's criminal statute was unconstitutionally overbroad. Furthermore, I.M.L was not guilty of criminal libel because it was not proved there was malicious intent behind the statements posted to the web.

Whereas I.M.L. addressed student rights and criminal libel, school officials have also been challenged in civil cases to protect victims of bullying. In general, courts have favored administrative discretion and given school officials immunity from claims against the school district and its employees.

Intentional Torts

Intentional torts are "perpetuated by one who intends to do that which the law has declared wrong" (Garner, 2004, p. 1527). Assault and battery are examples of intentional torts. However, the most common claims related to cyber-bullying would likely fall under defamation. *Black's Law Dictionary* (2004) states that: "A communication is defamatory if it tends so to harm the reputation of another as to lower him in the estimation of his community or to deter third persons from associating or dealing with him" (Garner, p. 448).

Defamation includes both libel (the written word) and slander (the spoken word), with the former applying to cyber-bullying. For the most part, these types of torts would involve private parties rather than the school district. For example, if a student had a web page that contained libelous remarks about another student, then the legal claim would come directly from the student who had been defamed and not from the school district. If a school official made libelous remarks on cyber space, that person would be sued as an individual not as a school official because such remarks are unlikely to fall within the scope of an educator's official duties. In other words, the school district would not be held responsible. However, there is a closer link between school districts and claims regarding non-intentional torts.

Non-Intentional Torts

Non-intentional torts are as they sound, i.e., actions where the alleged wrong-doer had no intent to do harm. Common examples of non-intentional torts include automobile crashes and medical malpractice cases. In the school setting, non-intentional torts may involve students getting hurt on the athletic field, in chemistry labs, or in classes where heavy machinery is used. They also apply to "slip and fall" cases; for instance, an individual falling on an icy sidewalk outside the school or in a hallway where something has been spilled. Thus, anything that we might view as an accident (i.e., not on purpose) that causes harm to students would likely fall in this category.

Negligence is the standard used to determine liability with respect to non-intentional torts. While the word negligence is commonly used in the English language to describe carelessness or acting irresponsibly, the legal definition of negligence is much more specific. Defined by state law, negligence generally is determined by a four-part test that asks if the entity sued had a duty to the person bringing suit, whether that duty was breached, whether the incident was foreseeable so that a reasonable person using "ordinary care" could have prevented the outcome, and if there were damages occurring as a direct result of the breach of duty. All of these prongs must be answered in the affirmative for there to be liability.

As of this writing, cyber-bullying cases have not, for the most part, focused on issues of negligence. However, there are some court decisions on bullying in general that provide guidance on this matter. Having said this, it is important to note that, unless the case involved sexual harassment, courts rarely find the school liable for bullying incidents, even when the outcome results in substantial damage to the student. *Jasperson v. Anoka-Hennepin* (2007) an unpublished decision which cannot be cited for legal precedent, nonetheless, provides a poignant example of a Minnesota appeals court's efforts to protect the district's discretion in making day-to-day decisions.

The *Jasperson* case involved J.S., a 13-year-old student in the eighth grade at Anoka-Hennepin Independent School District No. 11. J.S. lived with his parents and older brother. His father and brother hunted and all three males enjoyed target shooting. J.S. knew how to use guns and was familiar with the precepts of gun safety. There were guns at home, and J.S. assisted his father in reloading ammunition at a workbench in their home's basement. During the 6th and 7th grade, J.S. was grounded and told that he could not hunt due to failing grades, which subsequently improved. He attended a summer school class after 7th grade, taught by Dennis Lande, who then became J.S.'s 8th grade teacher.

When J.S. was in the 8th grade, two boys bullied him on the way home from school, threatening to kill him and telling him that they knew where he lived and which room was his bedroom. Very frightened, J.S. told his mother. The mother relayed these events and the names of the boys to the principal, requesting that her son be protected. The principal advised J.S. to change his route when walking home and to let him know of any further incidents. However, since the boys threatening J.S. attended another school, one for behavioral problems, the principal could only bring charges against the boys for trespassing in the school parking lot. He stated that J.S. and his mother would need to talk with Brad Wise, the school liaison officer, regarding protection. Hearing about the incident, Mr. Wise told J.S. that no crime had occurred and advised him to walk home with friends.

On his first quarter report, J.S. was failing all subjects except physical education, where he had earned an "A." J.S. reportedly blamed his teachers for these low grades and was upset that he would not be allowed to go hunting. While the exact words are in dispute, an unidentified student claimed that Mr. Lande, J.S.'s teacher, told J.S. that his life was "going nowhere" and that he (J.S.) was one of the dumbest students that he had ever taught (*Jasperson*, p. 2). J.S. discussed what had happened with Mr. Lande and the boys' continuing threats with his mother, saying that these threats prevented him from concentrating on his schoolwork. J.S. also told his mother that he had tried to speak with the school's Prevention Advisor, Ms. Rutt, who told him she was too busy and that he would have to come back the next day. J.S.'s mother promised to get him out of Mr. Lande's class but told him that he would not be able to go hunting. The next morning, J.S. killed himself with a .22 caliber semi-automatic handgun. He left a note to his mother saying that since his life was going nowhere, he decided that he didn't want to live any longer.

Rick Jasperson, as trustee for J.S.'s next-of-kin brought wrongful-death charges against the school district asserting that the district's negligence caused J.S.'s death. Deciding in favor of the school district, a Minnesota appeals upheld the lower court's summary judgment. This court maintained that school officials could not have foreseen the suicide and thus had no duty to protect J.S. from harm. The court also noted that actions on the part of school personnel did not cause the suicide. Finally, according to state law, school officials were immune from damages because they had acted within their official capacities and their actions were not willful or malicious.

A somewhat similar situation occurred in *Hasenfus v. LaJeunesse* (1999). Here, a 14-year-old 8th grader in Maine was subjected to harassment by her classmates. The previous year, this student had testified in court after having been raped. School officials were aware of her situation. Nonetheless, her physical education teacher reprimanded her in public and sent her alone to the locker room. Here, Jamie attempted suicide. While the suicide was unsuccessful, this student was left permanently disabled. Jamie's parents claimed that school officials were negligent and had a duty to protect students, considering that there had been an outbreak of suicides in the school district. Ruling against the parents, the court maintained that the school had no duty to protect under these circumstances and that school officials had not acted willfully.

Constitutional Torts

Constitutional torts involve claims of money damages for violation of the U.S. Constitution or federal laws. These claims fall under §1983 of the United States Code, which states that:

> Every person who under color of any statute, ordinance, custom, or usage, of any state or territory, subjects, or causes to be subjected, any citizen of the United States or any person within the jurisdiction thereof to the deprivation of any rights, privileges, or immunities secured by the Constitution and laws, shall be liable to the party injured in an action at law, suit in equity, or other proper proceeding for redress (22 U.S.C.A., §1983).

Claims for monetary damages under §1983 must be made at the same time as the other legal claims. For example, if a student claims that her First Amendment free speech rights are violated, she cannot receive money damages unless she also makes a claim under §1983 at the same time. If the student does not prevail in her free speech claim, then obviously she will not be awarded damages under §1983. On the other hand, just because the student wins on her free speech claim, this does not mean that she will be awarded money damages under §1983. The latter is determined through a different, and more stringent, standard.

Smith v. Guilford (2007) presents a good example of a constitutional tort claim. In this case, Jeremy, a high school student, brought suit against the Guilford Board of Education for violating his Fourteenth Amendment equal protection rights and the right to a free and appropriate education. He claimed that school officials failed to protect him from bullying by classmates. The bullies taunted Jeremy for being 4'7" and 75 pounds as well as having Attention Deficit Hyperactivity Disorder (ADHD). As a result, Jeremy claimed he was no longer able to engage in school activities and friendships. It was alleged in part that school employees knew of the bullying and allowed it to continue.

The United States Court of Appeals, Second Circuit, ruled that the school officials' lack of action had not violated Jeremy's right to substantive due process as their conduct did not "rise to the level of egregious conduct so brutal and offensive to human dignity as to shock the conscience" (*Guilford*, p. 58). Thus, under this "shock the conscience" standard, school officials could not be held liable for money damages. *Guilford* is typical of decisions involving substantive due process and claims for money damages under §1983 as this standard is often difficult to meet. An important exception is when the claim involves sexual harassment. Here the court is crystal clear in holding school districts accountable.

In *Davis v. Monroe* (1999), a landmark decision involving peer-on-peer sexual harassment in schools, the Supreme Court held that school districts could be liable for peer sexual harassment under Title IX of the Education Amendments of 1972 if three conditions were met. First, the student has to demonstrate that he was sexually harassed. Second, he must prove that school officials had actual knowledge of the harassment and were deliberately indifferent. Third, the harassment has to be so "so severe, pervasive, and objectively offensive it deprive[s] the student of access to educational opportunities" (*Davis*, p. 1664). Therefore, if cyber-bullying involves sexual harassment, it is likely that the school district would be liable as long as the necessary conditions are met.

ADMINISTRATIVE ACTION RELATED TO CYBER-BULLYING

As demonstrated in the above-mentioned cases, school officials are rarely held liable for student bullying. Therefore, it is equally likely that, at present, they would not be held liable for cyber-bullying. Schools and school officials are generally afforded legal immunity so they can use their discretionary judgment to handle educational matters without having to worry that actions within the scope of their employment will result in money damages.

On the other hand, cyber-bullying opens new dimensions for courts to consider that may ultimately restrict administrative discretion and immunity. For example, schools may not be legally obligated to take a proactive stance against all forms of cyber-bullying due to liability, but they nevertheless have a professional duty to ensure a safe and supportive learning environment for all students.

If the conduct of a student is considered "foreseeable" or it could have been prevented by school officials exercising "ordinary care," school districts and officials could be held responsible. There is a chance that perhaps sometimes cyber-bullying cases may cause the courts to reinterpret the legal definition of "foreseeable conduct" resulting from behavior shrouded behind the use of technology.

In the future, schools may be offered less protection from claims of liability if the definition of "ordinary care" for students is interpreted to encompass student use of computers, cellular phones, or imaging software. In addition, in the face of rising litigation, administrators now have more incentive to thoroughly document student complaints of cyber-bullying, raise awareness about cyber-bullying among the school community, and revise procedures to not only protect victims of cyber-bullying but also discipline the instigator.

Limitations of the Law

Given the climate of accountability in education and an increased awareness of legal literacy in educational administration, school officials often look to the law for guidance on striking a balance between respecting the rights of students and providing a safe and supportive environment for all learners. Courts have been hesitant to impose their will on school officials. However, courts have recognized that their position is not to interfere with the daily operation of schools but merely to uphold the constitutionality of its management (see *Island Trees v. Pico, 1982*). Accordingly, there are limitations to what can be learned from legal proceedings.

While school officials should be aware of legal precedent regarding student rights and school liability as a government agency entrusted with the safety of students, legal literacy is not a substitute for good decision-making skills in the face of any situation requiring administrative discretion and certainly not in the aftermath of cyber-bullying. The specific cases that have been addressed in this chapter are only a minor indication of the immense challenges educators face on a daily basis as a result of cyber-bullying. In fact, when reviewing these cases, one could argue that school officials are hard-pressed to find an operational definition of cyber-bullying.

Legal decisions are limited to the facts of the case presented before the court. As this chapter has shown, the majority of legal claims are brought forth by students, not school districts. One cannot conclude that courts fail to see the disruptions caused by cyber-bullying. Neither can it be assumed that courts disagree with disciplining students for speech or actions that negatively affect the school community. To date, judicial analyses have been limited to weighing the school's documentation of such disturbances and determining whether a violation occurred on campus, in the privacy of a student's home, or whether a legitimate threat actually existed.

Administrators and courts may in fact have similar concerns related to the effect of cyber-bullying in schools but separate responses to resolve these concerns. While courts have the task of interpreting the law, school officials must act to prevent conflicts from interfering with student learning. The immediate need for action caused by taunting, embarrassment, or harassment of one student by another demands that administrators discipline the offending party or parties appropriately and in such a way that is both respectful of the victim(s) and the offender's rights. In this regard, school leaders are given a wide range of administrative discretion. Perhaps the lesson that administrators can learn from these cases is how to discipline students for cyber-bullying and how to compile the documentation needed to withstand legal scrutiny.

When an instance of cyber-bullying creates a disturbance in school proceedings, administrators may tend to punish, for punishment's sake, rather than discipline, which would involve explaining to the student conditions that are intended to reward good behavior and discourage inappropriate actions. In the cases presented in this chapter, the most common consequence for cyber-bullying was suspension. Therefore students' legal claims are often based on the grounds that the student was improperly suspended, i.e., not afforded their due process rights or denied their right to free speech. Administrators are therefore tied to defending the constitutionality of punishing the student rather than seeking a resolution to the initial conflict.

Regardless of the effect that cyber-bullying has on a particular student or school community, school officials bear a heavy burden in documenting the nexus between the effects of the student's speech, for instance, and the school's purpose. Because legal claims related to cyber-bullying are generally initiated by students in response to their punishment, courts must weigh the students' rights to free speech against the school officials' decision to suspend students. Often because of the immediate need for action, no tangible documentation exists that can satisfy this requirement. The need for documentation becomes a double-edged sword for school officials.

If school officials perceive a threat, they are not afforded the luxury to wait and see if a disturbance will occur. If educators wait to properly document disturbances, they risk increasing the number of people who are actually affected by the bully's actions. How then, are school officials to manage instances of cyber-bullying, and perhaps more importantly, how do their decisions to punish or discipline affect the culture and future operation of their schools? The concluding portion of this chapter discusses how combining ethical decision-making skills with legal knowledge can be a tool for administrators to simultaneously address cyber-bullying and foster a safe and supportive school environment.

FINDING AN ETHICAL RESPONSE

As we have seen, most attempts to punish students for cyber-bullying have come under legal scrutiny for constitutional matters that are foundational to student rights but not necessarily aimed at providing a remedy for the root problem. Moreover, the gap in time and place that exists between a student who wishes to inflict damage and its effect on another student or school community suggests that this trend may continue for many years to come. As technology becomes more sophisticated, so too will the options that students have to express themselves and exercise their rights to privacy and free speech. As the law will always be one step behind technology, educational leaders and policy makers need not attempt to restrict student rights in order to control instances of cyber-bullying. Rather, school officials should work toward articulating the meta-values of their schools, thereby creating a moral awareness that can also be used to educate students about the responsibilities that accompany their rights (Begley, 2008).

Accordingly, in her book, *Best Interests of the Student: Applying Ethical Constructs to Legal Cases in Education,* Stefkovich (2006) observes that the law is limited in resolving many issues that confront educational leaders. Thus, while school officials often turn to the court system seeking an answer to their questions, more often than not, the question is one that cannot be answered legally but instead needs to be confronted on a moral basis. Given the legal restrictions regulating cyber-bullying, educators may want to consider ethical issues such as whether there is a place in their school for bullying, harassment, bigotry, unkind words, and so forth. If not, school leaders need to foster a climate of mutual respect and teach students to take responsibility for the repercussions of their actions out of caring rather than punishment.

References

Begley, P.T. (2008). The nature and specialized purposes of educational leadership. In Crow, G., Lumby, J., Pashiardis, P. (Eds) *UCEA International Handbook on the Preparation and Development of School Leaders.* NY: Routledge Press, pp. 21–42.

Beussink v. Woodland R-IV School District, 30 F.Supp.2d 1175 (E.D. Mo.1998).

Bethel School District No. 403 v. Fraser, 478 U.S. 675 (1986).

Garner, B.A. (Ed.) (2004). *Black's Law Dictionary (8th ed.).* St. Paul, MN: West Publishing Co.

Board of Education Island Trees Union Free School District No. 26 v. Pico, 457 U.S. 853 (1982).

Cohen v. California, 403 U.S. 15 (1971).

Coy v. Board of Education of North Canton City Schools, 205 F.2d 791 (N.D. Ohio, 2002).

Davis v. Monroe County Board of Education, 526 U.S. 629 (1999).

Emmett v. Kent School District No. 415, 92 F.2d 1088 (W.D. Wash., 2000).

Flaherty v. Keystone Oaks School District, 247 F.2d 698 (W.D. Pa., 2003).

Hazelwood School District v. Kuhlmeier, 484 U.S. 260 (1988).

Hasenfus v. LaJeunesse, 175 F.3d 68 (Me., 1999).

Hinduja, S. & Patchin, J. W. (2009). Quote from *Bullying Beyond the Schoolyard: Preventing and Responding to Cyberbullying.* Sage Publications (Corwin Press). Retrieved from the Cybullying. us web site November 19, 2008 from http://www.cyberbullying.us/research.php.

I.M.L. v. State, 61 P.3d 1038 (Utah, 2002).

Jasperson v. Anoka-Hennepin Independent School Dist. No. 11, 2007 WL 3153456 (Minn.App., 2007). (Unpublished opinion).

J.S. ex rel. H.S. v. Bethlehem Area School District, 569 Pa. 638 (Pa., 2002).

Killion v. Franklin Regional School District, 136 F.2d 446 (W.D. Pa., 2001).

Latour v. Riverside Beaver School Dist. Not Reported in F.Supp.2d, 2005 WL 2106562, (W.D. Pa., 2005).

Layshock v. Hermitage School Dist., 496 F.2d 587 (W.D. Pa., 2007).

Mahaffey v. Aldrich, 236 F.2d 779 (E.D. Mich., 2002).

Morse v. Frederick, 127 U.S. 2618 (2007).

National Crime Prevention Council (2008). *Delete Cyberbullying.* Retrieved November 16, 2008 from *http://www.ncpc.org/newsroom/current-campaigns/cyberbullying.*

National Coalition for Parent Involvement in Education. (August, 2008). *NCPIE Update: Internet Safety and Cyberbullying Statistics Highlight August 2008 NCPIE Meeting.* Retrieved November 18, 2008 from http://www.ncpie.org/ncpie_update/ncpieupdateAugust2008.pdf.

Raskauskas, J. & Stoltz, A. D. (2007). Involvement in Traditional and Electronic Bullying Among Adolescents. *Developmental Psychology, 43*(3), pp. 564–575. Retrieved November 16, 2008 from http://ft.csa.com.ezaccess.libraries.psu.edu/ids70/resolver.php?sessid=9o1ji287tab2m 8sm4p7bpglk53&server=csaweb109v.csa.com&check=b0ab257a7eb7951d146c01522b7127 02&db=psycarticles-set-c&key=DEV%2F43%2Fdev_43_3_564&mode=pdf.

Shariff, S., and Johnny, L. (March, 2007). *Cyber-Libel and Cyber Bullying: Can Schools Protect Student Reputations and Free-Expression in Virtual Environments?* Retrieved November 16, 2008 from *http://proquest.umi.com/pqdweb?index=0&did=1260353171&SrchMode=2&sid=3&Fmt=6& VInst=PROD&VType=PQD&RQT=309&VName=PQD&TS=1226865816&clientId=9874.*

Smith v. Guilford Bd. of Educ., 226 Fed.Appx. 58, 2007 WL 1725512, (Conn., 2007).

Smith, P.K., Mahdavi, J., Carvalho, M., Fisher, S., Russell, S., and Tippett, N. (2008). Cyberbullying: its nature and impact in secondary school pupils. *Journal of Child Psychology and Psychiatry, 49*(4), pp. 376–385. Retrieved November 16, 2008 from http://www3.interscience.wiley.com. ezaccess.libraries.psu.edu/cgi-bin/fulltext/119392241/PDFSTART

Stefkovich, J.A. (2006). *Best Interests of the Student: Applying Ethical Constructs to Legal Cases in Education.* Mahwah, N.J.: Lawrence Erlbaum Associates, Inc.

Tinker v. Des Moines Independent Community School District, 393 U.S. 503 (1969).

Ybarra, M.L. & Mitchell, K.J. (2004). Online aggressor/targets, aggressors, and targets: A comparison of associated youth characteristics *Journal of Child Psychology and Psychiatry,* 45(7), 1308–1316

Wisniewski v. Board of Educ. of Weedsport Cent. School Dist., 494 F.3d 34 (2nd Cir. 2007).

7 · *Morse v. Frederick* and Cyber-bullying in Schools

The Impact on Freedom of Expression, Disciplinary Authority, and School Leadership

Patrick D. Pauken

INTRODUCTION

Ⅰn my relatively short legal and teaching career, I have been fascinated by the prospects and problems associated with the application of "old," preexisting law to "new," transforming media (see, e.g., Daniel & Pauken, 2002; Daniel & Pauken, 1999). In discussions of school violence, for example, the most traditional law of exclusionary discipline and due process—detentions, suspensions, expulsions, and the like—was not effective in addressing problems of gangs in schools without associated educational programs for students, staff, parents and whole school communities. Likewise, in the era of school shootings like the 1999 massacre at Columbine High School in Littleton, Colorado, we discovered that school violence had an additional face—middle and upper class, otherwise intelligent, and often alone, with the time and facility to do great damage without warning and with telltale signs appearing only in hindsight (Daniel & Pauken, 2002). In the twenty-first century, however, school violence has combined the territorial fear that we grew to know from rival gangs, and the time and opportunity we have come to know from youth who have a fascination for and a facility with electronic media, and has expanded its reach to cyberspace, where violence is often more silent and less obvious, but where it is equally if not more dangerous to mind, body, and spirit.

In the twenty-first century, technology and other transforming media allow the entire world of knowledge and information to become a school's library. At the same time, however, cyberspace also becomes a child's difficult-to-monitor playground, where expression, seemingly, knows no bounds. Clearly, such contexts make for a difficult leadership dilemma. On one hand, we expect school leaders to use the latest technological advances to open up the world of legitimate and positive information and knowledge to young, exploring minds and allow them to participate in knowledge discovery and dissemination. On the other hand, we expect them to protect those minds from inappropriate, irrelevant, and dangerous material and the predators who deliver it. Add to the second hand the fact that some of these dangerous predators are students and staff, and the plot thickens. So do the expectations of our school leaders.

For years now, school leaders have attempted to regulate the conduct of students and their use of technology, typically through acceptable use policies and expanded discipline, anti-harassment, and anti-bullying codes (Daniel & Pauken, 1998; Daniel & Pauken, 2002). These leaders are often guided by state and federal statutes and related case law. For example, in spring 2007, the state of Ohio enacted a short series of provisions that require schools to implement anti-bullying policies (Ohio Rev. Code Ann. §§3313.666, 3313.667). According to Ohio Revised Code §3313.666(A), "harassment, intimidation, or bullying" means "any intentional written, verbal, or physical act that a student has exhibited toward another particular student more than once behavior both: (1) causes mental or physical harm to the other student; and (2) is sufficiently severe, persistent, or pervasive that it creates an intimidating, threatening, or abusive educational environment for the other student." The required policy must include, at a minimum, the statutory definition of harassment, intimidation, or bullying; procedures for reporting, documenting, and investigating the alleged incidents; procedures for notifying the parents or guardians of students involved; strategies for protecting alleged victims; and disciplinary procedures for students guilty of harassment, intimidation, or bullying, "which shall not infringe on any student's rights under the first amendment to the Constitution of the United States" (Ohio Rev. Code Ann. § 3313.666(B)).

Ohio's anti-bullying law is similar in many respects to the laws of several other states (see, e.g., Alaska Stat. §14.33.200; Conn. Gen. Stat. §10–222d; Idaho Code §18–917A; Kan. Stat. Ann. §72–8256; La. Rev. Stat. 17:416.13; and N.H. Rev. Stat. Ann. 193-F:2). But two aspects of the law are worthy of additional comment. First, many states' anti-bullying provisions make particular reference to technology and cyberspace (see, e.g., Ark. Code Ann. §6–18–514; 14 Del. Code §4112D; Neb. Rev. Stat. Ann. §79–2,137; N.J. Stat. §18A:37–13; and Ore. Rev. Stat. §339.351). Yet, despite the relative newness of Ohio's provision and the seemingly open opportunity to add a reference to cyber-bullying, Ohio's statute does not include such a reference. The provisions' language, however, is easily read to include cyber-bullying: There is no explicit restriction in the statute to student conduct that occurs on the physical premises of a school or during particular hours of school activities. In other words, the statute appears to target the *effects* of harassment, intimidation, and bullying (e.g., mental and physical harm; abusive, intimidating educational environment), regardless of where it originates, without speaking to the physical location and/or time where the harassment, intimidation, and bullying take place. Therefore, applications of harassment, intimidation, and bullying via electronic media appear viable under Ohio's law.

Second, the necessary provisions for due process for those accused of violating a school's anti-bullying policy include an explicit mention that due process and discipline shall not infringe on the students' First Amendment rights. In light of what appears to be the most common issue encountered in court cases addressing student conduct in cyberspace—student free speech—the reference to the First Amendment in Ohio's anti-bullying law is a welcome one, giving school leaders further guidance in the enactment and implementation of anti-bullying policy. Student expression in school settings has been guided very readily by a series of three landmark Supreme Court decisions from the 1960s and 1980s and one very recent decision from 2007 that may reach the same landmark status. This chapter explores these decisions and their application to cyberspace and cyber-bullying.

As explained by Stefkovich, Crawford and Murphy in Chapter 6, in *Tinker v. Des Moines Independent Community School District* (1969), the Supreme Court offered one of the most foundational statements in school law, policy, and civil rights: "It can hardly be argued that either students or teachers shed their constitutional rights to freedom of speech or expression at the schoolhouse gate" (*Tinker,* p. 506). The Court struck down a school district's ban on black armbands worn by students to protest the Vietnam War, emphasizing the personal politics and philosophy of students and the lack of disruption the speech had at school. In 1986, the Court spoke again in *Bethel School District No. 403 v. Fraser* (1986). Upholding a school principal's decision to suspend a high school student for delivering a speech laced with sexual innuendo at a school assembly, the Court gave schools the authority to disassociate themselves from the lewd, vulgar, and plainly offensive speech of students at school to make the point that such speech is inconsistent with the school's mission and fundamental values. Two years later, in *Hazelwood School District v. Kuhlmeier* (1988), the Court gave schools the authority to exercise editorial control over the content and style of student speech in school-sponsored activities (here, school newspapers produced as part of a class), so long as the restrictions are related to legitimate pedagogical concerns.

Finally, in June 2007, in *Morse v. Frederick* (2007), the United States Supreme Court held that a school principal did not violate the First Amendment free speech rights of a student when she suspended the student for unfurling a 14-foot home-made banner with the phrase "BONG HiTS 4 JESUS" across the street from his high school. Students were dismissed from classes to watch the 2002 Olympics Torch Relay, as it passed by the Juneau, Alaska, school. The student argued that the speech was student-generated, non-disruptive, and displayed off school premises and out of the hands of school disciplinary authority. The principal and school argued that the speech took place at a school-sanctioned event and violated school policy that prohibited students from displaying messages promoting the use of illegal substances. Acknowledging these noticeable fact differences, the Supreme Court, in a 5–4 decision, adopted petitioner Morse's reading of the facts and held for Morse: "we hold that schools may take steps to safeguard those entrusted to their care from speech that can reasonably be regarded as encouraging illegal drug use" (*Morse v. Frederick*, 2007, p. 2622).

In the nearly 20 years between *Hazelwood* (1988) and *Morse* (2007), student speech and other expressive conduct took rather dramatic turns, particularly with respect to conduct in cyberspace and/or conduct off of school premises and after school hours. In the meantime, however, school leaders and policymakers had only three major historical Court decisions—decided in times and contexts unlike those we see today—and dozens of somewhat helpful, yet often inconsistent, lower court decisions to guide them in the resolution of First Amendment free speech questions. In other words, when presented with questions of Internet, cyberspace, and other electronic conduct of students (committed off premises and after school hours), school leaders have had to look to older and/or inconsistent law for help. *Morse v. Frederick* is the first student free speech case decided by the United States Supreme Court in the cyberspace era. How helpful is it? After *Morse,* how much authority does or should a school have to regulate off-premises speech of students? How impactful are the content and effect of that speech, especially when it is contrary to the school's fundamental values? How guiding is the fractured Supreme Court decision in the case? Even more specific to the full discussion here, how does *Morse* help with the regulation of electronic speech and the discipline and punishment of cyber-bullying? On its own, *Morse's* decid-edly narrow opinion (addressing, it seems, only speech relating to the advocacy or glorification of illegal drug use) offers a little help. Along with the preexisting "big three"—*Tinker, Bethel,* and *Hazelwood*—more help is offered. Add in state statutes and school policies on bullying and cyber-bullying, and much more guid-ance is offered. The purpose of this chapter is to explore the legal implications of cyber-bullying in light of the older, preexisting law of student free speech and in light of the United States Supreme Court's decision in *Morse v. Frederick* (2007). While the majority opinion in *Morse* rather explicitly declared its decision to be a narrow one, not all lower courts since the summer of 2007 have read and applied the decision that way. With this in mind, the present chapter addresses the location, effect, and content of student speech in a technological era and offers school leaders guidance as they enact and apply anti-cyber-bullying policy.

THE BIG THREE: *TINKER, BETHEL,* AND *HAZELWOOD*

Freedom of Speech Inside the Schoolhouse Gate: *Tinker v. Des Moines Independent Community School District*

In 1965, parents and students in Des Moines, Iowa, met to plan and publicize their objections to the United States' involvement in Vietnam. They agreed to wear black armbands as the symbol of their protest. The principals of the Des Moines schools discovered the plan. They met and adopted a policy that any student wearing an armband to school would be asked to remove it, and those who refused would be suspended until they returned without the armband. Three students refused to comply with the new armband policy and were suspended until their protest ended. The students filed suit, alleging violations of free speech. The District Court held for the school district and the Eighth Circuit Court of Appeals affirmed.

In what has become a landmark case in American education law, the Supreme Court reversed and found for the students, holding that public school administrators may not restrict the silent, passive, political speech of students unless that speech substantially disrupts the operation of the school, materially interferes with school discipline, or infringes on the rights of others. In a classic discussion of constitutional rights, the Court engaged in a balancing act between the rights of individuals (to speak on matters of personal and public importance) and the good of the whole (the responsibility and authority of the school leaders to make and enforce rules for the safety of school community members and for the maintenance of a positive educational environment). In its first drawing of the line between individual rights and institutional authority, the Court offered the often-quoted "schoolhouse gate" statement. The Court said that student speech may not be restricted without evidence of disruption or impending disruption of the rights of others or of the school as a whole. Undifferentiated fear of disturbance is not enough to overcome individual rights to freedom of expression:

> Any variation from the majority's opinion may inspire fear. Any word spoken, in class, in the lunchroom or on the campus, that deviates from the views of another person, may start an argument or cause a disturbance. But our constitution says we must take this risk. (p. 508)

In other words, administrative action in light of such student expression must be caused by more than the mere desire to avoid the unpleasantness that accompanies an unpopular viewpoint.

As loudly as *Tinker's* ruling rings for students and their free speech rights, the decision speaks nearly as loudly for schools and their authority to maintain discipline. With this ruling, school administrators still retain wide discretion to determine whether there is sufficient evidence of material or substantial disruption or whether such disruption can be reasonably forecast under the circumstances. However, singling out the expression of one particular opinion, as the administrators in *Tinker* did, especially without evidence that doing so is necessary, was not constitutionally permissible. The Court stated so rather plainly: "In our system, state-operated schools may not be enclaves of totalitarianism….In our system, students may not be regarded as closed-circuit recipients of only that which the state chooses to communicate."

Lewd and Vulgar Speech, and the Fundamental Mission of Public Education: *Bethel School District No. 403 v. Fraser*

In *Bethel School District No. 403 v. Fraser* (1986), Matthew Fraser, a high school junior, delivered a speech at a school-sponsored assembly nominating a fellow student for elective office. Six hundred students, some of whom were 14 years old, attended. During the speech, Fraser referred to his candidate in terms of a graphic, explicit sexual metaphor. In advance of the assembly, two of his teachers advised him of the school's speech policy and warned him not to deliver the speech. The school's policy read as follows: "Conduct which materially and substantially interferes with the educational process is prohibited, including the use of obscene, profane language or gestures" (*Bethel,* 1986, p. 678). Fraser delivered it anyway, to rather notorious effect. Many of his classmates laughed; many hooted and hollered; several made physical gestures relating to the words; and others sat there, stunned and bewildered.

The next day, Fraser admitted to the assistant principal that he intended the sexual innuendo in the speech. He was suspended for three days and was removed from consideration as a graduation speaker. Fraser brought suit and alleged a violation of First Amendment free speech rights. Applying the *Tinker* disruption standard, both the District Court and the Court of Appeals held for Fraser. The Supreme Court reversed for the school and held that the First Amendment does not prevent a public school district from disciplining a student for giving a lewd and vulgar speech at a school assembly. Rather than emphasize the apparent disruption of the school event and the rights of others, thereby applying *Tinker* and ruling for the school, the Court instead focused on the content of the speech and who has control over it in school settings: "It was perfectly appropriate for the school to disassociate itself to make the point to the pupils that vulgar speech and lewd conduct is wholly inconsistent with the 'fundamental values' of public school education" (*Bethel*, 1986, pp. 685–686). Recognizing the long-standing doctrine of *in loco parentis* ("in the place of parents"), the Court noted that the rights of students in schools are not coextensive with the rights of adults in other settings. In other words, the determination of what student speech is appropriate or inappropriate, when spoken in a classroom or in a school assembly, properly rests with the school board. And while tolerance and respect for divergent political and religious views are to be valued in educational settings, so is the consideration for the personal sensibilities of participants and audiences. According to the Court, the objective of public education is "the inculcation of fundamental values necessary to the maintenance of a democratic political system" (p. 681). Among these values are civility in public discourse and respect for the rights of others.

Nonpublic Forums, Imprimatur, and Legitimate Pedagogical Concerns: *Hazelwood School District v. Kuhlmeier*

In *Hazelwood School District v. Kuhlmeier* (1988), three high school students filed suit against their public school district and principal, after the principal cut two pages of the school-sponsored newspaper to avoid the publication of two articles the principal felt were objectionable, invasive, and inappropriate. One article was on teenage pregnancy; it used false names, but the identities of the students could be discovered from the context. The other dealt with the impact of divorce and mentioned a student's name and made some disparaging remarks about the student's father. There was no time to make changes to the articles, so the principal deleted the whole pages. The newspaper was published as part of a journalism course but had a large circulation that included community members outside the school. The plaintiffs claimed censorship and argued that the school violated their free speech rights. The District Court held for the school, deferring to its reasonable educational decision-making. The Eighth Circuit Court of Appeals reversed and held for the students, on the grounds that the newspaper was a public forum; the Circuit Court then applied the *Tinker* rule and held that the articles would not have amounted to substantial interference with the work of the school.

The Supreme Court addressed two related issues and reversed in favor of the school district. First, on the question of whether a school-sponsored newspaper is a public forum for purposes of the First Amendment, the Court held that it was not. According to the Court, school facilities may be deemed public forums only if schools, by policy or practice, open these facilities to indiscriminate use by the general public. There was no evidence that the school had done so in this case. School board *policy* dictated that school-sponsored publications are developed within the schools' adopted curriculum and in accordance with regular classroom activities. The editing and review *practice* dictated that the teacher had final authority over students, subject to further review by the principal.

Second, on the question of whether public school administrators possess editorial authority over the style and content of school-sponsored publications and other sponsored expressive activities, the Court said that they do. "Educators do not offend the First Amendment by exercising editorial control over the style and content of student speech in school-sponsored expressive activities so long as their actions are reasonably related to legitimate pedagogical concerns" (p. 273). The Court noted early that this case was different from *Tinker*, which emphasized *tolerance* of particular student speech. *Hazelwood,* instead, involved the *promotion* of particular student-sponsored speech. Hence, a new and different standard applies in such cases. School administrators may exercise greater control over the second form of speech, which members of the public might perceive to bear the imprimatur of the school. Included in this second form are school-sponsored expressive activities, whether in or out of the classroom, especially those activities tied to the school's educational mission. Schools must also be sensitive of the younger audience members and may restrict school-sponsored student speech if the restriction is related to legitimate pedagogical concerns. The Court found that the principal acted reasonably. The identities of students could be discovered in the submitted articles, and the topics of sexual activity and birth control were not appropriate for the school audience. The student in the divorce article sharply criticized her father, without giving the father an opportunity to defend himself. The curriculum is concerned with the treatment of sensitive controversial speech and the administration was in the right to emphasize these curricular concerns.

MORSE V. FREDERICK

The Facts

On January 24, 2002, students at Juneau-Douglas High School were released from school early to watch the 2002 Winter Olympics Torch Relay, which was passing by the school. The relay was sponsored largely by Coca-Cola and other private entities. Some of the school's athletes, cheerleaders, and band members, however, participated in the leg of the relay that was passing by, lending an air of sponsorship, support, and accommodation by the school. For all intents and purposes, though, all other students were simply released for the day.

Meanwhile, Joseph Frederick, an 18-year-old senior at the school, never made it to school in the morning, as his car was reportedly stuck in the snow on his driveway. He did, however, make it to the torch relay. He and some friends stood across the street from the school and waited until the torch and the television cameras came by. At just the right time, Frederick and his friends unfurled a home-made 14-foot banner saying "BONG HiTS 4 JESUS." Deborah Morse, principal of the school, crossed the street immediately and asked Frederick to take the banner down. She claimed that the banner violated school policy against displaying offensive material, including material that advertises or promotes the use of illegal drugs. When Frederick refused to take the banner down, Morse confiscated it and suspended Frederick for ten days.

Morse conceded her decision was not based on a concern for potential disruption. Instead, she claimed the sign was inconsistent with the educational mission of the school to promote a healthy, drug-free life style. She also claimed that failure to act as she did under the circumstances would give the public the impression that the school condoned such speech. Specifically, Morse cited a school board policy that "prohibits any assembly or public expression that…advocates the use of substances that are illegal to minors." On the other hand, Frederick claimed that his speech was designed to be meaningless and funny. He was simply hoping to get on television. Furthermore, he argued that he was not in school that day and was not on school property when he displayed his banner. Frederick appealed his suspension to the superintendent, who upheld Morse's decision. In a statement setting forth his reasons for supporting Morse, the superintendent declared that the banner was, in fact, displayed during a "school-sanctioned activity" and that Frederick was disciplined not because Morse disagreed with the message of the speech, but because it advocated illegal drug use. Furthermore, the superintendent stated that the message of the speech contravened "the work of the schools."

Frederick then filed suit. The district court granted summary judgment to the school district and Frederick appealed. The United States Court of Appeals for the Ninth Circuit reversed in favor of Frederick, holding that the speech did not take place at a school-sponsored event and was not a part of school curriculum, nor was it plainly offensive to the school's drug-free mission. The court of appeals applied *Tinker* and found the speech non-school-sponsored and nondisruptive. In addition to ruling for the student on the First Amendment speech claim, the Ninth Circuit also rejected Morse's qualified immunity defense to Frederick's claim for monetary damages. The circuit court held that Morse violated Frederick's clearly established right to free speech, a right established by the line of cases from *Tinker* to *Bethel* to *Hazelwood*, discussed above. Morse then appealed to the Supreme Court, which reversed in favor of Morse on both the free speech and qualified immunity claims.

The Majority Opinion: Chief Justice Roberts, Drugs, and the School Leader's Reasonable Interpretations of Student Speech

Essentially, Chief Justice Roberts, in his majority opinion, carved out an additional exception to *Tinker's* long-standing statement that students and teachers do not shed their constitutional rights at the schoolhouse gate, although he does so in a fairly sharp manner. Joined by Justices Scalia, Kennedy, Thomas, and Alito, the Chief Justice's stated holding is a narrow one: School officials do not violate the First Amendment rights of students when they restrict speech and conduct that advocates illegal drug use, particularly when that speech and conduct occur at a school-related function.

The majority dismissed early and quickly one of Frederick's most important arguments—that his speech occurred off school property and was not sanctionable by the school. The majority stated that the event was school-related: "we agree with the superintendent that Frederick cannot 'stand in the midst of his fellow students; during school hours, at a school-sanctioned activity and claim he is not at school'" (p. 2624). Teachers and administrators were interspersed among the students, the marching band and cheerleaders performed; and Frederick and his friends directed the banner toward the school, making the words plainly visible to the students and staff. There may be some question as to the physical, geographic, and time-based limits on a school's authority to restrict student speech. However, according to the Court, the facts of this case did not raise such a question.

Most of the power of Roberts' majority opinion comes from the discussion on Morse's interpretation of Frederick's banner. Frederick himself argued credibly that his motive was purely to get the attention of the television cameras and not to advocate illegal drug use. Nonetheless, it was Morse who was in the position to enforce school policy and she testified that the banner could have been viewed by the school community and larger public as promoting drug use. The Court viewed Morse's interpretation as reasonable:

> At least two interpretations of the words on the banner demonstrate that the sign advocated the use of illegal drugs. First, the phrase could be interpreted as an impera-tive: "[Take] bong hits…"—a message equivalent, as Morse explained…, to "smoke marijuana" or use an illegal drug. Alternatively, the phrase could be viewed as celebrat-ing drug use—"bong hits [are a good thing]," or "[we take] bong hits"—and we discern no meaningful distinction between celebrating illegal drug use in the midst of fellow students and outright advocacy or promotion. (p. 2625)

Bolstering the reasonableness of Morse's interpretation of Frederick's speech was the lack of alternative reasonable meanings. Frederick argued that the banner was meant to be funny and meaningless. And his stated motive—to get on TV—is not an interpretation of the content. Moreover, Frederick failed to assert any political or religious message with the banner.

The majority reviewed the significant holdings of *Tinker, Bethel,* and *Hazelwood* and essentially did not apply any of them with any force. Instead, the majority fashioned what may be considered another exception to *Tinker's* traditional "material and substantial disruption" standard. According to the Court, this case was not about the desire to avoid controversy. *Tinker* involved silent and passive political speech, with no motive on the part of the Des Moines school district other than to avoid the unpleasantness and discomfort of an unpopular view. The school administration in *Morse,* on the other hand, legitimately viewed Frederick's banner as advocacy of illegal activity and used that interpretation to make the statement that schools' and students' interests in a lawful, drug-free educational environment outweigh the individual rights of students to use school events to celebrate drug use.

The majority presented the holdings in *Bethel* and *Hazelwood,* largely, to make the point that the *Tinker* analysis is not absolute in student speech cases. While the Court did not apply *Bethel* and *Hazelwood* directly, those decisions were important to remind readers that the constitutional rights of students are not automatically coextensive with the rights of adults in other settings. The Court refused to stretch *Bethel* so far as to allow school administrators to restrict all offensive speech conflicting with the school's espoused "fundamental mission," as doing so would cross the line into lawful religious and political speech, protected by *Tinker.* The concern was not that the speech was offensive but that it was reasonably viewed as promoting drug use.

In an interesting and important turn, the majority used two well-known Supreme Court decisions upholding random, suspicion-less urinalysis drug tests in schools to make their point (see *Board of Educ. v. Earls,* 2002; and *Vernonia Sch. Dist. 47J v. Acton,* 1995). The Court recognized that the deterrence of drug use among students is a compelling state interest for schools and that drug use remains a serious problem today at all age and grade levels. Schools are expected to educate children on the dangers of drug use and, as a result, must be able to "convey a clear and consistent message that...the illegal use of drugs is wrong and harmful" (*Morse,* 2007, p. 2628). Arguing further, Chief Justice Roberts wrote:

> Student speech celebrating illegal drug use at a school event, in the presence of school administrators and teachers, thus poses a particular challenge for school officials working to protect those entrusted to their care from the dangers of drug abuse. (p. 2628)

Most important for practitioners in schools, the majority in *Morse* gave educators credit for taking on their necessary roles and gave them the leeway to act reasonably in the face of conduct like Frederick's:

> When Frederick suddenly and unexpectedly unfurled his banner, Morse had to decide to act—or not to act—on the spot. It was reasonable for her to conclude that the banner promoted illegal drug use....[F]ailing to act would send a powerful message to the

students in her charge, including Frederick, about how serious the school was about the dangers of illegal drug use. The First Amendment does not require schools to tolerate at school events student expression that contributes to those dangers. (p. 2629)

Justice Thomas: *In Loco Parentis* and the Argument to Overrule Tinker

Justice Thomas, in his concurring opinion, made the somewhat startling statement that the standard set forth in *Tinker* in 1969 has no basis in the Constitution. Espousing values of a historical nature, Justice Thomas extolled the virtues of early public education for its emphasis on discipline, manners, and school authority. According to Justice Thomas, public schools were originally created as substitutes for private schools, which were more well known for their discipline, instilled sets of common values, and "subordination to lawful authority" than for "free wheeling debates or exploration of competing ideas" (*Morse,* 2007, p. 2630). The connection, then, is that public schools should not recognize free speech rights of students any more than the private schools they mirrored long ago.

Justice Thomas was particularly fond of the *in loco parentis* doctrine, which gives school officials wide latitude in the imposition of discipline, including the regulation of student speech. Praising the judicial restraint that comes with the notion of school teachers and leaders acting *in loco parentis,* Justice Thomas reviewed several state court decisions from the 1800s to make the point that courts have historically offered great deference to the important daily decisions made by school leaders. He then updated this argument with important references to the Court's majority opinions in *Vernonia School District 47J v. Acton* (1995) and *Bethel School District v. Fraser* (1986), both of which recognized the continued applicability of *in loco parentis* in public schools.

Against this historical backdrop, Justice Thomas then argued for the overruling of *Tinker.* According to Justice Thomas, teachers instill a core of common values through strict curriculum and strict discipline. Essentially, he states that Chief Justice Roberts' majority opinion respects those common values but does so through yet another round of "ad hoc" scaling back of *Tinker,* as opposed to the much simpler resolution of disposing with *Tinker* altogether. "In my view, petitioners could prevail for a much simpler reason: As originally understood, the Constitution does not afford students a right to free speech in public schools" (p. 2634). Justice Thomas clearly argues for a less active judiciary in such situations, best effected by an overruling of *Tinker.* He adds *Morse* to *Bethel* and *Hazelwood* as evidence that the Court is increasingly uncomfortable with the standard it articulated in *Tinker* in 1969.

Justice Alito: Reaffirming *Tinker* with a Drug-Related Exception

Justice Alito's concurring opinion, in which Justice Kennedy joined, is perhaps the most important opinion in *Morse v. Frederick*, with respect to the balance between the free speech rights of public school students and the institutional interests in student discipline and order. On one hand, the opinion strongly endorsed the limited free speech restrictions offered by Chief Justice Roberts' majority: "[T]he opinion of the Court...goes no further than to hold that a public school may restrict speech that a reasonable observer would interpret as advocating illegal drug use..." (p. 2636). To that end, Justice Alito notes that the majority's opinion would not support a restriction of student speech on political or social issues, including speech on the legalization of marijuana for medicinal purposes.

On the other hand, Justice Alito's concurrence also reaffirms *Tinker's* fundamental principle that students do not shed their constitutional rights to free speech at the schoolhouse gate. He noted the well known restrictions to speech outlined in *Bethel* and *Hazelwood* and made the necessary statement that the restriction outlined in *Morse* represents no further significant disintegration of *Tinker*. Importantly, Justice Alito noted that the majority opinion did not go as far as Morse and the school district wanted it to:

> The opinion of the Court does not endorse the broad argument advanced by the petitioners...that the First Amendment permits public school officials to censor any student speech that interferes with a school's "educational mission." This argument can easily be manipulated in dangerous ways, and I would reject it before such abuse occurs. (p. 2637)

According to Justice Alito, the educational mission argument would lead to unconstitutional viewpoint discrimination and "strikes at the very heart of the First Amendment" (p. 2637).

Justice Alito's stated reaffirmation of *Tinker* is particularly telling. It is certainly true that Justice Alito's arguments favor the views of the majority, with an acceptance of *Morse's* narrowly drawn exception to *Tinker*, and disfavor the views of Justice Stevens' dissent. But Justice Alito's concurring opinion is, perhaps, at its strongest against the viewpoints espoused by Justice Thomas in Thomas' concurrence. In stark contrast to Justice Thomas and the doctrine of *in loco parentis*, Justice Alito reminded readers that public school officials, while perhaps possessing some delegated authority courtesy of *in loco parentis*, do not lose their status as State actors and, as such, their contribution to the legal and ethical balance must include some consideration of the public school setting. From Justice Alito's point of view, the consideration most relevant to the case here is student safety (including, by implication, incidents relating to cyber-bullying):

> [D]ue to the special features of the school environment, school officials must have greater authority to intervene before speech leads to violence....Speech advocating

illegal drug use poses a threat to student safety that is just as serious [as speech that causes substantial disruption or physical violence], if not always as immediately obvious. (p. 2638)

The Dissent: Justice Stevens and the Feared Trivialization of *Tinker* with Trivial Student Speech

Justice Stevens, in a dissent joined by Justices Souter and Ginsburg, accused the majority, with its newly fashioned "promotion of illegal drug use" test for student speech, of trivializing two central principles set forth in *Tinker*. First, Justice Stevens asserted that censorship based on viewpoint and content of speech has always been subjected to the highest level of scrutiny. It was clear, according to Justice Stevens, that Frederick's speech was targeted and restricted on account of viewpoint and content. Frederick stated convincingly and regularly that he meant nothing by the message and merely wished to get on television. Justice Stevens did not believe Morse's interpretation—advocacy of illegal conduct—to be reasonable.

Second, the restriction of speech that advocates illegal conduct is lawful only when the advocacy is likely to provoke the harm that the government seeks to avoid. And while the school setting may modify these principles, *Tinker* supported them even in light of its application in schools. Although Justice Stevens did not say so directly, it seems he would have simply applied *Tinker's* disruption standard to these facts and would have, thus, supported Frederick. Instead, according to the dissent, the majority carved out a "pro-drug speech" exception to *Tinker* that has no support in the law. In making this argument, however, Justice Stevens may have done some damage to student speech while attempting to support it. On one hand, he asserted that the majority trivialized *Tinker's* essential principles. This may be the case. But on the other hand, Justice Stevens also spoke to the motive, content, and effect of the speech and, in his efforts to argue for Frederick's right to speak, he trivialized the speech itself as silly, nonsensical, and vague.

> This is a nonsense message, not advocacy....Frederick's credible and uncontradicted explanation for the message—he just wanted to get on television—is also relevant because a speaker who does not intend to persuade his audience can hardly be said to be advocating anything....Most students...do not shed their brains at the schoolhouse gate, and most students know dumb advocacy when they see it. (p. 2649)

Throughout Justice Stevens' dissent, he described the speech as "ambiguous," "nonsensical," "ridiculous," "obscure," "silly," and "stupid." And then he said the following, in seeming contradiction: "The Court's ham-handed, categorical approach is deaf to the constitutional imperative to permit unfettered debate, even among high school students, about the wisdom of the war on drugs or of legalizing marijuana for medicinal use" (p. 2649). It is fairly clear that Justice Stevens was not suggesting that Frederick and his speech were the vehicles to a great debate over drugs (or for that matter, other serious social issues affecting the youth of America). He simply feared that *Tinker* suffered a significant setback with the Court's opinion. It is unfortunate for those who agree with this argument, however, that he minimized the speech at issue in this case as a non-player in the dialogue. Curiously, Justice Stevens' argument ultimately begs the question, "If the speech is not worth much, then who will care if it's free?"

Justice Breyer: The Argument to Avoid the Constitutional Discussion

> In resolving the underlying constitutional question, we produce several differing opinions. It is utterly unnecessary to do so. Were we to decide this case on the ground of qualified immunity, our decision would be unanimous. (p. 2641)

In, arguably, the most unique and separate opinion of the five authored in *Morse,* Justice Breyer's reading of the facts in the case avoids the First Amendment question altogether, although he appeared to dissent from the viewpoint of the majority on this account and grants qualified immunity to Principal Morse because, according to Breyer, she did not violate clearly established law in her confrontation with Frederick.

Justice Breyer's complaints with Chief Justice Roberts' majority are simple and clear. First, he separated the action of removing the banner from any restriction on speech: "To say that school officials might reasonably prohibit students during school-related events from unfurling 14-foot banners (with any kind of irrelevant or inappropriate message) designed to attract attention from television cameras seems unlikely to undermine basic First Amendment principles" (p. 2638). Second, he stated that connecting Morse's reaction to questions of First Amendment free speech and then holding in favor of Morse on account of her alleged reasonable interpretation of the banner, yields a holding that has its basis in viewpoint discrimination. Justice Breyer argued that such viewpoint discrimination was without justification under the facts of the case, and the resultant holding is now ripe for massive abuse in the future.

Justice Breyer's complaints with Justice Stevens' dissent are similarly clear and strike at the same critical facts in the case. He agreed with the majority that Morse had to react quickly under the circumstances, but judgment of her conduct is less a question for the First Amendment than it is for qualified immunity. First, he strongly argues that courts should avoid constitutional questions except in cases where doing so is unavoidable and/or where answering the question will offer guidance. Here, he says treating the dispute as an issue of qualified immunity avoids the First Amendment question nicely. Second, and to address the speech question in the not-so-guiding manner that the majority did will only generate more unnecessary free speech disputes between educators and students.

The traditional argument for qualified immunity in public school cases is that the law applied by the school official (state actor) in the case was not clearly established at the time the decision was made, and that the state actor in question had not clearly violated the law. At the time of the confrontation in *Morse, Tinker, Bethel,* and *Hazelwood* were the controlling cases. Justice Breyer argued that none of the three clearly governed the situation presented to Morse.

CYBERSPACE SPEECH AND BULLYING AFTER *MORSE*: LOCATION, EFFECT, AND CONTENT OF SPEECH

Until *Morse*, school leaders were guided by three Supreme Court opinions on student speech: *Tinker's* substantial disruption and material interference standard, *Bethel's* prohibition of lewd and vulgar speech, and *Hazelwood's* restriction on student speech in school-sponsored educational activities. But with *Morse*, where does the balance between individual student speech and institutional authority to restrict such speech now lie? In other words, in light of *Morse*, the first K-12 student speech case to go to the Supreme Court in almost 20 years, what primary values guide the policy and discipline decisions school leaders can make, particularly when applied to expressive conduct in a technological era? The five different opinions in *Morse* give school leaders much to think about in terms of the location, effect, and content of student speech.

First, school administrators may certainly be guided by Chief Justice Roberts' sharply written and arguably narrow majority, focusing on the content of Frederick's drug-related speech and the reasonable interpretation Morse gathered from it. Chief Justice Roberts and the majority find the content and potential effect (i.e., the principal's interpretation) of the speech to be the salient features in the case. As a result, school administrators may restrict student speech which, under a reasonable administrative interpretation of content, can be seen to advocate illegal drug use. Read broadly, the majority opinion may speak to school leaders' reasonable interpretation of other speech on potentially illegal conduct, including speech conveyed via electronic media.

Second, Justice Thomas espoused fundamental values associated with the long-standing historical doctrine of *in loco parentis*, arguing that public school students have no recognized First Amendment right to free speech at school and that a nearly absolute right to impose strict discipline rests with the school. Essentially, this argument speaks to the location of student speech and a sharp diminution of students' rights at the schoolhouse gate. Third, Justice Alito finds the content and the effect of student speech most salient, reaffirming *Tinker* and reiterating Chief Justice Roberts' drug-related exception to student speech. Fourth, like Chief Justice Roberts and Justice Alito, Justice Stevens focuses his attention on the content and effect of Frederick's speech but finds instead the weak effect of the speech significantly heavier than the speech's drug-related content. Finally, in what might be a strange comparison to Justice Thomas' opinion, Justice Breyer focuses his energy on the values associated with deference to the important decisions school administrators make. He stops short of judging the content of the speech as the most salient. Instead, he favors the disciplinary authority school leaders must exercise under circumstances presented in this case and argues that they should be qualifiedly immune from lawsuit for acting reasonably and implementing simple behavior-based rules. Each of these opinions, when viewed through the lenses of location, effect, and content, contributes to what we now know about *Morse's* impact on the balance between students' rights and school authority in the context of cyber-bullying.

The Location of the Speech

Despite the heavy emphasis the Ninth Circuit Court of Appeals placed on the location of Frederick's speech (technically, off school grounds and arguably outside of school rules and jurisdiction), none of the five opinions at the Supreme Court, most importantly the majority, placed emphasis on it. So, how long is the arm of the school when it comes to restricting student speech? *Morse* does not necessarily muddy the waters containing answers to this question. But any expectation that *Morse* would clear those waters was dashed when the opinions were released. Nonetheless, location of student speech remains a factor, particularly in light of today's technological media. Dating itself to 1979 and from a case involving a group of students who were suspended for printing a sexually explicit magazine, the following statement from the Second Circuit Court of Appeals is rather fascinating in its balance between student and school:

> When school officials are authorized only to punish speech on school property, the student is free to speak his mind when the school day ends. In this manner, the community is not deprived of the salutary effects of expression, and educational authorities are free to establish an academic environment in which the teaching and learning process can proceed free of disruption. Indeed, our willingness to grant school officials substantial autonomy within their academic domain rests in part on the confinement of that power within the metes and bounds of the school itself. (*Thomas v. Board of Education, Granville Central School District,* 1979, p. 1052)

A more recent case, which involved a student who emailed a "top ten" list of disparaging remarks about his school's athletic director, makes a similar statement: "[C]ourts considering speech that occurs off school grounds have concluded (relying on Supreme Court decisions) that school officials' authority over off-campus expression is much more limited than expression on school grounds" (*Killion v. Franklin Reg'l Sch. Dist.,* 2001, p. 454). In other words, a student's right to free expression in school settings is not coextensive with the right to free expression in other settings. In *Killion v. Franklin Regional School District,* the "top ten" list was, indeed, published by a high school student and emailed to several of his classmates. The uncomplimentary list suggested, among other things, that the athletic director was fat and engaged in sexually harassing conduct with female students at the school. The student author was suspended for ten days after a hard copy of the list landed in the school's teachers' lounge. It was undisputed that a classmate was the one who brought the hard copy to school. The student and his family filed suit alleging both due process and free speech violations. The court found in favor of the student, in part, due to the fact that the student's conduct occurred off premises and that the speech was not disruptive.

So if the student's speech originates off school grounds and not at a school-sponsored activity or event, when and where does the school's authority outweigh the student's right to speak? When the *content* of the speech spills over to school grounds? When the *effect* of that speech does? Or in other words, when the *location* is no longer the most salient feature? The courts generally answer these last three questions in the affirmative. In the context of cyber-bullying, then, it is not often the location of the speech that is lawfully restricted by the school but rather its content or effect.

The violent and disturbing drawings and writings of young people, even when created off school grounds and after school hours, will undoubtedly unnerve the most reasonable school administrators, teachers, and classmates. In such cases, the seriousness of the expressive content will most often trump the location of the speech and allow the school leader to punish the author/artist, particularly when the expression is targeted to a specific person (*Doe v. Pulaski County Special Sch. Dist.,* 2002), or when it appears in close proximity (in time or location) to well known, national, news-making school shootings (*Lavine v. Blaine Sch. Dist.,* 2001; *Porter v. Ascension Parish Sch. Bd.,* 2004). In *Doe v. Pulaski County Special School District* (2002), a junior high school student wrote a profane, threatening letter to his ex-girlfriend, expressing a desire to rape, molest, and kill her. He wrote it during the summer and never delivered it to her but allowed a friend to deliver it. The Eighth Circuit Court of Appeals upheld a one-year expulsion. In *Lavine v. Blaine School District* (2001), a student showed his teacher a poem he wrote, entitled "Last Words," which detailed a school shooting with the poet as the shooter. He wrote the poem shortly after the shootings at Columbine High School. He was removed from school in an emergency expulsion and was allowed to return only after a psychiatric evaluation.

The authority of a school district to punish out-of-school student speech has been the subject of several recent cases involving the speech of young people in cyberspace. For example, consider a student's derogatory, controversial, and/or lewd and vulgar comments, directed at school employees or classmates, but made and posted on his or her personal web site (*Coy v. Board of Educ. of North*

Canton City Sch., 2002; *Mahaffey v. Aldrich*, 2002; *J.S. v. Bethlehem Area Sch. Dist.*, 2002; *Beussink v. Woodland R-IV School District*, 1998), blog (*Doninger v. Niehoff*, 2007), message board (*Flaherty v. Keystone Oaks Sch. Dist.*, 2003), or web-based social network (e.g., MySpace or Facebook) (*Layshock v. Hermitage Sch. Dist.*, 2007; *Snyder v. Blue Mountain Sch. Dist.*, 2008). Or consider the posting of a controversial video on YouTube, perhaps a video of a teacher secretly taped by a student (*Requa v. Kent Sch. Dist.* No. 415, 2007). Then consider a school's disciplinary authority when those sites are accessed on school grounds or when hard copies of those comments find their way to school. Or when one or more school officials merely hear about them. No doubt, many school leaders will want to make a strong statement to their technology-savvy student body that, while the students have the knowledge and power of technology, the school is the one with the ultimate disciplinary authority.

When the off-premises, after hours Internet speech of students does not disrupt the work of the school or the rights of others in content or effect, attempts to justify student punishment will typically fail. In *Mahaffey v. Aldrich* (2002) and *Beussink v. Woodland R-IV School District* (1998), for example, students created web pages on home computers and, while the content on the sites contained language and images of vulgarity and violence (including language critical of the school), there was no evidence of substantial disruption or interference. The student who posted her displeasure over school decisions to a publicly accessible blog was not as fortunate (*Doninger v. Niehoff*, 2007). In *Doninger*, court considered the student's conduct to be on-campus speech and upheld the school's punishment, particularly because the speech was related to school matters and was reasonably likely to be seen at school:

> *Fraser* and *Morse* teach that school officials could permissibly punish Avery [Doninger] in the way that they did for her offensive speech in the blog, which interfered with the school's 'highly appropriate function…to prohibit the use of vulgar and offensive terms in public discourse.' (p. 48)

The student who posted the YouTube video was similarly unlucky, with the court upholding his suspension, as well (*Requa v. Kent Sch. Dist.* No. 415, 2007).

Two fascinating cases involving MySpace profiles add wrinkles to this portion of the dialogue. In *Layshock v. Hermitage School District* (2007), a high school senior (Layshock) created a parody profile of his school principal and posted it on MySpace.com, a social networking Internet site where users can share photos, journals, and personal interests with fellow users. MySpace has a template profile of questions that allows users to fill in background information about themselves. In a parody of his principal, Layshock's answers to the profile's questions were presented as though his principal completed the information; the responses centered on the theme of "big" and ranged from nonsensical to crude, with references to sex, drugs, and alcohol. The profile was created off school premises and after school hours. But word of the parody reached most of the student body and several school employees. Layshock was suspended for 10 days and ordered to attend school in an alternative program at the high school. He was also banned from participation in school activities, including graduation. He filed suit against the district.

Ultimately weighing the location of the speech as the most salient feature, the court found in favor of Layshock. The district argued for its authority on both content and effect grounds. First, using the values espoused and defended in *Bethel,* the district claimed that Layshock's speech was lewd, profane, and sexually inappropriate. The court did not necessarily disagree; however, the content of the speech was not controlling in the case, in that *Bethel* does not give school administrators the authority to punish lewd and profane off-premises speech. Second, the district used *Tinker* to argue that the parody had a disruptive effect on the work of the school. The court disagreed, saying that the district failed to make the connection between Layshock's speech and any disruption. The only charges the school offered against Layshock were against his off-premises conduct. "On this record, there is no evidence that the school administrators even knew that Justin [Layshock] had accessed the profile while in school prior to the disciplinary proceedings" (p. 601).

In a case with similar facts to those in Layshock, the court came to a decidedly different conclusion. In *Snyder v. Blue Mountain School District* (2008), a student created a false MySpace profile for his middle school principal. The profile portrayed the principal as a married, bisexual man from Alabama. The web address for the profile contained the phrase "kids rock my bed." The author of the profile never accessed the profile at school, nor did he bring hard copies to school. However, the profile caused quite a stir in the hallways and a hard copy eventually landed on the principal's desk. The student-creator was suspended for ten days and the parents filed suit. The court rejected a "location of speech" argument and distinguished *Layshock* (2007), *Killion* (2001), and *Flaherty* (2003). Upholding the suspension, the court held that *Tinker* is not the only applicable standard in such cases and, instead, favored *Bethel* and *Morse*. While Snyder's speech may not have generated the type or level of disruption contemplated in an application of *Tinker,* it was enough to justify punishment under *Bethel* and *Morse*. In an important statement, the court moved *Morse's* application to speech beyond illegal drug use:

> This speech is not the *Tinker* silent protest. It is more akin to the lewd and vulgar speech addressed in *Fraser.* It is also akin to the speech that promoted illegal actions in the *Morse* case. The speech at issue here could have been the basis for criminal charges. (pp. 17–18).

So what does *Morse* contribute to the dialogue with respect to the location of the speech? To the disappointment of Frederick, his lawyers, and the overturned Ninth

Circuit, all of whom placed great stock in the off-premises unfurling of Frederick's banner, none of the five opinions in *Morse* highlighted the location of the speech as critical to the outcome. Despite the fact that, among the four Supreme Court cases on student free speech (*Tinker, Bethel, Hazelwood,* and *Morse*), Frederick's speech is the only speech across the four never to reach the physical premises of the school, cases following *Morse* may follow the Supreme Court's lead and leave *Morse* out of a discussion of student speech and its location. The *Layshock* court, for example, stated that *Morse* did not change the basic *Tinker-Bethel-Hazelwood* framework, due, in part, to the fact that the Supreme Court decision in *Morse* was not dependent on where the student's speech took place. In contrast, the Snyder decision invoked *Morse* for an analysis of content and effect of speech. So, what about the web site and other Internet cases involving off-premises speech of students? It is true that the students win several of these, especially when their conduct has no disruptive effect at school. But what if the speakers and actors on the MySpace page, YouTube video, blog, or web site advocate illegal drug use or commit other potentially illegal conduct, at least to the reasonable interpretation of a school administrator or educator surfing by? Is the off-premises location of the speech enough to withstand school punishment? The emphasis in *Morse* on the connection of the Torch Relay to the school, and several of the cases cited above tend to say "yes." But recall the words of Chief Justice Roberts, praising the school for its anti-drug policy enforcement. By and large, as long as the content and effect of the speech remain off school grounds, the student tends to win on a First Amendment challenge. However, when content and/or effect trump location, and invade school grounds, school property, school hours, or even school personnel outside of school, students tend to lose and courts favor the efforts of school to maintain safe and comfortable school environments.

The Actual or Forecasted Effect of the Speech

When we speak of the "effect" of student speech, we likely think quickly of *Tinker* and the very well known substantial disruption standard. If we believe the words of Chief Justice Roberts and Justice Alito, this standard has not been affected by the decision in *Morse*. If we believe Justice Stevens, however, the standard has been weakened significantly. Almost all readers can agree, however, that the majority opinion in *Morse* carves out a content-based exception (i.e., student advocacy of illegal drug use) to *Tinker* standard, however narrow that exception may be. From a different perspective, though, consider the school leader's "reasonable interpretation" of student speech as effect-based. Principal Morse was concerned not only about the content of Frederick's banner but also about the effect it would have on the appearance and judgment of the school from the perspective of those who would view it. Does the notion of a "reasonable interpretation" of student speech give more power to the decision-making authority of school leaders, even outside of drug-related speech, when they determine whether or not student speech is substantially disruptive or likely to be so? Perhaps. *Tinker's* standard will continue to be applied, but perhaps a little differently when courts consider the perspective of those who first decide whether a student's speech should be restricted. In the context of cyber-bullying, the pressure on school leaders is high. As a result, the tendency to err on the side of the alleged victim(s) and argue that the alleged perpetrator's conduct has an actual or reasonably likely disruption is very real. And courts may follow suit, agreeing with the school administrator who sees danger and harm to students and schools, and disagreeing with the student perpetrator who argues that the conduct was meant to be harmless commentary. In the most recent iteration of *Harper v. Poway Unified School District* (2008), a protracted case involving the disputed right of a student to wear a T-shirt condemning homosexuality, the District Court for the Southern District of California recognized and accepted *Morse's* narrow holding but expanded it anyway to include speech outside of alleged pro-drug advocacy:

> Although this Court's review of *Morse* reveals that the majority made it clear its decision is limited to speech concerning illegal drug use,…this Court agrees with defendants [school district and its officials] that the reasoning presented in *Morse* lends support for a finding that the speech at issue in the instant case may properly be restricted by school officials if it is considered harmful. (p. 1100)

A great number of *Tinker* disruption applications come in challenges to student dress codes. Recently, in a string of disputes over controversial dress, the students have won relatively often on findings of no actual or potential disruption, with cases involving pro-life messages (*K.D. v. Fillmore Cent. Sch. Dist.*, 2005; *M.A.L. v. Kinsland*, 2007), anti-homosexuality shirts (*Nixon v. Northern Local Sch. Dist. Bd. of Educ.*, 2005), dress-related statements honoring the military (*Griggs v. Fort Wayne Sch. Bd.*, 2005; *Grzywna v. Schenectady Cent. Sch. Dist.*, 2006), and T-shirts criticizing President Bush (*Barber v. Dearborn Pub. Sch.*, 2003; *Guiles v. Marineau*, 2006). In these cases, the school leaders wish to restrict the controversial content of the clothing in order to avoid disruption of school work or interference with the rights of others. True to the spirit of *Tinker*, though, courts have held that "offensiveness" of the message and/or "disagreement" with the content is not enough to suppress the expression.

Of course, schools need not show actual disruption in order to restrict student speech; reasonable likelihood of disruption is sufficient. In *Boucher v. School Board of Greenfield* (1998), for example, the Seventh Circuit Court of Appeals held that an underground newspaper article offering suggestions and encouragement on how to hack into a school's computer system justified the author's expulsion, despite the lack of any actual hacking or other disruption. The District Court for the Southern District of New York came to a similar conclusion ten years later in a case involving a fifth-grader's written comment in a school assignment (*Cuff v. Valley Cent. Sch. Dist.*, 2008). Students were directed to fill in a picture of an astronaut with statements of their personalities. One student claimed that he would "blow up the school with all the teachers in it." The court acknowledged the holding in *Morse v. Frederick* as a reaffirmation of *Tinker* and upheld the school's five-day suspension.

A common application of the "reasonable forecast of disruption" standard occurs in cases involving student display, use, or wearing of the Confederate flag. In nearly all such cases, schools have successfully justified restriction on student expression or other punishment on account of current and potential racial unrest in the school, relying on both content and effect (see, e.g., *Barr v. Lafon*, 2008; *B.W.A. v. Farmington R-7 Sch. Dist.*, 2007; *Denno v. School Bd. of Volusia County*, 2000; *Phillips v. Anderson County Sch. Dist. No. 5*, 1997; *Scott v. School Bd. of Alachua County*, 2003; *West v. Derby Unified Sch. Dist. No. 260*, 2000; and *White v. Nichols*, 2006). In addition, schools tend to win student protest cases on the grounds that student safety trumps disruptive or potentially disruptive student speech (see, e.g., *Brandt v. Board of Educ. of City of Chicago*, 2007; *Lowery v. Euverard*, 2007; *Madrid v. Anthony*, 2007; and *Pangle v. Bend-Lapine Sch. Dist.*, 2000). This is particularly the case when student expression is violent and/or targeted to specific people, even when the speech is otherwise silent, as in the case of a student's notebook writings detailing the creation of a neo-Nazi group and plans to commit a Columbine-style shooting at school (*Ponce v. Socorro Indep. Sch. Dist.*, 2007); or the detailed writing of a student's dream on how she would shoot her math teacher (*Boim v. Fulton County Sch. Dist.*, 2007); or a student's text message icon depicting the killing of her English teacher (*Wisniewski v. Bd. of Educ. of Weedsport Cent. Sch. Dist.*, 2007). Each of these cases cites and applies both *Tinker* and *Morse* to uphold necessary student discipline. Traditional, passive, and silent protests, however, carry a solid application of *Tinker*, with the students prevailing, in cases, for example, protesting school uniforms (*DePinto v. Bayonne Bd. of Educ.*, 2007; *Lowry v. Watson Chapel Sch. Dist.*, 2007) and Pledge of Allegiance recitation (*Frazier v. Alexandre*, 2006; and Holloman v. Harland, 2004).

So, the results are mixed when the "effect" of the speech is the salient feature, with students winning several challenges under circumstances with no disruption or forecast thereof, and schools winning several when they can show actual or potential disruption beyond "offensiveness" or disagreement with the message. How does *Morse* change this scorecard? Combine the ideas of offensiveness and disagreement with the speaker's message with *Morse's* language of "reasonable interpretation" of the viewer or listener, and students' victories may be tougher to achieve. Consider one such example from among the dress code and other related cases referenced here. While the decision in *Grzywna v. Schenectady Central School District* (2006) was released one year before the Supreme Court opinion in *Morse*, the court in *Grzywna* noted the importance of the audience's interpretation of speech in its judgment of the effect of that speech. Namely, the court analyzed the particularity of the student's message and comprehensibility of it to the audience. In *Grzywna,* a twelve-year-old middle school student wore a red, white, and blue beaded necklace she made. According to the student, she wore it to show her support for the military, including members of her own family. The defendant school district, however, viewed the necklace as gang-related and violative of school policy. The district court, in denying the defendants' motion to dismiss, made some important and telling statements: "The context in which a symbol is used for purposes of expression is important, for the context may give meaning to the symbol" (p. 144). According to the court in *Grzywna,* the plaintiff bears the burden of showing her speech is protected under the First Amendment. As such, she must convince the court that her conduct is expressive and that she offers a "particularized message." In *Grzywna,* the court found that the plaintiff may be able to supply facts demonstrating a particularized message. More important to our present discussion, though, are the *Grzywna* court's statements on the "comprehensibility" of the speaker's message. Quoting the Supreme Court decision in *Spence v. Washington* (1974), the court stated, "It also must be shown that there is a great likelihood that Plaintiff's message will be understood by those viewing it" (p. 145). Such a statement recalls Justice Stevens' dissent in *Morse,* where he argued that no reasonable viewer could interpret Frederick's speech as advocating anything. But, of course, that same statement recalls Chief Justice Roberts' majority and Justice Alito's concurrence, each claiming that Morse, as school leader, was in the perfect and necessary (even if unenviable) position to interpret student speech for school safety, discipline, message, advocacy, public appearance, and media effect. While the particularized message hoped for by the speaker appears to be important, the analysis from *Grzywna* and its reference to *Spence v. Washington* indicates that the comprehensibility of that message is equally important. If this analysis holds for cases post-*Morse,* an important connection can now be made between *all* student speech, whether or not drug-related, and the reasonable interpretations of that speech offered by the disciplinarian school administrators.

The Content of the Speech

We have seen thus far that, when the location of the disputed speech is the salient feature in the legal analysis of free speech claims in a technological era, it is often a quick analysis in favor of the student and against the stretching of a school's disciplinary authority to off-premises conduct. Schools are more successful in defending free speech claims when location is not salient, or when it is coupled with either the effect of the speech (discussed above) or the content of the speech. Perhaps the effect argument is the most successful one a school leader can make when restricting the dangerous and harmful conduct of students. However, a content-based restriction is also viable and, perhaps, equal to or more powerful than the effect argument, in that content-based arguments can target harmful conduct closer to its core. In other words, content-based restrictions, while tougher to argue legally, carry with them the proactivity that school leaders need to address bullying, both in hard copy and in cyberspace.

Tinker's disruption standard is certainly useful. But with *Bethel, Hazelwood,* and *Morse,* school administrators are more fully equipped to address First Amendment challenges that come from technologically creative students. Therefore, similar to the effect of student speech, discussed above, the "reasonable interpretation" idea from *Morse* likely carries some weight outside of drug-related speech, making content a salient feature in most, if not all, student speech cases, especially when *Morse* can be backed up by *Bethel's* "fundamental mission" language and *Hazelwood's* "legitimate pedagogical concerns."

There is no question that the "fundamental mission" language from *Bethel* is a powerful tool for school leaders when combating the creativity of inappropriate student speech. The superintendent in *Morse* invoked this language, along with *Tinker,* to defend the suspension of Frederick. Note, though, that while the Court offered great deference to Morse's reasonable interpretation of Frederick's speech, a majority of the Justices proceeded with great caution in stretching the "educational mission" argument too far. This point was made most forcefully by Justice Alito in his concurring opinion. Nonetheless, with *Morse* and a standard that invokes the interpretation of speech made by those who are tasked with school discipline and safety, there is an increased respect for a school's stated missions and values and perhaps some increased leeway on the leaders' content-based interpretation of student speech. Helping the school leaders in *Morse* is the majority's use of its Fourth Amendment cases on random, suspicionless urinalysis drug testing of students, *Vernonia School District 47J v. Acton* (1995) and *Board of Education v. Earls* (2002). Respecting the custodial and tutelary interests schools have over the students under their care, the Court helps school leaders bring home the point that drug use among youth is a serious problem, that schools are necessarily tasked with addressing it, and that courts ought to defer to the reasonable initiatives schools implement to curtail it. Certainly, the same can be said for anti-harassment and anti-bullying initiatives like those required by a majority of states.

In that vein, one post-*Morse* case has extended the reasoning in *Morse* to speech beyond the advocacy of illegal drug use. In *Miller v. Penn Manor School District* (2008), a student was forbidden under school policy from wearing a T-shirt that allegedly portrayed a pro-violence message and advocated vigilantism. The T-shirt was given to the student by his uncle, a member of the U.S. Army who was stationed in Iraq at the time. The shirt displayed the phrase "Volunteer Homeland Security" and images of an automatic handgun. The back of the T-shirt had the following phrase on it: "Special Issue—Resident-Lifetime License, United States Terrorist Hunting Permit, Permit No. 91101, Gun Owner—No Bag Limit." The student argued that the shirt did not advocate violence, was not targeted at anyone specific, and could not be reasonably interpreted that way. Furthermore, he argued that anyone can be a part of the nation's "Rewards for Justice" program, established in 1984 to combat international terrorism. The shirt, according to his argument, does no more than honor the work of his uncle and homeland security. The defendant school district disagreed and defended its decision using the ruling in *Morse.* According to the school, given the special characteristics of the school environment and the public interest in preventing violence in schools, the district need not show "substantial disruption" in order to restrict the T-shirt. Under *Morse,* all that is necessary is a "reasonable interpretation" that the student's speech advocates the use of the force, violence, and violation of the law. The court agreed with the school district. The court studied the "Rewards for Justice" web site and concluded that the school's interpretation of the T-shirt's message—one advocating violence and vigilantism—was reasonable. With reference to the mass shootings at Virginia Tech University, Columbine High School, Northern Illinois University, and other schools, the court made the following statement, akin to the Supreme Court's use of *Vernonia, Earls,* and anti-drug policies in its decision in *Morse:* "It is clear that the threat of violence in the school setting and the safety of our schools is [*sic*] of the utmost importance" (*Miller,* 2008, p. 46).

Hazelwood (1988) also plays a substantial role in content-based restrictions on student expression, particularly in reference to the potential for inappropriate student speech in school-sponsored activities to bear the imprimatur of the school. Morse, in her defense, argued that Frederick's banner, if unfurled on television, could give the impression that the school condoned such messages. With such defenses in mind, school leaders often see the "legitimate pedagogical concerns" associated with the speech as the most salient features of the case. Violent and/or sexually explicit or suggestive language in school-related speech is easily restricted by school leaders in cases involving essays written for a creative writing class (*Reihm v. Engelking,* 2007), gang symbols included in student work (*Kelly v. Board of Educ. of McHenry Comm. High Sch. Dist* 156, 2006), violent drawings made at school (*Demers v. Leominster Sch. Dep't,* 2003), and sexual innuendo in student council campaigns (*Henerey v. City of St. Charles Sch. Dist.,* 1999). School leaders have also been successful when claiming legitimate pedagogical concerns associated with the establishment and maintenance of a safe, respectful school environment with regard to student speech on the playground (*S.G. v. Sayreville Bd. of Educ.,* 2003) and in students' choice of dress and accessories (*Bar-Navon v. School Bd. of Brevard County,* Florida, 2007).

In the spirit of *Hazelwood,* but with use of *Bethel* and *Morse,* school leaders have launched a pedagogical interest defense in a couple very recent cases dealing with clothing containing messages condemning homosexuality (*Nuxoll v. Indian Prairie Sch. Dist.*, 2008), and a challenge to a school policy that prohibits students from making "stigmatizing or insulting comments regarding another student's sexual orientation" (*Morrison v. Bd. of Educ. of Boyd County*, 2008). In each of these two cases, the school's policy was challenged for its content-based restriction and, in each case, the policy was upheld. In *Nuxoll*, the school had a policy that prohibited students from making "derogatory comments" referring to "race, ethnicity, religion, gender, sexual orientation, or disability." A student club at the school sponsored a "Day of Silence" to support tolerance and acceptance for homosexuals. The plaintiff in *Nuxoll* was one of several students who wished to sponsor a "Day of Truth" in response to the Day of Silence; on that day, he wished to wear a T-shirt that said "Be Happy, Not Gay." The school determined that the shirt violated the "derogatory comments" policy and the plaintiff filed suit. Ultimately, the court, in a split decision, held that the school must allow the student to wear the particular disputed T-shirt because the school failed to justify a ban on that specific message. The court did not deem "Be Happy, Not Gay" to be "derogatory" or "demeaning" under the rule. However, the plaintiff was not entitled to a judgment striking down the school policy as a whole. The court held that the school need not show actual or reasonably forecasted disruption in order to justify its rule. Specifically, the court noted that *Tinker* is not the only free speech analysis available to schools and courts. Inspired by *Morse* and *Bethel,* the court made the following statement:

> [W]e infer that if there is reason to think that a particular type of student speech will lead to a decline in students' test scores, an upsurge in truancy, or other symptoms of a sick school—symptoms therefore of substantial disruption—the school can forbid the speech. The rule challenged by the plaintiff appears to satisfy this test. It seeks to maintain a civilized school environment conducive to learning, and it does so in an even-handed way....The list of protected characteristics in the rule appears to cover the full spectrum of highly sensitive personal-identity characteristics. And the ban on derogatory words is general. (p. 674)

It is not a stretch to say that such a statement is applicable to instances of cyber-bullying.

The impact of *Morse* is buoyed by the notion that young people are vulnerable in school settings, even more so when surrounded by unsafe, harmful, or illegal conduct. In *Morse,* the Court made important reference to drugs and used *Vernonia* and *Earls* to make its point. At least one lower court has used this inspiration to carry the argument—and *Morse*'s ruling—beyond drug-related speech. In *Ponce v. Socorro Independent School* (2007), a student kept a notebook diary, in which he detailed the establishment of a pseudo-Nazi group and the group's plan to a commit "a Columbine shooting" at his high school or a coordinated attack on multiple schools simultaneously. The writings contained statements targeting homosexuals and racial minorities. The high school assistant principal deemed the notebook to contain "terroristic threats" to the safety and security of the school and suspended the student and recommended that he be transferred to the district's alternative school. The student maintained that the writings were fiction. His parents filed suit. The district court applied *Tinker* and granted a preliminary injunction in favor of the student, finding that the school failed to show evidence of actual or reasonably forecasted disruption. On appeal, however, the Fifth Circuit Court of Appeals declined to apply *Tinker,* favored *Bethel* and *Morse* instead, and vacated the injunction. According to the court, the prevention of drug use (the speech at issue in *Morse*) is not related to disruption; it is related instead to health and safety. The court in *Ponce* paid great attention to Justice Alito's concurring opinion in *Morse.* "Justice Alito's concurring opinion goes on to expound with further clarity why some harms are in fact so great in the school setting that requiring a school administrator to evaluate their disruptive potential is unnecessary" (p. 13). The special characteristic at issue in such cases is not where the expression originated; it is not in the potential disruption or effect of the speech. It is instead in the threat to student safety:

> On Justice Alito's analysis, the heightened vulnerability of students arising from the lack of parental protection and the close proximity of students with one another make schools places of 'special danger' to the physical safety of the student.... [S]chool officials must have greater authority to intervene before speech leads to violence. (pp. 13–14)

Is the Fifth Circuit engaging in a stretch of the seemingly narrow reading of *Morse?* Perhaps. But according to the court, if speech reasonably perceived to advocate the illegal use of drugs led the Supreme Court to go outside the disruption standard of *Tinker* to allow for a special analysis in the face of threat to student safety, surely a student's notebook outlining a Columbine-type shooting at his high school will warrant similar intervention. "The harm of a mass school shooting is…so devastating and so particular to schools that *Morse* analysis is appropriate" (p. 17).

Content-based restrictions are not automatic, though, even when inspired by the best of intentions. Schools are strongly cautioned to draft their student speech codes carefully, to prevent courts from striking down those policies on grounds of vagueness and overbreadth (Daniel & Pauken, 2002). The best accessible example comes from *Saxe v. State College Area School District* (2001), in which the Third Circuit Court of Appeals—in an opinion written by then Circuit Judge Samuel Alito—struck down a school district's anti-harassment policy as unconstitutionally overbroad because it prohibited a great deal of speech and other conduct that would otherwise have been lawful. The policy defined "harassment" as follows:

> . . . verbal or physical conduct based on one's actual or perceived race, religion, color, national origin, gender, sexual orientation, disability, or other personal characteristics,

and which has the purpose or effect of substantially interfering with a student's educational performance or creating an intimidating, hostile or offensive environment. (p. 202)

According to the policy, harassment included any unwelcome verbal, written or physical conduct that "offends, denigrates or belittles an individual." Conduct includes "unsolicited derogatory remarks, jokes, demeaning comments or behaviors, slurs, mimicking, name calling, graffiti, innuendo, gestures, physical contact, stalking, threatening, bullying, extorting or the display or circulation of written materials or pictures." The court conceded that "non-expressive physically harassing" conduct is not protected under the First Amendment. However, free speech does include expression regarding a person's race, national origin, gender, disability, religion, or sexual orientation—even though many people would find some speech on these topics to be deeply offensive. On its face, the school's policy covers some conduct and speech that may be regulated and some that may not. In an application of the three then-existing landmark Court cases to the policy at issue, the court of appeals distinguished all three. Because the policy did not confine itself to lewd and vulgar speech alone, *Bethel* could save the school on only some of the policy's applications. Moreover, the policy applied well beyond school-sponsored activities and, therefore, applied well beyond *Hazelwood*'s reach. Under *Tinker*, the policy's defenses fail as well, because *Tinker* restrictions require that the conduct or expression give rise to at least a reasonable forecast of disruption or interference with the work of the school or the rights of others. This anti-harassment policy attempts to restrict more than that. As a result, the court of appeals found the policy to be unconstitutionally overbroad. The decision in *Saxe* is powerful, no doubt and likely serves as an important wake-up call for those schools enacting and enforcing anti-bullying policies. The administration of policy in this arena is tough when viewed through location, effect, and content lenses. And it is likely even tougher in cyberspace.

CONCLUSIONS

This chapter opened with the statement on the fascination of the prospects and problems of applying old, preexisting law to new, transforming media. Well, despite the fact that there are no reported court cases in the United States directly on point to cyber-bullying, there is new law on the books: (1) statutes in a majority of the states requiring schools to implement anti-bullying policies, with many of those statutes directly addressing cyber-bullying; (2) a new Supreme Court case in *Morse v. Frederick* (2007) addressing student free speech, involving student-born expression, delivered off of school premises, and allegedly advocating illegal drug use; and (3) several lower court opinions, either staying true to *Morse*'s reportedly narrow holding, or expanding the ruling to cover speech beyond the celebration of drug use. In other words, we have new law prepared to apply to new media.

This chapter has explored the impact of *Morse* on the law of cyber-bullying in schools. *Morse's* facts—about a 14-foot banner and the phrase "BONG HiTS 4 JESUS"—are quite far from the sadness and danger of cyber-bullying. However, *Morse* is new law, perhaps more readily applicable to new, transforming media than the law that came before it, especially when bolstered by the law that came before it—*Tinker, Bethel,* and *Hazelwood.* In this vein, *Morse* speaks to location, effect, and content of speech, as do the vast instances of cyber-bullying.

First, with respect to location, *Morse* involved speech that originated off premises yet found its way to school and school-related events. It is true that several courts, including one since *Morse* (see *Layshock,* 2007), have argued that schools have limited disciplinary jurisdiction over student conduct off premises and after hours. However, more recently, schools have been able to connect such conduct to the work of the schools or to the safety of students and staff. When the location of the speech is augmented by its effect and/or content, *Morse* reaffirms *Tinker's* disruption standard and *Bethel's* commentary on lewd and vulgar speech, and, in turn, a school's disciplinary authority increases (see *Doninger,* 2007; *Snyder,* 2008; and *Wisniewski,* 2007).

Second, with respect to the effect of the speech, *Morse* did much to reaffirm *Tinker's* disruption standard: Students win several challenges under circumstances with no disruption or forecast thereof, and schools win several when they can show actual or reasonably likely disruption. Chief Justice Roberts made the narrow holding in *Morse* rather explicit, and many lower courts since the summer of 2007 have noted that *Morse* did not alter the *Tinker* framework (see *Bar-Navon,* 2007; *Barr,* 2008; *B.W.A.,* 2007; *Cuff,* 2008; *DePinto,* 2007; *Lowry,* 2007; and *Madrid,* 2007), with several of those courts finding enough evidence of disruption or a reasonable forecast thereof. However, the reasoning in *Morse* does open another door—the "reasonable interpretation" of student speech. Morse defended her disciplinary action, in part, on her efforts to keep the message of Frederick's banner away from a school-sanctioned event and to prevent the public impression that the school condones such conduct. *Morse* reminds school leaders of the necessary power they have to read and react to the expressive conduct of their students, especially in the cyberspace era when the speech is often silent and anonymous.

Finally, with respect to content of speech, *Morse* may have its strongest card to play. Deborah Morse's interpretation of what she believed to be the intent of Frederick's speech—advocacy of illegal drug use—was given great deference by the Court, due in large part to the school's anti-drug programs and the responsibility schools have to ensure safe and drug-free school settings. Most courts since *Morse* have agreed that the decision is limited to restrictions on speech advocating illegal drug use. However, when backed up by *Bethel's* interest in restricting lewd and vulgar conduct, *Hazelwood*'s interest in respecting legitimate pedagogical concerns, and an overall interest in student safety, a few courts have expanded the coverage of *Morse* to speech outside of drug use, particularly other illegal or potentially illegal conduct: the harassment that comes with a false MySpace profile (*Snyder*, 2008), an allegedly pro-violence T-shirt (*Miller*, 2008), and a student's notebook writing detailing a mass school shooting (*Ponce*, 2007).

Perhaps the most powerful post-*Morse* card was played by the court in *Ponce v. Socorro Independent School District* (2007). A reiteration of that court's endorsement of Justice Alito's concurrence in *Morse* is necessary to end our discussion and inspire school leaders to act with legal support, leadership confidence, and hope:

> The concurring opinion therefore makes explicit that which remains latent in the majority opinion: speech advocating a harm that is demonstrably grave and that derives that gravity from the "special danger" to the physical [and emotional] safety of students arising from the school environment is unprotected....School administrators must be permitted to react quickly and decisively to address a threat of physical violence against their students, without worrying that they will have to face years of litigation second-guessing their judgment. (*Ponce*, 2007, pp. *14, 20)

References

14 Del. Code §4112D (2008).

Alaska Stat. §14.33.200 (2008).

Ark. Code Ann. §6–18–514 (2008).

Barber v. Dearborn Pub. Sch., 286 F. Supp.2d 847 (E.D. Mich. 2003).

Bar-Navon v. School Bd. of Brevard County, Florida, No. 6:06-cv-1434-Orl-19KRS, 2007 U.S. Dist. LEXIS 82044 (M.D. Fla. Nov. 5, 2007).

Barr v. Lafon, 538 F.3d 554 (6th Cir. 2008).

Bethel School District No. 403 v. Fraser, 478 U.S. 675 (1986).

Beussink v. Woodland R-IV School District, 30 F. Supp.2d 1175 (E.D. Mo. 1998).

Board of Educ. v. Earls, 536 U.S. 822 (2002).

Boim v. Fulton County Sch. Dist., 494 F.3d 978 (11th Cir. 2007).

Boucher v. School Bd. of Sch. Dist. of Greenfield, 134 F.3d 821 (7th Cir. 1998).

Brandt v. Board of Educ. of City of Chicago, 480 F.3d 460 (7th Cir. 2007).

B.W.A. v. Farmington R-7 Sch. Dist., 508 F. Supp.2d 740 (E.D. Mo. 2007).

Conn. Gen. Stat. §10–222d (2008).

Coy v. Board of Educ. of North Canton City Sch., 205 F. Supp.2d 791 (N.D. Ohio 2002).

Cuff v. Valley Cent. Sch. Dist., 559 F.Supp.2d 415 (S.D.N.Y. 2008).

Daniel, P. T. K., & Pauken, P. D. (2002). The electronic media and school violence: Lessons learned and issues presented, *West's Education Law Reporter, 164,* 1–43.

Daniel, P. T. K. & Pauken, P. D. (1999). The impact of the electronic media on instructor creativity and institutional ownership within copyright law, *West's Educ. Law Rep, 132,* 1–43.

Daniel, P. T. K. & Pauken, P. D. (1998). Authority, rights, and issues on the way to using the information highway: Cyberspace and schools, *J. of Urb. & Contemp. Law, 54,* 109–155.

Demers v. Leominster Sch. Dep't, 263 F. Supp.2d 195 (D. Mass. 2003).

Denno v. School Bd. of Volusia County, 218 F.2d 1267 (11th Cir. 2000).

DePinto v. Bayonne Bd. of Educ., 514 F. Supp.2d 633 (D.N.J. 2007).

Doe v. Pulaski County Special Sch. Dist., 306 F.3d 616 (8th Cir. 2002).

Doninger v. Niehoff, 514 F. Supp.2d 199 (D. Conn. 2007).

Flaherty v. Keystone Oaks Sch. Dis., 247 F. Supp.2d 698 (W.D. Pa. 2003).

Frazier v. Alexandre, 434 F. Supp.2d 1350 (S.D. Fla. 2006).

Griggs v. Fort Wayne Sch. Bd., 359 F. Supp.2d 731 (N.D. Ind. 2005).

Grzywna v. Schenectady Cent. Sch. Dist., 489 F. Supp.2d 139 (N.D.N.Y. 2006).

Guiles v. Marineau, 461 F.3d 320 (2d Cir. 2006).

Harper v. Poway Unif. Sch. Dist., 545 F.Supp.2d 1072 (S.D. Cal. 2008).

Hazelwood Sch. Dist. v. Kuhlmeier, 484 U.S. 260 (1988).

Henerey v. City of St. Charles Sch. Dist., 200 F.3d 1128 (8th Cir. 1999).

Holloman v. Harland, 370 F.3d 1252 (11th Cir. 2004).

Idaho Code §18–917A (2008).

J.S. v. Bethlehem Area Sch. Dist., 569 Pa. 638, 807 A.2d 847 (Pa. 2002).

Kan. Stat. Ann. §72–8256 (2008).

K.D. v. Fillmore Cent. Sch. Dist., No. 05-CV-0336(E), 2005 U.S. Dist. LEXIS 33871 (W.D.N.Y. 2005).

Kelly v. Board of Educ. of McHenry Comm. High Sch. Dist 156, No. 06 C 1512, 2006 U.S. Dist. LEXIS 68425 (N.D. Ill. Sept. 22, 2006).

Killion v. Franklin Reg'l Sch. Dist., 136 F. Supp.2d 446 (W.D. Pa. 2001).

La. Rev. Stat. 17:416.13 (2008).

Lavine v. Blaine Sch. Dist., 257 F.3d 981 (9th Cir. 2001), reh'g denied, 279 F.3d 719 (9th Cir. 2001).

Layshock v. Hermitage Sch. Dist., 496 F. Supp.2d 587 (W.D. Pa. 2007).

Lowery v. Euverard, 497 F.3d 584 (6th Cir. 2007).

Lowry v. Watson Chapel Sch. Dist., 508 F. Supp.2d 713 (E.D. Ark. 2007).

Madrid v. Anthony, 510 F. Supp.2d 425 (S.D. Tex. 2007).

Mahaffey v. Aldrich, 236 F. Supp.2d 779 (E.D. Mich. 2002).

M.A.L. v. Kinsland, No. 07-10391, 2007 U.S. Dist. LEXIS 6365 (E.D. Mich. Jan. 30, 2007).

Miller v. Penn Manor School District, Civ. Action No. 08-cv-00273, 2008 U.S. Dist. LEXIS 76767 (E.D. Pa. Sept. 30, 2008).

Morrison v. Bd. of Educ. of Boyd County, 521 F.3d 602 (6th Cir. 2008).

Morse v. Frederick, 127 S. Ct. 2618 (2007).

Neb. Rev. Stat. Ann. §79–2,137 (2008).

N.H. Rev. Stat. Ann. 193-F:2 (2008).

Nixon v. Northern Local Sch. Dist. Bd. of Educ., 381 F. Supp.2d 965 (S.D. Ohio 2005).

N.J. Stat. §18A:37–13 (2008).

Nuxoll v. Indian Prairie Sch. Dist., 523 F.3d 668 (7th Cir. 2008).

Ohio Rev. Code Ann. §§3313.666, 3313.667 (2008).

Ore. Rev. Stat. §339.351 (2008).

Pangle v. Bend-Lapine Sch. Dist., 10 P.3d 275 (Ore. Ct. App. 2000).

Phillips v. Anderson County Sch. Dist. No. 5, 987 F. Supp. 488 (D.S.C. 1997).

Ponce v. Socorro Indep. Sch. Dist., No. 06–50709, 2007 U.S. App. LEXIS 26862 (5th Cir. Nov. 20, 2007).

Porter v. Ascension Parish Sch. Bd., 393 F.3d 608 (5th Cir. 2004).

Reihm v. Engelking, No. 06–293 (JRT/RLE), 2007 U.S. Dist. LEXIS 616 (D. Minn. Jan. 4, 2007).

Requa v. Kent Sch. Dist. No. 415, 492 F. Supp.2d 1272 (W.D. Wash. 2007).

Saxe v. State College Area Sch. Dist., 240 F.3d 200 (3d Cir. 2001).

Scott v. School Bd. of Alachua County, 324 F.3d 1246 (11th Cir. March 20, 2003).

S.G. v. Sayreville Bd. of Educ., 333 F.3d 417 (3d Cir. 2003).

Snyder v. Blue Mountain Sch. Dist., No. 3:07cv585, 2008 U.S. Dist. LEXIS 72685 (M.D. Pa. Sept. 11, 2008).

Spence v. Washington, 418 U.S. 405, 410 (1974).

Thomas v. Board of Education, Granville Central School District , 607 F.2d 1043 (2d Cir. 1979).

Tinker v. Des Moines Indep. Comm. Sch. Dist., 393 U.S. 503 (1969).

Vernonia Sch. Dist. 47J v. Acton, 515 U.S. 646 (1995).

West v. Derby Unified Sch. Dist. No. 260, 206 F.3d 1358 (10th Cir. 2000).

White v. Nichols, No. 05–15064, 2006 U.S. App. LEXIS 14314 (11th Cir. June 12, 2006).

Wisniewski v. Board of Educ. of Weedsport Cent. Sch. Dist., 494 F.3d 34 (2d Cir. 2007).

8 · Mediated Speech and Communication Rights

Situating Cyber-bullying Within the Emerging Global Internet Governance Regime

Marc Raboy
Jeremy Shtern

INTRODUCTION

This chapter will consider how the issue of cyber-bullying could be addressed within what can be called the emerging global Internet governance regime. In particular, we will focus on the debates around what we call communication rights that are occurring in regard to global internet governance and propose a social cycle of communication as a model for balancing the seemingly intractable tensions between competing rights claims that regularly emerge in cyber-bullying controversies.

The global internet governance regime is a relatively new and emerging front in what one of the editors of this volume has previously referred to as the "battle" over cyber-bullying, by which she means the increasingly litigious tension between "students, civil liberties advocates and some parents [who] defend student rights to free expression in cyberspace" and "educators, teachers' unions, other parents and government officials [who] want to restrict them" (Shariff, 2008, p. 1).

The Internet destabilizes the existing balance that jurisprudence around general bullying had struck in regard to victim rights and school and parent responsibilities with respect to free speech rights. Even in the United States, where constitutional protection for free speech is generally perceived to be the strongest, a major focus of regulating the problem of bullying has historically centered on placing limitations on the speech rights of children. More than a quarter century of case law has established a framework in which schools have the right "to regulate speech deemed inappropriate for the school setting, even when the same speech is protected outside of school" (Servance, 2003, p. 1231) but are rarely granted the authority to moderate speech originating off campus that is disruptive to the school community. However, "it would be absurd," Servance (2003) has written "to attempt to place a particular website geographically because it is simply a set of digitalized computer instructions that have no particular time or geographic space. Given this inherently different mode of expression, the old distinctions physically demarcating authority over student speech to on or off campus are not adequate, especially as applied to children in a school setting" (p. 1235).

It has been clearly established that through mediation by the Internet, expressions of bullying can severely impact the learning environment of a given school no matter when or where they originate. However, it is not at all certain to what extent students can or should be able to claim the right to freedom of expression when communicating over the internet. Many students who have been punished by school administrations for cyber-bullying have pushed back with law suits and publicity campaigns charging that school-imposed sanctions based on what students communicate over the internet represent a violation of their freedom of expression (c.f. Shariff, 2008, Ch. 5).

Cyber-bullying may be a relatively new phenomenon, but the question of how acceptable speech is defined has been asked in regard to a series of successive 'new' mass media for decades. All public discourse and communication take place in a particular moral and ethical environment. But particular media forms exhibit certain characteristics that demand particular forms of framing by public authorities. The need to protect children has thus been a long-standing concern of media and communication policymaking. For example, television standards and late-night scheduling of potentially sensitive content as well as limitations placed on advertising directed at children are but two examples of media regulation intended to protect this vulnerable segment of the public. Why is this the case?[1]

The regulation of broadcasting dates from the introduction of radio "stations" in countries such as Canada, the United States and Great Britain in the years following the First World War. Every industrialized country in the world regulates broadcasting to some extent, if only to attribute "licences" to corporate entities that are consequently entitled to use a particular broadcasting frequency for a determined period of time.

The scarcity of broadcasting frequencies is an uncontested fact deriving directly from the characteristics of over-the-air broadcast technology and resulting in an obvious need to "control traffic" on the radio (as well as television) airwaves. (As soon as more people want to broadcast than there are frequencies, some allocation mechanism is necessary.) The public character of the air and the particular nature of broadcast media are subtler notions that have been open to various degrees of interpretation (discussed below). Regulation also seeks to provide equilibrium in order to ensure the overall viability of broadcasting systems (for example, by providing for a full range of services including public and private broadcasting, ensuring that different social groups have access to the system, regulating certain aspects of market conditions such as limits on advertising, etc).

The regulation of conventional broadcasting within democratic societies is justified by the particular features of the medium. These include broadcasting's pervasiveness, invasiveness, publicness, and influence (Tambini & Verhulst, 2000).

Broadcasting *pervasiveness* refers to the fact that, because of frequency limitation, all broadcasting content is "everywhere" when it is being broadcast. Unlike the press, which one must actively seek out (finding the newsstand that carries the journal you are interested in, for example), anyone who has a radio or television set has immediate and direct access to *all* content that is being broadcast in his or her community at a given time, and *only* to that content.

Invasiveness refers to the fact that one does not know what one is about to hear until one has actually heard it. With the press (not to mention other media, such as books, records or cinema) one has far greater opportunity to filter and control one's consumption (as well as that of one's children, for example). With broadcasting, particularly radio, one is not always in a position to choose what one is going to be exposed to.

Broadcasting, again because it can be relatively well circumscribed (on the radio or television dial, for example), plays a particular role in public life. Its *publicness* resides in the fact that the medium enables a broadcaster at least hypothetically to reach all of the people all of the time (possession of radio and television sets is much higher than literacy rates in a country like Canada, for example). Many societies have recognized this by establishing public broadcasting organizations such as the CBC or the BBC.

Finally, broadcasting has great *influence.* It describes the boundaries of public experience and public debate but does so in the privacy of the home. It has a strong role in agenda-setting, in framing the important issues of the day, in suggesting what it is important for people to think about.

All of these features of broadcasting relate, in varying degrees, to the Internet as well. What is new with the Internet is that the source of the message can be a single individual, more difficult to identify and track down—and hence to regulate—than a broadcasting company, and certainly impossible to license. *Regulation* therefore poses a more difficult challenge to communication via the Internet, but if we pursue the lineage connecting older and newer media, we see that some form of regulation is still a valid, indeed essential, form of social intervention.

The German legal scholar Wolfgang Hoffmann-Riem, a member of Germany's Constitutional Court and one of the world's leading experts on the social basis of broadcasting regulation, has argued that a regulatory regime is necessary in order to protect what he calls society's "vulnerable values." He writes, in his classic study *Regulating Media* (1996), that the nature of media regulation in any society is influenced by the value accorded to media freedom in that society, with the important caveat that most societies value freedom of speech not as an end in itself but as a means to reaching normative objectives such as the promotion of democracy.

> Therefore, mass communication is deemed to have an important sociocultural dimen-
> sion. Mass media render a service to society. Government, particularly the legislature,
> bears the responsibility of ensuring that the processes of informing the public, exchang-
> ing ideas, and thus shaping values take place in a truly free manner and are not jeop-
> ardized either by the state or private power-holders. (p. 268)

The notion of "vulnerable values" merits some elaboration. Broadly speaking, the term refers to values that are generally accepted by society at large but that can be considered to be at risk. Hoffmann-Riem cites 20 fields or areas which typically require protective regulatory measures in broadcasting. These include pluralism, diversity, fairness, and impartiality; public responsibility in airing different interests and countering of stereotypes; access for minorities; protection of juveniles and fostering of educational programming for children; maintenance of standards in matters of violence, sex, taste, and decency; maintenance of high-quality programming; and personal integrity. In addition to *values,* regulation can also aim to protect vulnerable social *groups:* women, children, ethnic and racial minorities, and so forth.

The need to defend vulnerable values and social groups, therefore, requires pro-viding safeguards to protect those which may be generally supported by the legal and social order but are potentially placed at risk by media content. When different values collide—say, freedom of expression and the need to protect children—authorities need to find the appropriate balance point. Societies differ as to where this optimal point lies. The spread of digital technologies in the twenty-first century, and the public policy debates that have ensued, has made this issue more complex. This is the context in which the issue of cyber-bullying has appeared.

Cyber-bullying is one among many relatively new and seemingly unrelated phenomena that have emerged in the wake of the social appropriation of new tech-nologies. As with other practices that have come to light as we discover more and more about the functioning of the Internet, cyber-bullying is both a specific activity, with its own specific characteristics, and one of many forms of social interaction in the digital world. In this respect, it can be useful—indeed, it is essential—to consider cyber-bullying in the context of two parallel sets of developments: the emergence of a global framework of Internet governance, and the impact of the Internet on a decades-old debate around the notion of communication rights.

In this chapter, we shall present an overview of global Internet governance and its relation to the broader notion of communication rights and shall situate the discussion of cyber-bullying within that nexus. We begin with a brief discussion of the notion of communication rights.

Communication Rights and the Social Cycle of Communication

From the start, the status of a universal right to freedom of expression has been contested turf. During the drafting of the Universal Declaration of Human Rights, free expression was originally framed not as an autonomous right in and of itself, but as part of a larger right—the right to freedom of information. However, political squabbling between western countries and the soviet bloc about whether the freedom of information meant "the freedom to impose cultural imperialism" or the "freedom to practice censorship and propaganda" (this was not particularly a citizen-focused debate) quickly escalated into an intractable polarized debate leaving freedom of expression as only part of this much larger debate with enough support to be reified as a universal human right (see Binder, 1952; Krotteinen, Myntti & Hannikainen, 1999).

By the 1960s efforts to buttress and expand upon freedom of expression began to be renewed. French public servant Jean D'Arcy is credited with launching the concept of a right to communicate, in a 1969 paper written for the European Broadcasting Union (see D'Arcy, 1977). The idea would elicit discussion, refinement and several rounds of polarized and intractable debate within the UN organization during the Cold War, and by the 1980s enthusiasm for discussing let alone formalizing a right to communicate had understandably ebbed (see Padovani, 2005). The 2003–2005 World Summit on the Information Society was the site of the formation of the activist network, the Campaign for Communication Rights in the Information Society (CRIS), and the (re)emergence of the closely related notions of communication rights and the right to communicate (see Padovani & Nordenstreng, 2005)—importantly, in that the WSIS was also the site and the precursor of important innovations in the sphere of internet governance that we will discuss in detail below.

The premise of a communication rights approach is the view that democracy in large, modern societies where notions of community can no longer plausibly remain based strictly on face-to-face interaction, are intimately tied to the creation of spaces within the communication system where the entire public can engage in transparent, informed and sustained democratic discussion. From this normative claim stems a broad notion of what rights are relevant to the processes of communication in society[2] as well as a series of concerns for the realization of such communication within policy frameworks centred on the right to free speech alone.

Communication rights thus refer to "the conditions for the full exercise of freedom of expression in a complex and mediated society where power and control of resources are distributed very unevenly" (CRIS, 2005, p. 22). This approach looks beyond speech rights and to the rights that underpin the entire process of communicating, which, rather than unidirectional transit of information, is approached as interaction between people. One way of thinking about this interaction is as a "social cycle of communication."

The idea of communication rights refers to all of the provisions that are required in order to assure the realization of this social cycle. Freedom of expression covers certain key communicative functions (the ones shaded in grey in Figure 1) but is not in itself a sufficiently comprehensive basis for the entire social cycle of communication. Communication rights therefore implies consideration of the other distinct *flanking* or enabling rights that are required to complete the right to freedom of expression into discussions of media and communication policy issues. The communication rights that flank or enable freedom of expression within the social cycle include:

- A right to honour, dignity and reputation;
- A right to safety of the person;
- A right to enjoy the benefits of scientific progress and its applications;
- A right to privacy;
- A right to peaceful assembly and association;
- A right to free primary education and progressive introduction of secondary education.

This is just a sampling of the universal human rights recognized in international law that should flank consideration of freedom of expression within any discussion of policy responses to online child protection and cyber-bullying.[3]

Figure 1: The Social Cycle of Communication

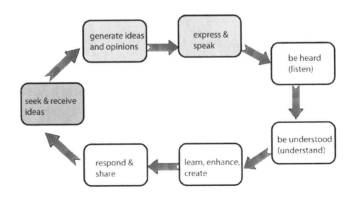

The social cycle of communication offers a normative guide that is useful in considering how the balance should be struck between various communication rights on any given media and communication policy question. At times, the objective of preserving the social cycle may be possible simply by adopting multifaceted policy responses that address various communication rights simultaneously. In other instances, it may be that preservation of the social cycle necessitates the application of constraints on freedom of expression so that the flanking rights can be realized. The powers that American courts have granted schools to restrict speech on campus that would be acceptable off-campus are a clear example of how crucial functions within democratic societies may require the realization of flanking rights such as the right to education and the right to honour and dignity that are contingent upon the imposition of limits on freedom of expression. That said, freedom of expression is a sacrosanct foundation of human rights and of democratic societies and restrictions upon it should not be imposed lightly.

Cyber-bullying: National and Global Responses

One approach to the juridical challenges created by Internet mediated communication has been the push to establish new categories of criminal behavior. Efforts on the part of various governments to adapt domestic bullying and child protection policy to the internet have varied in their approach. Different areas of domestic policy focuses have included: delinquency law (France); harassment law (UK); education policy (Canada) and in laws specifically targeted toward giving public authorities the power to impose limits on free speech in the online environment such as the Deleting Online Predators Act in the US.[4] Amidst calls to move away from an "offender-based" approach and focus on blocking opportunities for crimes to be committed, national online child protection laws are often criticized for doing little more than criminalizing and restricting certain uses of the internet (Shariff, 2008, drawing on Eck, 2002). The focus on criminalization of offender behavior is seen as particularly problematic as a response to cyber-bullying, given that most cyber-bullies, like their victims, are children who are themselves also arguably victims of systemic breakdowns of the civility and tolerance that is required in order to maintain positive and productive educational environments (c.f. Shariff, 2008).

When viewed through the prism of the social cycle of communication, the national criminal law approach is equally problematic: it restricts freedom of expression without producing any real corresponding gains in other elements of the cycle.

But what other recourse do governments have? After all, national governments have irrefutable claims to be able to control the behavior of individuals physically present within their borders. Cyber-bullies are commonly members of the same school or at least community as their victims. But they do not have to even be citizens of the same country. This fact fundamentally constrains the ability of governments to develop victim-centred responses to cyber-bullying. A government can promise the residents of its own territory that they will be punished if they engage in cyber-bullying. But the global or borderless nature of communication over the internet means that the potential exists for those residents to be cyber-bullied from people in other countries over whom the victims' government cannot reasonably claim to have any jurisdiction.

Whereas the jurisdictional challenges posed by the global nature of communication over the internet were once perceived to place it entirely beyond the control of governments,[5] a series of recent policy initiatives and controversies centred around greater global coordination of the internet have emerged within a variety of international organizations. Domestic policies that pursue speech regulation as a response to the problem of cyber-bullying, however well-intentioned, in effect prescribe a narrow offender-focused criminal law approach. The search for a more holistic view to the balance between speaker and victim rights in other words, necessitates engagement with this emerging global internet governance framework.

The global internet governance regime is made up of a range of national, supranational and global structures that are involved—directly or by implication—in developing policy related to issues in the management and use of the Internet. The global internet governance regime is diffuse and fluid, and there is nothing resembling a universally accepted accounting of the organizations it includes. Generally speaking, the examination of the global internet governance regime involves a cross-cutting look at internet policy emanating from national governments (such as the cyber-bullying laws discussed above), intergovernmental organizations, and multi-stakeholder global assemblages which engage a range of actors including governments, the private sector, civil society and non-governmental organizations, activist groups and the Internet technical community from across the globe on issues of common interest.

In the balance of this chapter we try to outline a pragmatic approach that takes account of institutional realities but within a principled normative framework that treats cyber-bullying as a communication rights issue.

Council of Europe and the Treaty on Cybercrime

The Council of Europe (CoE) is an intergovernmental organization comprising 47 European countries. It develops conventions, agreements and recommendations primarily in regard to human rights, democracy and the rule of law.

The CoE Convention on Cybercrime (see Council of Europe, 2004) represents an effort to establish a common criminal policy aimed at the protection of society against cybercrime by obligating ratifying states to adopt a set of prescribed legislation and to participate in a framework aimed at promoting international co-operation in preventing, investigating and prosecuting cybercrime.

Though cyber-bullying is not explicitly discussed by the convention, content or speech regulation is prescribed by Article 9: "Offences related to child pornography" as well is in the additional protocol that criminalizes racist and xenophobic propaganda spread via computer networks. When taken in combination with the data interception powers granted to law enforcement agencies by Article 21 and the "General Principles Related to International Cooperation" outlined in Article 23, the CoE Convention on Cybercrime approach establishes a framework for placing and enforcing an embargo on a particular undesirable category of internet-mediated speech in the aim of protecting children (Council of Europe, 2004). This could be one model for establishing an international policy response to the problem of cyber-bullying.

The CoE is also active in the creation of resources and campaigns that aim to raise awareness amongst all stakeholders about the policy challenges associated with children's use of the internet. For example, the CoE *Internet Literacy Handbook*[6] includes a chapter introducing the problem of cyber-bullying to children, parents and teachers and the CoE "Guidelines for Internet Service Providers and Online Games Providers"[7] also makes reference to the problem of cyber-bullying within its human rights guidelines.[8]

European Commission (EC): Safer Internet, Safer Internet Plus and New Safer Internet

The European Commission is the executive branch of the European Union (EU). It is responsible for implementing treaties, proposing legislation and includes the trans-national civil service that is responsible for day to day operations of the work of the EU. Within the EC, the Information Society & Media Commissioner is where most of the activity around internet policy issues occurs.

The place of cyber-bullying within the recently concluded European Commission (EC) Safer Internet plus program is assessed in detail elsewhere (see Shariff, 2008, pp. 132–33). Since that publication however, a new Safer Internet Program has been launched for 2009–2013 and, along with "grooming" (where a person befriends a child for sexual abuse), cyber-bullying is identified as one of the areas into which the scope of the program will be extended over the course of its new mandate. "Reducing illegal content and tackling harmful conduct online," the first action item of the Safer Internet Plus program, has been retained for the 2009–2013 program, its scope having been extended to include a more explicit focus on the problems related to cyber-bullying (Commission of the European Communities, 2008).

The 2009–2013 Safer Internet Program aims to explicitly "tackle" harmful online conduct including cyber-bullying by increasing understanding, awareness, cooperation and accountability amongst all stakeholders in regard to the illicit conduct. Activities planned range from establishing points where members of the public can report concerns and awareness raising campaigns to efforts to promote research into the effects of harmful online conduct and share best practice solutions (Commission of the European Communities, 2008).

The EC has also conducted a variety of public consultations on issues related to cyber-bullying including: "Safer Internet and Online Technologies for Children"; "Child Safety and Mobile Phone Services" and the recently concluded consultation on "Age Verification, Cross Media Rating and Social Networking."[9]

UN World Summit on the Information Society (WSIS)

The World Summit on the Information Society (WSIS) was a two-phased United Nations Summit hosted by the International Telecommunications Union (ITU). The first summit was held in Geneva in 2003 and the 2nd in Tunis in 2005. The preparatory process (PrepCom), the venue for formal discussion of issues, resolutions and modalities of participation occurred, began as early as 2001. The WSIS was initially devised as a framework for developing global policy for extending the "digital revolution" across the "digital divide."[10] From the start however, rather than this narrow prescriptive policy agenda, participants seemed intent on pushing a whole series of broader concerns about the role of global policy in the control and management of the internet (see Kummer, 2005). This can be attributed in part to the active participation of NGOs, academics and activists through the formal inclusion of civil society in the WSIS process (cf. Raboy & Landry, 2005) but also to the absence of existing institutional venues in which appropriate policy responses to public-interest concerns about the use and management of the internet could be discussed.

During the summer of 2005, a 40 member multi-stakeholder working group created by the Secretary-General of the United Nations wracked its collective brain to deal with the question of Internet governance (IG). The need to understand the challenges of Internet governance had been identified during the first phase of the 2003–2005 World Summit on the Information Society as one of the most problematic concerns arising from the technological changes of the turn of the century.

The Working Group on Internet Governance (WGIG) was asked to develop a working definition of Internet Governance; to identify the relevant public policy issues; and to "develop a common understanding of the respective roles and responsibilities of governments, existing international organizations and other forums as well as the private sector and civil society from both developing and developed countries" (WGIG, 2005). From amongst the policy issues related to the use of the internet that the WGIG report identified as having emerged over the first phase of the WSIS, there are a number of issues that are directly relevant to discussion of possible juridical responses to cyber-bullying. These include:

- tension between efforts to investigate misuse of the internet and the privacy rights of internet users;
- tension between criminal law approaches to combating internet misuse and fundamental rights such as freedom of expression;

as well as questions about:

- whether individuals should be required to identify themselves when using the Internet, or whether the information necessary to track them *ex post* should be mandatorily recorded and kept by ISPs and service operators, and to what extent;
- whether services that increase the degree of privacy or fully anonymize the usage of the Internet should be allowed, encouraged, or forbidden;
- whether individuals should be required to identify themselves or to register their websites, especially when posting news or political material;
- to which extent applications installed on a personal computer (including so-called spyware) should be allowed to monitor its usage, report information back to the software supplier or vendor, or take control of the content and capabilities of the personal computer;
- whether users should have the right to prevent archival of publicly posted information that they want to remove from the Internet (old website content, newsgroup messages, e-mail etc.), and how this can be accomplished.(WGIG, 2005, p. 36)

Such questions about what kind of communication the internet ought to be facilitating are fundamental to addressing the law and policy environment around cyber-bullying, and the WGIG report is clear that they can indeed be discussed as issues of law and policy. The WGIG is also clear that global or borderless communication that is facilitated by the Internet requires that questions like these be addressed by global institutions, that:

- There are a host of specific issues that have often been regulated nationally but that lack global coordination;
- To avoid the creation of 'cybercrime havens,' it will be necessary to ensure that criminalization of specific conduct committed in cyberspace, should be put in place on a global level, respecting the diversity of cultures and legal systems. (WGIG, 2005).

Thus, the sorts of concerns for the protection of children that have always been central to communication policymaking are gradually emerging in regard to the Internet but are doing so primarily at the global level. The WGIG defined internet governance as

> the development and application by governments, the private sector, and civil society, in their respective roles, of shared principles, norms, rules, decision making procedures and programmes, that shape the evolution and utilization of the Internet.

Prevention of cybercrime and online child protection in the final agreements and documents produced by the WSIS[11] as well as in the parallel civil society declaration produced for the Geneva phase of the summit.[12]

WSIS not only defined the field of global internet governance, it placed the issue within the global policy sphere through the creation of a new, semi-permanent institution for discussing internet policy issues: the Internet Governance Forum (which we will discuss below). The WSIS process also raised awareness of the diffuse institutional geography of global internet policy making and highlighted the overlaps that exist between internet-related policy development that is going on in a variety of different international institutions; for example, the extent to which the activities of the CoE, the EC and more technical organizations like the ITU and ICANN (which will be discussed shortly) intersect. While there is still pushback emanating from various stakeholders against the idea that social policy and human rights issues should be discussed by the same organizations that deal with the management of internet technical resources, internet governance is now clearly accepted as a global public policy issue.

UN Internet Governance Forum (IGF)

The IGF was created with the adoption of the 'Tunis Agenda for the Information Society' at phase II of the WSIS in Tunis in November of 2005. The mandate of the IGF is to:

- Discuss public policy issues related to key elements of Internet governance in order to foster the sustainability, robustness, security, stability and development of the Internet;
- Facilitate discourse between bodies dealing with different cross-cutting international public policies regarding the Internet and discuss issues that do not fall within the scope of any existing body;
- Interface with appropriate inter-governmental organizations and other institutions on matters under their purview;
- Facilitate the exchange of information and best practices and in this regard make full use of the expertise of the academic, scientific and technical communities;
- Advise all stakeholders in proposing ways and means to accelerate the availability and affordability of the Internet in the developing world;

- Strengthen and enhance the engagement of stakeholders in existing and/or future Internet governance mechanisms, particularly those from developing countries;
- Identify emerging issues, bring them to the attention of the relevant bodies and the general public, and, where appropriate, make recommendations;
- Contribute to capacity building for Internet governance in developing countries, drawing fully on local sources of knowledge and expertise;
- Promote and assess, on an ongoing basis, the embodiment of WSIS principles in Internet governance processes;
- Discuss, inter alia, issues relating to critical internet resources;
- Help to find solutions to the issues arising from the use and misuse of the Internet, of particular concern to everyday users;
- Publish its proceedings (see WSIS, 2005a, at para 72).

The IGF meets annually under the auspices of Security General of the United Nations. At time of writing, it has met three times: in 2006 in Athens, 2007 in Rio de Janeiro and in 2008 in Hyderabad, India. The mandate of the IGF calls for the Secretary General of the United Nations to conduct a review and lead a process of evaluating whether or not the mandate of the IGF will be extended beyond an initial five-year period.

While the IGF does not pass resolutions, seek to establish consensus or negotiate texts, it provides a platform where stakeholders can coalesce for action around issues of common concern. The "dynamic coalitions," as groups that emerge from the IGF are known, can use the platform to facilitate coordination, capacity building and awareness raising of internet governance issues in other, decision-making venues.

A dynamic coalition on child online safety was created during the 2007 IGF in Rio with the aim of creating: "a permanent, open platform for discussion on fundamental and practical issues related to child online safety within the agenda of the Internet Governance Forum, ensuring dialogue among representatives from children's organizations, government, industry, academia and other civil society groups."[13]

At the 2008 IGF in Hyderabad, India, online child protection issues were topics of frequent discussion. Workshops were organized with titles such as "Child safety online: measures to protect children from exploitation—the challenge of keeping pace with technological developments"; "Dignity, security and privacy of children on the Internet—applying international law to protect their best interests"; "Strategies to prevent and fight child pornography in developing countries"; "The internet goes mobile—child protection in the always connected age" and "An Interpol for the Internet?" British online child advocate John Carr was given a high profile speaking slot in one plenary session and presented a five-part online child protection agenda for the global internet governance regime that included:

- Content—the Internet's ability to expose children and young people to age-inappropriate material including illegal material such as child pornography; the way the Internet is able to facilitate exchanges, for example between sexual predators and vulnerable children; the way in which the new technology is facilitating and enabling new styles of insidious bullying and online harassment.

- Commerce—the way in which some Internet companies take advantage of children to sell "dodgy" products or to misrepresent the terms on which those products or services are offered; the way in which some companies take advantage of the naiveté of children to elicit commercially sensitive or commercially valuable information

- Addiction—the way in which some children appear to be drawn into overuse of the technology at the expense of normal and healthy development of social relationships

- Privacy—cross-cutting questions about the rights to privacy a child has vis-à-vis their parents and school; questions about how internet businesses selling age-restricted products determine whether or not they have in fact obtained true consent from someone old enough to give it.[14]

Online child protection was also the topic of many interventions made in plenary and open dialogue sessions. Some of these interventions dealt with possible responses such as the need to develop, market and presumably use policy to support or obligate the use of technical fixes such as sophisticated age authentication, blocking or filtering software; calls for greater policy coordination through informal cooperation or the extension of the international criminal law approach of the cybercrime convention, but, most frequently, interventions on online child protection at the 2008 IGF seemed to focus on simply raising awareness amongst internet governance stakeholders as to the existence of threats to children online. Some of these interventions stemmed poignantly out of the experience of practitioners and were grounded in alarming practical realities. A Brazilian federal prosecutor, for example, asked what more could be done

> to protect the security and the rights of these new users, especially children and adolescents considering that…crimes have been committed by nationals who take advantage of the borderless nature of the Internet to violate fundamental rights[15]

and pointed out that "unfortunately, the self-regulation model which has been successfully implemented in Europe has not been working well in developing countries."[16]

However many interventions from child protection activists seemed based on more general and rhetorical questions about what was being done to protect children online and exhibited an alarming and largely unproductive degree of instrumental faith in the ability of technical management to weed out undesirable human behavior.

Not all participants to the IGF were even in agreement that internet governance is the appropriate policy venue for consideration of such issues. In his summary of the Hyderabad meeting, for instance, the Chair of the IGF felt obliged to observe that:

> On child pornography, some people questioned the predominance this topic was taking at this IGF. A number of points were made that this perhaps was not the appropriate space to take up this discussion any further. (Chairman of the IGF, 2008)

Other participants seemed to see the emergence, focus and evolution of online child protection within global internet governance over the course of the 2007 and 2008 IGFs in much more positive terms. Brazilian government representative Everton Lucero suggested that:

> one of the issues that has been debated at length today was the question of child protection against sexual abuse and pornography. And it seems that discussion has matured enough in this area so that now we perhaps could think of creating a common environment where all relevant stakeholders could build trust and work together.[17]

Clearly the place of child protection within the IGF continues to be shaped by two tensions that have dominated debate over the appropriate role for global institutions in governing the Internet since the WSIS: the extent to which social policy issues should be considered as relevant to management of internet technologies as well, and the threat that well intentioned efforts to improve juridical protection for certain specific uses of the internet might lead to precedent-setting interventionist policy that could eventually undermine the precarious state of free expression and privacy rights online.

The International Telecommunication Union (ITU)

Formed as the International Telegraph Union in 1865, renamed in 1934 and integrated into the UN system in 1947, the International Telecommunication Union (ITU) is responsible for coordinating activities such as the allocation of radio spectrum frequencies, the development of common standards technical standards and telecommunication equipment and facilitation of shared tariffs between international carriers. In short, the ITU works with its 191 Member States and over 700 communication industry Sector Members on distinguishing between national telecommunications systems and on facilitating the interconnections that make global communication networks possible (see Ó Siochrú, Girard & Mahan, 2002).

In the follow-up and implementation of the WSIS agreements, the ITU was assigned Action Point C5: "building confidence and security in the use of ICTs."

As a response, ITU Secretary-General Dr. Hamadoun Touré formally announced the launch of the Global Cybersecurity Agenda (GCA) on 17 May 2007. The Child Online Protection (COP) initiative represents one direct outcome of the GCA. The COP

> aims to tackle cybersecurity holistically, addressing legal, technical, organizational and procedural issues as well as capacity building and international cooperation.[18]

The key objectives of the initiative are to:

- Identify the key risks and vulnerabilities to children in cyberspace;
- Create awareness of the risks and issues through multiple channels;
- Develop practical tools to help governments, organizations and educators minimize risk;
- Share knowledge and experience while facilitating international strategic partnerships to define and implement concrete initiatives.

At present the COP is still emerging and it is unclear exactly how these objectives will be addressed. It is too early to say whether the ITU's foray into the issue of online child protection should be seen as the next salvo in the ongoing battle for legitimacy and jurisdiction in global internet policy—between the ITU and the WSIS/IGF—or as evidence of greater awareness of the need to embed child protection into all levels of internet policy making, including the largely technical functions overseen by the ITU.

ICANN

The Internet Corporation for Assigned Names and Numbers (ICANN) is the agency that coordinates the unique alphanumerical identifiers that allow internet users from around the world to communicate with each other. ICANN is a not-for-profit corporation based in California that was established in 1998. According to its website, "ICANN doesn't control content on the Internet."[19] Yet, the domain system does organize how the content of the Internet is presented. By making some content easier or more difficult for certain users to find and view, individual policy decisions made in ICANN blur the lines between technical coordination and speech regulation. The controversial proposal to create a red-light top-level domain name that would allow pornographic websites to migrate from addresses ending in ".com" to addresses ending in ".xxx" is the clearest example of how the sort of technical coordination performed by ICANN could be directed towards de facto speech and content regulation in the interest of child protection.

The principle behind .xxx was simple enough: if an .xxx top level domain name is established, and adult sites volunteer to migrate to it from their existing .com website address, children will be less likely to accidentally come across pornography by clicking on hyperlinks to sites whose names are not (to children at least) obviously indicative of pornographic contents. By being able to block out all websites whose addresses contain the domain name .xxx, filtering software and parental controls would also be significantly improved. The creation of an .xxx domain name was first proposed by ICM Registry, a Florida-based internet service provider (ISP), in 2000 as was the creation of a ".kids" domain name that would have applied the same logic toward the opposite effect. However, both proposals were rejected. The .xxx idea re-emerged in 2003. ICM's updated proposal for .xxx included a plan to charge $60 for registering an .xxx domain (far more than is charged for .com for example) and use a portion of each registration to fund educational and community groups engaged in internet literacy programs and responding to problems of online child exploitation.

The perception amongst public authorities was that support for the proposal amongst child advocacy groups was strong. According to US Department of Commerce documents obtained through a freedom of information request filed by ICM Registry (and made available on the website of the Syracuse University-based Internet Governance Project),[20]

> The ICM Registry application for .xxx has strong support from the child advocacy community because they feel that ICM's approach to the .xxx puts into place best practices that would not be available in the .com space. Wired Safety and Wired Kids supported the application as did the Internet Content and Rating Association. In addition, there is strong support out of the UK child advocacy community.[21]

Support for .xxx was far from universal however. The Family Research Council, for example, encouraged supporters to flood congress, the Department of Commerce and the FCC with copies of the following petition stating:

> I oppose the establishment of the .xxx domain. I do not want to give pornographers more opportunities to distribute smut on the Internet. By establishing this new .xxx domain, you would be giving false hope to parents who want to protect their families from pornography. You would also be lending legitimacy to the hardcore pornography industry. Please stop this effort now.

While the charge that the creation of .xxx would in effect constitute an endorsement of internet pornography by public authorities certainly had much more to do with the ultimate collapse of the .xxx proposal, the "false hope" charge is revealing about the limitations inherent to efforts to legislate child protection into the technological architecture of mass communication systems.

While some adult content businesses might have happily agreed to pack up shop and move to an .xxx address in exchange for the legitimacy that the approval of .xxx seemed to bestow on the online pornography industry, others—particularly advertising as opposed to subscription revenue-based amateurish sites or sites with more illicit or overtly illegal content—would be unlikely to move to .xxx given the elevated cost of registering an .xxx domain, the increased surveillance their content was certain to be under in the .xxx domain, and the loss of their ability to use pop-up windows, misleading domain names and other unscrupulous techniques aimed at getting users to navigate to their sites by accident. Not only was it unlikely that many adult content websites would purchase .xxx domain names if they were not forced to, but the basic retail economic fact that two stores are probably going to move more merchandise than one provided a strong indication that those websites that did move into the .xxx domain would be highly unlikely to relinquish their .com domain name. By "false hope," The Family Research council means that many parents might assume that after .xxx was created, their children would not be able to access internet pornography as long as filtering software was set up to block all addresses ending in .xxx when in fact little would have been done to rid the .com domain of such sites.

In response, some child protection activists pushed the .xxx approach even further, making a case for buttressing the creation of the .xxx domain with congressional legislation that would force websites containing adult content and services to adopt .xxx domain names and forbid them from using addresses ending in .com or other domain names. Congress, the DOC and the FCC were also flooded with pro-.xxx petition templates from groups such as Protect Every Child that read:

> Protect your child from innocently entering the world of Internet pornography by sponsoring legislation limiting all pornographic material to the .XXX Top Level Web Domain Extension! Pornography is not going away. It is just like someone who discovers they have cancer. They can use medication and treatments to control it or they can allow it to continue to grow by leaving it alone to fester and spread. Without .xxx and a mandatory movement to this TLD, children and families will continue to be devastated by the pornography that threatens their existence when they stumble across it through deceptively named webites. .xxx will protect the 1st Amendment rights of the majority— every child, every adult—while continuing to protect the rights of the few, the pornographers.[22]

The first problem with this approach is that it was not supported by the main protagonists behind the .xxx proposal. Stakeholders within the pornography industry voiced concern about such laws being used to drive them into a ghetto on the internet in the same way that zoning laws been used to restrict brick and mortar pornography businesses to the outskirts of society. ICM, the registrar behind the .xxx proposal, vehemently opposed the push to make .xxx mandatory for adult content websites, going as far as putting aside $250, 000 to fund legal challenges to the establishment of any such laws (Jesdanun, 2005). The second problem with the proposal to mandate the migration of adult content providers to the .xxx domain illustrates a great deal about why global policy is essential for a global medium of communication like the internet. It is virtually impossible to establish a uniformly accepted definition of what constitutes pornography. Furthermore, the reach of the American congress and law enforcement being restricted to the United States, even DOC officials were forced to concede that "a bill like that faces definitional and jurisdictional problems."[23]

Despite initially approving the creation of the .xxx domain name, ICANN subsequently took the controversial move of reversing its position and deciding against creating the new domain name; illustrating that technical solutions instated through policy that are designed to in effect manage or organize objectionable internet speech in the aim of protecting children can create poor optics for public authorities who do not wish to be seen to be condoning or otherwise working with the speakers of the objectionable speech.[24]

Child Protection on the Global Internet Governance Agenda: The Cross-Cutting View

Looking at these different institutions and policy frameworks together, we can identify at least four distinct approaches to protecting children online: technological fixes; criminal law; victim rights-based speech regulation and what could be described as multi-stakeholder cooperation.

In the table on the next page, we have mapped out where and how the various institutions and policy initiatives discussed above fit within this framework. Before moving to discuss each of these categories in turn it is worth noting that each institution is attempting to deal with child protection online within two or more of these approaches. This suggests that there is no one stop solution and that a hybrid or mixed method is most applicable.

Engineered Technological Fixes

The activities of virtually all of the global internet governance organizations discussed included some mention of possible technological solutions for protecting children online. WSIS documents include rhetoric about being "committed to ensuring that the development of ICT applications and operation of services respects the rights of children as well as their protection and well-being." The CoE 2009–13 Safer Internet Programme's mandate includes the task of

> Stimulating application of technical solutions for dealing adequately with illegal content and harmful conduct online. Activities should encourage the development or adaptation of effective technological tools to deal adequately with illegal content and tackle harmful conduct online, for general use by stakeholders. (Commission of the European Communities, 2008, p. 17)

Such technological tools are often less than ideal solutions however. In regard to filtering and blocking software, for instance, Mitchell et al. (2005) report that parents who have used such tools express concern not only about the percentage of illicit sites that are not blocked but also about the tendency for access to legitimate health or educational sites to be restricted.

Protecting Children Online: Global Institutions and Approaches

	TECHNOLOGICAL FIX	CRIMINAL LAW	VICTIM RIGHTS	MULTI-STAKEHOLDER COOPERATION
CoE		Cybercrime convention	Cybercrime convention	Guidelines and literacy projects
EC	Safer Internet Program			Safer Internet Program
WSIS	Geneva Statement of Principles A11 -Civil Society Declaration 2.1.4	-Tunis Agenda 40	-Geneva Plan of Action 12B -Civil Society Declaration 2.2.7 -Tunis Agenda 24	Geneva Statement of Principles B10 Tunis Agenda 92 Creation of IGF Tunis Agenda 90q, 92
ITU	COP			COP
IGF	Filtering, blocking age verification etc. -Teaching the internet to forget		-Calls for increased power to censor for child protection	Dynamic Coalition on Child Protection
ICANN	".xxx" (creation)		".xxx" (deletion)	.xxx (not for profit helping parents with $10 from each registration)
Other relevant frameworks or institutions	internet technical community (standards setting agencies, ISOC, IT industry associations, etc.)	Interpol	Convention on the Welfare of the Child -International Bill of Rights	UNESCO

Ad-hoc efforts to alter the technical architecture of the internet in the aim of protecting children have proven no less reliable. The well intentioned .xxx initiative for instance, if it had gone forward, would have resulted in creation of a clearly demarcated red light zone but would have had no way of preventing the existence of illicit content with .com or other domain names.

Realization of the futility of silver bullets has led some to push for silver bulldozers however. Responding to the problem of cyber-bullying could include advocating for fundamental systemic changes to the way the internet is designed and works such as the development of a "track back" system that could effectively restrict anonymity on the internet. This would clearly mitigate one issue related to child protection online and cyber-bullying but would come at a great cost to privacy protection and would have a chilling effect on freedom of expression online. Cyber-bullying activists and privacy rights advocates need to find a common ground on the question of technically limiting online anonymity. The search for better track back or identification tools also would focus efforts at alleviating the problem of cyber-bullying toward punitive measures aimed at perpetrators.[25]

A victim-focused technical fix that has been discussed on various occasions in the internet governance forum without ever emerging as a major agenda item is the concept of teaching the Internet to forget (cf. Mayer-Schönberger, 2007). One of the most damaging impacts of cyber-bullying is its permanence. Victims of cyber-bullying should not have to explain to potential employers why ten-year-old websites are devoted to ridiculing them. Special provisions might be pursued allowing victims of cyber-bullying to request the removal of offending web-based content so that they are not forced to confront the negative effects of being bullied in perpetuity.

Generally however, the rather mixed experience of efforts to design technical fixes underlines the importance of focusing activism on internet governance rather than engineering. Technology embeds values and communication technology certainly shapes the social cycle of communication. It is important not only that values such as the need to protect children are embedded within the technologies we use to communicate, but that these values reflect some kind consensus, are widely known, subject to review, debate and change. We should not use the ability to relatively uncontroversially engineer restrictions on free speech as a way of avoiding a potentially divisive political debate over what kind of balance to achieve between different aspects of communication rights that we might want to use technology to establish. In his prescient 1999 book *Code and Other Laws of Cyberspace*, Stanford law professor Lawrence Lessig anticipated that many would see technical fixes—what he calls regulation by code—as preferable to constitutional remedies to problems stemming from the misuse of the Internet, in particular Americans opposed to discussing limits on their First Amendment rights. "The consequence of no legal regulation to child porn" he cautioned, "is an explosion of bad code. No law in other words, sometimes produces bad code" (Lessig, 2006, p. 267). Despite the emergence of a much broader framework for discussing internet law issues since the publication of Lessig's book, many stakeholders still seem focused on coding solutions into technology and the result continues to be, as we have seen, mostly bad code.

Criminal Law

The CoE Convention on Cybercrime is viewed as important precedent for its explicit extension of definitions of criminal activity to the online environment as well as for its facilitation of cooperation and investigative powers amongst the law enforcement community. For example, the Convention on Cybercrime was pointed to by the WSIS as an example of the "necessity of effective and efficient tools and actions, at national and international levels, to promote international cooperation among, inter alia, law-enforcement agencies on cybercrime" (WSIS, 2005a, at para 40). At the most recent IGF, child protection activist John Carr described the Cybercrime Convention as "creat[ing] specific legal obligations on states and actors within states to provide for the protection of children" and pointed to it as a cornerstone document in the debates that global internet governance seeks to address.[26]

But how significant a precedent is the CoE Cybercrime Convention for advocates of greater online child protection? The only explicit reference to child protection made with the Convention on Cybercrime comes in the Part 9 treatment of child pornography. This limited protection is also tepid. Part 9 is in fact an "optional protocol" meaning that "each Party may reserve the right not to apply" it, "in whole or in part" (Council of Europe, 2004). Of the 23 countries that have ratified the Convention on Cybercrime, nine—including the United States and France—have done so with expressed reservations about the application of article 9.[27] While harmonizing criminal law around areas such as forgery and copyright might be relatively uncontroversial, these reservations reflect on long-held culturally specific understandings of what constitutes childhood and free speech. It is difficult to imagine that these differences could easily be worked through and, accordingly, that the effort to harmonize global criminal law in the name of online child protection could be expanded by future agreements, on cyber-bullying in particular. Any attempt to create a harmonized international criminal law instrument aimed at confronting cyber-bullying would lead directly into the jaws of both dilemmas.

Much of the discussion about using criminal law to protect children online is geared toward the threats posed by adults toward children: child pornography, grooming, fraud, etc. In contrast, the victims of cyber-bullying can be children but are often adult teachers or school administrators[28] and the perpetrators are always children. Various cultures and legal systems view the criminal culpability of children very differently. If Western democracies are forced to agree to disagree in the Convention on Cybercrime about, for example, the age at which children have the right to consent to appearing in sexually explicit photographs, it is unimaginable that a significant global consensus could be ever reached over appropriate punitive measures were cyber-bullying to be explicitly criminalized.

The challenge of developing international consensus over where the line would be drawn between acceptable free speech and criminal cyber-bullying would be even greater. In addition to the opt-outable child pornography article, the Convention on Cybercrime includes an opt-inable "additional protocol" making any publication of racist and xenophobic propaganda via computer networks a criminal offence.[29] While the Convention itself has been ratified by 23 countries, the additional protocol has received only 11 ratifications. Overall, looking at number of states that have ratified the treaty, ratified the additional protocol and have expressed reservations about article 9, the CoE experience suggests that the criminalization of certain categories of online speech is much less popular and more controversial than the cybercrime convention itself.

We do not view the criminal law approach as appropriate to the problem of cyber-bullying. We have already discussed the political tensions that would most certainly undermine any effort to criminalize bullying. The focus of efforts should be on helping children get past the damage caused by cyber-bullying, including the cyber-bullies themselves.

Victims' rights

Assertions of the rights of victims of cyber-crime and of children are frequent within the global internet governance regime. Human rights law has undeniable normative advantages over criminal law as an end to achieving the means of justifying restrictions on certain undesirable categories of speech; in particular in regard to cyber-bullying.

A criminal law-based approach to cyber-bullying would be based around the application of life-changing punishment to child perpetrators, many of whom are often "good kids" who simply have not properly thought through the harm their use of the internet can cause (c.f. Shariff, 2008). In contrast, the human rights framework shifts the focus toward proactive, preventative measures as well as on restitution for victims.

In debates over global internet governance, victims' rights claims have tactical advantages over criminal law approaches as well. Assertions of victims' rights, in particular in regard to protecting children from cybercrime, are normatively difficult to reject out of hand. The United States, for instance, has, as we have discussed, been largely opposed to calls to restrict freedom of speech on the internet, approving the CoE Convention on Cybercrime with reservations about the articles related to the criminalization of child pornography. At the 2008 IGF, US ambassador David Gross nonetheless called the issue of child pornography "the easy case" and added: "I don't know anybody who is for child pornography."[30]

Criminal law involves a necessary negation of existing freedoms; a proposal to criminalize cyber-bullying or online hate speech is directly correlated with a simultaneous reduction in free speech. The sum of subjects about which we would be free to express ourselves would be slightly less after hate speech was criminalized than it was previously. Assertions of victims' rights in contrast, focus not on reducing existing freedoms but on expanding or re-enforcing them. Just as it is easy to be against child pornography, it is hard to be against the rights of the child or cybercrime victims' rights to honour dignity and reputation. There are thus undeniable strategic advantages to rhetoric that avoids confrontation by claiming victims' rights without directly addressing the corresponding limitations in freedom of expression and privacy rights that would be required in order to accomplish anything on the ground. It is not surprising then that many interventions from child protection activists within the Internet governance regime focus on victim rights whilst steering clear of the subject of limiting free speech. Ignoring this complication however, does not mean that there would not be a balance to be struck between victims' and speech rights in any effort to implement real policy around online child protection. Nor should it be a surprise that certain privacy and free expression activists seem increasingly frustrated with this vague manner in which advocates for online child protection are invoking victims' rights and with what is being left unsaid about the implications on free speech. The argument that, in certain cases, the protection of children online justifies elevating a series of communication rights of potential victims above the free expressions and privacy rights of all internet users could perhaps instigate more meaningful deliberation amongst internet governance stakeholders if such claims were framed as communication rights issues and considered within the social cycle of communication.

Multi-Stakeholder Cooperation

One of the trends that are unmistakable when one looks at our table mapping how different institutions active in global internet governance are approaching the issue of online child protection is that every one of these institutions is engaged in multi-stakeholder cooperation. This is significant for cyber-bullying activists trying to understand the mechanics of global Internet governance and consider how to push for responses to cyber-bullying within it. In each instance, organizations recognize the need to engage in media literacy and educational activities in the aim of developing and communicating greater understanding of the threats that exist to children's use of the internet and how to avoid and respond to them.

The global internet governance regime offers the opportunity to work with—through informal cooperation or the organization of dynamic coalitions—and ideally pressure organizations such as Facebook and MySpace who are frequently implicated in instances of cyber-bullying but may not be responsive to local or even national efforts at developing policy solutions. In addition such cooperation would be an opportunity to push governments such as the UK's that have been proactive in instating laudable policy responses to cyber-bullying to share best practices and discuss results.

Despite the reservations that some IGF participants expressed about the appropriateness of the issue of online child protection to the mandate of the IGF, there was considerable enthusiasm expressed about the role that multi-stakeholder cooperation could play in establishing an acceptable balance between competing communication rights. "We shouldn't necessarily talk about a tension between security and privacy" Natasha Primo (of the Association of Progressive Communication or APC) suggested. "These can be mutually reinforcing," that

> the tension should be reconceptualized as that between rights and responsibilities, and this also brings into focus the importance of education, and specifically media literacy for users...I think people feel very positive that it is a space for developing consensus, for developing deeper understanding of the different viewpoints, the different perspectives, and that this has value in and of itself.[31]

This call was echoed by Everton Lucero from the government of Brazil's contention that child protection issues

> represent challenges not only to law enforcement agencies, but also to parliamentarians, to civil society, to intergovernmental organizations, to the private sector, to the technical community. So whatever the way forward may be, it has to go through the multi-stakeholder cooperation, dialogue and partnership in the spirit of shared responsibilities. That is drawing the line between privacy, security, and openness is, indeed, a collective work. We have to start somewhere.[32]

If cyber-bullying is going to emerge as a higher profile issue within the global internet governance regime, it is indeed important that it start somewhere, and multi-stakeholder cooperation has undeniable appeal and potential as an approach. However, multi-stakeholder cooperation only seems to get so far. There have been repeated laments from activists and NGOs who have invested precious time and resources in the WSIS and IGF processes that little of concrete value is produced beyond the information and good will garnered by talking shop with other stakeholders. IGF dynamic coalitions, for instance, have proven difficult to administer and have, for the most part, failed to substantively impact other organizations within the work of the IGF. Thus, multi-stakeholder collaboration, in a certain sense the defining theme of the global internet governance regime, contains possibilities and pitfalls as an approach to engaging the global internet governance regime on the issue of cyber-bullying.

CONCLUSION

In a thorough review of the emerging and established legal standards applicable to cyber-bullying prepared in 2007, one of the editors of this collection focuses on the following areas of law and policy: Tort law (related to cyber-libel and to supervision); human and civil rights; constitutional principles and criminal law.[33] What, if anything, does the emerging global internet governance regime contribute to beginning to fill in the 'policy vacuum' (Shariff, 2005) surrounding cyber-bullying? Do recent policy initiatives aimed at protecting children online suggest that this list should be amended to include the emerging framework of global internet governance?

Cyber-bullying is most usefully understood as an extension of the age-old problem of "general" bullying rather than as something entirely new and unique (Shariff, 2005, p. 468). Yet, the mediation of unwanted, deliberate, persistent and relentless aggression and harassment by modern communication and information technologies (ICTs) such as the internet introduces a series of new characteristics. "Electronic media by their nature" Shariff (2008, p. 32) argues, "allow for traditional forms of bullying to take on characteristics" that are specific to cyberspace. The role played by *cyber* in the problem of cyber-bullying is unmistakable. The view that the borderless nature of internet mediated communication creates jurisdictional conflicts that render it impossible to regulate is being discredited by the emergence of the global internet governance regime and a more nuanced understanding that the internet should not be seen as a static technological tool, that its architecture and the values that are embedded into it are increasingly subject to debate and institutional governance. There are indications, as we have seen, that some stakeholders, child protection activists in particular, are interested in taking the next natural step in this evolution by pushing the specific issue of cyber-bullying further up the global internet governance agenda. In the sense that tackling the problem of cyber-bullying is increasingly being seen as requiring engagement in the cyber policy sphere as well as in the domain of bullying policy, the global internet governance regime is relevant to any discussion of policy remedies to the issue of cyber-bullying. In addition to providing venues for the discussion of various ad-hoc policy initiatives designed to curtail or investigate specific practices that are linked to the problem of cyber-bullying, the global internet governance regime is, in a larger sense, the venue in which the fundamental dilemma of cyber-bullying policy—the establishment of acceptable limits on free expression in the online environment—is playing out. "The Internet is a revolutionary medium of *communication* and communication is speech," Jack Goldsmith and Tim Wu remind us in their important book *Who Controls the Internet: Illusions of a Borderless World.* "In that sense," they continue, "just about every debate about Internet governance is at bottom a debate about speech governance" (2006, p. 150).

The balance between free speech and the need to protect the values that are made vulnerable by internet mediated communication is being questioned, established and challenged within the global internet governance regime, just as communication regulation has always been used to establish what limits a democratic society can justify on free expression. Clearer general indication of where the balance lies in regard to internet mediated communication would remove much of the uncertainty over the status of cyber-bullying and would help diffuse some of the controversy over stakeholder responsibility that blocks efforts to respond to and educate around the problem of cyber-bullying.

While internet governance matters to cyber-bullying, the reverse is also true. Should cyber-bullying emerge, as other areas of online child protection have, as a more frequent topic of discussion within global internet governance (indications are that it will[34]), consideration should be given to its role in setting the broader context for the governance of internet mediated communication. At the 2008 IGF, for example, the push for online child protection was perceived to be a threat to privacy and freedom of expression rights, both of which are extremely precarious given the pressure that some governments exert within the global internet governance regime for greater authority over each. While limiting free expression in order to protect victims of cyber-bullying might be an appropriate policy agenda to pursue at the local or national level in countries like the US or the UK where the principle of free speech is sufficiently established and protected that it can withstand a certain degree of tinkering at the margins, any gains that child protection activists would make to improving the lives of children by using the global internet governance regime to formally curtail free speech on the internet would pale in comparison to the losses that those same children would suffer by the corresponding increases in enclosure over their communication that such a precedent would establish. Rather than bringing child protection concerns such as cyber-bullying into direct conflict with openness, expression, the global internet governance regime could be place where, as Natasha Primo of APC suggested, such tensions could be "reconceptualized as that between rights and responsibilities."[35] The social cycle of communication offers some guidelines as to where this focus ought to lie in regard to cyber-bullying. Ultimately, the approach that is most likely to bear fruit is to situate the problem of cyber-bullying and proposed solutions within a broader framework of communication rights.

Endnotes

1. This section draws on Marc Raboy, *Report on the Matter of Broadcasting Regulation*. Prepared for the Department of Justice, Ottawa, Canada, In the case of *Genex Communications Inc. v. the Attorney General of Canada and the Canadian Radio-Television and Telecommunications Commission (CRTC)*. Federal Court of Appeal no. A-464–04.

2. This view draws from thinking that is well-established within the mainstream of political philosophy and free speech scholarship, in particular Habermas, 1989; see also Peters, 1989—especially at p. 201—for an overview of this line of thinking.

3. A more complete and general accounting of what is meant by "flanking rights" includes other rights that are less relevant to this discussion such as the right to freedom of information; cultural and linguistic rights (though certainly in cases where cyber-bullies mock the background of their victims it is very relevant); a right to self determination and to take part in government, etc. See CRIS (2005) for the overview of flanking rights, see also Raboy and Shtern (forthcoming) for discussion of more liberal interpretations of flanking rights.

4. See Shariff (2008, ch. 5) for a more detailed overview and discussion of each of these policy frameworks.

5. As a global medium that neither belongs to nor is situated in any one existing nation state in particular, many early commentators and policy makers came to the same conclusion as Nicholas Negroponte, co-founder of MIT's media lab that: "The internet cannot be regulated" (quoted in Higgins and Azhar, 1996) . For additional influential iterations of this view, see the juridical scholarship of Johnson and Post (1996). See Geist (2003) for an insightful mapping of the generation of domestic internet policy that accepted this truism as well as the gradual emergence of a more nuanced and realistic 'Cyberlaw 2.0.' Within the cyber-bullying literature, this view of the internet as immune to public authority is problematic not only because scholars may be unfamiliar with the more recent internet law literature wherein it has been entirely discredited (c.f. Lessig, 1999, 2006; Goldsmith and Wu, 2006; Benkler, 2006) and also because, as Shariff (2008) points out, the relatively common perception amongst teachers and children that there are no rules online complicates efforts to determine malicious intent and boundaries of authority in cases of cyber-bullying.

6. See http://www.coe.int/t/dghl/StandardSetting/InternetLiteracy/hbk_en.asp

7. See http://www.coe.int/t/dc/files/events/internet/2008_infosheet5_guidelines_ en.pdf#xml=http://www.search.coe.int/texis/search/pdfhi.txt?query=guidelines+for+ISPs +and+online+games+providers&pr=Internet_D2&prox=page&rorder=500&rprox=750& rdfreq=500&rwfreq=500&rlead=500&rdepth=250&sufs=1&order=r&mode=&opts=&cq =&sr=&id=491c9ee06

8. Shariff (2008, see p. 131) looks in greater detail at the section on cyber-bullying in the CoE *Literacy Handbook* and also makes reference to additional CoE documents that address issues related to cyber-bullying.

9. See http://ec.europa.eu/information_society/activities/sip/public_consultation/ index_en.htm

10. See http://www.itu.int/wsis/basic/why.html

11. Geneva Phase:

> Declaration of Principles (see WSIS 2003b):
>
> (A11) We are also committed to ensuring that the development of ICT applications and operation of services respects the rights of children as well as their protection and well-being; (B10) All actors in the Information Society should take appropriate actions and preventive measures, as determined by law, against abusive uses of ICTs, such as illegal and other acts motivated by…violence, all forms of child abuse (also 25b of Plan of Action).
>
> Plan of Action (see WSIS 2003a):
>
> 12b Governments, in cooperation with the private sector, should prevent, detect and respond to cyber-crime and misuse of ICTs by: developing guidelines that take into

account ongoing efforts in these areas; considering legislation that allows for effective investigation and prosecution of misuse; promoting effective mutual assistance efforts; strengthening institutional support at the international level for preventing, detecting and recovering from such incidents; and encouraging education and raising awareness.

Tunis Phase:

Tunis Agenda (see WSIS 2005a)

90q incorporating regulatory, self-regulatory, and other effective policies and frameworks to protect children and young people from abuse and exploitation through ICTs into national plans of action and e-strategies.

92. We encourage countries, and all other interested parties, to make available child helplines, taking into account the need for mobilization of appropriate resources. For this purpose, easy-to-remember numbers, accessible from all phones and free of charge, should be made available.

40. We underline the importance of the prosecution of cybercrime, including cybercrime committed in one jurisdiction, but having effects in another. We further underline the necessity of effective and efficient tools and actions, at national and international levels, to promote international cooperation among, inter alia, law-enforcement agencies on cybercrime. We call upon governments in cooperation with other stakeholders to develop necessary legislation for the investigation and prosecution of cybercrime, noting existing frameworks, for example, UNGA Resolutions 55/63 and 56/121 on "Combating the criminal misuse of information technologies" and regional initiatives including, but not limited to, the Council of Europe's Convention on Cybercrime.

42. We reaffirm our commitment to the freedom to seek, receive, impart and use information, in particular, for the creation, accumulation and dissemination of knowledge. We affirm that measures undertaken to ensure Internet stability and security, to fight cybercrime and to counter spam, must protect and respect the provisions for privacy and freedom of expression as contained in the relevant parts of the Universal Declaration of Human Rights and the Geneva Declaration of Principles.

Tunis Commitment (see WSIS 2005b):

24. We recognize the role of ICTs in the protection of children and in enhancing the development of children. We will strengthen action to protect children from abuse and defend their rights in the context of ICTs. In that context, we emphasize that the best interests of the child are a primary consideration.

12. 2.1.4 Importance of Youth: We commit to develop and use only those ICTs that ensure the well-being, protection, and harmonious development of all children.

2.2.7 Rights of the Child

Information and communication societies must respect and promote the principles of the Convention on the Rights of the Child. Every child is entitled to a happy childhood and to enjoy the rights and freedoms available to all persons under the Universal Declaration of Human Rights. All persons, civil society, private sector and governments should commit to uphold the Rights of the Child in information and communication societies.

13. Quoted from the website of the IGF Dynamic Coalition on Online Child Safety: http://www.intgovforum.org/cms/index.php/dynamiccoalitions/79-child-online-safety

14. Distilled from John Carr's comments made during the IGF 2008 main session "Fostering security, privacy and openness." See the transcript available online at: http://www.intgovforum.org/cms/hydera/HBD%20Security%20Privacy%20Openness%204Dec08.txt

15. Quoted from the transcript of the IGF 2008 main session "Fostering security, privacy and openness," available online at: http://www.intgovforum.org/cms/hydera/HBD%20Security%20Privacy%20Openness%204Dec08.txt

16. Quoted from the transcript of the IGF 2008 main session "Fostering security, privacy and openness," available online at: http://www.intgovforum.org/cms/hydera/HBD%20Security%20Privacy%20Openness%204Dec08.txt

17. Quoted from the transcript of the IGF 2008 "Open Dialogue" session on "Promoting Cyber-Security and Trust" http://www.intgovforum.org/cms/hyderabad_prog/Open%20Dialogue.html

18. Quoted from the COP section on the ITU website: http://www.itu.int/osg/csd/cybersecurity/gca/cop/about2.html

19. See http://www.icann.org/en/about/

20. See http://blog.internetgovernance.org/blog/_archives/2007/3/30/2847139.html

21. Quoted from US Department of Commerce staff emails sent 6/16/2005, included as "Exhibit 5" on page 7 of the document package obtained through an ICM Registry Freedom of Information Act request and posted on the website of the IGP.

22. Quoted from US Department of Commerce staff emails sent 6/22/2005, included as "Exhibit 13" on page 28 of the document package obtained through an ICM Registry Freedom of Information Act request and posted on the website of the IGP. (see footnote 15 for details on that document).

23. Quoted from US Department of Commerce staff emails sent 6/16/2005, included as "Exhibit 9" on page 17 of the document package obtained through an ICM Registry Freedom of Information Act request and posted on the website of the IGP. (see footnote 15 for details on that document).

24. Though this was ICANN policy, the complex oversight relationship between ICANN and the US government proved difficult for media covering the story to encapsulate and for the advocacy groups and, partially as a result, for members of the public mobilized around the issue to understand. As public pushback against the implication that the US government supports the pornographic industry increased, Department of Commerce officials responded by directing interventions to ICANN, reminding interested parties of the limits of their supervisory role in ICANN and the US government's commitment to fighting the pornography industry and, eventually, by 'requesting' that ICANN delay the creation of the .xxx domain and consider all of the (mostly negative) comments that were coming in. Ironically, those inclined to see such a request as an order disguised in diplomatic language argue that the .xxx episode entirely undermines any suggestion that the DoC plays only a supervisory role at ICANN, meaning that, rather than confused about where the decision came from, advocacy groups were entirely correct in targeting the DoC in addition to or instead of ICANN. (c.f.

Internet Governance Project, 2006; see also—for a more general overview of .xxx—Preston, 2008).

25. A clue to how this might be approached can be found in the new Obama administration's technology programme, which issues a call to "Protect Our Children While Preserving the First Amendment: Give parents the tools and information they need to control what their children see on television and the Internet in ways fully consistent with the First Amendment. Support tough penalties, increase enforcement resources and forensic tools for law enforcement, and encourage collaboration between law enforcement and the private sector to identify and prosecute people who try to exploit children online." http://www.whitehouse.gov/agenda/technology/

26. Quoted from the transcript of the IGF 2008 main session "Fostering security, privacy and openness," available online at: http://www.intgovforum.org/cms/hydera/HBD%20Security%20Privacy%20Openness%204Dec08.txt

27. Current as of 9/1/2009. Source: CoE Treaty Office: http://conventions.coe.int/Treaty/Commun/ListeDeclarations.asp?NT=185&CV=1&NA=9&PO=999&CN=999&VL=1&CM=9&CL=ENG

28. Shariff (2008) distinguishes between "peer-to-peer" bullying and "anti-authoritarian" bullying (see Ch. 1).

29. See http://conventions.coe.int/Treaty/en/Treaties/Html/189.htm see on ratifications: http://conventions.coe.int/Treaty/Commun/ChercheSig.asp?NT=189&CM=8&DF=8/27/2007&CL=ENG

30. Quoted from the transcript of the IGF 2008 main session "Fostering security, privacy and openness," available online at: http://www.intgovforum.org/cms/hydera/HBD%20Security%20Privacy%20Openness%204Dec08.txt

31. Quoted from the transcript of the IGF 2008 "Open Dialogue" session on 'Promoting Cyber-Security and Trust) http://www.intgovforum.org/cms/hyderabad_prog/Open%20Dialogue.html

32. Quoted from the transcript of the IGF 2008 "Open Dialogue" session on 'Promoting Cyber-Security and Trust) http://www.intgovforum.org/cms/hyderabad_prog/Open%20Dialogue.html

33. For summary, see table "Applicable Legal Standards: Emerging and Established" (Shariff, 2008, as table 7.1, p. 224), for a more detailed discussion consult the entirety of Chapter 7 of Shariff, 2008.

34. For instance, British child protection activist John Carr suggested to the 2008 IGF that "numerically, this is by far the more important issue for children and young people, the way in which the new technology is facilitating and enabling new styles of insidious bullying and online harassment." Quoted from the transcript of the IGF 2008 main session "Fostering security, privacy and openness," available online at: http://www.intgovforum.org/cms/hydera/HBD%20Security%20Privacy%20Openness%204Dec08.txt while cyber-bullying was the subject of its own section in a publication (see Muir, 2005) that was circulated by the NGO ECPAT International (End Child Prostitution, Child Pornography and Trafficking of Children for Sexual Purposes).

35. Quoted from the transcript of the IGF 2008 "Open Dialogue" session on 'Promoting Cyber-Security and Trust) http://www.intgovforum.org/cms/hyderabad_prog/Open%20Dialogue.html

References

Benkler, Y. (2006). *The wealth of networks: How social production transforms markets and freedom.* New Haven [Conn.]: Yale University Press.

Binder, C. (1952). Freedom of information and the United Nations. *InternationalOrganization,* 6(2), 210–226.

Chairman of the IGF. (2008). Third Meeting of the Internet Governance Forum (IGF) Hyderabad, India, 3–6 December 2008 Chairman's Summary. Retrieved January 20, 2009 from http://www.intgovforum.org/cms/index.php/component/content/article/295-event-in-mumbai

Commission of the European Communities. (2008) Proposal for a decision of the European Parliament and of the council establishing a multiannual community programme on protecting children using the Internet and other communication technologies. 2008/0047 (COD). Retrieved January 2009 from http://ec.europa.eu/information_society/activities/sip/programme/sip_09_history/index_en.htm

Council of Europe. (2004). Convention on cybercrime CETS No. 185. Retrieved January 20, 2009, from Council of Europe Treaty Office, http://conventions.coe.int/Treaty/EN/Treaties/Html/185.htm.

CRIS—The Communication Rights in the Information Society Campaign. (2005). Assessing communication rights: A handbook. Retrieved July 2008, from http://files.planetgrey.org/cris/crisinfo/CRAFT_en.pdf

D'Arcy, J. (1977). Direct broadcast satellites and the right to communicate. In L.S. Harms, J. Richstad, & K.A. Kie (Eds.), *Right to communicate : collected papers* (pp. 1–9). Honolulu: Social Sciences and Linguistics Institute, University of Hawaii at Manoa/ University Press of Hawaii.

Eck, J. (2002). Preventing crime at places. In L. Sherman, D. Farrington, B. Welsh and D. MacKenzie (Eds.), *Evidence-based crime prevention* (pp. 241–294). New York: Routledge.

Geist, M. (2003). Cyberlaw 2.0. *Boston College Law Review,* (44)2, 323–358.

Goldsmith, J. & Wu, T. (2006). *Who controls the Internet?: Illusions of a borderless world.* New York: Oxford University Press.

Habermas, J. (1989). *The structural transformation of the public sphere: An inquiry into a category of bourgeois society.* Cambridge: Polity.

Higgins, A. & Azhar, A. (1996, February 5) China begins to erect second Great Wall in cyberspace. *The Guardian.* p. 9.

Hoffmann-Riem, W. (1996). *Regulating media: The licensing and supervision of broadcasting in six countries.* New York: Guilford Press.

Internet Governance Project. (2006, May 19, 2006). Review of documents released under the Freedom of Information Act in the .XXX case: Internet Governance Project paper IGP06–003. Retrieved January 24, 2009, from http://internetgovernance.org/pdf/dist -sec.pdf

Jesdanun, A. (2005, June 14). Will a virtual red-light district help parents curb online porn? Associated Press Worldstream.

Johnson, D. R. & Post, D. (1996). Law and borders: The rise of law in cyberspace. *Stanford Law Review,* (48), p. 1367.

Korttein, J., Myntti, K. & Hannikainen, L. (1999). Article 19. In G. Alfredsoson and A. Eide (Eds.), *The Universal Declaration of Human Rights: A Common Standard of Achievement* (pp. 393–416). The Hague, Netherlands: Kluwer Law International.

Kummer, M. (2005). Introduction. In W. Drake (ed.) *Reforming Internet governance: Perspectives from the Working Group on Internet Governance (WGIG)* (pp. 1–6). New York: The United Nations ICT Task Force.

Lessig, L. (1999). *Code and other laws of cyberspace.* New York: Basic Books.

Lessig, L. (2006). *Code : Version 2.0* ([2nd ed.). New York: Basic Books.

Mayer-Schönberger, V. (2007, April). Useful Void: The art of forgetting in the age of ubiquitous computing. The John F. Kennedy School of Government faculty research working paper series. Retrieved January 27, 2009 from http://ksgnotes1.harvard.edu/Research/wpaper. nsf/rwp/RWP07-022

Mitchell, K. J., Finkelhor, D. and Wolak, J. (2005). Protecting youth online: Family use of filtering and blocking software. *Child Abuse and Neglect: The International Journal,* 29 (7), 753–65.

Muir, D. (2005). Violence against children in cyberspace. Bangkok: ECPAT International.

Ó Siochrú, S., Girard, B., & Mahan, A. (2002). *Global media governance: A beginner's guide.* Lanham, MD. ; Oxford: Rowman & Littlefield.

Padovani, C. (2005). Debating communication imbalances from the MacBride Report to the World Summit on the Information Society: An analysis of a changing discourse. *Global Media and Communication,* 1(3), 316–338.

Padovani, C. & K. Nordenstreng. (2005). From NWICO to WSIS: Another world information and communication order? *Global Media and Communication,* 1(3), 264–272.

Peters, J.D. (1989) Democracy and American communication theory: Dewey, Lippmann, Lazarfelds. *Communication, 11(3).* pp. 199-220

Preston, C.B. (2008). Internet porn, ICANN, and families: A call to action. *Journal of Internet Law,* 3–15.

Raboy, M. & Landry, N. (2005). *Civil society, communication and global governance: Issues from the World Summit on the Information Society.* New York: Peter Lang.

Raboy, M. & Shtern, J. (Eds.) (forthcoming). *Two Tiers of Freedom: Communication Rights and the Right to Communicate in Canada.* Vancouver: University of British Columbia Press.

Servance, R. L. (2003). Cyber-bullying, cyber-harassment and the conflict between schools and the First Amendment. *Wisconsin Law Review* (6), 1213–15.

Shariff, S. (2005). Cyber-dilemmas in the new millennium: Balancing free expression and student safety in cyber-space. [Special Issue: Schools and courts: Competing rights in the new millennium]. *McGill Journal of Education,* 40 (3), 467–487.

Shariff, S. (2008). *Cyber-bullying : Issues and solutions for the school, the classroom and the home.* London; New York: Routledge.

Tambini,D. & Verhulst, S. (2000). The transition to digital and content regulation. In D. Tambini (ed.), *Communications reform*. London: Institute for Public Policy Research.

WGIG. (2005). Background Report: The Working Group on Internet Governance. Retrieved January 23, 2009, from www.wgig.org/docs/BackgroundReport.doc

WSIS. (2003a). The World Summit on the Information Society: A plan of action. Retrieved January 23, 2009, from http://www.itu.int/wsis/docs/geneva/official/poa.html

WSIS. (2003b). The World Summit on the Information Society Declaration of principles. Retrieved January 23, 2009, from http://www.itu.int/wsis/docs/geneva/official/dop.html

WSIS. (2005a). The World Summit on the Information Society: The Tunis agenda for the information society. Retrieved January 24, 2009, from http://www.itu.int/wsis/docs2/tunis/off/6rev1.html

WSIS. (2005b). The World Summit on the Information Society: The Tunis commitment. Retrieved January 23, 2009, from http://www.itu.int/wsis/docs2/tunis/off/7.html

Educational Programs

9 · Changing Learning Ecologies

Social Media for Cyber-citizens

Jennifer Masters
Nicola Yelland

INTRODUCTION

The everyday life of children in the 21ˢᵗ century is vastly different from that of children of previous generations. The use of new technologies has permeated all aspects of life and learning and is now an integral part of activity, whether at work or play. Social interactions are also mediated by the technologies of the time. Children are enthusiastic in their uptake of new ways to communicate, and participation in online social networking has joined instant messaging as a popular form of keeping in touch with friends.

A major concern for parents and educators is the issue of cyber-safety in social networking environments. While children confidently display information about themselves or others, they are usually unaware of the broad nature of their audience and can expose themselves to situations that are potentially unsafe or inappropriate. Although a common reaction is to try and prevent children from participating, we propose that one way children can learn to be cybersafe is by playing and practicing in appropriately designed spaces.

This chapter will discuss a project that adopts the "learning through doing" approach. SuperclubsPLUS is an online learning community designed for children aged 6–12 years to participate in social networking. Only children and teachers from registered schools can access the environment, and highly trained mediators are provided to facilitate interactions and protect children from bullying or abuse.

BACKGROUND

Citizens of the 21st Century

The children in our schools today are citizens of the 21st century. They use new technologies fluently for a variety of purposes and are intuitive in their approach to appropriating them in activities that constitute their daily lives. These new technologies have created new work and social practices that have distinctively changed the ways that we do things in our lives. However, schooling systems have maintained heritage curricula conceived for past eras and often seem impervious to change. This resistance to change is currently being made very clear in Australia where a National Curriculum is being constructed. Discussions are not centred on what type of knowledge and skills citizens will need to contribute to life in 21st century Australia, but rather, on what content should remain in (traditional) discipline areas and what can be sacrificed. The new curriculum is an exercise of rationalisation rather than an opportunity to reconceptualize our curriculum work.

In fact, the rate of change we are experiencing in society is accelerating. Howe and Strauss (2001) in writing about the Millennial Generation remind us of the characteristics of this cohort who were born after 1985. Their lives are digital and they communicate in a variety of modes with a myriad of materials that are made of bits and bytes. Their homes are full of media options that include: TVs, mobile phones, computers, mp3 players, DVD machines, digital cameras, interactive toys and games and video game consoles and mobile devices. In a Kaiser Family Foundation study of zero to six-year-olds' use of electronic media, Rideout, Vandewater and Wartella (2003) report that 99% have a TV at home and 36% have one in their own bedroom. Nearly a half of their sample had a video game player and 63% lived in a home that had Internet access. Additionally, nearly half (48%) of the group under six years of age have used a computer and 30% of them played video games. Parent reports of time spent with screen media indicate that this group spent approximately 2 hours a day using them and that this was about the same amount of time that they spent playing outdoors, and three times as much time as they spent reading (a book) or being read to.

This is not passive consumption of new media. These are young people who are actively seeking out information and who have electronic media at their disposal. Seventy-seven per cent are turning on the TV by themselves, asking for particular shows (67%), using the remote control to change channels (62%) playing their favourite DVDs (71%), turning on the computer by themselves (33%) and loading CDRoms with games on (23%). The study revealed that listening to music (and dancing/ acting) is one of the most popular pastimes for young children in this age range with 79% listening to music daily and with just under half (42%) owning their own CDs so they can listen when they want to.

Further children in the age range of 6 to 17 years continue to extend their skills bases with new technologies. In excess of two million American children in this age range have created their own website (Grunwald Associates, 2003) and there are similar trends in the UK (Gibson, 2005). More recently the evolution of social media such as MySpace, Facebook, Club Penguin and the growing use of blogs, wikis and instant messaging have enabled young people to be in touch instantly and constantly with all their friends and families.

The lives of these students are so different from those of the generations before them that they require us to rethink what constitutes an effective education system that will prepare them for life. Our 21st century students exist in communities of practice that should be incorporated into their schooling experiences since these communities have the potential to enrich their learning and extend their skills base, allowing them to acquire knowledge and apply it in a variety of rich contexts.

Learning in the 21st Century

A report entitled *Learning for the 21st Century,* (Partnership for 21st Century Skills, 2004) not only recognises that we need to define and incorporate core subjects in order to establish the conditions to extend thinking from a foundational base but also recommends that we need to broaden our notion of what is "basic" in light of the major changes that have taken place in all aspects of our lives. The report recognises that *No Child Left Behind* identifies the core subjects as being English, reading or language arts, mathematics, science, foreign languages, civics, government, economics, arts, history and geography and applauds the fact that the list was expanded to meet the demands of the new century. However, it also suggests that citizens of the 21st century need to go beyond the core subjects in order to function effectively and that they need to know how to use their knowledge and skills to:

- Think critically,
- Apply knowledge to new contexts,
- Analyse information,
- Understand new ideas,

- Communicate,
- Problem solve,
- And make decisions.

The content of the report supports the notion that such skills are fundamental learning skills that are increasingly important in the workplace and have the potential to enrich all aspects of personal lives. It focuses on three areas of learning skills that are based around:

- Information and communication,
- Thinking and problem solving,
- Interpersonal and self-directional skills.

Even more specifically, the report states that "learning skills enable people to acquire new knowledge and skills, connect new information to existing knowledge, analyse, develop habits of learning and work with others to use information among other skills" (p. 10). This skill development energises learners to be autonomous and be flexible in their learning so that they can adapt well to the changing circumstances that tend to define our contemporary lives. Naturally, the resources that support the learning skills are digital and facilitate interactions and learning that were not possible prior to their development.

Furthermore, the report provides specific strategies to assist children to make connections in their learning to build on these notions. In this way it is important that teachers should be aware of them as they include:

- Making content relevant to children's lives,
- Bringing the world into the classroom,
- Taking students out into the world,
- Creating contexts for learning that enable students to interact with themselves and others in authentic ways.

Such a stance resonates with what Scardamalia (2003) labels as knowledge building, which she maintains should be central to the process of education. Her view of knowledge building incorporates:

> …the production and continual improvement of ideas of value to a community, through means that increase the likelihood that what the community accomplishes will be greater than the sum of individual contributions and part of broader cultural efforts…as applied to education…the approach means engaging learners in the full process of knowledge creation…(p. 2)

Scardamalia (2003) suggests that in order for schools to become places that nurture creativity, imagination and innovation, they need to assist students to build knowledge in dynamic ways. She believes that these skills are essential for effective functioning in the 21st century. In her scenario schools are sites where public knowledge is explored, experimented with and modified in active and specific ways with the purpose of using it in new and creative ways. New millennium learners achieve this autonomously in out-of-school or informal learning contexts, where they are able to design new creations, make sense of ideas, extend their knowledge using new technologies, and communicate their findings both to local and global audiences.

Informal Learning

The use of computers and associated new technologies in informal learning settings is of considerable interest in contemporary educational research. It is commonly identified that children naturally access and use new technologies as part of their everyday lives (Sefton-Green, 2004), and therefore it is important that educators find out how and what children learn through the informal use of technology. Research in this area suggests that informal learning contexts have some distinct differences to formal settings. Sorensen, Danielsen and Nielsen (2001) suggested that the prominence of learning is inverted in an informal learning situation. In school, learning is the goal of the task—teachers design activities in order to engage children in learning outcomes. However, in an informal learning setting, learning is simply a means to an end. Children learn skills and processes in order to reach their desired goal, whether it is reaching a level in a computer game, chatting on line or building a web page. Further they identified the importance of social learning in "spare-time culture" (p. 3). This learning incorporated a number of learning forms. These were referred to by Sorensen et al. (2001) in dimensions of a) a learning hierarchy, where younger/older, confident/less-confident or experienced/less-experienced learners work in an apprenticeship model; b) the learning community in which social structures form and reform in a loose transition; and c) a learning network where knowledge is stored and accessed by consistent reference to each other.

Social Networking and Cyber Safety

Although online social networking environments such as Bebo and Facebook are very attractive to children, a major concern for parents and educators is that children will publish information or images about themselves or converse with people who may be a threat to the child, either virtually or physically. Despite these concerns it appears that parents are giving in to pressure and allowing their children to use the Internet for social purposes. The National School Boards Association (2007), in a USA survey of 1,277 children aged 9–17, reported that a staggering 96% of children with Internet access use social networking technology. As a consequence, the report, while acknowledging the need to set rules about cyber-safety, recommends that "students may learn these lessons better while they're actually using social networking tools" (p. 8) and that social networking environments should be adjusted to be "explicitly educational in nature." Tynes (2007) also believes in a proactive approach. She suggests that strategies for keeping children safe online need to be based on the technological awareness and sophistication of the children involved. Rather than banning the use of social networking tools, the use of these tools needs to be harnessed to support the cognitive and social advantages that this type of environment can offer.

Campbell (2005) suggests that the advent of cyber-bullying should also be a concern when addressing the cyber-safety of children. In this situation the technological tools are used to harass and/or intimidate victims, with hurtful or humiliating emails or postings to public spaces such as web sites or forums. Campbell identifies that just as adult supervision in the playground decreases the incidence of face-to-face bullying, educators also need to be aware that bullying happens with technology and should take the same steps to intervene in any suspected incidents.

THE SUPERCLUBSPLUS PROJECT

Context

SuperclubsPLUS Australia was based on a highly successful version of the project in the UK and was established in Australia in 2008. The project provides an online learning community for children 6–12 to talk to current friends and meet new ones, publish and be creative, participate in forums and discussions, and learn new ICT skills. SuperclubsPLUS is a safe environment because:

- All members are authenticated through their schools, and only children and teachers from registered schools can access the environment;
- Teachers can see everything that their students write or create;
- Highly trained mediators are rostered on to facilitate interactions and
- scaffold creative work;
- Sophisticated content-checking tools are used by the mediators to monitor all communications, protecting children from bullying or abuse.

SuperClubsPLUS provides a rich environment for personalised and social learning. Although many teachers incorporate the program into their curriculum activity, much of the interaction is informal with children participating in their leisure time in out-of-school contexts. This type of use is supported by the extended opening hours, including weekends. The children have full access to all facilities during *Live Time*, usually from 8.00 am to 8.00 pm and then *Build Time* allows them to work on constructions such as articles, web pages or projects (but not communicate with others) at all other times.

The program was introduced in Australia in May 2008 and officially launched in September 2008. At the end of September 2009 there were 87,000 children participating in SuperclubsPLUS Australia, with 220,000 participants worldwide. It is anticipated that there will be 500,000 Australian participants within two years.

Activities in SuperclubsPLUS

The SuperclubsPLUS interface displays the range of activity provided for children in the environment (see figure 1). Broadly, SuperclubsPLUS provides the opportunity for children to:

- Communicate with their teacher, other children and mediators via secure internal email;
- Create Websites on their interests and favourite topics;
- Contribute to discussion *Forums, Clubs* and *Projects* on a wide range of subjects;
- Develop ICT in areas such as web safety, publishing and page construction via the Star Awards;
- Participate in online polls, quizzes and surveys;
- Talk with experts or guests in the *Hot Seat* events;
- Play collaborative games such as rhyming words, counting and role playing in make-believe settings.

Figure 1: The SuperclubsPLUS interface

ICT Skills

Children develop their ICT skills significantly as they work and create artefacts in the SuperclubsPLUS environment. In addition to informal development, the program has a Stars mechanism to ensure that children engage with key ICT aspects. There are five different coloured stars that are awarded to the children as they complete lists of tasks. When the tasks are completed satisfactorily, the star automatically appears on the child's personal web page. The first star, the White Star, relates to safety online and requires the child to successfully complete a quiz before proceeding. The subsequent stars (red, green, blue and yellow) support the children to build their web pages within a template, construct email and contribute to forums, create and upload images and use BB codes (a subset of html) to hone their page display. If a child becomes extremely competent and a model citizen of SuperclubsPLUS may apply to join the *Tech Team,* a select group of members who have additional rights and are available to support other users.

Literacy

Since the beginning of SuperclubsPLUS over 10 million emails have passed between children, teachers and mediators. Written text is the principal mechanism for communication, and children soon realise that they must master this skill to participate. In this situation children write because they have a purpose that is motivated by their desire to communicate. While email communication is not edited or moderated by teachers, the mediators on duty mediate discussions. A mediator will pay particular attention to any conversation that appears to be "uncomfortable" and will intervene if necessary. A child can email the mediator on duty at any stage, or they can use the emergency bell that is displayed on every page to send a distress message to the mediator if they feel threatened by a conversation. This process ensures that children develop a familiarity with the genre and etiquette of email.

In the forums, children engage in discussion for a wide range of subjects. They learn to pose and respond to questions and they write to engage their audience. They also learn to debate issues and present their opinions. During *Hot Seats* discussions, they chat with experts or people with particular experiences. In these conversations they learn to focus their questions in order to address the area of discussion. Children are also highly motivated to write material for their web pages which they share with their peers through *web rings*—a mechanism that links children with similar interests via an icon on their web page. Finally, children can also write articles for publication on the *Club* pages. Each *Club* has an editor (usually a mediator) who accepts, rejects or suggests modifications to the submission. Publication is by no means automatic. It is usual for a child to be asked to make changes, as a high quality of article is required. If the article is accepted the child receives a congratulatory email from the editor and an award icon for their page as well as a link that encourages visitors to their web page.

Active Citizenship

In our SuperclubsPLUS society, a sense of citizenship is developed through active participation and responsibility. In the SuperclubsPLUS environment, children are far less dominated by adult interaction and supervision. Although mediators are always available, their intervention tends to be subtle, and the children themselves take an active role in conducting conversations, supporting and encouraging each other. While SuperclubsPLUS acts as a natural community where children create their own culture, it also scaffolds a wider sense of citizenship by providing regular opportunities for children to engage with community, national and global issues through forums and hot seats. A recent example of this was a forum on the recent "Sorry Day" held in Australia, where the Australian Prime Minister, Kevin Rudd, apologized to Indigenous Australians for the policy of removing children from families as late as the 1970s. These children are known as "The Stolen Generation." The children in England were provided with some details and then asked to comment on what they thought about the Stolen Generation. The forum was posted on the 14th of February, and children were still commenting 3 weeks after the event, with almost 150 responses documented. While most of the children reacted with sympathy for the Stolen Generation, they also appreciated the significance of the event, with comments such as "I'm glad that they made a sorry day and are saying sorry like good people and not protenting (sic) it never happened." Adults did not guide or participate in this discussion, and yet it is interesting that many of the contemporary common issues relating to this matter that were evident in everyday discussions (e.g., newspapers and TV) also came to light in the students' discussions. For example, the idea of compensation was raised, but the issues around it were not unanimous, with some children arguing that compensation could not correlate with the sorrow caused. It was evident that some of the children involved felt that it was significant to just be involved in dialogue. One boy simply contributed "i think that the world is geting biger as we speek (sic)."

SuperclubsPLUS as a Safe Environment

While cyber-safety has been identified as a problem ever since the Internet has been available for children, a common approach to protection (such as Net Nanny) has been to try and simply block access to sites that might be dangerous (Tynes, 2007). We consider that this approach does nothing to educate children on what might be unsafe, and further it often inhibits effective use of the Internet by excluding some useful sites by adopting broad and often clumsy exclusion mechanisms. The SuperclubsPLUS environment is designed to help children aged 6–12 years to learn aspects of cyber-safety while maintaining interactions in a closed and safe environment. There are ten rules that all SuperclubsPLUS users—children, teachers and mediators—must adhere to:

1. Never write anything that is rude or insulting. Never threaten, bully or intimidate other SuperClubbers. If you can't think of anything nice to say about someone, then don't say anything at all.
2. Don't send lots of silly messages in emails, or Forums—that is called Spamming. This includes sending chain mail, asking people to "pass it on."
3. Don't use SuperClubsPLUS for "Chatting up" other members or anything to do with "boyfriend/girlfriend stuff." SuperClubsPLUS is for mates, NOT dates!
4. Never give or ask for any contact details—like your surname, home address, phone number, home email, MSN messenger or other similar contact information. You should not even talk about anything to do with this kind of personal information.
5. Keep your password a secret. NEVER give it to anyone else or ask them for theirs. Never let ANYONE ELSE use your account.
6. Don't give a lot of personal details about you or your family. If you do write about your family or friends, ask for their permission before you send it in. Also, don't upload personal pictures to the Library—or anything that can identify you, your family or where you live.
7. Don't put links to other websites or mention other web addresses or sites, because they might not be safe sites.
8. Respect the copyright code, only upload things that you have created yourself or you have permission to use. Don't copy people's ideas without their permission.
9. NEVER EVER make arrangements to meet someone from another school.
10. Only use the Emergency Bell if you see or read something that is VERY upsetting or that seriously breaks the rules.

As the Intuitive Community Engine (ICE) scans all communication—email, homepages and forums—the mediators on duty are immediately alerted when discussions breach these conditions. A mediator will then monitor the discussion or entries before deciding if a particular rule has been broken. For example, a student who mentioned an unsecured website in an email would get this warning:

Subject: REMEMBER—Discussing other websites

Steven,

Many websites (like the one you are talking about) aren't safe because they let you communicate with other people and you don't really know who they are (it could be an adult pretending to be a child). Please stop talking about it because next time you will get a warning. Please STOP and reply to this email to say you understand. If you are not sure use this link to read the rules: CLICK HERE

Mediator

Additionally any images used in SuperclubsPLUS have to be uploaded for review and approval by a moderator. The students need to make sure the size of their image is appropriate (both in dimension and size) and they are required to declares if they created the image or if they believe it is free from copyright restrictions before submitting. The mediator then checks the image for a number of conditions such as inappropriate content or copyright problems. For example, if a child tried to load a personal photo they would get the following message.

Subject: Your Library Upload

Sorry, your uploaded item 'my picture' has not been added to the library.a

This is because we don't allow personal pictures of you, your family, or anything that might identify you in real life.

While it would be naïve to think that children who use SuperclubsPLUS don't use websites that are unprotected, it is hoped that the learning scaffolds provided for the children in the SuperclubsPLUS environment will help to raise an awareness of cyber-safety issues during general Internet use. Further, as parents are often worried about what their children are accessing on the web, they can at least be sure that SuperclubsPLUS can provide a safe alternative for social networking so children won't need to access sites such as Bebo or Facebook where security is not available.

THEORETICAL FRAMEWORK

The SuperclubsPLUS project is intended to foster a rich environment where a number of research avenues will be investigated. A broad theoretical framework based on Cultural-Historical Activity Theory (CHAT) acts as a global structure to represent the SuperclubsPLUS community and environment. The core concept of this theory is that awareness emerges from an individual participating in a social structure where activity incorporating the use of tools to produce artefacts leads to socially valued outcomes. In doing so, the individual develops their own perspective, changing the way they think and behave in future situations. The CHAT model was represented by Engeström (1987) in the form of a triangle where the subject interacts with the community, rules, division of labour, the instruments and the object (artefact) to reach the outcome. This triangle has now become a common framework for representing understanding based on this framework.

As Cultural-Historical Activity Theory not only provides a theoretical basis but also a guide to practice, the CHAT triangle is used as an analytical framework. In this context, the study considers the environment as an activity system and maps the interactions between participants (children, teachers and mediators), the technology, and the virtual environment (see Figure 2). Understandings are drawn primarily from transcripts of online communication but also from virtual artefacts created by participants, such as member's home pages, projects, forums and webrings within the Superclubs PLUS community.

Figure 2: The SuperclubsPLUS Environment in a CHAT context

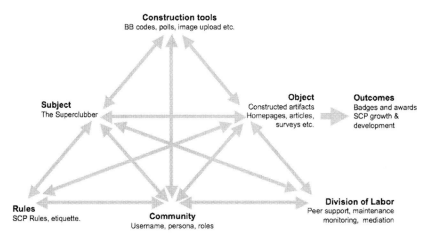

PRACTICES IN SUPERCLUBSPLUS

The role of the mediator in Superclubs PLUS is essential for the development of safe and appropriate interactions. The mediators are the equivalent of a teacher on duty in a virtual playground, and they spend most of their duty time scaffolding SuperclubsPLUS activity by performing tasks including:

- Being an email audience,
- Providing technical assistance,
- Encouraging, supporting and celebrating,
- Mediating conversations or discussions,
- Reminding children of the rules.

The following section will illustrate some typical examples of how SCP interactions supported by a mediator can help children to learn about cyber-safety, appropriate online behaviour and the prevention of cyber-bullying.

Acknowledgment of Error

An important component of the SuperclubsPLUS warning emails that the children receive is that they are required to respond to the mediator to acknowledge that they understand that they have broken a rule.

> Please STOP and reply to this email to say you understand. If you are not sure use this link to read the rules: CLICK HERE

In the majority of cases children are quite happy to acknowledge and move on. Some are matter of fact; others are apologetic:

Kellie:"Ok. I understand"

Jack:"Sorry i forgott (sic) i will never do it again"

Some actually find it amusing that they needed to be reminded. In these situations, the mediator can enjoy the funny side with the child. Being reminded of a rule isn't "getting told off" but rather part of the learning process:

Chris: "Ok I'm new. I haven't got used to the rules yet ha ha ha"

Mediator: "Tricky, isn't it?" ;o)

On occasions children respond to the message because they are obliged to rather than because they understand what the problem is. In these situations, a mediator needs to tease out the issue in order to explain why the rule has been broken. Simon had been warned because he asked his friend to talk to him in MSN Web Messenger.

Simon: I understand. What did I do?

Mediator: You wrote "go on em es en" (MSN)

Simon: How do you know what that is?

Mediator: Mediators know EVERYTHING

Simon: He goes to my school and we are best friends. We both
have em es en and we saw each other today. Why can't we
use it?

Mediator: The thing is that MSN isn't really a safe website. It is possible for children to talk to other people on MSN who might
be an adult who is pretending to be a child. We don't want
to encourage Superclubs children to use MSN and so we
ask you not to talk about it here. You need to look at rule
numbers 4 and 7. Click here to read the rules.

Reporting Emergencies

Children not only are required to abide by the rules set to guide their online
practice, they are also asked to be vigilant and report anything that they see or
read that makes them feel unhappy, uncomfortable or anything that they think
is generally not suitable. They can email the mediator by clicking on the name
under the mediator's photograph or, if they feel particularly stressed by an incident, they can press the *Emergency Bell*. The format of the emergency report is
shown in Figure 3.

While the emergency bell rarely is required for a significant emergency, this
device is a good mechanism in the first instance for children to quickly and easily
report anything they see that might be inappropriate. This is a good opportunity
for them to develop observation skills, and they quite often pick up and report
small details such as a child who might have displayed a nickname based on their
surname on their website. In the second instance the *Emergency Bell* can also be a

Figure 3: Emergency Bell Screen

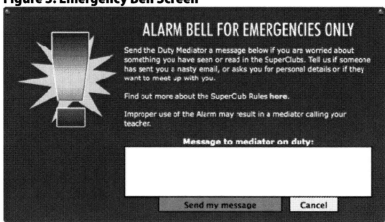

comfort to children who feel wronged in some way and can avert ongoing anxiety. The following is a typical example:

Morag: EMERGENCY HELP!! Jody said I had a funny name!

Mediator: Thanks for letting me know, Morag. Your name is lovely! I
(to Morag) think that Jody probably hasn't heard of anyone with your name before and so it is unusual to her. I will let her know that she must think about people's feelings.

Morag: Thank you.

Mediator: Jody, Morag was a bit upset that you said she had a funny
(to Jody) name. Morag is an unusual name but you must be polite, even if you have never heard of it before. If you want to comment on someone's name you can say that it is nice or even unusual but "funny" sort of means that it is not nice or silly. You have to be careful not to hurt her feelings. Remember, Rule 1 says "If you can't think of anything nice to say about someone, then don't say anything at all."

In this situation, it was unlikely that Jody had meant to be unkind, and so an official warning for rude or insulting behaviour was not necessary. It was important though to reassure Morag and then let Jody know that she needed to be careful.

Establishing What Is Appropriate and What Is Not

Children who join SuperclubsPLUS begin by learning the rules; however, as with most new settings, it takes a while to establish how things work and they need to practice to make sensible decisions based on the rules. We find that when children begin using SuperclubsPLUS they are likely to be rather evangelistic in their approach. While it is important that children learn about cybersafe practices, it is also important that they learn what is OK too. For example, this report came from Rosie in the first weeks of being a member:

Rosie: EMERGENCY HELP !! Emma said on her home page that she wishes her name was Gemma or Charlotte that might be affencef (sic) to her mum her family or her friends

Mediator: Hi Rosie, it is actually OK to say that you would like a different name. I think her Mum wouldn't worry too much.

Rosie: Ok, thanks for telling me

Mediator: No problem. Are you enjoying SuperclubsPLUS?

Rosie: I am really enjoying it. It is very fun and i love writing emails to my friends!

Rosie is now an experienced Superclubber, with all of her stars, several other awards and has sent almost 500 email messages.

Sometimes, the appropriateness of a message is based on the interpretation by the receiver. In this situation, a request for physical location, the child is supported to respond to the request while still make a decision to follow safe practices.

Sarah: EMERGENCY HELP!! Someone just sent me where do you live?

Mediator: Thanks for the email. I think you will find that they meant where do you live as in what country or what city. It's OK to tell someone this—just remember never to give out your street address.

Sarah: Ok thank you. I thought she ment (sic) home address sorry about that!!!!!!

An examination of the mediation records highlights the subtleties that children are exposed to every day. In this situation a child sees a *Web Ring* that he thinks is inappropriate. A *Web Ring* is represented by an icon on a child's page. It is a link that joins children's pages together under a common interest. Anyone can start a *web ring* and then invite others to join. In this instance the *web ring* is themed on "The Naked Brothers Band" a TV series on Nickelodeon. Ross takes the title literally.

Ross: Dear Mediator that is on duty, i read something not nice, if you would like to see it then click here and see it is on a webring and its the 2nd one under

Mediator: I can see what you mean, Ross but "Naked Brothers" is actually the name of a band. In this case "naked" doesn't mean without clothes. It can also mean without decorations or natural.

Ross: Dear Mediator, i am very sorry to disturb you i didn't know what it actually meant, so i am really sorry

Mediator: That is no problem at all Ross. You were right to report anything that you think might be bad

Addressing Inappropriate Practice

In a few cases, the interactions online may mimic the type of bullying that you would find in a school playground. Normally in these situations, a mediator needs to support the child who is being victimised and then target the behaviour of the perpetrator. In SuperclubsPLUS messages are scanned before they are sent to a child, and so it is also possible to intercept bullying or unfriendly behaviour before it is actually received. The following interaction happened between two children who didn't know each other but were online at the same time. Alison initiates the conversation by telling Nicole that she completed the blue star.

Alison:	I just got my blue star
Nicole:	Good for you
Alison:	Thank you
Nicole:	OMG! (Oh my God) I was being sarcastic!

At this stage the mediator intercepted the message and Alison didn't receive it. And, as Alison hadn't picked up on Nicole's sarcasm, she was quite happy with the response.

Mediator:	Dear Nicole, Please remember that if you can't say anything nice, don't say anything at all. Alison was really proud that she finished her blue star and she was just being friendly. I have deleted your sarcastic message so she doesn't have to read it. If you write mean things in emails you will get a warning next time.
Nicole:	Sorry. I didn't know that being sarcastic wasn't allowed in SuperclubsPLUS
Mediator:	If someone is sarcastic to you it makes you feel bad. It means that they are not respecting what you have to say.
Nicole:	OK I didn't know that. I will never be sarcastic again

Thus, the mediator is able to have an interaction with the perpetrators of bullying and inappropriate behaviour close to the time of its occurrence. We believe that this will not only limit the amount of bullying and inappropriate behaviour that might occur, but also that its timing and frequency will diminish the capacity for this type of action by perpetrators. Certainly, this is an interesting area for investigation in such online worlds which warrants further research inquiry, since anecdotal reports would tend to indicate that it has increased exponentially with the advent of new technologies. We need more information about the nature and extent of the problem in order to deal with it effectively.

Learning the Rules of Negotiation

Another typical social issue that children face is fighting with friends. Just as teachers need to deal with situations at school, the mediators on SuperclubsPLUS are often working with children who are squabbling at school and then continue their arguments online after school. It is important in this situation that the focus is on mediation, and even though the mediators don't know the children in person, he or she must quickly pick up on the wider context to make a positive contribution.

> Olivia: EMERGENCY HELP!! Chelsea told me to shut up but she said it like this sssssshhhhhhhhhhuuuuuuuuuuuuuttttt up.
> Mediator: OK, Olivia, I will look into it.

On investigation it is obvious that the two are in the same classroom and have once been friends. There are a number of accusing emails back and forward, with threats of telling teachers and the mediators—"I'm going to [emergency] bell you."

> Mediator: Hi Olivia, I had a look at your discussion and you have both been a bit grumpy. If you get something that you don't like, I suggest you either put that person on your spam list or just don't answer rather than sending grumpy messages back. I think you should just ignore any further messages from Chelsea tonight and perhaps have a chat to sort it out at school tomorrow.
> Olivia: Sorry, its just she and I had a fight a while ago and she still on me and she's like stealing my friends and stuff and she took my bestie [best friend] away from me so yeah…
> Mediator: I thought that the problem might be something like that. It is hard to ignore but sometimes that is best.

Olivia participates in other SuperclubsPLUS activities and there are no further interactions between the two girls for an hour. Then Olivia received this message from Chelsea.

> Chelsea: Olivia, if u do not tell on me i will not tell on u…

Hopefully this interchange laid some useful foundations for further peace making at school the following day. If these girls had used an unsupervised forum such as MSN for this discussions, it is very likely that the conflict would have escalated rather than been settled as a result.

Transferring Skills to Other Contexts

An important component of the SuperclubsPLUS mission is to provide children with cyber-safety skills and practices that they will then be able to transfer to broader Internet use. While our research has not focused on this aspect as yet, we are aware that many of our SCP members (and particularly the older ones) use SuperclubsPLUS as one of many web based applications. In SuperclubsPLUS it is important that mediators use fortuitous opportunities to address and reinforce ethical and safe practices where possible. The following interaction gives a glimpse into the type of scenarios that children face:

> Sarah: Excuse me are you allowed to send e-mails that have disgusting pics like anorexic people?
>
> Mediator: A mediator checks every picture that gets loaded into SCP so any pictures that are not appropriate don't get in the library. If you see a picture that you think isn't suitable you should send it to the mediator and they will check it. If the mediator thinks it should not be there he or she will remove it from the library so nobody else can use it.
>
> Sarah: But can you send it when it is from Google?
>
> Mediator: Not in SuperclubsPLUS because every image has to be checked. Do you mean outside SCP? If so that is a really good example of how people use the Internet inappropriately. A person who has anorexia is very ill and should not be used as entertainment. Do you agree?
>
> Sarah Yes I do. I'm just asking if we can that's all
>
> Mediator: The answer is
>   1. Not in SuperclubsPLUS
>   2. Some people might outside of SCP but it is not very nice

The aspect of transfer will be a significant component of future research for the SuperclubsPLUS project. If we can demonstrate that children who begin using the Internet through SuperclubsPLUS can later use the Internet more ethically, effectively and safely, the value of the project will be clearly justified.

CONCLUSIONS

In this chapter we have suggested that learning ecologies need to change in order to incorporate new ways in which children work, play and socialise. We have described the SuperclubsPLUS project as an example of appropriate design and have illustrated the ways in which it constitutes a safe learning environment for children from 6 to 12 years of age. SuperclubsPlus was a response to the growing concern that while online sites are spaces of immense learning and communication opportunities, they can also be potentially dangerous if children were not aware of how to interact with others in safe ways.

Research (e.g., Sorensen et al., 2001) has shown that informal learning contexts are rich in learning, and we believe that schools have much to learn from their design and the activities that are inherent to them. SuperclubsPLUS is a learning environment with a lot of potential to provide contexts in which children can explore and play with ideas in new and dynamic ways. They can participate in activities of their own choosing as well as meet and communicate with wider local as well as global communities. They can do this without fear of being harassed and in the process learn valuable life skills about appropriate ways to interact in online contexts.

We are cognisant that bullying is a behaviour that manifests in online environments (Campbell, 2005) and propose that children can learn strategies to deal with bullying behaviour in virtual, as well as real settings and that mediation can be used to provide support for this process. We have provided examples here of the ways in which the interactions occur in the SuperclubsPLUS environment. When difficult situations arise, such as in the instance of bullying or inappropriate comments, perpetrators may not be aware that such behaviour is hurtful. Once aware, they are often willing to change style immediately. The scaffolding of behaviour is usually immediate and thus actions can be initiated close to the act.

The SuperclubsPLUS is an authentic social networking environment because children experience genuine interactions not only within their established community of familiar peers and teachers but also with new contacts such as children from other schools and mediators. During these interactions children are supported to practice social interaction skills in order to learn about appropriate online behaviour. It is anticipated that the type of learning ecology illustrated in the SuperclubsPLUS project has the potential to make a difference in the way children operate in broader context—the wider cyber-world. Our aspiration is to equip the children with the skills they require to be future global cyber-citizens.

References

Campbell, M. (2005) Cyber bullying: An old problem in a new guise? *Australian Journal of Guidance and Counselling 15*(1), pp. 68–76.

Engeström, Y. (1987). *Learning by expanding: An activity-theoretical approach to developmental research.* Helsinki: Orienta-Konsultit.

Gibson, O. (2005). Young blog their way to a publishing revolution. Retrieved 29/10/07 from available: www.gadian.co.uk/technology/2005/oct/07/media.pressandpublishing

Grunwald Associates. (2003). Children, families and the Internet. Retrieved December 2004 from http://www.grunwald.com/surveys/cfi/newsrelease.php

Howe, N. & Strauss, W. (2000). *Millennials rising: The next great generation.* New York: Vintage.

Intuitive Media Australia (2009b). SuperclubsPLUS Australia Member User Rules. Retrieved September 2009 from http://www.superclubsplus.com.au/i/rules

Intuitive Media Australia (2009a). SuperclubsPLUS Australia. Retrieved September 2009 from http://www.superclubsplus.com.au

National School Boards Association (2007) Creating and Connecting//Research and Guidelines on Online Social and Educational Networking. Accessed on 01/03/08 at http://www.nsba.org/SecondaryMenu/TLN/CreatingandConnecting.aspx

Partnership for 21st Century Skills. (2004). *Learning for the 21st century: A report and MILE guide for 21st century skills.* Washington: Partnership for 21st Century Skills.

Rideout, V., Vandewater E. & Wartella, E. (2003). *Zero to six: Electronic media in the lives of infants, toddlers, and preschoolers,* Menlo Park, CA: The Henry J. Kaiser Family Foundation.

Scardamalia, M. (2003). *Extending the Limits of the Possible in Education.* Keynote, International Conference for Educational Technology. Hong Kong.

Sefton-Green, J. (2004) *Literature review in informal learning with technology outside school.* REPORT 7. Bristol, UK: Futurelab.

Sorensen, B., Danielsen, O., & Nielsen, J. (2001) Children's informal learning in the context of schools of the information society. *Proceedings of WCCE 2005,* Cape Town, South Africa, July 4–7.

Tynes, B. M. (2007). Internet safety gone wild? Sacrificing the educational and psychosocial benefits of online social environments. *Journal of Adolescent Research 22* (6), pp. 575–584.

10 · Kia Kaha

Police and Schools Working Together to Eliminate Bullying, a New Zealand Intervention

Gillian Palmer
Juliana Raskauskas

Kia Kaha Poem

Kia Kaha is what we learn
We like to play and take our turn
We are special because we care
We also like to play fair.
We are a class who are polite
Other classes think we are such a delight
Being different is okay
We like to have our say.
Our class is special and unique
We like to play hide and seek
Co-operating is our game
We do not like to lay the blame.
Hand in hand go rights and responsibilities
We are all different in our abilities
Together we are brave and strong

We know how to get along.
Our class likes to share
We don't like to shed a tear
We don't like to make people cry
Even when they're way up high.
Kia Kaha is fun, fun, fun
We like to play with everyone
No bullying at our school
Because we are cool, cool, cool!

INTRODUCTION AND FOUNDING PRINCIPLES

*K*ia Kaha, is part of a Māori whakatauki (proverb) "Kia Kaha, Kia Toa, Kia Manawanui." It is used in the context of bullying to affirm that all people need to stand strong against bullying. The name has also been chosen to acknowledge the tāngata whenua of Aotearoa (native people of New Zealand). *Kia Kaha* is an example of law enforcement and school communities working together to create environments where all members of the school community feel safe, respected and valued, and where bullying cannot flourish. The New Zealand Police Youth Education Service makes this series of programmes available to primary and secondary schools and works in partnership with school staffs to put the whole school approach in place. The approach is designed to help schools create communities where everyone feels safe, respected, and valued—all characteristics of communities that minimize bullying behaviours.

The New Zealand Police has within its Youth Services Group a special section, the Youth Education Service (YES), whose main aim is to work in partnership with schools and their communities to reduce the likelihood of children and young people becoming victims or perpetrators of road crashes or crime. This aim fits within the police goal of achieving safer communities together. YES consists of three elements—a curriculum framework, educational resources and programmes, and a team of specially trained police constables who work alongside teachers. Police Education Officers (PEOs) take the programmes to schools and work with teachers to plan classroom lessons and partner in their teaching, evaluate the curricula and resources, and assess students' learning. This service is funded by the New Zealand Police budgets with no charge to participating schools.

Bullying is a world-wide issue, in all types of schools, and New Zealand is no exception. Of young people surveyed in *Youth 2000*'s 2001 Survey, approximately 1 in 3 students (28% of females and 33% of males) reported being bullied at school at least once during the school year 9%; of male students and 5% of female students reported frequent (at least weekly) bullying and 10% of students reported having been bullied in a way they felt was "pretty bad," "really bad" or "terrible" (*Youth 2000*, 2001). Since this survey, we have seen the rapid migration of these traditional patterns of bullying into online spaces. In the preliminary findings of the 2008 Convergence Generation Research Project carried out by Netsafe, approximately 10% of students reported having experienced internet bullying in the last year, and approximately 20% of students reported experiencing text bullying. The most common form of cyberbullying was said to involve "saying or texting mean, hurtful or nasty things" (Personal Communication, 2008, Fenaughty). It is well documented that children and young people who have been or are being bullied are unlikely to reach their full potential, that the child who bullies likely has social problems of their own and that those who stand by and do nothing may also suffer from feelings of guilt (Shariff, 2008).

The New Zealand Police first became aware of this problem in the early 1990s, through reports from teachers and Police Education Officers. These reports were accompanied by a plea to do something to help. International bullying research was in its early stages and NZ Police could find no suitable interventions, and, being Kiwis, we decided to develop our own anti-bullying programme. The result was the first Kia Kaha programme. It was a good first effort and did acknowledge the importance of the whole school approach. By and large it was greeted with enthusiasm by schools and parents.

By the end of the 1990s work was underway to develop a series of Kia Kaha programmes for all levels (from 5- to 17-year olds) of the school community. These programmes would be designed to meet international best practice standards. Our first step was to define and understand bullying. To this end, the New Zealand Police formally recognised the following identifying features of bullying: it is deliberate, hurtful behaviour; it is repeated over a period of time; it is difficult for those being bullied to defend themselves; and those who bully have and exercise power inappropriately over others (Olweus,1993). We also recognise that bullying can take a number of forms: physical violence, for example, hitting and kicking; emotional and verbal, such as name-calling, exclusion, threatening and coercion; damage to property; and, importantly for our disucssion in this book, cyberbullying—such as emailing or texting nasty messages. Cyberbullying is a relatively new phenomenon and one that is causing great concern. While it shares the identifying features above, it creates its own additional stresses: it can occur 24 hours a day; it can invade home and personal space; the audience can be very large and reached rapidly; cyberbullies may attempt anonymity; and content can be online forever.

In the context of this understanding, we developed the following principles which are used to guide our Kia Kaha Program:

1. **Schools must accept the need to establish safe environments where antisocial behaviour such as bullying has no place.** The school needs to examine its policies and procedures with a view to eliminating those which allow bullying to flourish.

2. **Schools have to consistently intervene when bullying occurs.** The school must recognise the need to be consistent in striving to change the contexts within the school which allow bullying to flourish. They must be clear about what constitutes bullying behaviour and act on all reports of bullying (no matter how minor they may seem to be).

3. **Nobody deserves to be bullied.** Regardless of size, shape, religious or ethnic background, sexual orientation, disability, academic prowess, economic background or any other distinguishing characteristic, no one asks for or deserves to be bullied. We must teach children, young people, and indeed the adults that teach and care for them, to be empathetic, kind and tolerant.

4. **All children and young people can be supported to learn new behaviours.** As mentioned before there are three groups involved in any bullying incident—the victim, the child or young person who sometimes bullies, and the bystanders. Bullying is not just the victims' problem. It is not their responsibility to bring about the necessary change. In all likelihood, if there were anything they could have done to change the situation, they probably would have done so already. Making the child or young person who bullies aware of the consequences of his or her actions can have startling results, as is demonstrated through the use of an approach which shares the problem-solving and does not 'blame' the child or young person who bullies. Additionally the bystanders can be taught to take action, such as supporting the victim or reporting the incident. Bystanders who intervene will often experience a new sense of social responsibility.

5. **Schools must utilize a whole school approach.** No intervention will succeed if there is not total buy-in from the whole school community. Involving the whole community is not easy to achieve but, if successful, can make a difference. Success means not only looking at adminstrative policy and procedures about ways bullying incidents will be handled, but also must include consistent classroom interventions throughout the school. The school must question its entire ethos.

6. **Schools must create an environment where reports of bullying are listened to and acted upon.** Bullying survives because nobody wants to hear about it or do anything to prevent it. Students are too scared to report, either because they fear recrimination or because they believe they will not be listened to. They too often hear comments like "run away and don't be a nark" or "telling tales again?" from teachers and

parents. Students feel strongly bound by the philosophy that you never grass (tell) on another student, no matter what they have done. Schools need to encourage students to report not just bullying they experience but also to get help for other students being bullied. Schools must create an environment where students feel safe going to adults for help. The use of anonymous Kia Kaha reporting boxes for this purpose is very popular among Kia Kaha schools.

7. **Schools should adopt a shared problem-solving (No Blame) approach for dealing with bullying incidents.** Criminal behaviour and such things as hacking into someone else's computer or sending threatening messages, should, of course, always be reported to the Police for action. For more minor incidents, we strongly advocate Barbara Maines and George Robinson's 'No Blame' approach (Maines & Robinson, 1992) as a pedagogical approach capable of dealing with issues both with younger children in primary schools and also with cases of intimidation in large secondary schools.

Thus the Kia Kaha Program begins to work as a school community begins to abide by and support all of the underlying principles. Students must report the bullying to an adult and the school should be notified. The school must then handle the matter in accordance with school policy. If the school faithfully follows the whole school approach as advocated in Kia Kaha, it will have strategies in place to handle both face-to-face and cyberbullying. The classroom curriculum materials use scenarios, case studies and examples that depict a whole range of bullying situations, including cyberbullying. The advice for students involved in cyberbullying incidents is to refrain from responding, save the content/message/pictures/online conversation as evidence and to inform the provider of the service if content is abusive or repeated more than once. Because cyberbullying is a form of bullying, the strategies for dealing with it also include the strategies for any other form of bullying.

THE KIA KAHA PROGRAMME

The Whole School Approach

The whole school approach means that the whole school community (students, staff, Board of Trustees, parents, caregivers and whānau) must work together to confront bullying. Involving the whole community is the only effective way to bring about change (Olweus, 1993; Rigby, Smith & Pepler, 2004).

The Police Education Officers (PEOs) have an important role to play here. They introduce the Kia Kaha programme to the school and support them throughout its implementation. In our experience, this implementation strategy has been very effective. Schools, especially large secondary schools, are busy places with large staffs, both teaching and ancillary. Despite the best intentions, schools struggle to have enough time and energy to manage an intervention like Kia Kaha without expert guidance—the role the PEOs play. Additionally we recommend that the school appoint a Kia Kaha Co-ordinator to oversee the implementation and work with the PEO, and this partnership approach can work well.

Programme Components

The Kia Kaha Program is made up of two components. The first component is an implementation book, one for primary and one for secondary, which assists the school to put the whole school approach into place. This book is coupled with resources for parents, teachers and school administrators. The second part of the program is four curriculum packages: one each for Junior, Middle, Senior Primary, and Secondary levels. The names of the modules are: "Building a Safe, Happy Classroom," "A Bully-Free Zone," "Safer Communities Together," and "Our Place." Each package includes a teaching guide and quality resources such as photopacks, DVDs, posters, story books and scenario cards.

The Implementation Process

The implementation process involves the following series of six key steps. These steps need to be completed sequestially as each step sets the foundation for the one which follows.

The first step for a school wishing to implement the Kia Kaha Program is for the Police Education Officer to introduce the program to the school senior management team and a representative from the Board of Trustees. The school then decides if it wants to proceed with Kia Kaha. If yes, a Kia Kaha Co-ordinator is appointed.

The second step of the program is to begin working with the entire school faculty. This process begins with a staff training session to increase staff awareness of the issues surrounding bullying. At this point, the staff is asked to vote on whether or not Kia Kaha should be implemented in the school. If the staff does not vote to proceed (a successful vote being 75% or higher being in support) the meeting concludes and the Kia Kaha materials are returned. This vote is an important step as, unless there is a high level of commitment throughout the school, the intervention will not work.

The third step involves broadening the process to include community stakeholders. For the whole school approach to be successful, the whole school community must also have an opportunity to have their say and be informed about the criteria on which Kia Kaha is based. A meeting format is provided and supporting resources are available, including a pamphlet to be sent home to all parents and caregivers or posted on the school website. This is all part of the awareness raising process, and it helps the school move towards formulating a shared definition of bullying. For example, the owner of a dairy close to the school who observes bullying needs to know that it is unacceptable, should intervene if it is safe to do so and must advise the school so that steps can be taken to handle the incident.

The fourth step is for the school and the PEO to sign a formal agreement and work through a checklist to ensure the implementation is thorough. The checklist has a number of important components. The first component of the checklist is to identify the extent of the bullying problem. This identification process includes documenting the types of bullying, their frequency, and the times of the day they are most likely to occur as well as identifying safe and unsafe places. The second is to review and circulate the anti-bullying policy to all stakeholders. This policy must include the agreed definition of bullying and a commitment to consistently respond to bullying incidents. The policy must also have a procedure for handling bullying incidents, including details about how victims will be supported. Additional items on the checklist include: identifying and rectifying problem areas and practices that allow bullying to occur; promoting and fostering a telling environment; and developing and communicating safe policies and procedures around the use of computers and mobile phones (ICT). Thus the checklist serves to develop a community committed to promoting a safe physical and emotional school environment for all.

The fifth step of the implemenatation involves the Police Education Officer working with the individual teachers to plan, teach and evaluate the classroom lessons. Kia Kaha is a flexible programme which allows a unit of work to be crafted that meets the needs of an individual class. The PEO and the teacher decide which lessons the PEO will be present for. This partnership has a range of benefits for students. They see two adults working in a co-operative way; messages are reinforced by both partners; students feel that they are able to report bullying to the PEO and something will be done about it, and the teacher knows the class will be present to handle any outcomes and will be in a position to ensure that the new directions are maintained. PEOs also provide ongoing support and maintenance for the programme, which in most schools is taught every two years.

The final step of the implementation program is assessment. Tools have been provided to assist the school with programme evaluation and assessment of students' learning. We recommend that the whole school approach should be evaluated one year from completion of the last implementation step.

This careful implementation of the whole school approach is not difficult or complicated—but it can be successful in decreasing the level of bullying, as the following two anecdotes show. School A, a large rural secondary school, diligently went about administering surveys to students to find out what types of bullying were most common, when bullying was most likely to take place; and what safe and unsafe places existed around the school. The guidance counsellor was horrified to find that the area outside her room was considered one of the least safe areas. Further investigation revealed the cause of the problem. There were lockers along one side of the corridor, making it almost impossible for students to pass each other without jostling and physical contact—an ideal breeding ground for bullying. Added to the overcrowded physical space, the lighting in the general area was poor. Subsequently the shool moved the lockers and improved the lighting. Bullying in this area decreased dramatically. In School B, an intermediate school located alongside a large co-educational secondary school, students reported a high level of after-school bullying by older students. Both schools finished at the same time each day, and students from both schools poured out on their way home—some by bus and some on foot. The principals and Boards of Trustees of both schools conferred, and the secondary school agreed to a later start time and correspondingly later finish. Problem solved.

The Curriculum Materials

The Kia Kaha classroom curriculum is designed to provide children and young people with facts about bullying and to give them opportunities to learn interpersonal skills and responses to bullying. The four teaching packages are created as a spiralling curriculum, so that students get age-appropriate personal safety education right through their schooling. Kia Kaha supports the New Zealand Curriculum 2007 (Ministry of Education, 2007), fitting largely within the Health and Physical Education Learning Area and assisting students in the continued development of their key competencies.

In the junior primary package, *Building a Safe, Happy Classroom*, the emphasis is on behaviour in the classroom. Children consider special things about themselves, and similarities and differences between them, their classmates and their families. They define acceptable ways of working in the classroom and practise safe, positive and co-operative skills in both the classroom and on the playground. Emphasis is placed on making choices in a range of scenarios and then understanding the consequences of those choices. They come to an understanding of what bullying is and determine that it is unacceptable and must be reported. As with child protection skill building, they develop the conviction to go on telling until someone does something to help.

The importance of the whole school being engaged in Kia Kaha lessons was demonstrated when one school decided to only implement the Junior Primary programme. The five-year-olds had completed the activity which involved identifying safe and unsafe places in the playground. They had each fastened a balloon with a smiley face on it in the place where they felt most safe. Playtime came, and older students had a spree bursting all the balloons! This misstep provided the catalyst for the school to implement the teaching right through all class levels.

The middle primary package, *A Bully-Free Zone*, builds on and extends this learning. Students learn about the rights and responsibilities they have as individuals and examine the importance of everyone working collaboratively together to achieve something. One activity that works well is students working in teams, each member with a defined role, to follow a recipe and produce something delicious to eat. A second example is the making of a model waka, a Māori canoe. Some children make the waka, some design the backdrop, some make the paddles, and some make the people to sit in the waka. The last group chooses words to go on the paddles which describe qualities the class has, or which they are working towards, such as honesty and being supportive of each other. Some wonderful wakas have been created and displayed on classroom walls all around New Zealand. During the building process, students identify bullying and its impacts and effects, and, as well as reporting skills, they consider how they may be able to help a child being bullied. Students work together to design a bully-free community.

The senior primary package, *Safer Communities Together*, is more tightly focussed on bullying. Students clarify what bullying means to them and identify and use strategies to stop it. They learn to accept differences and they explore the unfairness of stereotyping people. Each student is encouraged to take stock of their own behaviour, identify behaviours that they might want to change and set goals to achieve these changes. They move towards understanding and perceiving the classroom as a place where everyone has a sense of hauora or well-being.

In the secondary package, *Our Place*, a slightly different approach has been used. Many PEOs find it harder to encourage secondary schools to use the Youth Education Service programmes. Teachers seem to be more resistant because they are exam, qualifications and subject focused, and they prefer to develop their own units of work gathering resources from a range of sources. Police Education Officers respond to this by assisting schools to identify the extent of their bullying problems through surveys and by offering their services for joint planning and teaching.

Kia Kaha fits primarily within the learning area of Health and Education of the New Zealand Curriculum 2007. At the secondary level a series of lessons have been developed for both junior secondary and and senior secondary health classes. Students take a much more in depth look at the causes and effects of bullying and at strategies for managing a bullying situation and supporting all those involved. They actively work to make change within their school and they clarify their thinking around societal bullying.

An Activity Book has also been developed which contains a number of stand alone lessons that can be used by a range of people, for example different subject teachers such as maths and English, relievers, peer leaders and form teachers. These lessons should be done within the framework of the whole school approach for safety reasons. In one secondary school, peer leaders are taking a leading role in working to eliminate bullying. They have set up an attractive Kia Kaha Box , which was placed on the school office counter. Students can post requests for help with bullying and often a range of other problems as well. These requests are then handled by the senior students. Since students went to the counter for a number of reasons, it was a fairly anonymous process.

THE ROLE OF THE POLICE EDUCATION OFFICER (PEO)

The PEO is undoubtedly a pivotal part of the Youth Education Service (YES) for schools. The PEO is required to have had frontline experience in the various aspects of policing, while at the same time being an effective communicator, programme manager and teacher. Police have close links with the various schools and colleges of education throughout New Zealand, and over time a number of these institutions have contributed to the training of PEOs. For the last seven years PEOs have been trained by the University of Auckland, which has helped equip them with the necessary specialised teaching skills and knowledge to be effective partners in the classroom. As well PEOs often provide professional development for teachers, particularly in the fields of child protection, bullying, especially cyberbullying, and road safety education.

The specialised skills that PEOs have include a number of specialised skills. These skills include not only the ability to relate positively to children and young people but also the ability to build effective partnerships with teachers in order to facilitate the planning, teaching and evaluation of lessons. PEOs must also be able to use a variety of teaching methods and resources at any level of schooling from five-year-olds to school leavers and advise and assist school consultations with parents, caregivers and whānau. Finally PEOs must be able to establish links between schools and Police as well as between schools and other helping agencies. In this way, PEOs support a school to establish the whole school approaches and develop educational programmes based on best practice available to schools.

One very important aspect of the PEO presence in the school is that it helps break down the stereotyped view that many children and young people have of

Police. If their previous contacts with the Police have been when their big brother was arrested or the Police came to the house because of domestic violence or because they were indoctrinated from a very young age with the idea that "if you were naughty the police officer would come and take you away!," it is understandable that perhaps some students might initially be apprehensive.

PEOs provide the human face of Police. Children and young people come to trust that the officer will know what the law says, will be able to give them advice, and will listen and act if they disclose a problem. Some years ago a PEO, who had been a police officer for many years, was working with a teacher and her class on the YES drug education programme. At the end of teaching, when the PEO had been present over a long period of time and the class were asked for their thoughts on the programme, one young man wrote words along the lines of the following: "When you first came into our class I thought you were a silly old man. Today I think you are my friend. I have learnt things from you and you have helped my mother get the treatment she needs."

BARRIERS TO IMPLEMENTATION

There are three main barriers to implemenation: insufficient Police Education Officers, getting buy-in from secondary schools, and sustainability. We will briefly address each of them.

PEOs are a scarce resource. There are currently under 125 of them nationally, trying to cover as many schools in their district as possible. The more programmes that become part of the YES curriculum, the greater the pressure to meet the needs of schools. The main aim is, of course, to empower schools to take ownership of the YES programmes that they are running in their school. Once the implementation groundwork has been done by the PEO their role can become more one of ensuring sustainability: keeping in contact, offering advice and support, keeping resources up to date, helping to upskill new staff. Similarly, in the classroom the PEO can help the teacher get underway and initially take more complex lessons or those requiring specialist knowledge. Then gradually the teacher takes an increased role. The importance of Police Education Officers, especially males, in the teaching of personal safety programmes has been well documented by Emeritus Professor Freda Briggs in her research into YES programmes (Briggs, 2002).

As mentioned earlier, it can be difficult to get a large secondary school to commit to a whole school approach. A topic such as bullying or child protection is seen as a health topic and therefore of little concern to teachers of math, technology, language or science. Teachers (as well as other shool personnel) may be quite dismissive when expected to attend training and to come to terms with issues that they see as outside their sphere. And yet a young person can disclose to anyone, a teacher in their favourite subject or even the property manager; therefore, everyone on the school staff needs to understand and commit to the culture of telling. PEOs find that getting a very supportive contact within the school, preferably from senior management, is critical to the eventual success of the programme. the most common ally is the Deputy Principal, Health Co-ordinator or Guidance Counsellor.

Kia Kaha is not a programme that the school does this term and then congratulates itself for having addressed bullying. Bullying does not just go away. As long as there are people there will be bullying. Establishing strategies to deal with it in an ongoing way is most important. Each new cohort of students must be informed of the culture of telling and be quite clear about what the consequences of bullying will be. All new staff must similarly be trained. New parents, caregivers and whānau must be given clear non-bullying messages to reinforce at home. A school must commit to being a Kia Kaha school for life. Schools that have appointed a Kia Kaha Co-ordinator and set up a Kia Kaha committee of staff and students will find this an easier task.

CONCLUSION AND BENEFITS OF IMPLEMENTATION

Committing to Kia Kaha helps schools meet the national eductional guidelines as set out by the minstry of education. One of the National Education Guidelines set by the Ministry of Education states: each Board of Trustees is also required to: (i) provide a safe physical and emotional environment for students; (ii) promote healthy food and nutrition for all students; (iii) where food and beverages are sold on school premises, make only healthy options available; and (iv) comply in full with any legislation currently in force or that may be developed to ensure the safety of students and employees (National Administration Guideline 5 Ministry of Education).

Clearly, a student who is being bullied is not working and playing in a safe physical and emotional environment. In 2006 the Minister of Education stated "Bullying in any form is not acceptable and will not be tolerated in our schools or communities…Schools can expect to get more help and to see a greater focus on the role played by the Ministry of Education and the Education Review Office in dealing with this issue" (NZ: 2006, Minister of Education, Steve Maharey http://www.beehive.govt.nz). In 2007 ERO published a national report drawn from reviews of schools over three terms (ERO, 2007). This report found that most schools acknowledge that bullying is a risk to be managed and take their responsibilities seriously in seeking to prevent bullying. Beginning in Term 3 2008, in all school education reviews, ERO is seeking assurance about the provision and content of anti-bullying programmes through questions in the Board Assurance Statement

(BAS) in the Health, Safety and Welfare section. This move should help to alleviate some of the implementation barriers.

More importantly than meeting regulatory requirements, Kia Kaha has been shown to reduce incidents of bullying within school communities that have adopted the program. Two recent research projects have been carried out on Kia Kaha.

The first of these was done by Keith Sullivan, Professor of Education and Head of Department, National University of Ireland, Galway (Sullivan, 2005). In 1998 Sullivan carried out an evaluation of the first Kia Kaha programme and made recommendations for its improvement. Sullivan chose three separate examinations of "Our Place" for study: i) a critique of "Our Place" using the recommendations of the first evaluation; ii) a focus-group critique and evaluation of "Our Place" by 25 students from a third-year university education course; and iii) a case study to examine the implementation of "Our Place" in a secondary school. The focus of this study was Feilding High School, a middle New Zealand secondary school with a bicultural ethnic mix, serving a rural community of roughly 1000 students. Kia Kaha was being implemented with the assistance of PEO Senior Constable Diana Hayden.

Sullivan had two positive conclusions. The first conclusion was that "the second edition of 'Kia Kaha' is an excellent anti-bullying programme." He claimed that the second edition of Kia Kaha is "A massive improvement over the first edition." He goes on to say that the four kits provide a package of useful resources that give foundation and structure for teaching about bullying and suggesting a variety of ways it can be dealt with. Resources are useful and to the point. He also remarked that "The kit is flexible enough so that the school can take ownership." In Feilding High School, Kia Kaha was a catalyst for bringing together two opposing philo-sophical approaches, pastoral and disciplinary, into an anti-bullying intervention that worked. Success here seemed to stem from the fact that the two guidance counsellors spearheaded the effort, with assistance from the PEO.

Sullivan also had two recommendations. The first was that "the Police need to think how best to get the Kia Kaha anti-bullying kits into schools." Sullivan suggests that because of events that happen in a school a lot of attention can suddenly be given to a topic or issue. For example a new topic, like truancy, may tip bullying out of the limelight. He makes the point that bullying needs to be addressed on a continuous basis and that "Our Place" is a particularly useful package for this purpose. The second was that "The Police need to develop a strategy to re-launch Kia Kaha and to get it fully taken up." Sullivan suggested that Police put in place positive marketing and publicity strategies, plus a series of staff development courses to raise the profile and develop familiarity with "Our Place."

The second study involved the Kia Kaha programme as it is used for students in years 5–8 (middle and junior primary). This study was conducted by Dr. Juliana Raskauskas in 2007 (Raskauskas, 2007).

This research included 45 schools (27 that had done Kia Kaha in the past 3 years and 18 who had not) participating in an evaluation of the programme in 2006. Schools were drawn from the lower North Island and upper South Island and were matched on size, decile ranking, location and type of school. The evaluation included a comparison of Kia Kaha and non-Kia Kaha schools. In the research described here 53% of students at Kia Kaha schools and 62% of students at non-Kia Kaha schools reported being bullied in 2006. There were not significant gender differences but year-in-school differences were found with year 5 students reporting significantly more bullying than students in years 6–8.

Survey data were collected from 3,155 students and 67 teachers. Interviews or classroom discussions were conducted with students, teachers, and all nine PEOs who delivered the programme in the participating schools. The key findings from this research are summarised below. While the statistical analysis of surveys will not be reviewed, you can find this information in the full report available at: www.police.govt.nz/service/yes (Raskauskas, 2007).

Schools with Kia Kaha reported less bullying and victimisation than schools that have not used Kia Kaha. Statistical analysis indicated that Kia Kaha schools had less bullying than non-Kia Kaha schools. Sixty-five percent of Year 7 and 8 students who did Kia Kaha said that it had reduced bullying while the remaining 35% felt it had stayed the same. In their interviews teachers said whether they felt bullying had increased, decreased, or stayed the same. Several teachers were clear that the programme had reduced bullying. Some examples of teacher statements included: "Kia Kaha was chosen by the school as a preventative measure to keep bullying from becoming a problem and it has done that"; "Using Kia Kaha has reduced bullying, especially the minor name-calling and put downs. The awareness is what makes them think about bullying and then they try to stop it." Other teachers felt that while Kia Kaha had reduced bullying, new students could impede its effectiveness. For example: "Kia Kaha reduced bullying among the children who did it; however new children contribute to increases in bullying. Bullying is not static, it seems to change with different students." And "Last term 10–15 new kids came who did not get Kia Kaha and there was a lot of bullying." Finally one teacher commented on Kia Kaha students' ability to stand up for themselves against bullying: "I don't think it has reduced bullying, but it makes people more aware and teaches them to stand up for themselves when they see it."

Kia Kaha had a positive effect on school climate, which was related to less bullying in the school. When students in Year 7 and 8 at Kia Kaha and non-Kia Kaha schools were compared, it was found that students who had done the programme reported a more supportive school climate than those who had not. In interviews, teachers and PEOs discussed the positive changes to school climate resulting from Kia Kaha. The following quotes exemplify their comments: "The whole tone of the school has improved with Kia Kaha"; "Kia Kaha has made everyone more aware. It has made this a school that will not tolerate bullying. Even peer mediators say that after Kia Kaha they have less to do on the playground. The playground is a happier place. Doing the whole programme made the difference"; and "Kia Kaha is about teachers too and has changed some of the teachers' attitudes toward bullying at our school." PEOs say that schools select Kia Kaha to create a positive school climate: "Schools use Kia Kaha to establish rules and be consistent on right and wrong behaviour"; and "Schools use Kia Kaha to establish their school expectations and behaviour plans."

The programme was associated with better attitudes toward victims done in part by creating a safe environment for reporting of bullying. Students at Kia Kaha schools were more likely to report bullying they had witnessed than those at non-Kia Kaha schools. Willingness to report may be a function of attitudes toward victims and bullying. Kia Kaha and non-Kia Kaha students were compared on Rigby's Attitude Toward Victim Scale—higher scores indicated more supportive attitudes of bullying behaviour while lower scores show a more supportive attitude to victims. Kia Kaha students reported significantly less support for bullies and more support for victims than schools who had not done Kia Kaha. Year 5 and 6 students made the following comments about what they had learned from Kia Kaha: "Be strong, stop bullying"; "Learn to care about people—to look after victims;" "Try to stop bullying you see at school"; "Think before you say it"; "Tell someone if you are being bullied." Years 7–8 students also reported significant knowledge gains on what bullying is, what it looks like, and what can be done about it.

Implementing the programme according to the guidelines and using the whole school approach was related to less bullying in Kia Kaha schools. Teachers and PEOs reported on how well the participating schools implemented the Kia Kaha programme. Teachers were asked how closely they followed the manual: Eighty-four percent of teachers said they followed the manual closely, 16% "somewhat closely." Using teacher reports it was found that the more closely teachers followed the manual and the more frequently Kia Kaha lessons were taught (once a week or more), the less bullying occurred at the school. Several teachers credited the materials ease of use as the reason why they followed them so closely. One teacher who had used the programme quite a bit over the years had this to say: "The teacher's guide is easy to follow and I like it for that reason. I have done Kia Kaha in several schools and it has been effective in all of those schools. The school where I have been doesn't want bullying in their school—it helps kids recognise what bullying is and makes them look at their behaviour." PEOs reported in their interviews that the teacher training they offer makes the Kia Kaha programme easier for teachers to pick up and use. They also felt that teacher training contributed to teacher buy-in to the values and principles of the programme.

The effectiveness of the whole-school approach was examined in interviews with teachers and PEOs. Teachers were asked about the whole-school commitment to the Kia Kaha programme. Most teachers felt schools are committed to a whole-school approach. Some of their comments were that: "Definitely there is a whole-school commitment when it is offered every two years"; "All teachers across all classes adopt the Kia Kaha philosophy"; "Most staff deliver the programme uniformly, so you know that all students are getting pretty much the same thing"; and "The whole-school did Kia Kaha at the same time for consistency."

Other teachers commented that the whole-school approach is an important and valuable component of the Kia Kaha programme: "Whole-school approach is the best way. Staff need to be consistent with what they say and do about bullying"; "We planned together—the staff and the PEO. We used a whole-school approach with the lessons standardised between classrooms so it is more effective"; "In a school I was at before we couldn't have all classes doing the programme at the same time because of scheduling so different classes did at different times. The scatter gun approach is not effective. It should be whole school at the same time."

PEOs played a vital role in delivering the programme. They provided support and training for teachers, and students felt safe reporting bullying to them. Teachers described the role of the PEO in their interviews. They see the PEO's role as more than just delivering the programme. Their comments include: "PEO does many programmes in the school including road patrol, road safety, DARE, and Keeping Ourselves Safe. Knows well how to relate with the students and talk at their level"; "PEO gave parent training night and gave a presentation to the teachers. Did a waka activity for the whole school so parents could come and see it." In their interviews teachers have a lot to say about their relationship with their PEO: "I have a good relationship with our PEO. Our PEO is wonderful. She has good rapport with students"; "Staff and students know PEO well. The police uniform is important. It impresses the students that a police officer cares and comes to their school"; "PEO is very approachable"; and the "PEO is a good resource and is available for more than just Kia Kaha. Provides support for schools in dealing with bullying." In their interviews, PEOs were asked if students had disclosed personal experiences of bullying to them. All of the PEOs had students who had disclosed. In fact one PEO said: "Students do disclose. They talk about the bullying at school and where you can't play. Sometimes kids are too scared to talk about it, but I'm able to deal with that." When asked why students disclose to them, all of the PEOs say it is because the students know them and trust them. "Kids often come up and talk about their own personal experiences and ask for advice," one PEO explains. When students disclosed, it usually came up in the class discussions in Kia Kaha, or was told in confidence.

Based on the findings of the evaluations, we believe Kia Kaha is meeting its objective of reducing bullying through a supportive whole-school approach. The keys to making the Kia Kaha programme most effective as a prevention programme in schools seem to be: using the whole-school approach in which students, teachers, parents, and administrators work together to create a safe school environment; following the instruction materials closely and using the activities provided; giving lessons once a week or more and reinforcing concepts and strategies throughout the year; and working with the school's PEO to deliver the programme and reinforce concepts.

To find out more about the NZ Police Youth Education Service and Kia Kaha visit the No Bully website:www.police.govt.na/service/yes/nobully.

Acknowledgment

Kia Kaha Poem reprinted by permission of the Manchester Street School.

References

Briggs, F. (2002) To what extent can *Keeping Ourselves Safe* protect children? Report to New Zealand Police.

Education Review officer (2007). Report: Safe Schools: Strategies to Prevent Bullying Education Review Office May 2007. Accessed on July 17, 2007 at http://ero.govt.nz/ero/publishing.nsf/Content/safe-schs-strats-bullying-may07

Fenaughty, J. (2008) Personal Communication on the first of December.

Mahery, S. (2006) NZ: 2006, Minister of Education, Steve Maharey http://www.beehive.govt.nz)

Maines, B., and Robertson, G. (1992). *Michael's Story: The No Blame Approach*. Bristol: Lucky Duck Publishing.

Ministry of Education. (2007). *The New Zealand Curriculum* Wellington 2007.

National Adminstration Guideline 5, New Zealand.

Olweus, D. (1993) *Bullying at School: What We Can Do About It*. Oxford: Blackwell.

Rigby, K., Smith, P. K. & Pepler, D. (2004) Working to prevent school bullying: Key issues. In . P. K. Smith, D. Pepler, & K. Rigby (Eds) *Bullying in Schools: How Successful Can Intervention Be?* New York: Cambridge University Press.

Raskauskas, J. (2007). Evaluation of the Kia Kaha Anti-Bullying Programme for Students in Years 5–8. Report to New Zealand Police.

Shariff, S. (2008). *Cyber-bullying: Issues and Solutions for the School, the Classroom, and the Home.* Abington, Oxfordshire, UK: Routledge (Taylor & Francis Group).

Sullivan, K (2005) A Critique and Formative Evaluation of *Kia Kaha—Our Place*, the New Zealand Police's Anti-bullying Programme for Secondary Schools Report to New Zealand Police.

Youth 2000 (2001). The 2001 survey. Downloaded from www.youth2000.ac.nz/publications/
    reports).

11 · Cyber-bullying

A Whole-School Community Approach

Will Gardner

THE CHILDNET PROGRAMME

I n the UK, many schools are experiencing difficulties with the issue of cyber-bullying. Childnet has been working with the Department for Children, Schools and Families to help schools respond to this problem. Our guidance and resources help schools to understand that the approach required to tackle cyber-bullying is a whole-school community one. It needs the involvement of all teachers and school staff, not just the ICT staff, as well as children, parents, and the Heads and Governors. Everyone needs to understand what cyber-bullying is, that it does have an impact and that it is unacceptable. Everyone needs to know not only where to report incidents of cyber-bullying but also strategies to prevent it from happening at all. Critical to these strategies is all stakeholders developing the skills to use technology responsibly.

BACKGROUND

Today's children and young people have grown up in a world that is very different from that of most adults. Our work with young people has clearly shown that many rely on technology not just to keep in touch, but as a positive, productive and creative part of their activities and development of their identities. Above all, it is a social activity that allows young people to feel connected to their peers.

Unfortunately, technologies are also being used negatively. We know that when children are the target of bullying via a mobile phone or the Internet, they can feel alone and misunderstood. They may not be able to identify that what is happening to them is a form of bullying or be confident that the adults around them will perceive it that way. Previously safe and enjoyable environments can become threatening and a source of anxiety.

A broad body of research confirms these beliefs. As mobile phone and Internet use has become increasingly common so has the misuse of this technology to bully. One study carried out for the Anti-Bullying Alliance in the UK (Smith et al., 2008) found that 22% of young people reported being the target of cyber-bullying. With other research returning figures ranging from 11% (Microsoft, 2006) to 34% (Balls, 2007), we can say that current research in this area indicates that cyber-bullying is a feature of many young people's lives. Cyber-bullying also affects members of school staff and other adults; there are numerous examples of staff being ridiculed, threatened and otherwise abused online by pupils (Coughlan, 2007; Garner, 2007).

Like all forms of bullying, cyber-bullying should be taken seriously. In the UK, the children's charity Childnet International was commissioned by the Department for Children, Schools and Families (DCSF) to draw up a programme to help schools deal with this problem, including writing *Guidance for Schools on Preventing and Responding to Cyber-bullying*. This *Guidance* forms a part of the DCSF's broader anti-bullying Guidance *Safe to Learn* which includes programmes addressing homophobic bullying, bullying involving children with Special Educational Needs and Disabilities, and tackling bullying related to race, religion and culture (DCSF, 2008).

THE PROGRAMME'S HISTORY

The Cyber-bullying Guidance was launched in September 2007 and can be accessed online at Teachernet (www.teachernet.gov.uk/publications) and at digizen.org (www.digizen.org). In producing this *Guidance*, Childnet worked in close consultation with a wide range of sectors including children and young people, schools, industry service providers (including social networking sites and mobile operators), law enforcement, professional bodies, parent groups, and child welfare organisations. Childnet has worked to produce further supporting resources which have been made available including a leaflet summary of the *Guidance*, a film, lesson plans for a drama workshop, and an online interactive resource.

Our success is reflected by the huge demand for the information and materials, which continues to be in high demand and has warranted several reprints. In addition the DVD *Let's Fight it Together* has won an award, and the replication of these resources and their adaptation and translation for use in other countries around the world are ongoing.

OUR OBJECTIVES

Overall this work promotes a whole-school community approach to cyber-bullying. Cyber-bullying is not an issue that can be left solely for the ICT teacher to address. All members of the school community (i.e., the head teacher, the school governors, teachers, other school staff, parents and caregivers as well, of course, as children and young people themselves) have a role to play in its prevention and responding to cyber-bullying. All members of the school community need to understand how to recognize cyber-bullying for what it is and be aware of what can be done to prevent and respond to cyber-bullying when it occurs. *The Guidance* and the accompanying resources combine to promote this approach.

In addition to promoting a whole community approach, there were four overarching objectives for Childnet that were absolutely essential to our success. These objectives were key factors in guiding our decision making as we developed the programme.

The first objective was that the programme was both accessible and easily understandable. In particular, we wanted to ensure it catered to those who were less confident or familiar with the area of technology, especially in regard to children's use of technology. Although the resources would be web-based, the advantages of having hard copies of these resources were considerable.

The second objective was that this work had to be practical, so that people could use and take action with it. In the *Guidance,* for example, there is information and advice that the school can use to help inform children, parents and caregivers about the steps they can take to prevent and respond to cyber-bullying. The resources also include contact details for the relevant service providers and mobile operators. Finally, case studies of approaches taken by some schools and education authorities serve as an example of what others have done in developing successful strategies to deal with cyber-bullying.

The third objective was that the programme was comprehensive. It not only had to introduce the technology but also explain how technology has changed and placed the context of this technology in the lives of young people. Mobile phones and the Internet have become integral to children's educational and social lives. One 14-year-old girl in a focus group run by Childnet told us: "If you take away my mobile phone you take away a part of me." We include in the program an appendix with comments on the subject of cyber-bullying from the children and young people to help communicate their perspectives. We also include links to a range of other related topics and organisations.

The final objective was that the approach taken sets out to explain technology, and not to demonise it. The overarching approach taken in this *Guidance Programme* is focused on securing online safety through awareness and education. The policy approach of some schools of banning certain technology or web services from school is not addressed in this *Guidance*, though the approach advocated is to recognise the benefits and importance of equipping children with the skills and awareness to use new technology safely and responsibly. Even if children are not accessing certain technology in school, they will be using it out of school. Learning how to use technology safely and with respect for others should be an important part of becoming a net-citizen.

THE GUIDANCE PROGRAMME

In order to meet our goal of engaging the entire school community, we knew it was important that the programme did not end up gathering dust on the bookshelf of the head teacher but was made available to all school staff. Furthermore we wanted to ensure that there were accompanying resources that would not only enable schools to bring the *Guidance* to life, but actually to encourage them to do so. To achieve this, alongside the full *Guidance*, we produced a summary leaflet with the aim of bringing this information onto the staff coffee table and beyond. We also produced a DVD with a teachers' guide (including lesson plans) and these were made available, with the assistance of government funding, free of charge for schools.

The *Guidance* for schools is structured around three key areas: *Understanding cyber-bullying; Preventing cyber-bullying;* and, *Responding to cyber-bullying*

Understanding Cyber-bullying

The first section, *Understanding cyber-bullying,* defines cyber-bullying and describes the different forms it can take and the impact that it can have. In this *Guidance*, cyber-bullying is defined as the use of Information and Communications Technology (ICT), particularly mobile phones and the Internet, to deliberately upset and cause anxiety or distress in someone else. Cyber-bullying is a tactic that can be used to carry out all the different types of bullying (such as racist bullying, homophobic bullying, or bullying related to special educational needs). Instead of the perpetrator carrying out the bullying in person, they use technology as a means of conducting the bullying. Cyber-bullying can include a wide range of unacceptable behaviours, including harassment, threats and insults. Just like face-to-face bullying, cyber-bullying is designed to cause distress and harm. It can be an extension of face-to-face bullying, with technology providing the bully with another route to harass their target. Sometimes it can also be in retaliation to other forms of bullying.

Cyber-bullying can take a range of different forms: threats and intimidation; harassment or "cyber-stalking" (e.g., repeatedly sending unwanted texts or instant messages); vilification/defamation (e.g., name-calling, rumour-spreading); exclusion or peer rejection; hacking and impersonation; unauthorised publication of private information or images (including what are sometimes misleadingly referred to as 'happy slapping' images); and manipulation. It is important to be aware of and recognise each of these kinds of incidents as forms of cyber-bullying. When talking with students in the UK, we noted with some concern that many children see hacking and other unacceptable behaviours as part and parcel of using the technology, and therefore as something one simply must put up with.

Cyber-bullying can be a particularly pernicious form of bullying, and the *Guidance* illustrates the particular features of cyber-bullying that differ from other forms of bullying and highlights that these factors need to be taken into account when seeking to understand the phenomenon. They include:

- The potential 24/7 nature of the bullying with the invasion of home/ personal space;
- The difficulty in controlling electronically circulated messages. This impacts the scale of the audience and participants, as well as making the target uncertain that the event has been contained and will not resurface/ recur. Cyber-bullying can be challenging for the target to gain closure, as bullying content can reappear online at any time;
- The profile of the bully and target. Teachers have been on the receiving end of horrendous cyber-bullying; it is not just children who are potential victims
- The potential anonymity of the bully which can be very distressing for the target of the bullying and can lead them to distrust their relationships;
- The motivation behind the bullying; some cyber-bullying can be accidental or with unintended consequences of an online action;
- The evidence of its occurrence, in the form of text message or computer screen grabs for example. This is important to keep and can assist in the official response.

274 ▪ **Section III • Educational Programs**

These varied dimensions of cyber-bullying are important ones for people working with children and young people to understand.

The Guidance also sets out how cyber-bullying fits within the legal framework. In the UK a range of Education Acts and government initiatives outline that bullying is never acceptable, and that schools have an obligation to protect all their members and provide a safe, healthy environment. Cyber-bullying is a form of bullying, and is therefore implicitly included.

A recent piece of legislation has particular relevance to cyber-bullying, and this is highlighted to the school community in the *Guidance*. The *Education and Inspections Act* (EIA) Section 89(5) (2006) outlines some legal powers which relate more directly to cyber-bullying, giving head teachers the power "to such an extent that is reasonable." The government also has further information and guidance for schools and their responsibilities for regulating the conduct of pupils when they are offsite (DCSF, 2007). This is of particular significance to cyber-bullying, which is often likely to take place outside of school but which can impact very strongly on the school life of those pupils involved.

The EIA also provides a defence for school staff in confiscating items from pupils. This can include mobile phones when they are being used to cause a disturbance in class or otherwise contravene the school behaviour/anti-bullying policy.

In terms of criminal law, although bullying is not a specific criminal offence in UK law, there are relevant and applicable laws, including against harassing and threatening behaviour, and, of particular pertinence to cyber-bullying, against menacing or threatening communications. In fact some cyber-bullying activities could be prosecuted as criminal offences under a range of different laws, including the *Protection from Harassment Act* (1997), which has both criminal and civil provision, the *Malicious Communication Act* (1988), section 127 of the *Communications Act* (2003,), and the *Public Order Act* (1986). It is important that the *Guidance* makes this clear, both so that in serious cases people recognise that contacting and reporting to law enforcement are options to pursue but also to make clear to everyone that the law does address this issue. Being encased within the criminal code demonstrates that there can be serious consequences to actions, and the law is there to protect all citizens, including both children and adults.

Understanding cyber-bullying also tries to give an indication of the extent of cyber-bullying. There has been some research in this area recently, and the percentages of children reporting having been the victim of cyber-bullying range from 11% (Microsoft, 2006), to 22% (Smith et al., 2006), to 34% (Balls, 2007). The research is essentially telling us that cyber-bullying is increasingly a disturbing aspect of many children's lives (BBC, 2006).

Cyber-bullying also affects members of school staff, and there are many examples of staff being ridiculed and threatened online. Seventeen percent of teachers responding to a recent survey carried out by the Teachers Support Network and The Association of Teachers and Lecturers reported they had been victims of cyber-bullying (2007). To respond to this issue, Childnet has been working on some guidance for schools for the protection of school staff and faculty to help protect them from becoming victims of cyber-bullying and to inform them about what they can do if this occurs. This guidance was launched early in 2009. Knowing how to protect themselves and what options are available to them if they find themselves on the receiving end of cyber-bullying is essential information for teachers. Furthermore educators must consider where the boundaries lie in their own use of new technologies. For example, whether teachers should accept friend requests from pupils on their own social networking accounts such as Facebook and MySpace is an important question.

The *Understanding Cyber-bullying Guidance* puts the discussion around cyber-bullying firmly in its context of young people and technology; we have seen how technology has become an integral part of the lives of young people. It is an important factor in many young people's educational and social lives, enabling them to keep in touch, create identities, socialising, linking up with and belonging to groups. Social networking has many positive aspects. Children can truly express themselves through their ideas and opinions. The technology has become fantastically accessible, allowing children to create content to put online, without needing to know html or other complex web languages.

Technology plays a part in so many everyday activities that the distinction between online and offline lives may be of less relevance to young people. With technology playing such an important role in young people's lives, education about responsible use and e-safety is key to helping children deal confidently with any problems that may arise with its use, whether in or out of school.

The expressions "digital natives" and "digital immigrants" were coined (Prensky, 2001) to describe the difference between children and adults in relation to technology. The "digital natives" are children and young people who have grown up in a technological world, whereas adults are having to learn and adjust to technical realities. Keeping up with technology can be daunting, with the pace of seemingly continual change. Consider, for example, the rapid evolution from simple email to chat functions to sophisticated social networking sites.

Children benefit greatly when there are adults in their lives who are technologically savvy. If a child has a problem in a chatroom, for example, it might be difficult for them to fathom that their parent could help if they felt their parent had never been in a chatroom and probably didn't know about how they even operate. In this way, even if the school has a policy of blocking access to certain online services or mobile phones, some students may potentially feel more able to speak up if there are teachers available who understand the services that young people are using.

To address this issue, included in the *Guidance* for schools is a section providing a brief introduction to the technologies that young people are using, including mobile phones, social networking sites, video-hosting sites, instant messenger, webcams, email, chatrooms and message boards, virtual learning environments, and gaming sites and virtual worlds, such as Second Life. There is a brief introduction outlining what these technologies are, what the benefits are for young people, what the potential risks are, and how they can relate to cyber-bullying. This is a start, but there is much more that young people can teach us about these technologies and how they are using them.

The Guidance that Childnet has written for schools has tried to keep up with technology and how children use technology. From our perspective education and discussion around e-safety and responsible use are key to helping children deal confidently with any problems that may arise, both on and off of school campuses.

Preventing Cyber-bullying

The section on *prevention* in *The Guidance* looks at prevention strategies and activities that are designed to support the whole school community—i.e., learners, teachers, parents, school leaders, governors, and all the people who provide support, including teaching assistants, break and lunchtime supervisors, and extended school provision staff. Each activity should consider who can contribute to its development, consultation and implementation and how to best inform and involve as many people as possible. Some activities will be targeted at particular groups; however, effectively addressing cyber-bullying means making sure the whole school community knows that cyber-bullying is not acceptable and knows how to identify and take action against cyber-bullying.

Schools can take pro-active measures to help prevent cyber-bullying from occurring and to reduce the impact of any incidents that do happen. In the UK schools are already required to have a clear policy (DCSF, 2007) on tackling all forms of bullying, which is owned, understood and implemented by the whole school community. Cyber-bullying prevention can build on this, promoting and maintaining a safe and welcoming environment as a responsibility and function of the whole school community.

The Guidance stresses that school staff with responsibility for pastoral care, behaviour and IT systems as well as the school council, parents and teacher representatives must work together, but it also highlights as a first necessary step the need to decide who within the school community takes responsibility for the coordination and implementation of cyber-bullying prevention and responding strategies. To be most effective, it is likely that the person nominated will be a member of the senior management team and/or the staff member responsible for coordinating overall anti-bullying activity.

Included in *The Guidance* are examples of existing effective practice, useful resources, and activity ideas to support and illustrate the framework. The approach the school takes will reflect the culture, needs and preferences of that particular school community. However, the cyber-bullying strategy taken will need to align with existing anti-discrimination, citizenship, Personal, Social and Health Education (PSHE), and Social and Emotional Aspects of Learning (SEAL) work as well as with the school's mission and vision statements. As with other issues that potentially impact on the whole school community, wherever possible appropriate policies and processes should be discussed, agreed upon, and developed collectively.

There is no single, simple solution to the problem of cyber-bullying; it needs to be regarded as a live and ongoing issue. The prevention section in the *Guidance* outlines a prevention framework made up of the five essential action areas that together offer a comprehensive and effective approach to prevention. These include:

- Understanding and talking about cyber-bullying;
- Updating existing policies and practices;
- Making reporting cyber-bullying easier;
- Promoting the positive use of technology;
- Evaluating the impact of prevention activities.

In order to promote understanding and talking about cyber-bullying the Program helps schools and school communities develop and agree on a shared understanding of what cyber-bullying is, and supporting school-wide discussion around the issue of cyber-bullying provides a key foundation to all your prevention activities. Promoting awareness about cyber-bullying through the whole school community is an essential first step to ensuring that the whole school is confident and clear in its understanding of cyber-bullying. Pupils need to be aware of the importance of a safe environment and how to behave responsibly when using ICT. Pupils, parents and staff should be aware of the consequences of cyber-bullying for the bully. Young people and their parents should be made aware of pupils' rights and responsibilities in their use of ICT and what the sanctions are for misuse. In addition, students and parents will need information about out of school bullying to know that the school can, as outlined in the Education and Inspections Act, provide them with support if cyber-bullying takes place out of school.

The section on updating existing policies and practices outlines the importance of reviewing existing anti-bullying policies and school behaviour policies as well as Acceptable Use Policies (AUPs), so that they cover cyber-bullying and communicating any resulting changes. Cyber-bullying issues will also impact on a range of other policies—staff development, ICT support and infrastructure, and e-learning strategies, for example.

A further preventative step for schools is to make the process of reporting cyber-bullying easier. Reporting an incident of bullying can be extremely hard for the person being bullied and for bystanders involved. When we spoke to children and young people while drafting this *Guidance* they shared with us a number of reasons for not reporting bullying, including (i) They were scared of making the situation worse, for themselves or for other people. Sometimes they had been threatened about what would happen if they did tell anyone. (ii) They also sometimes remarked that they felt ashamed about their own behaviour, particularly if it involved something rude that they felt embarrassed about their parents finding out about. (iii) They were also worried that adults would be dismissive of cyber-bullying because it "was only words" and that their feelings would either be dismissed as silly or that grown-ups would not understand what had happened to them and might not believe them because they could not properly explain the event. (iv) Compounding these fears was the concern that it was their fault and that they would also get punished, that they had done something to deserve it, or even that the thing they were being cyber-bullied about was true and they didn't want everyone to know. (v) They were also scared that the person cyber-bullying them, or the group of people, might hurt them physically. (vi) Finally they were feeling "closed up inside" and either didn't know how to explain what was happening to them or didn't know who to tell. As is clear from the student responses, reporting can be very difficult for any number of reasons.

It is thus even more important that adults in the community are aware of potential non-verbal signs and indications of cyber-bullying. These may include indicators of depression, anxiety, or fear. Staff should be alert to children seeming upset after using the Internet or their mobile phone and be aware of subtle comments or changes in relationships with friends. Some young people might be unwilling to talk or be secretive about their online activities and mobile phone use.

Because reporting can be difficult, it is important to have different mechanisms available for reporting cyber-bullying incidents. Making reporting as easy as possible, and making sure everyone knows how they can report incidents is also an excellent way of raising awareness that cyber-bullying is unacceptable. Steps to accomplish this objective include publicising school reporting routes to all in the whole school community including all school staff and exploring different reporting routes. These different reporting routes can include involving children and young people in developing "bystander guidelines" that provide information about the responsibilities of bystanders in cyber-bullying incidents as well as signposting information about external reporting routes for reporting such as directly to the Internet service provider or mobile phone companies.

A further step to help prevent cyber-bullying for school communities is to promote the positive use of technology. ICT is increasingly recognised as an essential life skill, and embedding technology across the curriculum and in learning and teaching delivery provides opportunities and benefits for both learners and staff members. Learning about technology can be a real staff development issue too, in addition to helping to support children. Developing an organisational culture of confident ICT users supports innovation, e-safety and digital literacy skills, and helps to combat misuse and high-risk activities.

At Childnet International we have produced a range of resources that can be used in the classroom or to support individual learners, staff members and parents. These resources are all available online and are all free of charge. The site www.kidsmart.org.uk is dedicated to the primary level, and www.childnet-int.org/ kia/schools/ is for the secondary level. We have also developed specific resources for teachers and trainee teachers at www.childnet.com/kia. For parents, we have developed the site http://www.childnet.com/kia/parents/ in conjunction with DCSF and Becta. As a resource for young people, we developed www.childnet. com/sorted/ about online security. We also developed The SMART Rules—five rules for keeping in control of one's online activity. For primary schools see www. kidsmart.org.uk/yp/smart/default; for secondary schools, see www.chatdanger. com/smart.

The Guidance also highlights evaluating the impact of prevention activities and the importance of reviewing impact of strategies, via surveys for example, and celebrating successes across the whole school community.

Responding to cyber-bullying

The *Responding* section of the *Guidance* reiterates that cyber-bullying is a form of bullying, meaning all schools which already have anti-bullying and behaviour policies and procedure will be well placed to deal with the majority of incidents of cyber-bullying. As in all cases of bullying, incidents should be properly documented, recorded and investigated; support should be provided for the person being bullied; other staff members and parents should be informed as appropriate; and those found to be bullying should be interviewed and receive appropriate sanctions.However, in addition to existing procedures, there are elements relating to the cyber nature of the bullying that staff should be particularly aware of when responding to cyber-bullying incidents, relating to supporting the person being bullied, recording and investigating incidents, working with the bully, and sanctions.

SUPPORT FOR THE TARGET

The most important consideration is that the target of cyber-bullying will need emotional support. Just as with other forms of bullying, the existing pastoral support/procedures for supporting those who have been bullied in the school will be relevant.

In addition to supporting the victim, there is some key advice to give that relates to cyber-bullying, including keeping the evidence and not retaliating or replying to the message, at least not in anger. Also essential is advising students to think about the information they post in the public domain and where they go online. Changing their contact details, such as their Instant Messenger identity or mobile phone number, can be an effective way of stopping unwanted contact. However, it is important to be aware that some children may not want to do this and will see this as a last resort for both practical and social reasons. In fact, these measures may even make them feel that they are being punished.

Some forms of cyber-bullying involve the distribution of content or links to content, which can exacerbate, extend and prolong the bullying. There are advantages in trying to contain the 'spread' of this. If bullying content, e.g., embarrassing images, have been circulated, it is important to look at whether this content can be removed from the web. The quickest and most effective route to getting inappropriate material taken down from the web will be to have the person who originally posted it remove it. A second strategy is to contact the host (e.g., social networking site) to make a report to get the content taken down. The material posted may breach the service provider's terms and conditions of use and can then be removed. Schools also may confiscate phones containing offending content and/or ask pupils to delete the content as well as reveal who they have sent it on to. School staff should know that they can confiscate a mobile phone as a disciplinary penalty and have a legal defence in respect of this in the Education and Inspections Act 2006 (s 94). However, staff do not have a right to search through pupils' mobile phones. In some cases, it is appropriate to contact the police in cases of actual/suspected illegal content. The police will be able to determine what content is needed for evidential purposes, potentially allowing the remaining content to be deleted.

> Quote from a parent:
>
> "Thankfully my son's school were (sic) very helpful, they identified the child who posted the video from another video he had posted, they have disciplined the other child and had him remove the video, in fact they took the matter very seriously and also had any users who had posted anything with reference to the school remove their videos so that was very reassuring."

In order to prevent recurrence, there are some steps that the person being bullied can take, depending on the service that the bully has used, which can allow users to manage who they share information with and also who can contact them. These features can help a person being bullied to stop further contact from a bully. For example, blocking the bully from their email or instant messenger buddy list will mean that they will not receive messages from that particular sender anymore.

Contact the service provider or host (i.e., the chatroom, the social network provider, or mobile operator) to inform them of what has happened and get their advice on how to stop this happening again. The service provider may be able to block particular senders or callers (for landlines) or advise on how to change contact details and potentially delete the accounts of those are abusing the service.

The Guidance goes on to explain in what circumstances and how to contact the service provider—it gives the contact details of the major service providers for mobile phones, social networking sites, instant messenger services, video-hosting sites, email providers and chatrooms as well as outlining what service providers can and cannot do when they receive such reports. It is important to frame the expectations of those making a report, so they should know what they can expect but also what they should not.

For example, for mobile phones, as well as providing the contact details of the mobile operators in the UK, the *Guidance* outlines that all UK Mobile operators have nuisance call centres set up and/or procedures in place to deal with such instances. The responses may vary, but possibilities for the operator include changing the mobile number of the person being bullied so that the bully will not be able to continue to contact them without finding out their new number. It is not always possible for operators to bar particular numbers from contacting the phone of the person being bullied, although some phone handsets themselves do have this capability. Action can be taken against the bully's phone account (e.g., blocking their account) but only with police involvement.

For social networking sites it explains the tools available for the user, such as blocking, privacy settings and pre-moderation options for comments as well as details of how to report to the social network providers. If social networking sites do receive reports about cyber-bullying, they will investigate and can remove content that is illegal or breaks their terms and conditions in other ways. They can delete the accounts of those have broken these rules.

The Guidance explains that it is possible to get content taken down from video-hosting sites, though the content will need to be illegal or have broken the terms of service of the site in other ways. On YouTube, perhaps the most well known of such sites, it is possible to report content to the site provider as inappropriate. In order to do this, you will need to create an account (this is free) and log in, and then you will have the option to 'flag content as inappropriate.' The option to flag the content is under the video content itself. YouTube provides information on what is considered inappropriate in its terms of service (YouTube, 2008).

INVESTIGATION

Additionally, in order to help with an investigation there are a number of things schools should advise students and staff to do. The first is to preserve the evidence. Schools should advise pupils and staff to try and keep a record of the abuse: particularly the date and time; the content of the message(s); and where possible a sender's ID (e.g., username, email, mobile phone number) or the web address of the profile/content. Taking an accurate copy or recording of the whole web-page address, for example, will enable the service provider to locate the relevant content.

Keeping the evidence will help in any investigation into the cyber-bullying by the service provider, but it can also be useful in showing what has happened to those who may need to know, including parents, teachers, pastoral care staff, and the police.

The Guidance also gives practical details of how to keep the evidence on the device itself covering mobiles, instant messenger, and social networking and video-hosting and other sites to ensure that people know what to report and how.

Schools also should try to identify the bully. Although the technology seemingly allows anonymity, there are ways to find out information about where bullying originated. However, it is important to be aware that this may not necessarily lead to an identifiable individual. For instance, if another person's phone or school network account has been used, locating where the information was originally sent from will not, by itself, determine who the bully is. There have been cases of people using another individual's phone or hacking into their IM or school email account to send nasty messages.

The Guidance outlines some key questions to look at when you do not know the identity of the bully. Firstly, find out if the bullying was carried out on the school system and, if so, are there logs in school to identify the perpetrator? The second question is to see if there are identifiable witnesses who can be interviewed? For instance, there may be children who have visited the offending site and left comments. If the bullying was not carried out on the school system, the service provider, when contacted, may be able to take some steps to stop the abuse by blocking the aggressor or removing content it considers defamatory or breaking their terms of service. However, the police will need to be involved to enable them to look into the data of another user. For instance, if the bullying was via mobile phone, the perpetrator may have withheld their number. If so, it is important to record the date and time of the message and contact the mobile operator. Steps can be taken to trace the call, but the mobile operator can only disclose this information to the police, so police would need to be involved. If the number is not withheld, it may be possible for the school to identify the caller. For example, another student may be able to identify the number, or the school may already keep records of the mobile phone numbers of their pupils. Content shared through 'Bluetooth' on mobile phones does not pass through a network and is much harder to trace. Similarly text messages sent from a website to a phone also provide difficulties for tracing for the Internet service or mobile operator.

If a cyber-bullying incident involves a potential criminal offence having been committed, the police may have a duty to investigate. Police can issue a RIPA (Regulation of Investigatory Powers Act) request to a service provider, enabling them to disclose the data about a message or the person sending a message. This may help to identify the bully. Relevant criminal offences here include harassment and stalking, threats of harm or violence to a person or property, any evidence of sexual exploitation (for example, grooming or inappropriate sexual contact or behaviour). A new national agency called the Child Exploitation and Online Protection Centre (CEOP) was set up in 2006 to deal with child sexual exploitation, and it is possible to report directly to them online at www.ceop.gov.uk. However, it is important to note that it is the sexual exploitation of children and young people, not cyber-bullying, which forms the remit of CEOP.

WORKING WITH CHILDREN WHO BULLY AND SANCTIONS

The Guidance also addresses issues pertaining to working with children who bully and sanctions. *The Guidance* recognizes that schools already have systems and sanctions in place for bullying, and it is important that these apply to cyber-bullying too. Steps should be taken to change the attitude and behaviour of the perpetrator as well as ensuring access to any support that they may need.

When determining the appropriate response and proportionate sanctions, it is important to consider the ways in which cyber-bullying incidents might differ in impact to other forms of bullying. The key considerations here may include: attempts by the bully to disguise their identity; the public nature of posted material (and the extent of the humiliation); and the difficulty in controlling copies of the material (the difficulty in gaining closure over the event).

It should also be recognised, where induction and education activities are not in place, that some cyber-bullying has been known to be unintentional or at least carried out with little awareness of the consequences. Determining appropriate sanctions for incidents will then require sensitivity to the impact on the person being bullied as well as any misunderstanding or thoughtlessness on the part of the cyber-bully. Consideration should also be given to the possibility that the cyber-bullying could be a part of retaliation to previous bullying endured by the perpetrator.

In addition to any sanctions that are in existing anti-bullying / behaviour policies, it is important to refer to any Acceptable Use Policy or agreement for internet and mobile use and apply sanctions for breaches where applicable and practical. Technology-specific sanctions for pupils engaged in cyber-bullying behaviour could include limiting Internet access for a period of time or removing the right to bring a mobile phone into school (although issues of child safety should be considered in relation to the latter).

OTHER RELATED RESOURCES/INITIATIVES

Childnet has also produced other award-winning resources that are relevant to include here. We produced a series of resources called *Know IT All for Parents Know IT All for Teachers* and *Know IT All for Trainee Teachers.* The *Know IT All for Parents* resource was originally aimed at those parents who were late adopters of technology but soon developed and 1 million copies in CDRom format were produced, requested and ordered for free by schools. *Know IT All for Parents* aims to familiarise parents with the benefits of new technologies, inform them how their children are using these technologies as well as providing key information on how to stay safe and where to report if things go wrong. Nearly 1 million copies of this resource were ordered and distributed in less than 6 months, and Childnet has produced a further 500,000 to meet continuing demand.

We are currently finishing an interactive resource for those pupils who have seen the cyber-bullying DVD to go online and role play scenes within the school where the film is set, thus having to make their own decisions of how to behave in such an environment. We are also producing some guidance for schools to protect school staff from cyber-bullying as well as a resource for primary teachers and children looking at internet and technology safely generally but including a part on cyber-bullying aimed at children aged 7+.

THE DISSEMINATION STRATEGY

It was important to provide resources with the *Guidance* to encourage schools to adopt many of the recommendations in the *Guidance*. For this reason, the resources produced are available online and offline. *The Guidance*, its summary document, the film, lesson plans, etc., are all on the DCSF's and Childnet sites. Hard copies were also produced because this is necessary to reach the target audience, and in tandem with availability of these resources online can give these resources greater reach.

These resources were not sent to every school in a kind of 'spray and pray' approach. The school or other relevant body needed to request copies, which would then be sent out free of charge. The advantage here of such a system compared to sending materials to every school is not just in knowing the uptake and levels of demand for these resources, but also, and crucially, that they will go to someone in the school who knows what they are, what they are for, and actually wanted them. To date the summary document of the *Cyber-bullying Guidance* is entering its fourth print run as it has been so popular. 40,000 DVDs have been requested and distributed to schools, and online views of the film on the Digizen website have exceeded 80,000. Feedback to us from schools who have shown the DVD has been positive:

> The film was exceptionally well-received by Year 7–11 pupils (i.e., aged 12–16)—pins dropping comes to mind! The response from the students was amazing and sensitive even amongst the somewhat disaffected yr 11s. It was very powerful and made quite an impact. Many students were overheard by staff commenting on it and some making apologetic comments about students they may have not been overly kind to.

> …the same reaction of a very sincere and concerned atmosphere, and at the end of the assemblies there was a time (about a minute) of absolute silence and reflection amongst students—you could cut the atmosphere with a knife—it was inspiring and a hopeful sign for us all in our quest to beat bullying of all types.

> We have seen a clear reduction in bullying behaviour from the pupils who have seen the fllm. It seems to work where talking, explaining and mediation have failed in the past.

We have also put the film up on our YouTube channel (http://uk.youtube. com/user/childnet) to encourage a wider audience, and we are getting children who have seen the film at school coming to watch it again on YouTube, and it has over 30,000 views, some leaving comments, for example:

> I cant believe that someone would do this i was cyberbullied in school and its not nice because you dont know who it is and people laugh at you and they find it hilarious but you dont find it funny at all and i did actually want to kill my self but i didn't let it get to me because the person that did it hasn't got anything better to do than hurt other peoples feelings. (anonymous, 2008a)

> Watched this today in school because of anti-bullying week. Really made me think. Dont cyberbully, it ruins peoples lives and makes them feel like there is something wrong with them when there obviously isn't. Would you like it done to you? (anonymous, 2008b)

As well as visiting a number of schools, and addressing conferences around the country and internationally, Childnet and the DCSF also held two national conferences to help launch and spread awareness of the *Guidance* for schools and the accompanying resources now available. Representatives from schools and anti-bullying leads came and heard about the new *Guidance*, were introduced to the resources that were now available. There was also the opportunity for those attending to brainstorm together practical ways in which the steps outlined in the *Guidance* could be implemented—for example, how can a whole-school community approach be taken in practice, what ideas and steps can be taken to make this happen? These ideas were captured and sent out to those attending.

It was important to include the voices of children and young people at these conferences, and to do this we worked with Haberdashers' Aske's Hatcham College, a school local to Childnet in South East London. Childnet staff worked with the drama department at the school to coach the pupils to write and then perform their own play on this subject, interpreting cyber-bullying in the way that they see and understand it. They produced a very powerful play, definitely one of the highlights of the conferences, and then answered some questions afterwards and engaged in discussion with conference attendees.

In order not to lose this amazing work and momentum that the young people had generated, Childnet worked to make a short film outlining this work and how it was achieved, that can be viewed alongside a series of lesson plans/drama workshop plans to share how you can create a similar drama. For this information, please see http://www.digizen.org/cyber-bullying/film.aspx.

CONCLUSION

The approach outlined to tackle cyber-bullying is a whole school community one. It needs the involvement of all teachers and school staff, not just the ICT staff, as well as the children, the parents, the heads and the governors. Everyone needs to understand what it is, that it does have an impact and that it is unacceptable. It is important that everyone knows where to report if they need to as well as know how to prevent cyber-bullying happening (including how to use technology responsibly).

The Guidance, and other supporting documents, outlines a range of activities that are ongoing, that are focussed on cyber-bullying, and that are designed to support each other and support those looking to take steps to engage with the whole school community and seek to prevent and respond to cyber-bullying. The DCSF have supported Childnet's production of a range of resources. They also have run an online campaign targeting children and young people in the online environment where they "hang out," using banner ads.

There is a lot of work being conducted in this area, and there has been substantial interest from other countries in the work that has been carried out in the UK. The issue of cyber-bullying is one that is relevant for children the world over. It is crucial that we share and learn from each other's experience as we seek to ensure that children can get the most out of using technology and do so safely and responsibly.

References

Anonymous. (2008a) Retrieved February 1, 2009 from http://ca.youtube.com/comment_servlet?all_comments&v=dubA2vhIlrg&fromurl=/watch%3Fv%3DdubA2vhIlrgBalls.

Anonymous. (2008b) Retrieved February 1, 2009 from http://ca.youtube.com/comment_servlet?all_comments&v=dubA2vhIlrg&fromurl=/watch%3Fv%3DdubA2vhIlrg

Balls, Ed. (2007) No hiding places for bullies. Department for Children, Schools and Families. Retrieved January 30, 2009 from http://www.dcsf.gov.uk/pns/DisplayPN.cgi?pn_id=2007_0168

BBC. (2006, March, 31). More kids suffer cyber-bullying. Retrieved February 1, 2009 from http://news.bbc.co.uk/cbbcnews/hi/newsid_4860000/newsid_4865000/4865092.stm .

Communications Act. (2003) Retrieved from www.opsi.gov.uk/acts/acts2003/20030021.htm.

Coughlan, S. (2007). Cyber-bullying threat to teachers. *BBC News*. Retrieved January 30, 2009 from 2007http://news.bbc.co.uk/1/hi/education/6522501.stm.

Department for Children, Schools and Families. (2007). 3.4 Regulating pupils' conduct and disciplining them for misbehaviour outside school. Retrieved February 1, 2009 from http://www.teachernet.gov.uk/wholeschool/behaviour/schooldisciplinepupilbehaviourpolicies/nonstatguidanceforheadsandstaff/regulatingpupilsconduct/.

Department for Children, Schools and Families. (2008). Tackling School Bullying. Retrieved February 1, 2009 from http://www.teachernet.gov.uk/wholeschool/behaviour/tacklingbullying/.

Education and Inspections Act, The (EIA) (Section 89(5). (2006) Retrieved from http://www.opsi.gov.uk/Acts/acts2006/ukpga_20060040_en_1.

Garner, R. (2007). Teachers fear growing 'cyberbullying' by pupils. *The Independent*. Retrieved January 30, 2009 from http://www.independent.co.uk/news/education/education-news/teachers-fear-growing-cyberbullying-by-pupils-443265.html.

Malicious Communications Act. (1988) Retrieved from www.opsi.gov.uk/ACTS/acts1988/Ukpga_19880027_en_1.htm.

Microsoft. (2006). One in ten UK teens have been victims of cyberbullying and one in four knows someone who's been a victim. Retrieved January 30, 2009 from http://www.microsoft.com/uk/press/content/presscentre/releases/2006/03/pr03603.mspx.

Prensky, M. (2001). Digital Natives, Digital Immigrants. *On the Horizon*, 9(5). Retrieved March 25, 2009 from http://www.marcprensky.com/writing/Prensky%20-%20Digital%20Natives,%20Digital%20Immigrants%20-%20Part1.pdf

Protection from Harassment Act. (1997). Retrieved from www.opsi.gov.uk/acts/acts1997/1997040.htm

Public Order Act. (1986). Retrieved from www.opsi.gov.uk/si/si1987/Uksi_19870198_en_2. htm.

Smith, P., Mahdavi, J., Carvalho, M., Fisher, S., Russell S., & Tippett N. (2008) Cyber-bullying: its nature and impact in secondary school pupils. *Journal of Child Psychology and Psychiatry and Allied Disciplines,* 49 (4), pp. 376–385.

Teachers Support Network and The Association of Teachers and Lecturers. (2007). Cyber-bullying Report 2007. Retrieved February 1, 2009 from http://tsn.custhelp.com/cgi-bin/tsn.cfg/php/ enduser/fattach_get.php?p_sid=MZzsz4pj&p_li=&p_accessibility=&p_redirect=&p_tbl=9&p_ id=1669&p_created=1189439753&p_olh=0.

YouTube. (2008) Terms of Service. Retrieved February 1, 2009 from http://ca.youtube.com/t/ terms.

· About the Editors

Shariff, Shaheen: Shaheen Shariff is an Associate Professor in the Faculty of Education at McGill University, and an international expert on cyber-bullying. Her research and teaching are grounded in the study of law as it impacts educational policy, pedagogy and practice. Specifically, her work addresses the emerging policy vacuum on parent and school responsibilities to supervise and intervene when children and teenagers engage in bullying at school and in cyber-space. Her work identifies limits on student free expression in school and cyber-space; privacy rights, cyber-safety, cyber-libel; and school supervision (in the physical school setting and on-line). She has developed guidelines for school administrators, teachers and parents regarding the extent of their legal responsibilities to address cyber-bullying in various contexts. Her work also focuses on human rights, constitutional and tort law as they inform institutional responsibilities to provide safe and productive school and work environments; censorship and diversity in schools.

Her publications are listed at http://people.mcgill.ca/shaheen.shariff and include the following books: 1) *Cyber-bullying: Issues and Solutions for the School, the Classroom, and the Home,* Routledge (Taylor & Francis Group,

U.K.); 2) *Confronting Cyber-bullying: What Schools Need to Know to Control Misconduct and Avoid Legal Consequences,* Cambridge University Press, New York. Dr. Shariff is Principal Investigator on two collaborative national and international projects studying the phenomenon of cyber-bullying, funded by the Social Sciences and Humanities Research Council of Canada (SSHRC). She has presented her work internationally at the American Education Research Association (AERA) in San Francisco, Chicago and New York; Learning Conference in Grenada, Spain; Oxford Internet Institute, Oxford University, UK and Netsafe in New Zealand. She has been invited to Australia and Denmark to deliver keynotes in 2009 and 2010. In Canada, her keynote addresses include "I Am Safe" National Conference in Ottawa; Canadian Association for the Practical Study of Law in Education (CAPSLE); Centre for Innovation, Law and Policy; Quebec Provincial Association of Teachers; Television Ontario; Canadian Broadcasting System (CBC).

Churchill, Andrew H.: Andrew H. Churchill is a doctoral student at McGill University. He is a writing instructor in the McGill Centre for Teaching and Writing and a research assistant for the International Project on Cyber-bullying. In collaboration with Shaheen Shariff, the principal investigator, he has presented this research in Canada, the United States and New Zealand. He is doing his doctoral work under the supervision of Shirley Steinberg. As part of this work, he edited *Rocking Your World: The Emotional Journey into Critical Discourses.* This book features stories by a dozen authors about their personal and professional relationships with criticality. Currently, Andrew is focusing on his doctoral research: An analysis of the potential impact of Charter Schools on *critical* public education reform. This work focuses on examining the potential (or lack thereof) for Charter Schools to enact critical change within public education in the United States. Specifically, the work asks whether Charter Schools have the potential to redress any of the fundamental issues of inequality and social injustice pervasive to American public education. Its look is wide ranging in scope and considers issues such as student agency, assumptions around intelligence, the role of standardized curriculum and testing, the ongoing de-professionalization of teachers and, of course, the purpose of schools themselves.

▪ About the Contributors

Crawford, Emily R.: Emily Crawford is a doctoral student in Educational Theory & Policy at The Pennsylvania State University. She has a B.A. in Communications from Santa Clara University and worked for the communications department and the Knowledge Media Laboratory at the Carnegie Foundation for the Advancement of Teaching in Palo Alto, CA.

Gardner, Will: Will Gardner is Chief Executive Officer of Childnet International, an international children's charity (set up in 1995) that is working to help to make the Internet a great and safe place for children (see www.childnet.com). Will joined Childnet in 2000, working in research and policy, and has led a range of national and international projects relating to child safety online. He has given advice to thousands of children and adults on issues relating to Internet safety as well as to a range of industry players and governments, as well as other organisations. Will is a member of UK's Cyberbullying Taskforce, and the UK Council on Child Safety on the Internet.

Heirman, Wannes: Wannes Heirman is a researcher at the Department of Communication Studies of the University of Antwerp, Research Group Strategic

Communication. He has conducted extensive research in the area of ICT-use by minors in general and cyber-bullying in particular for the Belgian Internet Observatory. He has obtained a master's degree in Communication Sciences at the University of Antwerp.

Hoff, Dianne: Dianne L. Hoff, Ed.D, is an Associate Professor of Educational Leadership at the University of Maine. Her research focuses on the social and political environment of schools. She is the author of *Legal Issues for Maine Educators,* soon to be released in its 3rd edition. She has numerous national and international articles published on contemporary legal/ethical issues facing schools, including cyber-bullying, pay-to-play, and defensible accommodations for students with peanut allergies. Her ongoing research on barriers and challenges for women in school leadership roles has also received national attention.

Kraft, Ellen: Ellen Kraft is an Assistant Professor of Business Studies at Richard Stockton College of New Jersey. Her research interest in cyber-bullying evolved from teaching Internet and Society and e-commerce courses as well as her experience working as a safety engineer. Since 2006, she has written several papers examining the phenomena of cyber-bullying and emerging prevention programs and presented at a number of conferences. Recently, Dr. Kraft began focusing her research in higher education and the workplace. She presented her most recent paper "Will the Cyberbully Ever Grow Up?: Preventing Cyberbullying in Schools, Universities, and the Workplace" at the 2009 Global Conference on Business and Finance. In the summer of 2009, she built on pilot research of Richard Stockton College students to survey college students nationwide about their experiences with cyber-bullying and cyber-stalking.

Masters, Jennifer: Jennifer Masters is a senior lecturer in Education and the Bachelor of Education Course Coordinator at La Trobe University, Bendigo. She has taught in schools at both Early Childhood and Primary levels and specializes in the integration of ICT in curriculum. Her research interest areas include informal learning and social constructivism, social networking, using ICT for "real" purposes, publishing and presenting with computers and computer-based problem-solving opportunities. She completed her Ph. D. thesis relating to young children using computers, with a focus on how teachers can "scaffold" or support children working with computers. Her thesis was published as a book in 2008 entitled *Teachers Scaffolding Children Working with Computers: An Analysis of Strategies.* Jennifer's current research relates to the use of computers and associated technologies in informal contexts. She is particularly interested in children engaging in social networking and the use of technology for creative purposes such as digital story telling and animation.

Mitchell, Sidney: Sidney N. Mitchell, Ph.D., is an Assistant Professor of Educational Psychology and Research Methods at the University of Maine. His research centers on student motivation, perceptions of control, and aspirations. His most recent project examines the motivation for and psychological effects of cyber-bullying. His research is widely published nationally and internationally.

Murphy, Mark P.: Mark Murphy is a doctoral student in Educational Leadership at The Pennsylvania State University. He holds a B.A. in Music Education from Mansfield (PA) University and an M.Ed. in Educational Leadership from Penn State. He is the high school band director and fine arts department chair in Tyrone, Pennsylvania.

Palmer, Gillian: Gillian Palmer is currently curriculum officer for the New Zealand Police Youth Education Service, where she has responsibility for developing school-based programmes in all four themes of the Youth Education Service Curriculum. Examples are *Kia Kaha, Keeping Ourselves Safe* and *the Road Safe Series.* This includes coordinating writing parties to develop teaching materials, producing draft materials for comment and trial, overseeing the trials and steering the programmes through all stages of the production process. She conducts training for police education officers in new programmes produced for YES. Gill came to Police from the Department of Education's curriculum division, where she had responsibility for Consumer Education.

She has a background in secondary teaching, in Social Studies, Geography and Health, including distance learning. She has co-authored a number of Social Studies resource books and has been contracted to do curriculum development work in the health area.

Pauken, Patrick: Patrick Pauken, J.D., Ph.D. is an associate professor and graduate coordinator in the School of Leadership and Policy Studies at Bowling Green State University (BGSU). He is also Secretary to BGSU's Board of Trustees. He teaches school law, special education law, and moral and ethical leadership. Pat's research interests include school violence, technology, copyright, religion, academic freedom, special education, and higher education law. He has published in *West's Education Law Reporter, Journal of School Leadership, Journal of Educational Administration, Forum of Public Policy, Australia and New Zealand Journal of Law and Education,* and *Temple University Political and Civil Rights Law Review.* Pat is parliamentarian of the BGSU Faculty Senate and served as its Chair in 2007–2008. He was named the 2007 American Mensa Teacher of the Year. Pat is a member of the Education Law Association, the Ohio Bar and is of counsel with McGown, Markling & Whalen Co., L.P.A.

Raboy, Marc: Marc Raboy is Professor and Beaverbrook Chair in Ethics, Media and Communications in the Department of Art History and Communication

Studies at McGill University. A former journalist in a wide variety of media, educated at McGill, Professor Raboy taught previously at the Université de Montréal and Laval University. He is the author or editor of sixteen books and more than 130 journal articles or book chapters, as well as reports for a range of organizations such as UNESCO, the World Bank, the Japan Broadcasting Corporation, and the European Broadcasting Union. He has been a visiting scholar at New York University, Stockholm University, and the University of Oxford, and is a member of the international council of the International Association for Media and Communication Research (IAMCR), past president of the Canadian Communication Association, and member of several editorial boards. He is also a founding member of an international advocacy campaign for Communication Rights in the Information Society.

Raskauskus, Juliana: Dr. Juliana Raskauskas is an Assistant Professor at California State University, Sacramento in Child Development. Her doctorate is in Educational Psychology from the University of California, Davis. Dr. Raskauskas has been researching in the area of bullying for eight years in the United States and New Zealand. Her research interests include prevention/intervention, anti-bullying policy and programme evaluation, child and adolescent development, fostering resiliency, and electronic/text-message bullying. She is part of two large research projects, one in New Zealand examining the relationship of emotional intelligence to bullying behaviour and the other in the United States developing a integrated anti-violence program addressing bullying, sexual harassment, and molestation for students with and without disabilities.

Shtern, Jeremy: Jeremy Shtern is a post-doctoral fellow of Le Fonds québécois de la recherche sur la société et la culture (FQRSC) in the Rogers Communication Centre at Ryerson University, Toronto. His research explores issues of communication policy in the context of globalization with a particular focus on Internet governance. Jeremy was a delegate to the UN World Summit on the Information Society and has participated in the UN Internet Governance Forum since its inception in 2006. With Marc Raboy, Jeremy is co-editing a book based on a recently conducted assessment of the state of communication rights and the right to communicate in Canada to be published by University of British Columbia Press in 2009 as *Two Tiers of Freedom: Communication Rights and the Right to Communicate in Canada*. With Marc Raboy and Normand Landry, Jeremy is also co-authoring a book for Peter Lang on multi-stakeholder governance and UN internet policy making.

Stefkovich, Jacqueline A.: Jacqueline Stefkovich is Associate Dean for Graduate Studies, Research and Faculty Development at The Pennsylvania State University. She holds an Ed.D. from Harvard University and a J.D. from the

University of Pennsylvania. She has published numerous journal articles and five books on issues related to law and ethics in schools.

Walrave, Michel: Dr. Michel Walrave is senior lecturer at the Department of Communication Studies of the University of Antwerp and leads the Research Group Strategic Communication. His field of expertise is situated in the area of societal implications of ICT. He has conducted several national and European research projects on teens & ICT, e-working, e-government and e-privacy. Recently the research project *Teens & ICT, Risks & Opportunities* was finalized concerning cyber-bullying. Also for the Belgian Internet Observatory has has studied cyber-bullying. He teaches societal implications of ICT, marketing communications & ICT, e-marketing at the University of Antwerp and as a guest lecturer in several other universities. Michel Walrave has a Masters in Communication Science and a Masters in Information Science. In 1999 he published his Ph.D. thesis about data protection in direct marketing communications.

Yelland, Nicola: Nicola Yelland is Research Professor of Education in the School of Education at Victoria University in Melbourne, Australia. Over the last decade her research has been related to the use of ICT in school and community contexts. This has involved projects that have investigated the specific learning of students in computer environments as well as a broader consideration of the ways in which new technologies can impact on the pedagogies that teachers use and the curriculum in schools. Her multidisciplinary research focus has enabled her to work with early childhood, primary and middle school teachers to enhance the ways in which ICT can be incorporated into learning contexts to make them more interesting and motivating for students, so that educational outcomes are improved. Her latest publications are *Rethinking learning in Early Childhood Education* (OUP) and *Rethinking Education with ICT: New directions for effective practices* (Sense Publishers). She is the author of *Shift to the Future: Rethinking learning with new technologies in education* (Routledge, New York). She is also the author of *Early Mathematical Explorations* with Carmel Diezmann and Deborah Butler and has edited four books: *Gender in Early Childhood* (Routledge, UK), *Innovations in Practice* (NAEYC) *Ghosts in the Machine: Women's voices in Research with Technology* (Peter Lang) and *Critical Issues in Early Childhood* (OUP). Nicola has worked in Australia, the USA, UK and Hong Kong.

Zinga, Dawn: Dawn Zinga is an associate professor in the Department of Child and Youth Studies at Brock University. She is a cognitive developmental psychologist whose research focuses on the accommodation of culture within educational settings and children's rights within educational contexts. Her work has focused on examining how children and adolescents conceptualize and perceive their educational experiences within the context of culture and children's rights within education. She is particularly interested in aboriginal education issues, multiculturalism within education, and cyber-bullying.

▪ Index

new
literacies
q

AND DIGITAL EPISTEMOLOGIES

Colin Lankshear, Michele Knobel,
& Michael Peters
General Editors

New literacies and new knowledges are being invented "in the streets" as people from all walks of life wrestle with new technologies, shifting values, changing institutions, and new structures of personality and temperament emerging in a global informational age. These new literacies and ways of knowing remain absent from classrooms. Many education administrators, teachers, teacher educators, and academics seem largely unaware of them. Others actively oppose them. Yet, they increasingly shape the engagements and worlds of young people in societies like our own. The *New Literacies and Digital Epistemologies* series will explore this terrain with a view to informing educational theory and practice in constructively critical ways.

For further information about the series and submitting manuscripts, please contact:

Michele Knobel & Colin Lankshear
Montclair State University
Dept. of Education and Human Services
3173 University Hall
Montclair, NJ 07043
michele@coatepec.net

To order other books in this series, please contact our Customer Service Department at:

(800) 770-LANG (within the U.S.)
(212) 647-7706 (outside the U.S.)
(212) 647-7707 FAX

Or browse online by series at:

www.peterlang.com